Jacobean Tragedies

Jacobean Tragedies

EDITED WITH AN INTRODUCTION BY

A. H. GOMME

OXFORD UNIVERSITY PRESS

LONDON   OXFORD   NEW YORK

1969

Oxford University Press

LONDON OXFORD NEW YORK
GLASGOW TORONTO MELBOURNE WELLINGTON
CAPE TOWN SALISBURY IBADAN NAIROBI LUSAKA ADDIS ABABA
BOMBAY CALCUTTA MADRAS KARACHI LAHORE DACCA
KUALA LUMPUR SINGAPORE HONG KONG TOKYO

Introduction and notes
© Oxford University Press 1969

First published as an Oxford University Press
paperback by Oxford University Press, London, 1969

PRINTED IN GREAT BRITAIN
BY RICHARD CLAY (THE CHAUCER PRESS), LTD.,
BUNGAY, SUFFOLK

Contents

Introduction

The five plays in this volume are among the most interesting of the quantities that have survived from the reign of James I, the most prolific period of English dramatic writing. They show something of the variety of types attempted within the field of tragedy and tragicomedy, and present the different outlooks of at least four and possibly five dramatists, who nonetheless are linked in several ways. Marston's figure of the malcontent must have influenced the author of *The Revenger's Tragedy* in the creation of Vindice, and certain types and situations in Marston's play relate it to Tourneur's *Atheist's Tragedy*, though both that play and *The Revenger's Tragedy* show evidence of a close knowledge (or a good memory) of Shakespeare. Middleton's two tragedies stand at a remove in time and character from the other three plays (for Deflores in *The Changeling* is a malcontent of a different kind); nevertheless Middleton is seen by a number of scholars as the most likely contender for the authorship of *The Revenger's Tragedy*, though others stick to the old attribution to Tourneur.

Other connexions between all five plays which readers are bound to notice are the obsessions with death and more especially with sexual passion. Death and physical decay form the central preoccupation of the main figures in *The Revenger's* and *Atheist's Tragedies*, always seen, however, in close relation to, indeed as the inevitable outcome of, sin. And sin in these plays is always sexual sin. 'The black act of sin itself' is lust: the principal motivating force throughout the plays is physical passion (sometimes allied to lust for power), the self-centring and eventually self-destroying intensity of which prevents almost all the protagonists from having any awareness that they stand in moral relationships to others. In all the plays lust issues in adultery; and sexual pleasure is largely identified with sin:

> Give me my bed by stealth—there's true delight;
> What breathes a loathing in't, but night by night?

The few faithful lovers or chaste women are notably pallid. It is a familiar theme throughout Jacobean drama, which Shakespeare alone transcends. Even in those figures whose moral and dramatic function is to expose the lustful and bring them down, it is impossible to escape a sense of fascination amounting to relish in the details, range, and variety of sexual sin (see for example *The Revenger's Tragedy* I. iii). The reasons for this all-powerful obsession are doubtless complicated. The rising power of Puritanism is certainly one; and D. H. Lawrence has very plausibly suggested a related influence in the ravages of syphilis, which was unknown in England before the second half of the sixteenth century, but rapidly spread, particularly among the upper classes, with visibly devastating results.

But though the peculiar character of this obsessiveness—the combination of a self-consuming passion with a strong sense of sin—may seem foreign to us, the best plays of the Jacobean period are a good deal more than merely historically curious. Middleton's in particular, with their strong interest in the psychological processes of moral and spiritual atrophy, have a sombre power which remains impressive and disturbing; and the exploration of the implications of physical decay in *The Revenger's Tragedy* is scarcely less remarkable.

Of the five plays reprinted in this volume *The Malcontent* is the earliest. It was written probably in 1603 or 1604 (though the date is uncertain and some scholars put it as early as 1600), primarily for the boys' company at Blackfriars. Three editions were printed in 1604, the last of which contains considerable additions by Marston himself and an induction by Webster, the latter including a discussion between audience and players of the play's having been taken over from the boys by the King's Men acting at the Globe. Marston had begun his career as a satirist, and though it is perhaps wrong to call *The Malcontent* a satire, it contains obviously satirical elements in the treatment of Bilioso and the college of ladies. Like *The Atheist's Tragedy*, it has affinities with the old morality tradition and may perhaps be called a moral fable; like *The Revenger's*, it is an exposure of the corruption of court life, set for safety and propriety's sake in conventionally corrupt Italy. Both aspects lead to much deliberate moralizing, which tends to become stiff and sententious; and a comparison between Malevole's meditation on lust (II. v. 141ff.) with Leantio's (*Women Beware Women* III. i. 95ff.) shows the comparative limitations of Marston's dramatic technique: Malevole's moralizing is clearly the expression of the author's or the play's point of view; Leantio's is placed within a larger moral outlook by which he too is judged.

The figure of the malcontent is one of the most familiar in early seventeenth-century drama. But unlike Jaques or Hamlet or Flamineo or Vindice, Malevole is a malcontent only by agreement—he wears his cynicism as a mask. Hence he can regulate and control his expressed attitude and behaviour as Hamlet and Vindice cannot. Unlike Jaques who stands back from and despises all action, Malevole is an agent of retribution; unlike Vindice, he is himself uncorruptible, and though at one point he seems about to take a dangerous delight in vengeance, he is less the revenger than the reclaimer of the state and the redeemer of those who can be redeemed. Like Charlemont in *The Atheist's Tragedy* (who, however, is entirely passive), Malevole knows that God is on his side and thanks Providence for his reinstatement and for the moral redemption of Pietro and Aurelia; and his return to power at the end of the play, and the exposure and defeat of Mendoza, are therefore not a personal vengeance so much as a restoration of an order in the state which has been corrupted by personal passions.

The action and characterization throughout are of the broadest and simplest, of a kind which would not do for Shakespeare or Middleton; the figures are near to being types or humours, and the moral fable has no room for niceties of psychological motivation. Thus, though Pietro shows early on that (like Alonso in *The Tempest*[1]) he has a conscience and so can be redeemed, we are given no warning of Aurelia's change of heart until it happens and must simply accept it as a reported fact.

The Malcontent has little of the bitter sourness of Tourneur or the moral outrage of Middleton. It is on the whole a rather sunny play with a good deal of light-hearted entertainment in it. *The Revenger's Tragedy* has a dark savagery which, from the very first lines, puts us in a world of uncontrolled self-seeking passion, relieved only by the stubborn but colourless virtue of Castiza and the ambiguous action and moralizing of Vindice. It was probably written in 1605 or 1606, and was first printed anonymously in 1607, bound together with Middleton's *A Trick To Catch the Old One*. Tourneur's name was first attached to the play in an advertisement printed in 1656, and from then his title to it remained unquestioned until the late nineteenth century. Very little is known about Tourneur: though there is evidence of his having written or partly written two other plays now lost, only *The Atheist's Tragedy* has survived of his acknowledged dramatic work, and it is possible that he was not a professional dramatist. During this century there has been much argument on the authorship of *The Revenger's Tragedy*, centring mainly on the rival claims of Tourneur and Middleton. The dispute (which is conveniently summarized in R. A. Foakes's edition of the play) has not been settled, and it is probably best, unless documentary evidence comes to light, to take Allardyce Nicoll's advice and regard it as still anonymous.

The play, which owes something to Marston, is closer to the morality tradition than *The Malcontent*, going farther, for example, in its selection of names to demonstrate characteristics or functions—Castiza for Chastity, Lussurioso for Lechery, Vindice the revenger, and so on—an Italianizing trick of which the nearly contemporary *Volpone* gives the best-known examples. Foakes has pointed out that the habit of personification in the play —'that bald madam, opportunity'—brings other metaphorical characters momentarily alive, so that characterization and language are fused. Once

---

[1] The basic situation of *The Tempest* may owe something to that of *The Malcontent* and at one point there is evidence of a (deliberate?) verbal theft on Shakespeare's part: cf. *Malcontent*, IV. iii. 47 with *Tempest*, III. iii. 55.

again 'character' only in a special sense: when Vindice in his first speech refers to 'four excellent characters', it is only in the morality sense that the four who have passed over the stage can be seen as having any character at all. They are rather *exempla* of particular vices, and their function is to illustrate these without any of the complications we should expect in a fully portrayed human being. The whole story in fact, like that of *The Atheist's Tragedy*, has the form of a moral *exemplum*, a survival of medieval tradition whose best-known instance appears in Chaucer's *Pardoner's Tale*. The aim is above all to frighten the sinner with a reminder of mortality, of the perpetual nearness and threat of death. So the skull appears as a physical *memento mori*, and Vindice constantly plays on the impermanence of human desire and the corruption of the flesh in death. Vindice is the revenger with a more-than-Hamlet-like obsession with and horror at the physical characteristics of sexual desire: he stands, so far as any figure in the play does, for an attempt to assert morality through action. Yet his own morality is dominated by the desire for personal revenge and only occasionally given the outward dress of orthodoxy. He sees himself as God's agent in scourging the world of evil; yet he hardly has a richer philosophy than the lustful—only a keener aware-ness of the triumph of death; and the mortality of beauty takes the place of outraged virtue as the prime source of his attitude. He becomes to some extent corrupted by the corruption of the court, has a certain relish in trying against his will and judgment to seduce his sister for Lussurioso, and a great deal in his actual revenge which he later describes as 'somewhat witty carried'; he is sufficiently detached from his own fate to see the point of the ironic turning of the tables on himself at the end.

The vision of *The Revenger's Tragedy* is of a world of almost unrelieved bestiality, moved only by destructive passion: the narrowness of the vision is intensified by the remarkable insistence of the language on the central theme; if ever for a moment we might forget what this is, the verse concen-trates our attention with its perpetual reminders of death, so that the physical atmosphere created by the series of violent spasms which make up the plot, is one with the linguistic expression of it. And the verse is on occasion of such power as to impress this vision on the reader or audience with unforgettable vividness. There are few more intense or painful evoca-tions of the mortality of flesh, or the consequent futility of living only in the moment, than the famous address to the skull at III. v. 71ff.

The Atheist's Tragedy, written a few years after *The Revenger's* and first printed, under Tourneur's name, in 1611, is a revenge play of a different kind. The 'honest man's revenge' of the subtitle is patience; for Charlemont, the honest man, has been warned by the ghost of his father to 'leave revenge unto the King of kings'. So the revenger is Heaven itself; and the basic sin is the blasphemy of denying a power superior to visible nature. Nature in D'Amville's sense is akin to Edmund's view of it in *King Lear*; and the

philosophy explicitly opposed to this is the religious view of the creation of
the world and man's responsibility, expressed thinly enough by Charlemont
and more significantly in the series of events by which D'Amville's atheistic
philosophy is shown to be ultimately futile. These are of a kind which
make the play at times seem dangerously like a parody of the stylistic
formality of Jacobean tragedy. At D'Amville's supreme moment of self-
confidence, when he claims that

> My real wisdom has rais'd up a state,
> That shall eternize my posterity, (V. i. 46–7)

the boast is answered by the entry of a servant with the body of one of his
sons, while the dying groans of the other are heard off-stage: his whole
edifice collapses, and he makes a reproachful appeal to the Nature that has
betrayed him, only to have his view of Nature patly put in its place by the
doctor who could not, with his human skill, save the sons' lives. It is all of
course deliberately artificial, but not necessarily absurd. If there is a weakness
at such points, it is one of calculation rather than judgment: the formality
of the whole proceedings is designed to point the omnipresence of God in
the world; so it is precisely at the moment of greatest self-glorification that
human power is shown to be feeble and unreliable. The dramatic tricks by
which this is achieved are deliberately non-naturalistic; the dramatist
employed conventional devices which his audience recognized as such, in
order to dramatize more vividly and in a more concentrated form the
particular moral attitude or philosophy which was his prime concern. And it
is missing the point to remark that life isn't literally like that; for this is not a
literal but a symbolic representation of human actions and beliefs.

In the formal patterns of its verse *The Atheist's Tragedy* likewise provides
one of the clearest and most interesting demonstrations of Jacobean dramatic
technique. Here there is only space to point to two instances. The play, as
has been said, deals with a particular view of Nature. Against this view,
the characteristics of a richer, fuller, and of course truer idea of Nature (as
the author sees it) are revealed in the *natural* imagery particularly associated
with the virtuous (and hence 'truly natural') pair, Charlemont and Castabella,
above all in metaphors connected with liquids and flowing. Borachio's
strange faked description of Charlemont's supposed death, when the sea
both embraces and weeps for him (II. i. 7off.), though its direct function is
to further D'Amville's plans, has yet the effect of linking Charlemont with
Nature far more comprehensively than D'Amville ever is. And like the sea,
Castabella sacrifices tears on Charlemont's 'grave', tears which are linked
with the balm of dew. A savage contrast is provided by the rivers of blood
that flow when Belforest and Sebastian are killed, rivers started by the
fountain of Levidulcia's lust, for which tears are no balm, for Levidulcia is
not 'natural' as Castabella is. Finally, this imagery culminates in the water,

wine, and blood of the trial scene, with its hints of Christ's passion and its symbolism of the purity and the corruption of Nature. The two opposing views of Nature, which would otherwise be empty or abstract, are given living substance by the imagery which carries them.

Even more obviously deliberate are the images of building, all associated with D'Amville's attempt to construct a human fortress against the power of Heaven. So Borachio kills Montferrers with a stone and destroys a house with what D'Amville will later use as his cornerstone. When D'Amville's own house is brought low (the literal house is of course being used as a metaphor for the figurative), he hears his son's groans as the cracking of a great building; and when finally he understands the full enormity of his error, he tells of the 'proud monument' he had erected to his own pride—a monument which is both record and tomb.

With Middleton's two great tragedies we are not on debatable ground. Despite fairly obvious defects, which modern criticism has only partially explained away, they have some claim to be considered the most powerful plays written in English since the death of Shakespeare. Middleton had a fairly long career as a dramatist; his earlier work consists mainly of highly polished and very lively comedies of contemporary urban life, written, like *The Malcontent*, for the children's company at Blackfriars. Later he collaborated widely in a very mixed batch of plays, and only turned to a new kind of tragedy near the end of his life. *The Changeling*, written with Rowley in 1621 or 1622, has usually been thought the finer, and it must be admitted that the conventional holocaust which brings *Women Beware Women* (of 1623) to an end is a comedown after the sustained magnificence of the first four acts. In both plays we see a dramatist as ready as Tourneur to use the elaborate formal stagecraft of the time but interested in psychological analysis and exploration in a way unknown to any of his contemporaries save Shakespeare and on rare occasion Webster. As with Webster, Middleton's chief protagonists are women. In both the plays in this volume, the heroine is subjected to an intense psychological and moral shock which upsets the fragile balance by which she had preserved a code of honour, and leads to swift spiritual decay. Bianca's situation in *Women Beware Women* is somewhat the simpler: tricked into a position for which her self-control is unprepared and inadequate, and then seduced, she finds she has no spiritual defences to fall back upon, and yields to forces, the power of which in herself she had never known—to the point where she can freely plot murder to further her own desires. The portrayal of her sense of shock at being betrayed to forces stronger than her will is extremely powerful and moving (II. ii. 418ff.): a moral and psychological abyss has opened beneath her; and from now on her moral nature disintegrates unhampered by the fences of convention, which, once broken, are no longer a check to one without spiritual resources of her own. The collapse of her husband, Leantio, follows a similar path.

His sense of moral superiority early in the play is obviously too good to bear any severe pressure; and in the scenes between the two after Bianca's seduction, the moral weaknesses of both are mercilessly revealed. When Leantio returns after a fortnight's absence, she will not kiss him:

> Is there no kindness betwixt man and wife,
> Unless they make a pigeon-house of friendship,
> And be still billing? (III. i. 158–60)

The question exposes both of them, for Leantio's complacent uxoriousness shows a moral hollowness as gross as Bianca's callousness. Nevertheless, Leantio's laments, as he slowly realizes his loss, are deeply moving (III. ii), for Middleton is here concerned simply to display the suffering man: the suffering is at the moment the only thing that matters. The final scene between the two (IV. i), after Leantio, in revenge for her desertion, has given himself to the woman who first betrayed Bianca, is intensely painful, as the erstwhile lovers try their utmost to wound one another to the quick, in efforts to push each his own guilt on to the other. The psychological truth that informs this scene is what lies at the heart of the whole play—the discovery that moral sanctions accepted with no true belief in their foundation are powerless against the stronger and wilful passions which, at the moment of release from convention, turn vicious and ultimately self-destructive.

In the world of *Women Beware Women* the only rules, once the flimsy guard of convention is broken, are those of passion and self-will. In *The Changeling*, on the other hand, the shock that the heroine, Beatrice, suffers is that of an amoral being suddenly forced to realize the existence of a world beyond her own desires in which she is trapped and where she cannot buy herself out of the consequences and responsibilities of her actions. In the great scene after the murder of Alonzo, Deflores is always Beatrice's master; for he has a moral sense to the extent at least of knowing that events have consequences, and because he is not deceived by the absurd fantasy of her own honour on which Beatrice rests. Though she is not disturbed by the thought of murder undertaken to encompass her ends, the physical sign of it in the severed finger horrifies her. Deflores' action in hacking off the finger is brutal and repulsive, but hardly worse, as he observes, than the murder which she herself arranged. When she tries to buy off Deflores, it is he who reminds her that money will not buy ease of conscience—something which doesn't trouble him but nevertheless lies at the root of Beatrice's moral ignorance. Gradually he forces her to accept the fact that her responsibility is as deep as his, that her code of honour, which allows murder but stops short at an infringement of her modesty, is impossible; if he is hardly her moral superior, he is nonetheless morally educated as she is not; and so he has inescapable power over her and can force her to his own level. As in

Bianca's case, the initial act destroys the possibility of salvation, because Beatrice has no moral foundation to which she can hold.

The Changeling uses the device of a sub-plot which has little direct connexion with the main action but is designed to comment on it (it is the sub-plot, together probably with the opening and closing scenes, which is the work of Rowley). The relationship is hardly very close, and the sub-plot itself has usually been found tedious, though it is worth pointing out that its faults of tone are more apparent than real, inasmuch as Isabella, the truly upright woman, finds the madmen no funnier than we are likely to. But the double action in Act II, Scene ii of *Women Beware Women* is much more impressive. Here the moves in the chess game[1] (which would have been played on the main stage) parallel those of the seduction on the balcony above, of which of course only one player is aware. The ironic comedy of the interaction between these two scenes in which Bianca's mother-in-law is alike trapped, and which is pointed by the supercilious pleasure taken by Guardiano in his skill as a pander, displays the moral charlatanry of this world with irresistible piquancy. The whole scene is one of the most consummately stage-managed in Jacobean drama.

In preparing texts for this volume I have tried to keep as close as possible to the early editions, from which I have chiefly worked, though I have also used the modern editions cited in the headnotes to each play. The spelling has been modernized, except in the case of words which have changed their form or inflexion, as *corse* for *corpse*, *murther* for *murder* and so on. Sometimes two different forms of the same word appear in the same play or even scene: there cannot be any significance in this, but I have thought it best to leave the variations as they stand rather than make further arbitrary decisions of my own. Past participles in particular take many forms, and these have to some extent been regularized to indicate pronunciation; where, however, a form in -*t* has now given place to one in -*ed*, I have kept the old form except where (as in *mist* for *missed*) it seemed likely to be confusing. Where a past participle ends in -*ed*, it can be taken that an extra syllable is to be pronounced (as *resolved*—three syllables). The punctuation has also been left as close to the original as possible. The various points in Elizabethan and Jacobean writing do not all mean the same as they do today, and readers unfamiliar with old texts may at first find some usages strange. In addition some points were certainly meant to mark how an actor should speak rather than as grammatical indicators. Only where these seemed obviously wrong or genuinely in need of interpretation or likely to cause real confusion have I

---

[1] Middleton was evidently fascinated by chess: one of the most successful plays of the whole period is his *A Game of Chess*, a satire on the Spanish court which takes the form of an allegorical chess game; it was immensely popular, being most unusually played night after night at the Globe until stopped after a protest by the Spanish ambassador.

altered them to a more modern form. It is true that both spelling and punctuation were extremely haphazard in the early seventeenth century, and much in the printed texts clearly depends on accident or the whim of the compositor. Nevertheless the wholesale modernization of old punctuation can make a major change in the tone, if not the substantial meaning, of a sentence or whole passage. As one small instance, the full stop at the end of III. i. 131 of *The Atheist's Tragedy* is sometimes changed to a comma; but the heavier point helps to ensure the meditative character of the speech, which is a matter of some significance.

Lineation presents a more difficult problem in both Tourneur and Middleton. The printers of *The Revenger's* and *Atheist's Tragedies* apparently wanted to save paper, and frequently passages of verse have been written out as prose, short lines run into one another, and different speeches printed continuously. The same is true to a lesser extent of *The Changeling*, which has much mislineation in an otherwise clean text. Moreover it is often hard to tell exactly where prose ends and verse begins. Middleton in particular moves easily from verse to a strongly rhythmical prose, and some passages (for example *The Changeling* IV. i. 31ff.) are a mixture of the two. His verse contains many lines of greater or less than normal length. Very often the first syllable of a line is missing, but in such cases the slow opening makes up the length (for example *The Changeling* II. ii. 86). Conversely some lines have two or more extra syllables which constitute something like what G. M. Hopkins called outrides, that is, extra-metrical syllables which do not count in the scansion (for example *Women Beware Women* II. ii. 170 and 263). Some lines which are apparently hexameters are perhaps better seen as pairs of trimeters (for example *Women Beware Women* II. i. 53). Tourneur's verse seems at times not to be conceived linearly at all and asks to be read rather in paragraphs. An editorial tendency towards complete regularity, therefore, in which short lines are filled out with extra words or syllables and long ones reorganized, ought to be resisted, for it lends an artificial smoothness to the verse which is foreign to its character. Nevertheless all editors are obliged to do something about the villainous state in which the compositors have left the lineation. I have generally followed the editions cited in the headnotes, but have on occasion supplied my own emendation.

Stage directions have been left as in the early texts. Elaborate localizations of scene, so often supplied by editors, are foreign to Elizabethan and Jacobean plays, which, where necessary, usually supply the information in the text itself. But compositors (or authors) frequently omit essential exits and entrances: to distinguish them from what appears in the old text, these have been added in square brackets, as have occasional other stage directions which are implied in the text but not always made entirely clear. Readers will discover that Middleton's stage directions are more detailed than those of the earlier writers, and this greater elaboration is a tendency that has continued to the present day.

The Malcontent is the only one of the five plays which exists in more than one contemporary edition containing major variations. In this case the third quarto (containing Webster's induction and Marston's additions) must obviously be the one to work from, for it includes Marston's latest thoughts and corrections. Nevertheless this edition was carelessly proof-read and contains mistakes not present in the earlier ones; and some copies have been slightly emended in the interests of political safety. In most cases where the editions differ the preferred reading is obvious; and differences between the quartos have very rarely been mentioned in the notes. These do not in any event make the slightest claim to be exhaustive: their function is simply to help those unfamiliar with Jacobean English and to help sort out some of the more problematical phrases. For more detailed information and criticism readers are referred to the editions cited in the headnotes, and to the following books and essays:

M. C. Bradbrook, *Elizabethan Stage Conditions* (Cambridge, 1932); *Themes and Conventions of Elizabethan Tragedy* (Cambridge, 1935)
Una Ellis Fermor, *The Jacobean Drama* (London, 1936 and later editions)
P. B. Murray, *A Study of Cyril Tourneur* (Philadelphia and London, 1965)
Samuel Schoenbaum, *Middleton's Tragedies* (New York and London, 1955)
John D. Jump, 'Middleton's Tragedies'
L. G. Salingar, 'Tourneur and the Tragedy of Revenge'
(both the last two in B. Ford, ed., *Pelican Guide to English Literature*, Vol. 2: *The Age of Shakespeare*, Harmondsworth, 1955)

It is a pleasure to find an opportunity here to acknowledge, however inadequately, the unstinted and meticulous labours of my wife in checking typescript and proofs, and the admirable help which Mr. Richard Brain of the Oxford University Press has given throughout, including a number of ingenious suggestions which have been incorporated into text and notes.

1968   A. H. GOMME

THE MALCONTENT

BY

JOHN MARSTON

JOHN MARSTON (1576–1634)

The Malcontent

Written between 1600 and 1604; printed in 1604; the induction by John Webster added in the third edition (1604).

[*The Works of Marston*, ed. A. H. Bullen, 1887; *The Plays of John Marston*, ed. H. Harvey Wood, 1934; *The Malcontent*, ed. Martin Wine, Regents Renaissance Drama Series, 1965.]

THE

MALCONTENT.

Augmented by *Marston*.

With the Additions played by the Kings
Maiesties seruants.

Written by *Ihon Webster*.

1 6 0 4.

AT LONDON
Printed by V.S. for William Aspley, and
are to be sold at his shop in Paules
Church-yard.

BENIAMINO IONSONIO

POETAE

ELEGANTISSIMO

GRAVISSIMO

AMICO

SVO CANDIDO ET CORDATO,

IOHANNES MARSTON

MVSARVM ALVMNVS

ASPERAM HANC SVAM THALIAM

D. D.

Dedication] To Benjamin Jonson, the most elegant and weighty poet and his sincere and judicious friend, John Marston gives and dedicates this his rough comedy. ('Weighty' may be a punning reference to Jonson's bulk.)

TO THE READER

I am an ill orator; and in truth, use to indite more honestly than eloquently, for it is my custom to speak as I think, and write as I speak. 2

In plainness therefore understand, that in some things I have willingly erred, as in supposing a Duke of Genoa, and in taking names different from that city's families: for which some may wittily accuse me; but my defence shall be as honest, as many reproofs unto me have been most malicious: since (I heartily protest) it was my care to write so far from reasonable offence, that even strangers, in whose state I laid my scene, should not from thence draw any disgrace to any, dead or living. Yet in despite of my endeavours, I understand, some have been most unadvisedly over-cunning in mis-interpreting me, and with subtility (as deep as hell) have maliciously spread ill rumours, which, springing from themselves, might to themselves have heavily returned. Surely I desire to satisfy every firm spirit, who in all his actions proposeth to himself no more ends than God and virtue do, whose intentions are always simple: to such I protest, that with my free understanding, I have not glanced at disgrace of any, but of those whose unquiet studies labour innovation, contempt of holy policy, reverent comely superiority, and establisht unity: for the rest of my supposed tartness, I fear not but unto every worthy mind it will be approved so general and honest, as may modestly pass with the freedom of a satire. I would fain leave the paper; only one thing afflicts me, to think that scenes invented merely to be spoken should be inforcively published to be read, and that the least hurt I can receive is to do my self the wrong. But since others otherwise would do me more, the least inconvenience is to be accepted. I have my self therefore set forth this comedy; but so, that my enforced absence must much rely upon the printer's discretion: but I shall entreat, slight errors in orthography may be as slightly overpassed; and that the unhandsome shape which this trifle in reading presents may be pardoned, for the pleasure it once afforded you, when it was presented with the soul of lively action. 30

Sine aliqua dementia nullus Phoebus.

I.M.

---

5 wittily] cleverly   11 subtility] excessive ingenuity   17 labour] labour to bring about
25 set forth] published   31 *Sine . . . Phoebus*] No Phoebus (Apollo, *sc.* no poet) is without some madness

DRAMATIS PERSONAE

Giovanni Altofronto, disguised *Malevole*, sometime Duke of Genoa.
Pietro Jacomo, Duke of Genoa.
Mendoza, a Minion to the Duchess of *Pietro Jacomo*.
Celso, a friend to *Altofront*.
Bilioso, an old choleric Marshall.
Prepasso, a Gentleman Usher.
Ferneze, a young Courtier, and enamoured on the Duchess.
Ferrardo, a Minion to Duke Pietro Jacomo.
Equato,
Guerrino, } Two Courtiers.

Aurelia, Duchess to Duke *Pietro Jacomo*.
Maria, Duchess to Duke *Altofront*.
Emilia,
Beancha, } Two Ladies attending the Duchess [*Aurelia*].
Maquerelle, an old Pandress.
Passarello, Fool to Bilioso.
[Captain, guarding the citadel.]
[Mercury, in the masque.]
[Suitors.]
[Pages.]
[Guards.]

[*William Sly*,
 John Sinklo,
 Richard Burbage,
 Henry Condell,
 John Lowin,
 A Tireman, } Members of the Company of His Majesty's Servants, in the Induction.]

Minion] lover   *William Sly*, &c.] All five named men were members of the King's Men at the time when the play was written.   Tireman] wardrobe or props man

INDUCTION

Enter W. Sly, *a* Tireman *following him with a stool.*

Tireman. Sir, the gentlemen will be angry if you sit here.

Sly. Why? we may sit upon the stage at the private house: thou dost not take me for a country gentleman, dost? dost think I fear hissing? I'll hold my life thou took'st me for one of the players.

Tireman. No, sir.

Sly. By God's slid, if you had, I would have given you but sixpence for your stool. Let them that have stale suits, sit in the galleries, hiss at me: he that will be laught out of a tavern or an ordinary shall seldom feed well or be drunk in good company. Where's Harry Condell, D. Burbage, and W. Sly? let me speak with some of them.   10

Tireman. An't please you to go in sir, you may.

Sly. I tell you no; I am one that hath seen this play often, & can give them intelligence for their action: I have most of the jests here in my table-book.

Enter Sinklo.

Sinklo. Save you, coose.

Sly. O cousin, come, you shall sit between my legs here.

Sinklo. No indeed cousin, the audience then will take me for a viol de gambo, and think that you play upon me.

Sly. Nay, rather that I work upon you, coose.

Sinklo. We stayed for you at supper last night at my cousin Honeymoon's the woollen draper: after supper we drew cuts for a score of apricocks, the longest cut still to draw an apricock: by this light, 'twas Mistress Frank Honeymoon's fortune still to have the longest cut: I did measure for the women. What be these, coose?   23

Enter D. Burbage, H. Condell, J. Lowin.

Sly. The players. God save you.

Burbage. You are very welcome.

Sly. I pray you know this gentleman my cousin, 'tis Master Doomsday's son the usurer.

---

2 private house] the Blackfriars theatre where the play was first performed; the induction was written for the public performance at the Globe   3 hissing] Those who sat on the stage were often hissed by the other spectators for getting in the way.   6 slid] eyelid   7 stale] unfashionable   8 ordinary] eating-house   9 Condell] The quarto has 'Cundale', indicating the pronunciation.   9-10 D. Burbage, W. Sly] Perhaps the actor is to say Dick and Will.   12-13 give ... action] prompt them   13 table-book] pocket-book   14 coose] coz, friend   20 cuts] lots (made of straws of different lengths)   20 apricocks] apricots   22 still] always

Condell. I beseech you sir, be cover'd.

Sly. No in good faith, for mine ease: look you, my hat's the handle to this fan: God's so, what a beast was I, I did not leave my feather at home. Well, but I'll take an order with you.   *Puts his feather in his pocket.*

Burbage. Why do you conceal your feather, sir?   32

Sly. Why? do you think I'll have jests broken upon me in the play, to be laught at? this play hath beaten all your gallants out of the feathers: Blackfriars hath almost spoil'd Blackfriars for feathers.

Sinklo. God's so, I thought 'twas for somewhat our gentlewomen at home counsell'd me to wear my feather to the play, yet I am loth to spoil it.

Sly. Why, coose?

Sinklo. Because I got it in the tilt-yard: there was a harrald broke my pate for taking it up: but I have worn it up & down the Strand, and met him forty times since, and yet he dares not challenge it.   41

Sly. Do you hear, sir? this play is a bitter play.

Condell. Why, sir, 'tis neither satire nor moral, but the mean passage of a history: yet there are a sort of discontented creatures that bear a stingless envy to great ones, and these will wrest the doings of any man to their base malicious appliment: but should their interpretation come to the test, like your marmasite, they presently turn their teeth to their tail & eat it.

Sly. I will not go so far with you, but I say, any man that hath wit may censure (if he sit in the twelve-penny room) and I say again, the play is bitter.   51

Burbage. Sir, you are like a patron that, presenting a poor scholar to a benefice, enjoins him not to rail against any thing that stands within compass of his patron's folly. Why should not we enjoy the ancient freedom of poesy? Shall we protest to the ladies that their painting makes them angels, or to my young gallant that his expense in the brothel shall gain him reputation? No, sir, such vices as stand not accountable to law should be cured as men heal tetters, by casting ink upon them. Would you be satisfied in any thing else, sir?

Sly. Ay, marry, would I. I would know how you came by this play.   60

Condell. 'Faith sir, the book was lost, and because 'twas pity so good a play should be lost, we found it and play it.

Sly. I wonder you would play it, another company having interest in it?

---

30 fan] i.e., his feather   30 God's so] suggesting *cazzo*, still Italian slang for penis
34 this play . . . feathers] the scoffing references to feathers in the play have put the Blackfriars feather-trade out of business (cf. V. ii. 35-6)   39 tilt-yard] tournament ground   39 harrald] herald   43 moral] morality play   46 appliment] application, interpretation   47-8 like . . . eat it] The badger, not the marmoset, was popularly supposed, when hunted out, to eat its tail (there is a quibble here on 'tale').   50 twelve-penny room] a large box used by the fashionable   58 tetters] eruptions on the skin
61 the book was lost] i.e., by those who originally owned it (cf. ll. 64-5)

Condell. Why not Malevole in folio with us, as Jeronimo in decimo-sexto
   with them? They taught us a name for our play, we call it *One for another*.
Sly. What are your additions?
Burbage. Sooth, not greatly needful, only as your sallet to your great feast,
   to entertain a little more time, and to abridge the not received custom of
   music in our theatre. I must leave you, sir.   *Exit* Burbage.
Sinklo. Doth he play the Malcontent?   70
Condell. Yes, sir.
Sinklo. I durst lay four of mine ears, the play is not so well acted as it hath
   been.
Condell. O no sir, nothing *ad Parmenonis suem*.
Lowin. Have you lost your ears, sir, that you are so prodigal of laying them?
Sinklo. Why did you ask that, friend?
Lowin. Marry sir, because I have heard of a fellow would offer to lay a
   hundred-pound wager, that was not worth five bau-bees: and in this
   kind you might venter four of your elbows: yet God defend your coat
   should have so many.   80
Sinklo. Nay truly, I am no great censurer, and yet I might have been one
   of the College of Critics once: my cousin here hath an excellent memory
   indeed, sir.
Sly. Who, I? I'll tell you a strange thing of my self, and I can tell you, for
   one that never studied the art of memory, 'tis very strange too.
Condell. What's that, sir?
Sly. Why, I'll lay a hundred pound I'll walk but once down by the gold-
   smiths' row in Cheap, take notice of the signs, and tell you them with a
   breath instantly.
Lowin. 'Tis very strange.   90
Sly. They begin as the world did, with Adam and Eve. There's in all just
   five and fifty. I do use to meditate much when I come to plays too. What
   do you think might come into a man's head now, seeing all this company?
Condell. I know not, sir.
Sly. I have an excellent thought: if some fifty of the Grecians that were
   cramm'd in the horse belly had eaten garlic, do you not think the Trojans
   might have smelt out their knavery?

64–5 Why not . . . with them?] The children of the Blackfriars theatre had purloined *The
First Part of Jeronimo*, and in return the King's Men captured *The Malcontent*.   67 sallet]
salad   68–9 the not . . . music] By contrast, the children were primarily choristers and
there was much music at their performances.   74 *ad Parmenonis suem*] compared with
Parmeno's pig: Parmeno could imitate a pig so well that, when a genuine pig was introduced
to compete with him, the onlookers still cried, 'Nothing to Parmeno's pig'   75 lost your
ears] alluding to the cropping of felons' ears   78 bau-bees] bawbees, Scotch coins worth
varying amounts all small: perhaps an allusion to the needy followers of James I   88 Cheap]
Cheapside   95] Sly's thought is probably suggested by the smell of garlic rising from the
groundlings in the pit.

Condell. Very likely.

Sly. By God, I would they had; for I love Hector horribly.

Sinklo. O but coose, coose,   100

> *Great Alexander when he came to the tomb of Achilles*
> *Spake with a big loud voice, O thou thrice blessed & happy.*

Sly. Alexander was an ass to speak so well of a filthy cullion.

Lowin. Good sir, will you leave the stage? I'll help you to a private room.

Sly. Come coose, let's take some tobacco. Have you never a prologue?

Lowin. Not any, sir.

Sly. Let me see, I will make one extempore. Come to them and, fencing of a congee with arms and legs, be round with them.

Gentlemen, I could wish for the women's sakes you had all soft cushions: and gentlewomen, I could wish that for the men's sakes you had all more easy standings.   111

What would they wish more but the play now? and that they shall have instantly.   [*Exeunt.*]

101–2] Sinklo is remembering inaccurately John Harvey's hexameter translation of Petrarch, quoted by Gabriel Harvey in a letter to Spenser (*Three Proper and Wittie Familiar Letters*):

> *Noble* Alexander, *when he came to the tombe of* Achilles,
> *Sighing spake with a bigge voyce; O thrice blessed* Achilles, ...

103 cullion] rascal   107–8 fencing . . . legs] making a show of elaborate and obsequious curtseys (the phrase may be intended as a stage direction)   111 more easy standings] probably alluding to the size of women's dresses, but with a sexual quibble as well

THE MALCONTENT

Vexat censura columbas.

ACTUS PRIMUS. SCE. PRIMA

The vilest out-of-tune music being heard. Enter Bilioso *and* Prepasso.

Bilioso. Why, how now? are ye mad? or drunk? or both? or what?
Prepasso. Are ye building Babylon there?
Bilioso. Here's a noise in court, you think you are in a tavern, do you not?
Prepasso. You think you are in a brothel house, do you not? This room is
ill-scented.

Enter one with a perfume.

So; perfume; perfume; some upon me, I pray thee: the Duke is upon
instant entrance; so, make place there.   7

SCENA SECUNDA

Enter the Duke Pietro, Ferrardo, Count Equato, Count Celso *before, and*
Guerrino.

Pietro. Where breathes that music?
Bilioso. The discord rather than the music is heard from the Malcontent
Malevole's chamber.
Ferrardo. Malevole!
Malevole (out of his chamber). Yaugh, godaman, what dost thou there?
Duke's Ganymed, Juno's jealous of thy long stockings: shadow of a
woman, what would'st, weasel? thou lamb a'court: what dost thou
bleat for? ah you smooth-chinn'd catamite!   8
Pietro. Come down, thou ragged cur, and snarl here, I give thy dogged
sullenness free liberty: trot about and be-spurtle whom thou pleasest.
Malevole. I'll come among you, you goatish-blooded toderers, as gum into
taffeta, to fret, to fret: I'll fall like a sponge into water to suck up; to suck
up. Howl again. I'll go to church, and come to you.   [*Exit above.*]
Pietro. This Malevole is one of the most prodigious affections that ever
converst with nature; a man, or rather a monster, more discontent than

---

Vexat ... columbas] harsh criticism vexes the doves (Juvenal, *Satires*, ii. 63)   I. i, s.d.]
cf. Ind. 68–9   2 *Babylon*] city of vices, with a pun on Babel   I. ii, 5 godaman] God
o' man   8 catamite] male prostitute (corruption of 'Ganymede')   11 toderers] probably
sheep-dealers (= male prostitutes)

Lucifer when he was thrust out of the presence, his appetite is unsatiable
as the grave; as far from any content as from heaven, his highest delight
is to procure others' vexation, and therein he thinks he truly serves
heaven; for 'tis his position, whosoever in this earth can be contented is a
slave and damn'd; therefore does he afflict all in that to which they are
most affected; the elements struggle within him; his own soul is at
variance within herself: his speech is halter-worthy at all hours: I like
him 'faith, he gives good intelligence to my spirit, makes me understand
those weaknesses which others' flattery palliates. Hark, they sing.   24
                                                                  [*A song.*]

SCENA TERTIA

Enter Malevole *after the song.*

[*Pietro.*] See: he comes: now shall you hear the extremity of a malcontent: he
   is as free as air: he blows over every man. And sir, whence come you now?
Malevole. From the public place of much dissimulation, the church.
Pietro. What didst there?
Malevole. Talk with a usurer: take up at interest.
Pietro. I wonder what religion thou art of?
Malevole. Of a soldier's religion.
Pietro. And what dost think makes most infidels now?
Malevole. Sects, sects; I have seen seeming piety change her robe so oft,
   that sure none but some arch-devil can shape her a new petticoat.   10
Pietro. O! a religious policy.
Malevole. But damnation on a politic religion: I am weary, would I were one
   of the Duke's hounds now!
Pietro. But what's the common news abroad, Malevole? thou dogg'st
   rumour still.
Malevole. Common news? why, common words are 'God save ye', 'Fare ye
   well': common actions, flattery and cozenage: common things, women
   and cuckolds. And how does my little Ferrard? ah, ye lecherous animal,
   my little ferret, he goes sucking up & down the palace into every hen's
   nest like a weasel: & to what dost thou addict thy time to now, more than
   to those antique painted drabs that are still affected of young courtiers,
   flattery, pride, & venery?   22
Ferrardo. I study languages: what dost think to be the best linguist of our
   age?
Malevole. Phew, the devil; let him possess thee, he'll teach thee to speak all
   languages, most readily and strangely; and great reason, marry, he's
   travell'd greatly i'the world: and is everywhere.

21 affected] inclined

Ferrardo. Save i'th'court.

Malevole. Ay, save i'th'court. (*To* Bilioso.) And how does my old muckhill,
overspread with fresh snow? thou half a man, half a goat, all a beast:
how does thy young wife, old huddle?   31

Bilioso. Out, you improvident rascal.

Malevole. Do, kick, thou hugely horn'd old duke's ox, good Maister
Make-please.

Pietro. How dost thou live nowadays, Malevole?

Malevole. Why, like the knight Sir Patrick Penlolians, with killing o' spiders
for my lady's monkey.

Pietro. How dost spend the night? I hear thou never sleep'st.

Malevole. O no, but dream the most fantastical. O heaven: O fubbery,
fubbery.   40

Pietro. Dream, what dream'st?

Malevole. Why, me thinks I see that signor pawn his footcloth: that metreza
her plate: this madam takes physic that t'other mounsieur may minister
to her: here is a pander jewell'd: there is a fellow in shift of satten this
day, that could not shift a shirt t'other night: here a Paris supports that
Helen: there's a Lady Guinever bears up that Sir Lancelot. Dreams,
dreams, visions, fantasies, chimeras, imaginations, tricks, conceits.——
(*To* Prepasso.) Sir Tristram Trimtram, come aloft, Jackanapes, with a
whim-wham, here's a knight of the land of Catito shall play at trap with
any page in Europe; do the sword-dance with any Morris-dancer in
Christendom; ride at the ring till the fin of his eyes look as blue as the
welkin, and run the wild-goose chase even with Pompey the Huge.

Pietro. You run——   53

Malevole. To the devil. Now, Signor Guerchino; that thou, from a most
pitied prisoner shouldst grow a most loath'd flatterer! Alas poor Celso,
thy star's opprest, thou art an honest lord, 'tis pity.

Equato. Is't pity?

Malevole. Ay, marry, is't, philosophical Equato, and 'tis pity that thou,
being so excellent a scholar by art, shouldst be so ridiculous a fool by
nature. I have a thing to tell you, Duke; bid 'em avaunt, bid 'em avaunt!

Pietro. Leave us, leave us. Now, sir, what is't?   61

> *Exeunt all saving* Pietro *and* Malevole.

Malevole. Duke, thou art a becco, a cornuto.

---

29 muckhill] The quarto has 'muck ill', which just possibly means 'muckle', hence a huge
pile or lump.   31 huddle] miser   34 Make-please] Flattery   39 fubbery] cheating
44 satten] satin   48–52] a passage of fanciful satire, with several sexual innuendoes
48 Sir Tristram... Jackanapes] the cry of an ape-trainer to his animals to perform
49 land of Catito] playland   49 trap] trap-ball, a bat-and-ball game   51 ride at the
ring] a sport in which the rider tries to throw his spear through a ring   51 fin] lid
52 welkin] sky   62 becco, cornuto] cuckold

Pietro. How?

Malevole. Thou art a cuckold.

Pietro. Speak; unshale him quick.

Malevole. With most tumbler-like nimbleness.

Pietro. Who?—by whom? I burst with desire.

Malevole. Mendoza is the man makes thee a horn'd beast; Duke, 'tis Mendoza cornutes thee.

Pietro. What conformance?—relate! short, short!   70

Malevole. As a lawyer's beard.
> There is an old crone in the court, her name is Maquerelle,
> She is my mistress, sooth to say, and she doth ever tell me.
Blurt a rhyme, blurt a rhyme; Maquerelle is a cunning bawd, I am an honest villain, thy wife is a close drab, and thou art a notorious cuckold, farewell, Duke.

Pietro. Stay, stay.

Malevole. Dull, dull Duke, can lazy patience make lame revenge? O God, for a woman to make a man that which God never created, never made!   80

Pietro. What did God never make?

Malevole. A cuckold: to be made a thing that's hudwinkt with kindness whilst every rascal philips his brows; to have a coxcomb, with egregious horns, pinn'd to a Lord's back, every page sporting himself with delightful laughter, whilst he must be the last man know it. Pistols and poniards, pistols and poniards.

Pietro. Death and damnation!

Malevole. Lightning and thunder!

Pietro. Vengeance and torture!

Malevole. Catzo!   90

Pietro. O revenge!

Malevole. Nay, to select among ten thousand fairs
> A lady far inferior to the most,
> In fair proportion both of limb and soul:
> To take her from austerer check of parents,
> To make her his by most devoutful rites,
> Make her commandress of a better essence
> Than is the gorgeous world, even of a man:
> To hug her with as rais'd an appetite,
> As usurers do their delv'd up treasury,   100
> (Thinking none tells it but his private self,)
> To meet her spirit in a nimble kiss,

---

65 unshale] unshell, i.e., reveal   70 conformance] confirmation   74 Blurt] a fig for   75 close] secret   83 philips] fillips, flicks at (alluding to the cuckold's horns)   90 Catzo] cf. Ind. 3on.

Distilling panting ardour to her heart:
True to her sheets, nay, diets strong his blood,
To give her height of Hymeneal sweets——
Pietro. O God!
Malevole. Whilst she lisps, & gives him some court *quelquechose*,
Made only to provoke, not satiate:
And yet even then, the thaw of her delight
Flows from lewd heat of apprehension,   110
Only from strange imagination's rankness,
That forms the adulterer's presence in her soul,
And makes her think she clips the foul knave's loins.
Pietro. Affliction to my blood's root!
Malevole. Nay think, but think what may proceed of this,
Adultery is often the mother of incest.
Pietro. Incest!
Malevole. Yes, incest: mark, Mendoza of his wife begets perchance a
daughter: Mendoza dies. His son marries this daughter. Say you? Nay,
'tis frequent, not only probable, but no question often acted, whilst
ignorance, fearless ignorance clasps his own seed.   121
Pietro. Hideous imagination!
Malevole. Adultery? why, next to the sin of simony, 'tis the most horrid
transgression under the cope of salvation!
Pietro. Next to simony?
Malevole. Ay, next to simony, in which our men in next age shall not sin.
Pietro. Not sin? Why?
Malevole. Because (thanks to some church-men) our age will leave them
nothing to sin with. But adultery—O dulness!—should show exemplary
punishment, that intemperate bloods may freeze, but to think it. I would
dam him and all his generation, my own hands should do it: ha, I would
not trust heaven with my vengeance any thing.   132
Pietro. Any thing, any thing, Malevole, thou shalt see instantly what temper
my spirit holds; farewell, remember I forget thee not, farewell.

                                                      Exit Pietro.

Malevole. Farewell.
Lean thoughtfulness, a sallow meditation,
Suck thy veins dry, distemperance rob thy sleep!
The heart's disquiet is revenge most deep.
He that gets blood, the life of flesh but spills,
But he that breaks heart's peace, the dear soul kills.   140
    Well, this disguise doth yet afford me that
Which kings do seldom hear, or great men use,

107 *quelquechose*] trifle   124 cope of salvation] heaven   129 should show] Quarto:
'shue, should'.   131 dam] choke up   137 distemperance] upsetting of the humours

Free speech: and though my state's usurpt,
Yet this affected strain gives me a tongue
As fetterless as is an emperor's.
I may speak foolishly, ay, knavishly,
Always carelessly, yet no-one thinks it fashion
To poize my breath, for he that laughs and strikes
Is lightly felt, or seldom struck again.
Duke, I'll torment thee: now my just revenge   150
From thee than crown a richer gem shall part.
Beneath God naught's so dear as a calm heart.

SCENA QUARTA

Enter Celso.

Celso. My honour'd Lord.
Malevole. Peace, speak low; peace, O Celso, constant lord,
   (Thou to whose faith I only rest discovered,
   Thou one of full ten millions of men
   That lovest virtue only for it self,
   Thou in whose hand old Ops may put her soul;)
   Behold for ever banisht Altofront,
   This Genoa's last year's duke. O truly noble,
   I wanted those old instruments of state,
   Dissemblance, and suspect: I could not time it, Celso,   10
   My throne stood like a point in midd'st of a circle,
   To all of equal nearness: bore with none:
   Reign'd all alike, so slept in fearless virtue,
   Suspectless, too suspectless: till the crowd,
   (Still lickerous of untried novelties)
   Impatient with severer government,
   Made strong with Florence: banisht Altofront.
Celso. Strong with Florence, ay, thence your mischief rose,
   For when the daughter of the Florentine
   Was matched once with this Pietro now duke,   20
   No stratagem of state untri'd was left,
   Till you of all——
Malevole.   Of all was quite bereft,
   Alas, Maria too close prisoned:
   My true-faith'd duchess i' the citadel.

148 poize my breath] take account of my words   I. iv, 3 discovered] known   6 Ops]
goddess of plenty   9 wanted] lacked   10 suspect] suspicion   12 bore with] favoured
15 lickerous] greedy

Celso. I'll still adhere, let's mutiny and die.

Malevole. O no, climb not a falling tower, Celso,
    'Tis well held desperation, no zeal:
    Hopeless to strive with fate. Peace, temporize!
    Hope, hope, that never forsak'st the wretched'st man,
    Yet bids me live, and lurk in this disguise.   30
    What? play I well the free-breath'd discontent?
    Why man, we are all philosophical monarchs
    Or natural fools: Celso, the court's afire,
    The duchess' sheets will smoke for't ere it be long:
    Impure Mendoza, that sharp-nos'd lord, that made
    The cursed match linkt Genoa with Florence,
    Now brode-horns the duke, which he now knows:
    Discord to malcontents is very manna;
    When the ranks are burst, then scuffle, Altofront.

Celso. Ay, but durst?   40

Malevole. 'Tis gone, 'tis swallowed like a mineral,
    Some way 'twill work; phewt, I'll not shrink,
    He's resolute who can no lower sink.

    Bilioso *ent'ring,* Malevole *shifteth his speech.*

Malevole. O the father of maypoles! Did you never see a fellow whose whole
    strength consisted in his breath, respect in his office, religion in his lord,
    and love in himself? why then, behold.

Bilioso. Signor.

Malevole. My right worshipful Lord, your court night-cap makes you have
    a passing high forehead.

Bilioso. I can tell you strange news, but I am sure you know them already.
    The Duke speaks much good of you.   51

Malevole. Go to then, and shall you and I now enter into a strict friendship?

Bilioso. Second one another?

Malevole. Yes.

Bilioso. Do one another good offices?

Malevole. Just. What though I call'd thee old ox, egregious wittol, broken-
    bellied coward, rotten mummy, yet since I am in favour——

Bilioso. Words of course, terms of disport. His Grace presents you by me a
    chain, as his grateful remembrance for—I am ignorant for what, marry,
    ye may impart. Yet howsoever—come—dear friend: dost know my son?

Malevole. Your son?   61

27-8 'Tis well . . . fate] your plan is one of despair, not zeal in my cause   31 discontent]
malcontent   37 brode-horns] broad-horns, cuckolds   42 phewt] exclamation of disgust
48-9 your court . . . forehead] alluding to his cuckoldry   56 wittol] contented cuckold

Bilioso. He shall eat woodcocks, dance jigs, make possets, and play at
   shuttlecock with any young lord about the court: he has as sweet a lady
   too: dost know her little bitch?

Malevole. 'Tis a dog, man.

Bilioso. Believe me, a she-bitch! O 'tis a good creature, thou shalt be her
   servant, I'll make thee acquainted with my young wife too: what, I keep
   her not at court for nothing. 'Tis grown to supper time, come to my table,
   that any thing I have stands open to thee.

Malevole. (*To* Celso) How smooth to him that is in state of grace,   70
   How servile is the rugged'st courtier's face!
   What profit, nay, what nature would keep down,
   Are heav'd to them, are minions to a crown.
   Envious ambition never sates his thirst,
   Till, sucking all, he swells, and swells and bursts.

Bilioso. I shall now leave you with my always best wishes, only let's hold
   betwixt us a firm correspondence, a mutual-friendly-reciprocal-kind of
   steady-unanimous-heartily-leagued——

Malevole. Did your Signorship ne'er see a pigeon house that was smooth,
   round, and white without, and full of holes and stink within, ha' ye not,
   old courtier?   81

Bilioso. O yes, 'tis the form, the fashion of them all.

Malevole. Adieu, my true court-friend, farewell my dear Castilio.

Exit Bilioso.

Celso. Yonder's Mendoza.   *Descries* Mendoza.

Malevole.   True, the privy key.

Celso. I take my leave, sweet Lord.   *Exit* Celso.

Malevole.   'Tis fit, away!

SCENA QUINTA

Enter Mendoza, *with three or four* Suitors.

Mendoza. Leave your suits with me, I can and will: attend my secretary,
   leave me.   [*Exeunt* Suitors.]

Malevole. Mendoza, hark ye, hark ye. You are a treacherous villain, God
   bwy ye.

Mendoza. Out, you base-born rascal.

Malevole. We are all the sons of heaven, though a tripe-wife were our
   mother; ah, you whoreson hot-rein'd he-marmoset—Egistus, didst ever
   hear of one Egistus?

73 them, are] them that are   83 Castilio] i.e., Castiglione, author of *The Book of the
Courtier*   I. v, 1 I can and will] i.e., have them satisfied   3 God bwy ye] God be with
you   7 he-marmoset] male prostitute   7 Egistus] Aegisthus, lover of Clytemnaestra,
cuckolder of Agamemnon, later killed by Orestes

Mendoza. Gistus?

Malevole. Ay, Egistus, he was a filthy incontinent fleshmonger, such a one
as thou art.   11

Mendoza. Out, grumbling rogue.

Malevole. Orestes, beware Orestes.

Mendoza. Out, beggar.

Malevole. I once shall rise.

Mendoza. Thou rise?

Malevole.   Ay, at the resurrection.
    'No vulgar seed but once may rise, and shall,
     No king so huge, but 'fore he die may fall.'   *Exit.*

Mendoza. Now good Elysium, what a delicious heaven is it for a man to be
in a prince's favour: O sweet God, O pleasure! O Fortune! O all thou best
of life! what should I think, what say, what do, to be a favourite, a
minion? to have a general timorous respect observe a man, a stateful
silence in his presence: solitariness in his absence, a confused hum and
busy murmur of obsequious suitors training him; the cloth held up, and
way proclaimed before him: petitionary vassals licking the pavement with
their slavish knees, whilst some odd palace lampreels that engender with
snakes, and are full of eyes on both sides, with a kind of insinuated humble-
ness fix all their delights upon his brow: O blessed state, what a ravishing
prospect doth the Olympus of favour yield! Death, I cornute the Duke.
Sweet women, most sweet ladies, nay angels; by heaven, he is more
accursed than a devil that hates you, or is hated by you, and happier
than a God that loves you, or is beloved by you; you preservers of
mankind, life-blood of society, who would live, nay, who can live without
you? O Paradise, how majestical is your austerer presence! how imperiously
chaste is your more modest face! but O! how full of ravishing attraction is
your pretty, petulant, languishing, lasciviously-composed countenance:
those amorous smiles, those soul-warming sparkling glances, ardent as those
flames that sing'd the world by heedless Phaëton! in body how delicate,
in soul how witty, in discourse how pregnant, in life how wary, in favours
how judicious, in day how sociable, and in night how—O pleasure
unutterable! Indeed it is most certain, one man cannot deserve only to
enjoy a beauteous woman: but a duchess! In despite of Phoebus I'll write
a sonnet instantly in praise of her.   *Exit.*

17-18] This sentence is given in quotation marks in the early editions, as are those at
I. vi. 46-7; I. vii. 78, 79-80, 83-4; II. i. 8-9, 29; II. iii. 18-22, 85; II. v. 6-8, 69-71,
101-2; III. i. 8, 34; III. v. 34; IV. iv. 134-5. Most have something of a proverbial ring
but are not otherwise identified, and presumably are *sententiae*, or aphoristic sayings,
coined or adapted by Marston himself.   22 timorous] obsequious   22 observe] follow
24 training] making a train after him   26 lampreels] lampreys   29 cornute] cuckold
38 Phaëton] son of Helios, but incapable of guiding the chariot of the sun   42 Phoebus]
as god of poetry (cf. p. 7, note to l. 31)

SCENA SEXTA

Enter Ferneze *ushering* Aurelia, Emilia *and* Maquerelle *bearing up her train*, Beancha *attending: all go out but* Aurelia, Maquerelle, *and* Ferneze.

Aurelia. And is't possible? Mendoza slight me! possible?
Ferneze. Possible?
　　What can be strange in him that's drunk with favour,
　　Grows insolent with grace? speak, Maquerelle, speak.
Maquerelle. To speak feelingly, more, more richly in solid sense than worthless words, give me those jewels of your ears to receive my inforced duty; as for my part 'tis well (Ferneze *privately feeds* Maquerelle's *hands with jewels during this speech*) known I can put up any thing; can bear patiently with any man: but when I heard he wronged your precious sweetness, I was inforced to take deep offence; 'tis most certain he loves Emilia with high appetite; and as she told me (as you know we women impart our secrets one to another) when she repulsed his suit, in that he was possessed with your endeared grace, Mendoza most ingratefully renounced all faith to you.   14
Ferneze. Nay, call'd you—speak, Maquerelle, speak.
Maquerelle. By heaven, 'witch', 'dri'd bisque', and contested blushlessly, he lov'd you but for a spurt or so.
Ferneze. For maintenance.
Maquerelle. Advancement and regard.
Aurelia. O villain! O impudent Mendoza!   20
Maquerelle. Nay, he is the rustiest-jaw'd, the foulest-mouth'd knave in railing against our sex: he will rail against women——
Aurelia. How? how?
Maquerelle. I am asham'd to speak't, I.
Aurelia. I love to hate him, speak.
Maquerelle. Why, when Emilia scorn'd his base unsteadiness, the black-throated rascal scolded, and said——
Aurelia. What?
Maquerelle. Troth 'tis too shameless.
Aurelia. What said he?   30
Maquerelle. Why, that at four women were fools, at fourteen drabs, at forty bawds, at fourscore witches, and at a hundred cats.
Aurelia. O unlimitable impudency!
Ferneze. But as for poor Ferneze's fixed heart,
　　Was never shadeless meadow drier parcht
　　Under the scorching heat of heaven's dog,
　　Than is my heart with your inforcing eyes.

8 put up] endure　　15 you] i.e., Aurelia　　16 bisque] biscuit　　36 heaven's dog]
The dog star is in the ascendant in July and August.

Maquerelle. A hot simile.

Ferneze. Your smiles have bin my heaven, your frowns my hell;
　O pity then, grace should with beauty dwell.   40

Maquerelle. Reasonable perfect, by'r Lady.

Aurelia. I will love thee, be it but in despite
　Of that Mendoza: 'witch', Ferneze, 'witch'!
　Ferneze, thou art the Duchess' favourite,
　Be faithful, private, but 'tis dangerous.

Ferneze. 'His love is liveless, that for love fears breath;
　The worst that's due to sin, O would 'twere death.'

Aurelia. Enjoy my favour: I will be sick instantly, & take physic, therefore
　in depth of night, visit——

Maquerelle. Visit her chamber, but conditionally you shall not offend her
　bed, by this diamond——   51

Ferneze. By this diamond.——   *Gives it to* Maquerelle.

Maquerelle. Nor tarry longer than you please: by this ruby——

Ferneze. By this ruby.——   *Gives again.*

Maquerelle. And that the door shall not creak——

Ferneze. And that the door shall not creak.

Maquerelle. Nay but swear——

Ferneze. By this purse:——   *Gives her his purse.*

Maquerelle. Go to, I'll keep your oaths for you: remember, visit.

　　Enter Mendoza *reading a sonnet.*

Aurelia. 'Dri'd bisquet!' look where the base wretch comes.   6c

Mendoza. 'Beauty's life, heaven's model, love's queen——'

Maquerelle. That's his Emilia.

Mendoza. 'Nature's triumph, best on earth——'

Maquerelle. Meaning Emilia.

Mendoza. 'Thou only wonder that the world hath seen.'

Maquerelle. That's Emilia.

Aurelia. Must I then hear her prais'd?——Mendoza.

Mendoza. Madam, your Excellency is graciously encount'red; I have bin
　writing passionate flashes in honour of——   *Exit* Ferneze.

Aurelia. Out, villain, villain.   70
　O judgment, where have bin my eyes? what
　Bewitch'd election made me dote on thee?
　What sorcery made me love thee? But be gone,
　Bury thy head; O that I could do more
　Than loathe thee! Hence, worst of ill,
　No reason ask, our reason is our will.   *Exit with* Maquerelle.

50 conditionally] on condition that

Mendoza. Women? nay, furies, nay worse, for they torment only the bad, but women good and bad. Damnation of mankind, breath, hast thou prais'd them for this? And is't you, Ferneze, are wriggled into smock-grace? sit sure. O that I could rail against these monsters in nature, models of hell, curse of the earth, women that dare attempt anything, and what they attempt they care not how they accomplish; without all premeditation or prevention, rash in asking, desperate in working, impatient in suffering, extreme in desiring, slaves unto appetite, mistresses in dissembling, only constant in unconstancy, only perfect in counter-feiting: their words are fained, their eyes forg'd, their sights dissembled, their looks counterfeit, their hair false, their given hopes deceitful, their very breath artificial: their blood is their only God: bad clothes and old age are only the devils they tremble at: that I could rail now!   89

SCENA SEPTIMA

Enter Pietro, *his sword drawn.*

Pietro. A mischief fill thy throat, thou foul-jaw'd slave!
  Say thy prayers.
Mendoza. I ha' forgot 'em.
Pietro. Thou shalt die.
Mendoza. So shalt thou; I am heart-mad.
Pietro. I am horn-mad.
Mendoza. Extreme mad.
Pietro. Monstrously mad.
Mendoza. Why?
Pietro. Why? thou, thou hast dishonoured my bed.   10
Mendoza. I? come, come, sit, here's my bare heart to thee,
  As steady
  As is this centre to the glorious world.
  And yet hark, thou art a cornuto; but by me?
Pietro. Yes slave, by thee.
Mendoza. Do not, do not with tart and spleenful breath
  Lose him can loose thee: I offend the duke?
  Bear record, O ye dumb and raw-air'd nights,
  How vigilant my sleepless eyes have bin
  To watch the traitor; record, thou spirit of truth,   20
  With what debasement I ha' thrown my self
  To under offices, only to learn
  The truth, the party, time, the means, the place,
  By whom, and when, and where thou wert disgrac'd:

79 smock-grace] intimate favour   83 prevention] precaution   86 sights] sighs
89 only the] the only   I. vii, 17 lose] Quarto: 'loose'.

And am I paid with 'slave'? hath my intrusion
To places private, and prohibited,
Only to observe the closer passages——
Heaven knows with vows of revelation——
Made me suspected, made me deem'd a villain?
What rogue hath wronged us?

Pietro.   Mendoza, I may err.   30

Mendoza. Err? 'tis too mild a name, but err and err,
Run giddy with suspect, for through me thou know
That which most creatures save thy self do know.
Nay, since my service hath so loath'd reject,
'Fore I'll reveal, shalt find them clipt together.

Pietro. Mendoza, thou know'st I am a plain-breasted man.

Mendoza. The fitter to make a cuckold; would your brows were most plain
too!

Pietro. Tell me, indeed I heard thee rail——

Mendoza. At women, true; why, what cold fleam could choose,   40
Knowing a lord so honest, virtuous,
So boundless loving, bounteous, fair shap'd, sweet,
To be contemn'd, abus'd, defam'd, made cuckold?
Heart, I hate all women for't: sweet sheets, wax lights, antique bed-posts,
cambric smocks, villainous curtains, arras pictures, oil'd hinges, and all
the tongue-ti'd lascivious witnesses of great creatures' wantonness: what
salvation can you expect?

Pietro. Wilt thou tell me?

Mendoza. Why, you may find it your self, observe, observe.

Pietro. I ha' not the patience: wilt thou deserve me? tell, give it.   50

Mendoza. Tak't. Why, Ferneze is the man, Ferneze, I'll prove't: this night
you shall take him in your sheets, will't serve?

Pietro. It will, my bosom's in some peace; till night——

Mendoza. What?

Pietro.   Farewell.

Mendoza.   God, how weak a lord are you!
Why, do you think there is no more but so?

Pietro. Why?

Mendoza. Nay, then will I presume to counsel you.
It should be thus;
You with some guard upon the sudden break
Into the princess' chamber: I stay behind   60
Without the door, through which he needs must pass:

27 closer passages] more secret exchanges   28 of revelation] that I would reveal
34 reject] rejection   40 fleam] phlegm, the cold and moist humour, breeding apathy
45 arras] tapestry   50 deserve me] earn my favour, or perhaps, serve me

Ferneze flies, let him, to me he comes,
He's killed
By me, observe, by me: you follow, I rail,
And seem to save the body: duchess comes
On whom (respecting her advanced birth,
And your fair nature) I know—nay, I do know—
No violence must be us'd. She comes, I storm,
I praise, excuse Ferneze, and still maintain
The duchess' honour, she for this loves me,   70
I honour you, shall know her soul, you mine,
Then naught shall she contrive in vengeance
(As women are most thoughtful in revenge)
Of her Ferneze, but you shall sooner know't
Than she can think't. Thus shall his death come sure;
Your duchess brain-caught; so your life secure.

Pietro. It is too well, my bosom and my heart.
'When nothing helps, cut off the rotten part.'   *Exit.*

Mendoza. 'Who cannot feign friendship can ne'er produce the effects of
hatred.' Honest fool Duke, subtile lascivious Duchess, silly novice
Ferneze, I do laugh at ye; my brain is in labour till it produce mischief,
& I feel sudden throes, proofs sensible the issue is at hand.   82
'As bears shape young, so I'll form my devise,
Which grown proves horrid: vengeance makes men wise.'   *Exit.*

[SCENA OCTAVA]

Enter Malevole *and* Passarello.

Malevole. Fool, most happily encount'red, canst sing, fool?

Passarello. Yes, I can sing fool, if you'll bear the burden, and I can play
upon instruments, scurvily, as gentlemen do; O that I had been gelded,
I should then have been a fat fool for a chamber, a squeaking fool for a
tavern, and a private fool for all the ladies.

Malevole. You are in good case since you came to court, fool; what, guarded,
guarded!

Passarello. Yes 'faith, even as footmen and bawds wear velvet, not for an
ornament of honour, but for a badge of drudgery: for now the Duke is
discontented I am fain to fool him asleep every night.   10

Malevole. What are his griefs?

Passarello. He hath sore eyes.

Malevole. I never observed so much.

76 brain-caught] betrayed by cunning   I. viii, 2 bear the burden] sing the refrain
6 guarded] adorned (with court insignia)

Passarello. Horrible sore eyes; and so hath every cuckold, for the roots of the horns spring in the eye-balls, and that's the reason the horn of a cuckold is as tender as his eye; or as that growing in the woman's forehead twelve years since, that could not endure to be toucht. The Duke hangs down his head like a columbine.

Malevole. Passarello, why do great men beg fools?

Passarello. As the Welshman stole rushes, when there was nothing else to filch; only to keep begging in fashion.   21

Malevole. Pooh, thou givest no good reason, thou speakest like a fool.

Passarello. 'Faith, I utter small fragments as your knight courts your city widow with jingling of his gilt spurs, advancing his bush-coloured beard, and taking tobacco. This is all the mirror of their knightly complements. Nay, I shall talk when my tongue is a-going once; 'tis like a citizen on horseback, evermore in a false gallop.

Malevole. And how doth Maquerelle fare nowadays?

Passarello. 'Faith, I was wont to salute her as our English women are at their first landing in Flushing. I would call her whore; but now that antiquity leaves her as an old piece of plastic t'work by, I only ask her how her rotten teeth fare every morning, and so leave her: she was the first that ever invented perfum'd smocks for the gentlewomen, and woollen shoes for fear of creaking for the visitant: she were an excellent lady, but that her face peeleth like Muscovy glass.   35

Malevole. And how doth thy old lord that hath wit enough to be a flatterer, and conscience enough to be a knave?

Passarello. O excellent, he keeps beside me fifteen jesters, to instruct him in the art of fooling, and utters their jests in private to the Duke and Duchess; he'll be like to your Switzer, or lawyer; he'll be of any side for most money.   41

Malevole. I am in haste, be brief.

Passarello. As your fiddler when he is paid. He'll thrive, I warrant you, while your young courtier stands like Goodfriday in Lent: men long to see it, because more fatting days come after it: else he's the leanest and pitifull'st actor in the pageant. Adieu Malevole.

Malevole. O world most vilde, when thy loose vanities,
    Taught by this fool, do make the fools seem wise!

Passarello. You'll know me again, Malevole.

Malevole. O ay, by that velvet.   50

16–17 that growing . . . since] A pamphlet of 1588 describes the case of a Welshwoman with a horn on her forehead.   18 columbine] Its horned nectaries suggest allusions to cuckoldry.   19 beg fools] seek the guardianship of idiots in order to enjoy the use of their estates (cf. *Women Beware Women* III. ii. 113)   25 complements] accomplishments 30 Flushing] then in English hands as security for a loan   31 plastic] a wax model for sculpture 35 Muscovy glass] mica 40 Switzer] mercenary (from Switzerland) 47 vilde] vile

Passarello. Ay, as a pettifogger by his buckram bag, I am as common in the court as an hostess's lips in the country; knights, and clowns, and knaves, and all share me: the court cannot possibly be without me. Adieu, Malevole. [*Exeunt.*]

ACTUS SECUNDUS. SCE. PRIMA

Enter Mendoza *with a sconce, to observe* Ferneze's *entrance, who, whilst the Act is playing, enter unbraced, 2 Pages before him with lights, is met by* Maquerelle, *and convey'd in. The pages sent away.*

Mendoza. He's caught, the woodcock's head is i'th' noose,
    Now treads Ferneze in dangerous path of lust,
    Swearing his sense is merely deified.
    The fool grasps clouds, and shall beget centaurs.
    And now in strength of panting faint delight,
    The goat bids heaven envy him; good goose,
    I can afford thee nothing but the poor comfort of calamity, pity.
    'Lusts, like the plummets hanging on clock lines,
    Will ne'er 'a' done, till all is quite undone.'
    Such is the course salt sallow lust doth run.   10
    Which thou shalt try; I'll be reveng'd. Duke, thy suspect;
    Duchess, thy disgrace; Ferneze, thy rivalship,
    Shall have swift vengeance: nothing so holy,
    No band of nature so strong,
    No law of friendship so sacred,
    But I'll profane, burst, violate,
    'Fore I'll endure disgrace, contempt and poverty:
    Shall I, whose very hum strook all heads bare,
    Whose face made silence, creaking of whose shoe
    Forc'd the most private passages fly ope,   20
    Scrape like a servile dog at some latch'd door?
    Learn now to make a leg? and cry 'Beseech ye,
    Pray ye, is such a Lord within'? be aw'd
    At some odd usher's scoft formality?
    First sear my brains: *Unde cadis non quo refert:*
    My heart cries 'Perish all'. How? how? What fate
    Can once avoid revenge that's desperate?
    I'll to the Duke. If all should ope—if? tush,
    'Fortune still dotes on those who cannot blush.'   [*Exit*]

51 pettifogger] lawyer of inferior status   II. i, s.d. *Act*] entr'acte music   3 merely] entirely   4 The fool . . . centaurs] the fate of Ixion   8 plummets] clock weights 10 salt] salacious   18 very hum] slightest utterance   18 strook] struck   22 make a leg] bow   25 *Unde . . . refert*] Whence one falls, not whither, is what counts (from Seneca)

SCENA SECUNDA

Enter Malevole *at one door*, Beancha, Emilia, *and* Maquerelle *at the other door.*

Malevole. Bless ye, cast o' ladies! ha, Dipsas, how dost thou, old coal?
Maquerelle. Old coal?
Malevole. Ay, old coal, me thinks thou liest like a brand under these billets
   of green wood. He that will inflame a young wench's heart, let him lay
   close to her an old coal that hath first bin fir'd, a pandress, my half-burnt
   lint, who, though thou canst not flame thy self yet art able to set a 1000
   virgins' tapers afire: and how does Janivere thy husband, my little
   periwinkle? is 'a troubled with the cough a' the lungs still? does he hawk
   a'nights still? he will not bite.
Beancha. No by my troth, I took him with his mouth empty of old teeth.
Malevole. And he took thee with thy belly full of young bones, marry, he
   took his maim by the stroke of his enemy.   12
Beancha. And I mine by the stroke of my friend.
Malevole. The close stock, O mortal wench! Lady, ha' ye now no restoratives
   for your decayed Jasons, look ye? crabs' guts, bak't, distill'd ox-pith,
   the pulverized hairs of a lion's upper lip, jelly of cock-sparrows, he-
   monkeys' marrow, or pouldre of fox-stones? and whither are all you
   ambling now?
Beancha. Why to bed, to bed.
Malevole. Do your husbands lie with ye?   20
Beancha. That were country fashion i'faith.
Malevole. Ha' ye no foregoers about you? come, whether in good deed, law
   now?
Beancha. In good indeed, law now, to eat the most miraculously, admirably,
   astonishable compos'd posset with three curds, without any drink:
   will ye help me with a he-fox? Here's the Duke.
                                                           The Ladies go out.
Malevole. (*To* Beancha) Fri'd frogs are very good & French-like too.

---

1 cast] pair   1 Dipsas] a fabulous serpent, here a bawd   3-4 brand . . . wood] A
maquera is a bawd, who, burnt herself, will set light to those young and fresh.   6 lint]
Flax was used for kindling.   7 Janivere] alluding to Chaucer's *Merchant's Tale* of
old January and his young wife May   14 stock] stoccado, a thrust in fencing (with here
a sexual quibble)   14 restoratives] aphrodisiacs (like the following)   15 ox-pith] pith
supposed to grow in the ox's back   17 pouldre] powder   17-stones] testicles
22 foregoers] harbingers, ushers   22 whether] whither   22 law now] an exclamation
25 posset . . . curds] Possets were made with ale and milk.

SCENA TERTIA

Enter Duke Pietro, Count Celso, Count Equato, Bilioso, Ferrard, *and*
Mendoza.

Pietro. The night grows deep and foul, what hour is't?
Celso. Upon the stroke of twelve.
Malevole. Save ye, Duke.
Pietro. From thee: begone, I do not love thee, let me see thee no more, we
    are displeas'd.
Malevole. Why, God be with thee, heaven hear my curse, may thy wife and
    thee live long together.
Pietro. Be gone, sirrah.
Malevole. When Arthur first in court began,—Agamemnon, Menelaus—was
    ever any duke a cornuto?   10
Pietro. Begone hence.
Malevole. What religion wilt thou be of next?
Mendoza. Out with him!
Malevole. With most servile patience time will come,
    When wonder of thy error will strike dumb
    Thy bezzl'd sense,
    Slave's i' favour, ay, marry, shall he rise——
    'Good God, how subtile hell doth flatter vice,
    Mounts him aloft, and makes him seem to fly,
    As foul the tortoise mockt, who to the sky   20
    Th'ambitious shellfish rais'd: th'end of all
    Is only that from height he might dead fall.'
Bilioso. Why, when? out, ye rogue, be gone, ye rascal.
Malevole. 'I shall now leave ye with all my best wishes.'
Bilioso. Out, ye cur.
Malevole. 'Only let's hold together a firm correspondence.'
Bilioso. Out.
Malevole. 'A mutual friendly reciprocal perpetual kind of steady unanimous
    heartily leagued——'
Bilioso. Hence, ye gross-jaw'd, peasantly, out, go.   30
Malevole. Adieu, pigeon-house: thou burr that only stickest to nappy
    fortunes, the sarpego, the strangury, an eternal, uneffectual priapism seize
    thee!
Bilioso. Out, rogue.

9 When .. began] the opening line of a ballad also sung in 2 *Henry IV*: the three
men are all cuckolds   16 bezzl'd] fuddled with drink   24, 26, 28–9] cf. I. iv.76–8
31] cf. I. iv. 79   31 nappy] shaggy   32 sarpego] serpigo, ringworm   32 strangury]
a disease of the urinary organs   32 priapism] persistent erection of the penis

Malevole. Mayest thou be a notorious wittolly pander to thine own wife,
and yet get no office but live to be the utmost misery of mankind, a
beggarly cuckold.   *Exit.*

Pietro. It shall be so.

Mendoza. It must be so, for where great states revenge,
    'Tis requisite the parts (which piety   40
    And loft respect forbears) be closely dogg'd.
    Lay one into his breast shall sleep with him,
    Feed in the same dish, run in self-faction,
    Who may discover any shape of danger,
    For once disgrac'd, displayed in offence,
    It makes man blushless, and man is (all confess)
    More prone to vengeance than to gratefulness.
    Favours are writ in dust, but stripes we feel
    Depraved nature stamps in lasting steel.

Pietro. You shall be leagued with the Duchess!   50

Equato. The plot is very good.

Mendoza. You shall both kill and seem the corse to save.

Ferrardo. A most fine brain-trick.

Celso. (*tacite*) Of a most cunning knave.

Pietro. My Lords: the heavy action we intend
    Is death and shame, two of the ugliest shapes
    That can confound a soul: think, think of it;
    I strike but yet, like him that 'gainst stone walls
    Directs his shafts, rebounds in his own face,
    My Lady's shame is mine, O God, 'tis mine.   60
    Therefore I do conjure all secrecy,
    Let it be as very little as may be;
    Pray ye, as may be.
    Make frightless entrance, salute her with soft eyes,
    Stain naught with blood—only Ferneze dies,
    But not before her brows: O gentlemen,
    God knows I love her; nothing else, but this:
    I am not well. If grief that sucks veins dry,
    Rivels the skin, casts ashes in men's faces,
    Bedulls the eye, unstrengthens all the blood,   70
    Chance to remove me to another world,
    As sure I once must die, let him succeed:

40–41 A corrupt passage in the quarto: the sense seems to be that it is requisite that the
parties involved be closely watched, which the dignity of royalty precludes the Duke's
doing himself.   41 loft] elevated   42ff.] i.e., a spy is to be set in the guise of a close
companion   48–9] Favours are quickly forgotten but injuries etched permanently into
our memories   52 corse] corpse   54 *tacite*] aside   61 conjure] beseech   64 fright-
less] without arousing fright   69 rivels] wrinkles

I have no child, all that my youth begot
Hath bin your loves, which shall inherit me:
Which, as it ever shall, I do conjure it,
Mendoza may succeed, he's noble born:
With me of much desert.

Celso. (*tacite*) Much!

Pietro. Your silence answers 'ay',
I thank you, come on now. O that I might die,   80
Before her shame's display'd, would I were forc'd
To burn my father's tomb, unhele his bones,
And dash them in the dirt, rather than this:
This both the living and the dead offends,
'Sharp surgery where naught but death amends.'

Exit with others.

SCENA QUARTA

Enter Maquerelle, Emilia, *and* Beancha, *with a posset.*

Maquerelle. Even here it is, three curds in three regions individually distinct.
Most methodically according to art compos'd, without any drink.

Beancha. Without any drink?

Maquerelle. Upon my honour. Will you sit and eat?

Emilia. Good. The composure, the receipt, how is't?

Maquerelle. 'Tis a pretty pearl; by this pearl (how does't with me?), thus it
is: seven and thirty yolks of Barbary hens' eggs, eighteen spoonfuls and a
half of the joice of cocksparrow bones, one ounce, three drams, four
scruples, and one quarter of the syrup of Ethiopian dates, sweet'ned with
three quarters of a pound of pure candy'd Indian eryngoes, strow'd
over with the powder of pearl of America, amber of Cataia, and lamb-
stones of Muscovia.   12

Beancha. Trust me, the ingredients are very cordial, and no question good,
and most powerful in restauration.

Maquerelle. I know not what you mean by restauration, but this it doth, it
purifieth the blood, smootheth the skin, inlifeneth the eye, strength'neth
the veins, mundefieth the teeth, comforteth the stomach, fortifieth
the back, and quick'neth the wit, that's all.

Emilia. By my troth I have eaten but two spoonfuls, and me thinks I could
discourse most swiftly, and wittily already.   20

Maquerelle. Have you the art to seem honest?

82 unhele] uncover   II. iv, 6 how does't with me?] how does it suit me?   8 joice]
juice   9 scruple] one twenty-fourth of an ounce   10 eryngoes] the candied root of
the sea-holly, *eryngium maritimum*   10 strow'd] strewn   11 Cataia] China (Cathay)
11 lamb-stones] cf. II. ii. 17 and note   17 mundefieth] cleans   21 honest] chaste

Beancha. Ay, thank advice and practice.

Maquerelle. Why then, eat me of this posset, quicken your blood, and preserve your beauty. Do you know Doctor Plaster-face? by this curd he is the most exquisite in forging of veins, spright'ning of eyes, dyeing of hair, sleeking of skins, blushing of cheeks, surfling of breasts, blanching and bleaching of teeth, that ever made an old lady gracious by torch-light: by this curd, law!

Beancha. Well, we are resolv'd, what God has given us we'll cherish.

Maquerelle. Cherish any thing saving your husband, keep him not too high least he leap the pale: but for your beauty, let it be your saint, bequeath two hours to it every morning in your closet: I ha' bin young, and yet in my conscience I am not above five and twenty, but believe me, preserve and use your beauty, for youth and beauty once gone, we are like beehives without honey: out a' fashion, apparel that no man will wear, therefore use me your beauty.   36

Emilia. Ay, but men say——

Maquerelle. Men say—let them say what they will: life o' woman! they are ignorant of your wants. The more in years the more in perfection they grow: if they lose youth and beauty, they gain wisdom and discretion: but when our beauty fades, godnight with us! there cannot be an uglier thing to see than an old woman, from which, O pruning, pinching, and painting, deliver all sweet beauties!   [*Music.*]

Beancha. Hark, music.

Maquerelle. Peace, 'tis the Duchess' bed-chamber. Good rest, most prosperously grac'd ladies.   46

Emilia. Good night, sentinel.

Beancha. Night, dear Maquerelle.   *Exeunt all but* Maq.

Maquerelle. May my posset's operation send you my wit and honesty, and me your youth and beauty: the pleasing'st rest!   *Exit* Maq.

SCENA QUINTA

A Song [*within*].

Whilst the song is singing, enter Mendoza, *with his sword drawn, standing ready to murder* Ferneze *as he flies from the* Duchess' *chamber.*
[*Tumult within.*]

All [*within*]. Strike, strike.

Aurelia [*within*]. Save my Ferneze, O save my Ferneze.

---

22 thank] thanks to   25 forging] disguising   25 spright'ning] brightening   26 surfling] washing with a cosmetic   32–3 yet … I am] even now I feel   34 use] invest, put to usury   42 pruning] dressing up, adorning

Enter Ferneze *in his shirt, & is receiv'd upon* Mendoz. *sword.*

All [*within*]. Follow, pursue.
Aurelia [*within*]. O save Ferneze.
Mendoza. Pierce, pierce! Thou shallow fool, drop there.
                                        Thrusts his rapier in Fer[neze].
   'He that attempts a princess' lawless love
   Must have broad hands, close heart with Argus' eyes,
   And back of Hercules, or else he dies.'

Enter Aurelia, Duke Pietro, Ferrardo, Bilioso, Celso *and* Equato.

All. Follow, follow.
Mendoza. Stand off, forbear, ye most uncivil Lords.   10
Pietro. Strike.
Mendoza. Do not; tempt not a man resolv'd;
                              Mendoza *bestrides the wounded body*
                                  of Ferneze *and seems to save him.*
   Would you inhuman murtherers more than death?
Aurelia. O poor Ferneze.
Mendoza. Alas, now all defence too late.
Aurelia.   He's dead.
Pietro. I am sorry for our shame: go to your bed:
   Weep not too much, but leave some tears to shed
   When I am dead.
Aurelia. What, weep for thee? my soul no tears shall find.
Pietro. Alas, alas, that women's souls are blind.   20
Mendoza. Betray such beauty?
   Murther such youth? contemn civility?
   He loves him not that rails not at him.
Pietro. Thou canst not move us: we have blood enough;
   And please you Lady, we have quite forgot
   All your defects: if not, why then——
Aurelia.   Not.
Pietro.   Not.
   The best of rest, good night.   *Exit* Pietro *with other* courtiers.
Aurelia.   Despite go with thee.
Mendoza. Madam, you ha' done me foul disgrace.
   You have wrong'd him much, loves you too much.
   Go to; your soul knows you have.   30
Aurelia. I think I have.
Mendoza.   Do you but think so?

7 close] secret   29 loves] i.e., who loves

Aurelia. Nay, sure I have, my eyes have witnessed
    Thy love, thou hast stood too firm for me.
Mendoza. Why, tell me, fair-cheekt Lady, who even in tears
    Art powerfully beauteous, what unadvised passion
    Strook ye into such a violent heat against me?
    Speak, what mischief wrong'd us? what devil injur'd us?
    Speak.
Aurelia. That thing ne'er worthy of the name of man:
    Ferneze;   40
    Ferneze swore thou lov'st Emilia,
    Which to advance, with most reproachful breath,
    Thou both didst blemish and denounce my love.
Mendoza. Ignoble villain, did I for this bestride
    Thy wounded limbs? for this rank opposite
    Even to my sovereign? for this? O God, for this
    Sunk all my hopes, and with my hopes my life,
    Ript bare my throat unto the hangman's axe?
    Thou most dishonour'd trunk—Emilia?
    By life I know her not—Emilia?   50
    Did you believe him?
Aurelia.   Pardon me, I did.
Mendoza. Did you? and thereupon you graced him?
Aurelia. I did.
Mendoza.   Took him to favour, nay, even clasp'd
    With him?
Aurelia.   Alas, I did.
Mendoza.   This night?
Aurelia.   This night.
Mendoza. And in your lustful twines the Duke took you?
Aurelia. A most sad truth.
Mendoza. O God, O God, how we dull honest souls,
    Heavy-brain'd men, are swallowed in the bogs
    Of a deceitful ground, whilst nimble bloods,
    Light-jointed spirits, pent, cut good men's throats,   60
    And scape.
    Alas, I am too honest for this age,
    Too full of fleam and heavy steadiness:
    Stood still whilst this slave cast a noose about me;
    Nay then, to stand in honour of him, and her,
    Who had even slic'd my heart!
Aurelia.   Come, I did err,
    And am most sorry, I did err.

45–6 rank opposite . . . to] oppose

Mendoza. Why, we are both but dead, the Duke hates us,
    'And those whom princes do once groundly hate,
    Let them provide to die; as sure as fate,   70
    Prevention is the heart of policy.'
Aurelia. Shall we murder him?
Mendoza. Instantly?
Aurelia. Instantly, before he casts a plot,
    Or further blaze my honour's much-known blot,
    Let's murther him.
Mendoza. I would do much for you, will ye marry me?
Aurelia. I'll make thee Duke, we are of Medicis,
    Florence our friend, in court my faction
    Not meanly strengthful; the Duke then dead,   80
    We well prepar'd for change: the multitude
    Irresolutely reeling: we in force:
    Our party seconded: the kingdom maz'd:
    No doubt of swift success, all shall be grac'd.
Mendoza. You do confirm me, we are resolute,
    Tomorrow look for change, rest confident.
    'Tis now about the immodest waist of night,
    The mother of moist dew with pallid light
    Spreads gloomy shades about the numbed earth.
    Sleep, sleep, whilst we contrive our mischief's birth.   90
    This man I'll get inhum'd; farewell, to bed,
    I kiss thy pillow, dream the Duke is dead.   *Exit* Aurelia.
    So, so, good night. How fortune dotes on impudence!
    I am in private the adopted son
    Of yon good prince,
    I must be duke: why, if I must, I must.
Most silly lord, name me? O heaven, I see God made honest fools, to
maintain crafty knaves: the Duchess is wholly mine too; must kill her
husband to quit her shame. Much! Then marry her: ay;
    O I grow proud in prosperous treachery: 100
    'As wrestlers clip, so I'll embrace you all,
    Not to support, but to procure your fall.'

    Enter Malevole.

Malevole. God arrest thee.
Mendoza. At whose suit?

Malevole. At the devil's: ha, you treacherous damnable monster, how dost? how dost, thou treacherous rogue? Ha, ye rascal, I am banisht the court, sirrah.

Mendoza. Prethee let's be acquainted, I do love thee 'faith.

Malevole. At your service, by the Lord. Law! shall's go to supper? Let's be once drunk together, and so unite a most virtuously strengthened friend-ship, shall's, Huguenot, shall's?   111

Mendoza. Wilt fall upon my chamber tomorrow morn?

Malevole. As a raven to a dunghill. They say there's one dead here, prickt for the pride of the flesh.

Mendoza. Ferneze—there he is, pray thee bury him.

Malevole. O most willingly, I mean to turn pure Rochel churchman, I.

Mendoza. Thou churchman, why? why?

Malevole. Because I'll live lazily, rail upon authority; deny king's supremacy in things indifferent, and be a Pope in mine own parish.

Mendoza. Wherefore dost thou think churches were made?   120

Malevole. To scour plough-shares: I have seen oxen plough up altars: '*et nunc seges ubi Sion fuit*'.

Mendoza. Strange!

Malevole. Nay, monstrous: I ha' seen a sumptuous steeple turned to a stinking privy: more beastly, the sacred'st place made a dog's kennel: nay, most inhuman, the ston'd coffins of long dead Christians burst up, and made hogs'-troughs. '*Hic finis Priami.*' Shall I ha' some sack and cheese at thy chamber? Good night, good mischievous incarnate devil, godnight Mendoza. Ha, ye inhuman villain, godnight, night, fub.   130

Mendoza. God night: tomorrow morn.   *Exit* Mendoza.

Malevole. Ay, I will come, friendly damnation, I will come. I do descry cross-points, honesty and courtship straddle as far asunder as a true Frenchman's legs.

Ferneze. O!

Malevole. Proclamations, more proclamations.

Ferneze. O a surgeon!

Malevole. Hark, lust cries for a surgeon; what news from Limbo? How doth the grand cuckold Lucifer?

Ferneze. O help, help, conceal & save me.   140

> Ferneze *stirs, &* Mal. *helps him up, and conveys him away.*

---

111 Huguenot] here apparently used in the sense of hypocrite or traitor   116 Rochel] La Rochelle, where the Huguenots found refuge   119 things indifferent] matters where no religious rule is laid down   122 *et nunc ... fuit*] and now there is a cornfield where Sion was (adapted from Ovid)   127 *Hic ... Priami*] this is the end of Priam (adapted from Virgil)   130 fub] cheat   133 cross-points] trickery (properly a dance step) 133 courtship] courtiership

Malevole. Thy shame more than thy wounds do grieve me far,
　　Thy wounds but leave upon thy flesh some scar:
　　But fame ne'er heals, still rankles worse and worse,
　　Such is of uncontrolled lust the curse.
　　Think what it is in lawless sheets to lie,
　　But O Ferneze, what in lust to die:
　　Then thou that shame respects, O fly converse
　　With women's eyes and lisping wantonness:
　　Stick candles 'gainst a virgin wall's white back,
　　If they not burn, yet at the least they'll black.   150
　　Come, I'll convey thee to a private port,
　　Where thou shalt live (O happy man) from court.
　　The beauty of the day begins to rise,
　　From whose bright form night's heavy shadow flies.
　　Now 'gins close plots to work, the scene grows full,
　　And craves his eyes who hath a solid skull.   *Exeunt.*

ACTUS TERTIUS. SCE. PRIMA

Enter Pietro the Duke, Mendoz: Count Equato *and* Bilioso.

Pietro. 'Tis grown to youth of day, how shall we waste
　　This light?
　　My heart's more heavy than a tyrant's crown.
　　Shall we go hunt? Prepare for field.   *Exit* Equat.
Mendoza. Would ye could be merry.
Pietro. Would God I could: Mendoza, bid 'em haste.   *Exit* Mendoza.
　　I would fain shift place; O vain relief!
　　'Sad souls may well change place, but not change grief:'
　　As deer being struck fly thorough many soils,
　　Yet still the shaft stick fast, so,——   10
Bilioso. A good old simile, my honest Lord.
Pietro. I am not unlike to some sickman,
　　That long desired hurtful drink; at last
　　Swills in and drinks his last, ending at once
　　Both life and thirst: O would I ne'er had known
　　My own dishonour: good God, that men should
　　Desire to search out that, which being found

---

147 respects] i.e., respect'st   149–50 Stick . . . black] even if honour is not impaired,
reputation is bound to be blackened   151 private port] place of retreat   155 'gins]
begins   156 solid skull] sound head   III. i, 9 soils] pools used by hunted animals as refuges

Kills all their joy of life! to taste the tree
Of knowledge,
And then be driven out of Paradise!   20
Canst give me some comfort?

Bilioso. My Lord, I have some books which have been dedicated to my
honour, and I ne'er read 'em, and yet they had very fine names: *Physic for
Fortune: Lozenges of sanctified sincerity:* very pretty works of curates,
scriveners and schoolmasters. Marry, I remember one Seneca, Lucius
Anneus Seneca.

Pietro. Out upon him, he writ of temperance and fortitude, yet lived like a
voluptuous epicure, and died like an effeminate coward.
Haste thee to Florence:
Here, take our letters, see 'em seal'd, away!   30
Report in private to the honour'd duke
His daughter's forc'd disgrace, tell him at length
We know too much. Due compliments advance.
'There's naught that's safe and sweet but ignorance.'   *Exit* Duke.

Enter Beancha.

Bilioso. Madam, I am going embassador for Florence, 'twill be great charges
to me.

Beancha. No matter my Lord, you have the lease of two manors come out
next Christmas; you may lay your tenants on the greater rack for it: and
when you come home again, I'll teach you how you shall get two hundred
pounds a year by your teeth!   40

Bilioso. How, Madam?

Beancha. Cut off so much from house-keeping: that which is saved by the
teeth, you know, is got by the teeth.

Bilioso. 'Fore God, and so I may, I am in wondrous credit, Lady.

Beancha. See the use of flattery, I did ever counsel you to flatter greatness,
and you have profited well: any man that will do so shall be sure to be
like your Scotch barnacle, now a block, instantly a worm, and presently a
great goose: this it is to rot and putrefy in the bosom of greatness.

Bilioso. Thou art ever my politician: O how happy is that old lord that hath
a politician to his young lady! I'll have fifty gentlemen shall attend upon
me; marry, the most of them shall be farmers' sons, because they shall
bear their own charges, and they shall go apparell'd thus, in sea-water
green suits, ash-colour cloaks, wetchet stockings, and popinjay green
feathers: will not the colours do excellent?   54

23–4 *Physic . . . sincerity*] The names are probably intended to suggest Puritan pamphlets.
37 come out] expired   38 lay . . . rack] force more from your tenants   47 Scotch
barnacle] Barnacles were believed to grow on trees in Scotland and to turn into wild geese.
47 block] stump of a tree   51–2 they . . charges] Yeomen were obliged to supply men
for the militia at their own expense.   53 wetchet] i.e., watchet, light blue

Beancha. Out upon't, they'll look like citizens riding to their friends at Whitsuntide, their apparel just so many several parishes.

Bilioso. I'll have it so, and Passarello my fool shall go along with me, marry, he shall be in velvet!

Beancha. A fool in velvet?

Bilioso. Ay, 'tis common for your fool to wear satin, I'll have mine in velvet.

Beancha. What will you wear then, my Lord?   61

Bilioso. Velvet too, marry, it shall be embroidered, because I'll differ from the fool somewhat. I am horribly troubled with the gout, nothing grieves me but that my doctor hath forbidden me wine, and you know your ambassador must drink. Didst thou ask thy doctor what was good for the gout?

Beancha. Yes, he said ease, wine and women were good for it.

Bilioso. Nay, thou hast such a wit; what was good to cure it, said he?

Beancha. Why, the rack: all your empericks could never do the like cure upon the gout the rack did in England; or your Scotch boot. The French herlakeen will instruct you.   71

Bilioso. Surely I do wonder how thou, having for the most part of thy lifetime been a country body, shouldest have so good a wit.

Beancha. Who, I? why, I have been a courtier thrice two months.

Bilioso. So have I this twenty year, and yet there was a gentleman usher call'd me coxcomb t'other day, and to my face too: was't not a back-biting rascal? I would I were better travell'd, that I might have been better acquainted with the fashions of several countrymen: but my secretary, I think he hath sufficiently instructed me.

Beancha. How, my Lord?   80

Bilioso. Marry, my good Lord, quoth he, your Lordship shall ever find amongst a hundred Frenchmen, forty hot shots: amongst a hundred Spaniards, threescore braggarts: amongst a hundred Dutchmen, fourscore drunkards: amongst a hundred Englishmen, fourscore and ten madmen: and amongst an hundred Welchmen——

Beancha. What, my Lord?

Bilioso. Fourscore and nineteen gentlemen.

Beancha. But since you go about a sad imbassy, I would have you go in black, my Lord.

Bilioso. Why, dost think I cannot mourn, unless I wear my hat in cipers like an alderman's heir? That's vile, very old, in faith.   91

Beancha. I'll learn of you shortly; O we should have a fine gallant of you,

---

56 several parishes] i.e., mismatching   69 empericks] i.e., empirics, practitioners re-
lying solely on experience, often used in the sense of quacks   70 Scotch boot] tightly
fitting boots of iron into which wedges were driven between boot and foot   71 herlakeen]
harlequin, i.e., any old fool   82 hot shots] hotheads   87 gentlemen] a hit at the Welsh
pride in pedigree   90 cipers] cypress, a crepe-like material sometimes used for mourning

should not I instruct you! How will you bear yourself when you come into the Duke of Florence' court?

Bilioso. Proud enough, and 'twill do well enough; as I walk up and down the chamber, I'll spit frowns about me, have a strong perfume in my jerkin, let my beard grow to make me look terrible, salute no man beneath the fourth button, and 'twill do excellent.

Beancha. But there is a very beautiful lady there, how will you entertain her?

Bilioso. I'll tell you that when the lady hath entertain'd me: but to satisfy thee, here comes the fool: fool, thou shalt stand for the fair lady. 101

Enter Passarello.

Passarello. Your fool will stand for your lady most willingly and most uprightly.

Bilioso. I'll salute her in Latin.

Passarello. O, your fool can understand no Latin.

Bilioso. Ay, but your lady can.

Passarello. Why then, if your lady take down your fool, your fool will stand no longer for your lady.

Bilioso. A pestilent fool: 'fore God I think the world be turn'd upside down too. 110

Passarello. O no, sir; for then your lady, and all the ladies in the palace should go with their heels upward, and that were a strange sight you know.

Bilioso. There be many will repine at my preferment.

Passarello. O ay, like the envy of an elder sister that hath her younger made a lady before her.

Bilioso. The Duke is wondrous discontented.

Passarello. Ay, and more melancholic than a usurer having all his money out at the death of a prince.

Bilioso. Didst thou see Madam Floria today?

Passarello. Yes, I found her repairing her face today, the red upon the white showed as if her cheeks should have been served in for two dishes of barbaries in stewed broth, and the flesh to them a woodcock. 122

Bilioso. A bitter fowl. Come Madam, this night thou shalt enjoy me freely, and tomorrow for Florence. [*Exeunt* Bilioso *and* Beancha.]

Passarello. What a natural fool is he that would be a pair of bodies to a woman's petticoat, to be trusst and pointed to them. Well, I'll dog my Lord, and the word is proper: for when I fawn upon him he feeds me; when I snap him by the fingers, he spits in my mouth. If a dog's death were not strangling, I had rather be one than a serving-man: for the corruption of coin is either the generation of a usurer, or a lousy beggar. *Exit.*

97-8 beneath . . . button] with more than a slight bow   118 at the . . . prince] i.e., at a period of great uncertainty   122 barbaries] Barbary hens   125 pair of bodies] bodice
129-30 the corruption . . . beggar] the service of a usurer leads either to coining or to beggary

SCENA SECUNDA

Enter Malevole *in some frieze gown, whilst* Bilioso *reads his patent.*

Malevole. I cannot sleep, my eyes' ill-neighbouring lids
    Will hold no fellowship: O thou pale sober night,
    Thou that in sluggish fumes all sense dost steep:
    Thou that gives all the world full leave to play,
    Unbend'st the feebled veins of sweaty labour!
    The galley-slave, that, all the toilsome day,
    Tugs at his oar against the stubborn wave,
    Straining his rugged veins, snores fast:
    The stooping scytheman that doth barb the field,
    Thou makest wink sure: in night all creatures sleep,   10
    Only the malcontent that 'gainst his fate
    Repines and quarrels, alas he's goodman tell-clock;
    His sallow jaw-bones sink with wasting moan,
    Whilst others' beds are down, his pillow's stone.
Bilioso. Malevole.
Malevole. (*To* Bilioso) Elder of Israel, thou honest defect of wicked nature
    and obstinate ignorance, when did thy wife let thee lie with her?
Bilioso. I am going embassador to Florence.
Malevole. Embassador! Now, for thy country's honour, preethee do not
    put up mutton and porridge in thy clock-bag: thy young lady wife goes
    to Florence with thee too, does she not?   21
Bilioso. No, I leave her at the palace.
Malevole. At the palace? now discretion shield, man! for God's love let's
    ha' no more cuckolds, Hymen begins to put off his saffron robe. Keep
    thy wife i' the state of grace. Heart o' truth, I would sooner leave my lady
    singled in a bordello than in the Genoa palace.
    Sin there appearing in her sluttish shape
    Would soon grow loathsome, even to blushes' sense,
    Surfeit would cloak intemperate appetite,
    Make the soul scent the rotten breath of lust: 30
    When in an Italian lascivious palace,
    A lady guardianless,
    Left to the push of all allurement,
    The strong'st incitements to immodesty,

---

s.d. *frieze*] coarse woollen cloth   *patent*] letter of appointment   9 barb] mow   10 wink
sure] sleep soundly   12 tell-clock] the crier, telling the hours   20 clock-bag] for 'cloak-
bag', a valise   23 shield] forbid   24 saffron robe] customarily worn by Hymen in a
masque   26 bordello] brothel (Ital.)   27 there] i.e., in the bordello

To have her bound, incens'd with wanton sweets,
Her veins fill'd high with heating delicates,
Soft rest, sweet music, amorous masquerers,
Lascivious banquets, sin it self gilt o'er,
Strong fantasy tricking up strange delights,
Presenting it dressed pleasingly to sense,   40
Sense leading it unto the soul, confirm'd
With potent example, impudent custom,
Enticed by that great bawd opportunity——
Thus being prepar'd, clap to her easy ear
Youth in good clothes, well-shap'd, rich, fair-spoken, promising-noble,
ardent blood-full, witty, flattering: Ulysses absent, O Ithaca, can chastest
Penelope hold out?
Bilioso. Mass, I'll think on't. Farewell.   *Exit* Bilioso.
Malevole. Farewell, take thy wife with thee, farewell.

To Florence, um? it may prove good, it may,   50
And we may once unmask our brows.

SCENA TERTIA

Enter Count Celso.

Celso. My honour'd Lord.
Malevole. Celso, peace, how is't? speak low, pale fears suspect that hedges,
walls & trees have ears; speak, how runs all?
Celso. I'faith my Lord, that beast with many heads,
The staggering multitude, recoils apace,
Though thorough great men's envy, most men's malice,
Their much intemperate heat hath banisht you,
Yet now they find envy and malice near,
Produce faint reformation.
The Duke, the too soft Duke, lies as a block,   10
For which two tugging factions seem to saw,
But still the iron through the ribs they draw.
Malevole. I tell thee Celso, I have ever found
Thy breast most far from shifting cowardize
And fearful baseness: therefore I'll tell thee Celso,
I find the wind begins to come about,
I'll shift my suit of fortune.
I know the Florentine whose only force,
By marrying his proud daughter to this prince,

---

35 incens'd] excited, playing on the sense of perfumed   36 heating] i.e., exciting the blood
45 promising-noble] heir to noble rank   III. iii, 18 only force] power alone

Both banisht me, and made this weak lord Duke,   20
Will now forsake them all, be sure he will:
I'll lie in ambush for conveniency,
Upon their severance to confirm my self.

Celso. Is Ferneze interr'd?

Malevole. Of that at leisure: he lives.

Celso. But how stands Mendoza, how is't with him?

Malevole. 'Faith, like a pair of snuffers, snibs filth in other men, and retains
it in it self.

Celso. He does fly from public notice me thinks, as a hare does from hounds;
the feet whereon he flies betrays him.   30

Malevole. I can track him, Celso:
O my disguise fools him most powerfully:
For that I seem a desperate malcontent
He fain would clasp with me: he is the true slave,
That will put on the most affected grace,
For some vilde second cause.

Enter Mendoza.

Celso.   He's here.

Malevole.   Give place.   *Exit* Celso.
Illo, ho ho ho, art there, old true penny? Where hast thou spent thy self
this morning? I see flattery in thine eyes, & damnation i' thy soul. Ha,
thou huge rascal!

Mendoza. Thou art very merry.   40

Malevole. As a scholar, *futuens gratis.* How doth the devil go with thee now?

Mendoza. Malevole, thou art an arrant knave.

Malevole. Who, I? I have been a sergeant, man.

Mendoza. Thou art very poor.

Malevole. As Job, an alchemist, or a poet.

Mendoza. The Duke hates thee.

Malevole. As Irishmen do bum-cracks.

Mendoza. Thou hast lost his amity.

Malevole. As pleasing as maids lose their virginity.

Mendoza. Would thou wert of a lusty spirit, would thou wert noble!   50

Malevole. Why, sure my blood gives me I am noble, sure I am of noble
kind, for I find my self possessed with all their qualities; love dogs, dice
and drabs, scorn wit in stuff clothes, have beat my shoemaker, knockt
my sempsters, cuckold' my pottecary, and undone my tailor. Noble, why

---

23 Upon . . . my self] on their falling out to make my place sure   41 *futuens gratis*]
having sexual relations without paying   43 sergeant] sheriff's officer   47 bum-cracks]
breaking wind   49 lose] Quarto: 'loose'.   51 gives] tells   53 stuff] coarse

not? since the Stoic said, '*Neminem servum non ex regibus, neminem regem non ex servis esse oriundum*', only busy fortune touses, and the provident chances blends them together; I'll give you a simile: did you e'er see a well with 2 buckets, whilst one comes up full to be emptied, another goes down empty to be filled; such is the state of all humanity: why look you, I may be the son of some duke, for believe me, intemperate lascivious bastardy makes nobility doubtful; I have a lusty daring heart, Mendoza.

Mendoza. Let's grasp! I do like thee infinitely, wilt intact one thing for me?

Malevole. Shall I get by it? (Mendoza *gives him his purse.*) Command me, I am thy slave, beyond death and hell.   64

Mendoza. Murther the Duke!

Malevole. My heart's wish, my soul's desire, my fantasy's dream, my blood's longing, the only height of my hopes! How, O God, how!

  O how my united spirits throng together!

  So strengthen my resolve.

Mendoza.   The Duke is now

  A-hunting.   70

Malevole. Excellent, admirable, as the devil would have it; lend me, lend me, rapier, pistol, crossbow: so, so, I'll do it.

Mendoza. Then we agree?

Malevole.   As Lent and fishmongers.

  Come a-cap-a-pe, how? Inform.

Mendoza. Know that this weak-brain'd duke, who only stands

  On Florence' stilts, hath out of witless zeal

  Made me his heir, and secretly confirm'd

  The wreath to me after his life's full point.

Malevole. Upon what merit?

Mendoza.   Merit! by heaven, I horn him,

  Only Ferneze's death gave me state's life: 80

  Tut, we are politic, he must not live now.

Malevole. No reason, marry: but how must he die now?

Mendoza. My utmost project is to murder the Duke, that I might have his state, because he makes me his heir: to banish the Duchess, that I might be rid of a cunning Lacedemonian, because I know Florence will forsake her, & then to marry Maria, the banished Duke Altofront's wife, that her friends might strengthen me and my faction, this is all, law.

Malevole. Do you love Maria?

Mendoza. 'Faith, no great affection, but as wise men do love great women, to

<hr/>

55–6 *Neminem . . . oriundum*] There is no slave not descended from a king, nor king not descended from a slave (Seneca, quoting Plato)   56 touses] tousles   57 them] i.e., kings and slaves   62 grasp] embrace   62 intact] undertake   74 a-cap-a-pe] from head to foot   80 gave . . life] allowed me to escape sentence of death   85 Lacedemonian] strumpet

innoble their blood and augment their revenue. To accomplish this now,
thus now: the Duke is in the forest next the sea, single him, kill him,
hurl him i' the main, and proclaim thou sawest wolves eat him.   92

Malevole. Um, not so good. Me thinks when he is slain
 To get some ipocrite, some daungerous wretch
 That's muffled, or with feigned holiness,
 To swear he hard the Duke on some steep cliff
 Lament his wife's dishonour, and in an agony
 Of his heart's torture hurled his groaning sides
 Into the swollen sea. This circumstance,
 Well made, sounds probable, and hereupon   100
 The Duchess——

Mendoza. May well be banish'd: O unpeerable!
 Invention rare!
 Thou god of policy! it honeys me.

Malevole. Then fear not for the wife of Altofront,
 I'll close to her.

Mendoza. Thou shalt, thou shalt, our excellency is pleased:
 Why wert not thou an emperor? When we
 Are Duke, I'll make thee some great man, sure!

Malevole.   Nay,
 Make me some rich knave, and I'll make my self   110
 Some great man.

Mendoza.   In thee be all my spirit;
 Retain ten souls, unite thy virtual powers,
 Resolve; ha, remember greatness. Heart, farewell.

 Enter Celso.

 The fate of all my hopes in thee doth dwell.   [*Exit.*]

Malevole. Celso, didst hear? O heaven, didst hear?
 Such devilish mischief! Sufferest thou the world
 Carouse damnation even with greedy swallow,
 And still dost wink, still does thy vengeance slumber?
 If now thy brows are clear, when will they thunder?

             Exit [*with* Celso].

SCENA QUARTA

 Enter Pietro, Ferrardo, Prepasso, *and three* Pages.

Ferrardo. The dogs are at a fault.   *Cornets like horns.*

Pietro. Would God nothing but the dogs were at it! let the deer pursue

96 hard] heard 99 circumstance] detailed narration 102 unpeerable] peerless
106 close to] come to agreement with 112 virtual] virtuous 116 thou] i.e., heaven
117 carouse] drink a toast to

safely, the dogs follow the game, and do you follow the dogs: as for me,
'tis unfit one beast should hunt another; I ha' one chaseth me: and,
please you, I would be rid of ye a little.

Ferrardo. Would your grief would as soon as we leave you to quietness.

Pietro. I thank you.   *Exeunt* [Ferrardo & Prepasso].
                    Boy, what dost thou dream of now?

Page. Of a dry summer, my Lord, for here's a hot world towards: but my
Lord, I had a strange dream last night.

Pietro. What strange dream?   10

Page. Why, me thought I pleased you with singing, and then I dreamt you
gave me that short sword.

Pietro. Prettily begg'd: hold thee, I'll prove thy dream true, take't.

Page. My duty. But still I dreamt on, my Lord, and me thought, and shall
please your Excellency, you would needs out of your royal bounty give
me that jewel in your hat.

Pietro. O, thou didst but dream, boy, do not believe it, dreams prove not
always true: they may hold in a short sword, but not in a jewel. But now
sir, you dreamt you had pleas'd me with singing, make that true as I
ha' made the other.   20

Page. 'Faith my Lord, I did but dream, and dreams, you say, prove not
always true: they may hold in a good sword, but not in a good song:
the truth is, I ha' lost my voice.

Pietro. Lost thy voice, how?

Page. With dreaming, 'faith, but here's a couple of sirenical rascals shall
enchaunt ye: what shall they sing, my good Lord?

Pietro. Sing of the nature of women, and then the song shall be surely
full of variety, old crotchets and most sweet closes; it shall be humorous,
grave, fantastic, amorous, melancholy, sprightly, one in all, and all in one.

Page. All in one?   30

Pietro. By'r Lady, too many. Sing, my speech grows culpable of unthrifty
idleness, sing.

                          The Song.

                        SCENA QUINTA

Enter Malevole, *with crossbow and pistol.*

Pietro. Ah, so, so, sing, I am heavy. Walk off, I shall talk in my sleep, walk
off.   *Exeunt* Pages.

Malevole. Brief, brief! Who? the Duke? good heaven, that fools should
stumble upon greatness! Do not sleep, Duke: give ye good morrow. I
must be brief, Duke. I am feed to murther thee: start not: Mendoza,

---

4 beast] alluding to the Duke's horns   25 sirenical] melodious   III. v, 4 I must]
Quarto omits 'I'.   5 feed] paid

> Mendoza hired me, here's his gold, his pistol, crossbow, and sword,
> 'tis all as firm as earth.
>> O fool, fool, chok'd with the common maze
>> Of easy idiots, credulity!
>> ——Make him thine heir? what, thy sworn murderer?   10

Pietro. O can it be?

Malevole.   Can?

Pietro.   Discovered he not
> Ferneze?

Malevole. Yes, but why? but why? for love
>> To thee? Much, much. To be reveng'd upon
>> His rival, who had thrust his jaws awry,
>> Who being slain, suppos'd by thine own hands,
>> Defended by his sword,
>> Made thee most loathsome, him most gracious
>> With thy loose princess: thou, closely yielding
>> Egress and regress to her, madest him heir,   20
>> Whose hot unquiet lust straight tous'd thy sheets,
>> And now would seize thy state:
> Politician, wise man! death! to be led to the stake like a bull by the horns!
>> To make even kindness cut a gentle throat! Life!
>> Why art thou numb'd? thou foggy dulness, speak!
>> Lives not more faith in a home-thrusting tongue,
>> Than in these fencing tiptap courtiers?

Enter Celso *with a hermit's gown and beard.*

Pietro. Lord Malevole, if this be true——

Malevole. If? Come, shade thee with this disguise. If? Thou shalt handle it, he shall thank thee for killing thy self; come, follow my directions, and thou shalt see strange sleights.   31

Pietro. World, whither wilt thou?

Malevole. Why, to the devil: come, the morn grows late,
> 'A steady quickness is the soul of state.'   *Exeunt.*

ACTUS QUARTUS.   SCE. PRIMA

Enter Maquerelle *knocking at the Ladies door.*

Maquerelle. Medam, medam, are you stirring, medam? if you be stirring, medam, if I thought I should disturb ye——

[*Enter* Page.]

---

19 closely] secretly   21 tous'd] tousled   27 tiptap] obsequious, lightweight   34 state] statecraft   IV. i, 1 Medam] probably an affected pronunciation

Page. My Lady is up, forsooth.

Maquerelle. A pretty boy, 'faith, how old art thou?

Page. I think fourteen.

Maquerelle. Nay, and ye be in the teens—are ye a gentleman born? do ye know me? My name is Medam Maquerelle, I lie in the old cunny-court. See here, the ladies.

Enter Beancha *and* Emilia.

Beancha. A fair day to ye, Maquerelle.

Emilia. Is the Duchess up yet, sentinel? 10

Maquerelle. O ladies, the most abominable mischance, O dear ladies, the most piteous disaster! Ferneze was taken last night in the Duchess' chamber: alas! the Duke catcht him and kill'd him.

Beancha. Was he found in bed?

Maquerelle. O no, but the villainous certainty is, the door was not bolted, the tongue-tied hatch held his peace, so the naked troth is, he was found in his shirt, whilst I like an arrand beast lay in the outward chamber, heard nothing, and yet they came by me in the dark, and yet I felt them not, like a senseless creature as I was. O beauties, look to your busk-points, if not chastely, yet charily: be sure the door be bolted. Is your Lord gone to Florence? 21

Beancha. Yes, Maquerelle.

Maquerelle. I hope you'll find the discretion to purchase a fresh gown for his return. Now by my troth, beauties, I would ha' ye once wise: he loves ye, pish! he is witty, buble! fair-proportioned, meaw! nobly born, wind! Let this be still your fixt position, esteem me every man according to his good gifts, and so ye shall ever remain most dear, and most worthy to be most dear ladies.

Emilia. Is the Duke returned from hunting yet?

Maquerelle. They say not yet. 30

Beancha. 'Tis now in midst of day.

Emilia. How bears the Duchess with this blemish now?

Maquerelle. 'Faith, boldly, strongly defies defame, as one that has a duke to her father. And there's a note to you, be sure of a stout friend in a corner, that may always awe your husband. Mark the haviour of the Duchess now, she dares defame, cries, 'Duke, do what thou canst, I'll quite mine honour': nay, as one confirmed in her own virtue against ten thousand mouths that mutter her disgrace, she's presently for dances.

Enter Ferrardo.

7 cunny-court] women's apartments   16 hatch] half-door (whose hinges were oiled)
17 arrand] arrant   19 busk-points] stays   25 buble] bubble   27–8 and so . . . ladies]
from the Dedication to Sidney's *Arcadia*   33 defame] defamation, infamy   36 quite]
quit, acquit

Beancha. For dances?

Maquerelle. Most true.   40

Emilia. Most strange: see, here's my servant, young Ferrard. How many
servants think'st thou I have, Maquerelle?

Maquerelle. The more the merrier: 'twas well said, use your servants as
you do your smocks; have many, use one, and change often, for that's
most sweet and courtlike.

Ferrardo. Save ye, fair ladies, is the Duke returned?

Beancha. Sweet Sir, no voice of him as yet in court.

Ferrardo. 'Tis very strange.

Beancha. And how like you my servant, Maquerelle?

Maquerelle. I think he could hardly draw Ulysses' bow, but by my fidelity,
were his nose narrower, his eyes broader, his hands thinner, his lips
thicker, his legs bigger, his feet lesser, his hair blacker, and his teeth
whiter, he were a tolerable sweet youth i'faith. And he will come to my
chamber, I will read him the fortune of his beard.   54

Cornets sound.

Ferrardo. Not yet return'd, I fear, but the Duchess approacheth.

Enter Mendoza *supporting the* Duchess: Guerrino: *the Ladies that are
on the stage rise:* Ferrard *ushers in the* Duchess, *and then takes a Lady to
tread a measure.*

SCENA SECUNDA

Aurelia. We will dance. Music! we will dance.

Guerrino. Les quanto (Lady), *Pensez bien, Passa regis,* or Beancha's brawl?

Aurelia. We have forgot the brawl.

Ferrardo. So soon? 'tis wonder.

Guerrino. Why, 'tis but two singles on the left, two on the right, three
doubles forward, a traverse of six round: do this twice, three singles side,
galliard trick of twenty, curranto-pace: a figure of eight, three singles
broken down, come up, meet two doubles, fall back, and then honour.

Aurelia. O Daedalus! thy maze, I have quite forgot it.

Maquerelle. Trust me, so have I, saving the falling back, and then honour.

Enter Prepasso.

Aurelia. Music, music!   11

Prepasso. Who saw the Duke? the Duke?

53 And] an, if   IV. ii, 2 *Les . . .* brawl] names of dances; the brawl was introduced from
France in the mid-16th century   7 galliard] a lively dance   7 curranto] coranto,
courante, a running dance   8 honour] a curtsy at the end of a dance   9 Daedalus] the
creator of the Minotaur's maze   10 honour] spoken as a pun

Enter Equato.

Aurelia. Music!
Equato. The Duke, is the Duke returned?
Aurelia. Music!

Enter Celso.

Celso. The Duke is either invisible, or else is not.
Aurelia. We are not pleas'd with your intrusion upon our private retirement:
we are not pleas'd: you have forgot your selves.

Enter a Page.

Celso. Boy, thy maister: where's the Duke?
Page. Alas, I left him burying the earth with his spread joyless limbs: he
told me, he was heavy, would sleep, bade me walk off, for that the strength
of fantasy oft made him talk in his dreams: I straight obeyed, nor ever
saw him since: but where so e'er he is, he's sad.   23
Aurelia. Music, sound high, as is our heart, sound high!

SCENA TERTIA

Enter Malevole, *and* Pietro *disguised like an hermit.*

Malevole. The Duke—peace!—the Duke is dead.
Aurelia. Music!
Malevole. Is't music?
Mendoza. Give proof.
Ferrardo. How?
Celso. Where?
Prepasso. When?
Malevole. Rest in peace, as the Duke does, quietly sit: for my own part,
I beheld him but dead, that's all: marry, here's one can give you a more
particular account of him.   10
Mendoza. Speak, holy father, nor let any brow
     Within this presence fright thee from the truth:
     Speak confidently and freely.
Aurelia.   We attend.
Pietro. Now had the mounting sun's all-ripening wings
     Swept the cold sweat of night from earth's dank breast,
     When I (whom men call hermit of the rock)
     Forsook my cell, and clamber'd up a cliff,
     Against whose base the heady Neptune dasht
     His high-curl'd brows, there 'twas I eas'd my limbs,

When lo, my entrails melted with the moan   20
Some one, who far 'bove me was climb'd, did make——
I shall offend.
Mendoza. Not.
Aurelia. On.
Pietro. Me thinks I hear him yet: 'O female faith!
    Go sow the ingrateful sand, and love a woman:
    And do I live to be the scoff of men,
    To be their wittol cuckold, even to hug
    My poison? Thou knowest, O truth!
    Sooner hard steel will melt with southern wind,   30
    A seaman's whistle calm the ocean,
    A town on fire be extinct with tears,
    Than women vow'd to blushless impudence,
    With sweet behaviour and soft minioning,
    Will turn from that where appetite is fixt.
    O powerful blood, how thou dost slave their soul!
    I washt an Ethiop, who, for recompense,
    Sully'd my name. And must I then be forc'd
    To walk, to live thus black? must, must? Fie,
    He that can bear with "must", he cannot die.'   40
    With that he sigh'd so passionately deep,
    That the dull air even groan'd! at last he cries:
    'Sink shame in seas, sink deep enough': so dies.
    For then I view'd his body fall and souse
    Into the foamy main, O then I saw
    That which me thinks I see, it was the Duke,
    Whom straight the nicer-stomach't sea
    Belcht up: but then——
Malevole.   Then came I in; but 'las,
    All was too late, for even straight he sunk.
Pietro. Such was the Duke's sad fate.   50
Celso. A better fortune to our Duke Mendoza!
Omnes. Mendoza!   *Cornets flourish.*
Mendoza. A guard, a guard!

   Enter a Guard.
                  We full of hearty tears
    For our good father's loss—
    For so we well may call him,
    Who did beseech your loves for our succession—

---

32 extinct] extinguished   34 minioning] caressing   44 souse] swoop down   47 nicer-
stomach't] more particular (cf. *The Tempest*, III. iii. 55ff.)

Cannot so lightly over-jump his death
As leave his woes revengeless: (*to* Aurelia) woman of shame,
We banish thee for ever to the place
From whence this good man comes, nor permit,   60
On death unto the body, any ornament:
But base as was thy life, depart away.

Aurelia. Ungrateful——

Mendoza. Away!

Aurelia. Villain, hear me!   Prepasso *and* Guerrino *lead
away the* Duchess.

Mendoza. Be gone. My Lords,
Address to public counsel, 'tis most fit:
[*Aside*] The train of fortune is borne up by wit.
——Away, our presence shall be sudden, haste!

                    All depart saving Mendoza, Malevole *and* Pietro.

Malevole. Now, you egregious devil! Ha, ye murthering politician! how
dost, Duke? how dost look now? brave Duke, i'faith.   71

Mendoza. How did you kill him?

Malevole. Slatted his brains out, then sous'd him in the briny sea.

Mendoza. Brain'd him and drown'd him too?

Malevole. O 'twas best, sure work: for he that strikes a great man, let him
strike home, or else ware he'll prove no man: shoulder not a huge fellow,
unless you may be sure to lay him in the kennel.

Mendoza. A most sound brainpan: I'll make you both emperors.

Malevole. Make us Christians, make us Christians!

Mendoza. I'll hoist ye, ye shall mount.   80

Malevole. To the gallows, say ye? Come: '*Praemium incertum petit certum
scelus.*' How stands the progress?

Mendoza. Here, take my ring unto the citadel,
Have entrance to Maria, the grave Duchess
Of banist Altofront. Tell her we love her:
Omit no circumstance to grace our person: do't.

Malevole. I'll make an excellent pander: Duke, farewell, 'dieu, adieu, Duke.

Mendoza. Take Maquarelle with thee; for 'tis found
None cuts a diamond but a diamond.   *Exit* Malevole.
Hermit, thou art a man for me, my confessor,
O thou selected spirit, born for my good,   90
Sure thou wouldst make
An excellent elder in a deform'd church.
Come, we must be inward, thou and I all one.

---

61 On] on pain of   67 Address to] prepare for   71 brave] fine   73 sous'd] soaked
77 kennel] gutter   81-2 *Praemium . . . scelus*] The prize he seeks is uncertain, the crime is
certain (Seneca)—perhaps an aside to Pietro   82 progress] plan of action

Pietro. I am glad I was ordained for ye.

Mendoza. Go to then, thou must know that Malevole is a strange villain: dangerous, very dangerous: you see how broad 'a speaks, a gross-jaw'd rogue: I would have thee poison him: he's like a corn upon my great toe, I cannot go for him: he must be cored out, he must: wilt do't, ha?

Pietro. Any thing, any thing.   100

Mendoza. Heart of my life, thus then to the citadel,
     Thou shalt consort with this Malevole,
     There being at supper, poison him: it shall
     Be laid upon Maria, who yields love,
     Or dies: Scud quick, like lightning!

Pietro. Good deeds crawl, but mischief flies.   *Exit* Pietro.

    Enter Malevole.

Malevole. Your devilship's ring has no virtue. The buff-captain, the sallow Westphalian gammon-faced zaza, cries 'Stand out!' Must have a stiffer warrant, or no pass into the castle of comfort.

Mendoza. Command our sudden letter: not enter? Sha't! what place is there in Genoa, but thou shalt? Into my heart, into my very heart: come, let's love, we must love, we two, soul and body.   112

Malevole. How didst like the hermit? A strange hermit, sirrah.

Mendoza. A dangerous fellow, very perilous: he must die.

Malevole. Ay, he must die.

Mendoza. Thou'st kill him: we are wise, we must be wise.

Malevole. And provident.

Mendoza. Yea, provident; beware an hypocrite.
     A churchman once corrupted, oh avoid!   *Shoots under his belly.*
     A fellow that makes religion his stalking horse,   120
     He breeds a plague: thou shalt poison him.

Malevole. Ho, 'tis wondrous necessary: how?

Mendoza. You both go jointly to the citadel,
     There sup, there poison him: and Maria,
     Because she is our opposite, shall bear
     The sad suspect, on which she dies, or loves us.

Malevole. I run.   *Exit* Malevole.

Mendoza. We that are great, our sole self-good still moves us.
     They shall die both, for their deserts craves more
     Than we can recompense, their presence still   130

---

97 'a] he   99 go for] walk because of   107 buff-captain] referring to the leather coat he wears   108 gammon-faced] pig-faced (Westphalia was renowned for gammon) 108 zaza] bully   110 Sha't] Thou shalt   116 Thou'st] Thou must   119 s.d. *Shoots . . . belly*] presumably suggesting that Mendoza makes motions of shooting under the belly of a stalking horse, as the corrupt churchman does with religion   125 our opposite] opposed to us   126] sad suspect] heavy suspicion

Imbraids our fortunes with beholdingness,
Which we abhor, like deed, not doer: then conclude,
They live not to cry out ingratitude.
'One stick burns t'other, steel cuts steel alone:
'Tis good trust few: but O, 'tis best trust none.'   *Exit* Mendoza.

SCENA QUARTA

Enter Malevole *and* Pietro, *still disguised, at several doors.*

Malevole. How do you? how dost, Duke?
Pietro.   O let
      The last day fall, drop, drop on our curs'd heads!
      Let heaven unclasp it self, vomit forth flames.
Malevole. O, do not rand, do not turn player, there's more of them than can
      well live one by another already. What, art an infidel still?
Pietro. I am amaz'd, struck in a swown with wonder!
      I am commanded to poison thee.
Malevole. I am commanded to poison thee, at supper.
Pietro. At supper?
Malevole. In the citadel.   10
Pietro. In the citadel?
Malevole. Cross-capers, tricks! Truth o' heaven, he would discharge us as
      boys do eldern guns, one pellet to strike out another: of what faith art
      now?
Pietro. All is damnation, wickedness extreme,
      There is no faith in man.
Malevole. In none but usurers and brokers, they deceive no man, men take
      'em for blood-suckers, and so they are: now God deliver me from my
      friends.
Pietro. Thy friends?   20
Malevole. Yes, from my friends, for from mine enemies I'll deliver my self.
      O, cut-throat friendship is the rankest villainy: mark this Mendoza,
      mark him for a villain: but heaven will send a plague upon him for a
      rogue.
Pietro. O world!
Malevole. World? 'Tis the only region of death, the greatest shop of the
      devil, cruell'st prison of men, out of the which none pass without paying
      their dearest breath for a fee. There's nothing perfect in it but extreme,
      extreme calamity, such as comes yonder.

131 Imbraids] upbraids   IV. iv, 4 rand] rant   12 cross-capers] steps in dancing
13 eldern] of elderwood, i.e., pop-guns

SCENA QUINTA

Enter Aurelia, *two holberts before, and two after, supported by* Celso *and* Ferrardo, Aurelia *in base mourning attire.*

Aurelia. To banishment, led on to banishment!
Pietro. Lady, the blessedness of repentance to you.
Aurelia. Why? why? I can desire nothing but death,
     Nor deserve any thing but hell.
     If heaven should give sufficiency of grace
     To clear my soul, it would make heaven graceless:
     My sins would make the stock of mercy poor,
     Oh they would tire heaven's goodness to reclaim them:
     Judgment is just yet from that vast villain:
     But sure he shall not miss sad punishment,   10
     'For he shall rule. On to my cell of shame!
Pietro. My cell 'tis, Lady, where, instead of masques,
     Music, tilts, tourneys, and such courtlike shows,
     The hollow murmur of the checkless winds
     Shall groan again, whilst the unquiet sea
     Shakes the whole rock with foamy battery:
     There usherless the air comes in and out:
     The rheumy vault will force your eyes to weep,
     Whilst you behold true desolation:
     A rocky barrenness shall pierce your eyes,   20
     Where all at once one reaches, where he stands,
     With brows the roof, both walls with both his hands.
Aurelia. It is too good: blessed spirit of my lord,
     O, in what orb so e'er thy soul is thron'd,
     Behold me worthily most miserable:
     O let the anguish of my contrite spirit
     Entreat some reconciliation:
     If not, O joy, triumph in my just grief,
     Death is the end of woes, and tears' relief.
Pietro. Belike your lord not lov'd you, was unkind.   30
Aurelia. O heaven!
     As the soul lov'd the body, so lov'd he,
     'Twas death to him to part my presence, heaven
     To see me pleased:
     Yet I, like a wretch given o'er to hell,
     Brake all the sacred rites of marriage,
     To clip a base ungentle faithless villain:

s.d. *holberts*] halberds, i.e., halberdiers   9 yet] even   28 just] deserved

    O God, a very pagan reprobate—
    What should I say?—ungrateful throws me out,
    For whom I lost soul, body, fame, and honour: 40
    But 'tis most fit: why should a better fate
    Attend on any, who forsake chaste sheets,
    Fly the embrace of a devoted heart,
    Join'd by a solemn vow 'fore God and man,
    To taste the brackish blood of beastly lust,
    In an adulterous touch? Oh ravenous immodesty,
    Insatiate impudence of appetite!
    Look, here's your end, for mark what sap in dust,
    What sin in good, even so much love in lust:
    Joy to thy ghost, sweet Lord, pardon to me.   50
Celso. 'Tis the Duke's pleasure this night you rest in court.
Aurelia. Soul lurk in shades, run shame from brightsome skies,
    In night the blind man misseth not his eyes.

                    Exit [*with* Celso, Ferrardo, *and* Holberts].
Malevole. Do not weep, kind cuckold, take comfort, man, thy betters have
    been beccos: Agamemnon Emperor of all the merry Greeks, that tickled
    all the true Troyans, was a cornuto: Prince Arthur, that cut off twelve
    kings' beards, was a cornuto: Hercules, whose back bore up heaven, and
    got forty wenches with child in one night——
Pietro. Nay, 'twas fifty.
Malevole. 'Faith, forty's enow a' conscience, yet was a cornuto: patience,
    mischief grows proud, be wise.   61
Pietro. Thou pinchest too deep, art too keen upon me.
Malevole. Tut, a pitiful surgeon makes a dangerous sore, I'll tent thee to the
    ground. Thinkest I'll sustain my self by flattering thee, because thou art a
    prince? I had rather follow a drunkard, and live by licking up his vomit,
    than by servile flattery.
Pietro. Yet great men ha' done't.
Malevole. Great slaves fear better than love, born naturally for a coal-basket,
    though the common usher of princes' presence, fortune, hath blindly
    given them better place.   70
    I am vow'd to be thy affliction.
Pietro.   Prethee be,
    I love much misery, and be thou son
    To me.

    Enter Bilioso.

Malevole. Because you are an usurping duke.
    (*To* Bilioso.) You Lordship's well return'd from Florence.

55 ff.] cf. II. iii. 9   63 tent] prove

Bilioso. Well return'd, I praise my horse.

Malevole. What news from the Florentines?

Bilioso. I will conceal the great Duke's pleasure, only this was his charge, his pleasure is, that his daughter die; Duke Pietro be banished, for banishing his blood's dishonour, and that Duke Altofront be re-accepted: this is all, but I hear Duke Pietro is dead.   81

Malevole. Ay, and Mendoza is Duke: what will you do?

Bilioso. Is Mendoza strongest?

Malevole. Yet he is.

Bilioso. Then yet I'll hold with him.

Malevole. But if that Altofront should turn straight again?

Bilioso. Why then, I would turn straight again.

    'Tis good run still with him that has most might:

    I had rather stand with wrong, than fall with right.

Malevole. What religion will you be of now?   90

Bilioso. Of the Duke's religion, when I know what it is.

Malevole. O Hercules!

Bilioso. Hercules? Hercules was the son of Jupiter and Alkmena.

Malevole. Your Lordship is a very wittol.

Bilioso. Wittol?

Malevole. Ay, all-wit.

Bilioso. Amphitryo was a cuckold.

Malevole. Your lordship sweats, your young lady will get you a cloth for your old Worship's brows.   *Exit* Bilioso.

    Here's a fellow to be damn'd, this is his inviolable maxim: flatter the greatest, and oppress the least. A whoreson flesh-fly, that still gnaws upon the lean gall'd backs.   102

Pietro. Why dost then salute him?

Malevole. I'faith, as bawds go to church—for fashion sake. Come, be not confounded, th'art but in danger to lose a dukedom. Think this: this earth is the only grave and Golgotha wherein all things that live must rot: 'tis but the draught wherein the heavenly bodies discharge their corruption, the very muckhill on which the sublunary orbs cast their excrement: man is the slime of this dung-pit, and princes are the governors of these men: for, for our souls, they are as free as emperors, all of one piece: there goes but a pair of shears betwixt an emperor and the son of a bagpiper: only the dyeing, dressing, pressing, glossing, makes the difference. Now, what art thou like to lose?   113

    A gaoler's office to keep men in bonds,

    Whilst toil and treason all life's good confounds.

78–80 for . . . dishonour] so that his dishonour may be banished   96 all-wit] The old spelling of 'wittol' is 'wittall'—hence a play on words.   107 draught] cesspool   111–12 there goes . . . bagpiper] all are cut of the same cloth (proverbial)   112 glossing] finishing

Pietro. I here renounce for ever regency:
    O Altofront, I wrong thee to supplant thy right:
    To trip thy heels up with a devilish sleight;
    For which I now from throne am thrown, world-tricks abjure,
    For vengeance, tho't comes slow, yet it comes sure.   120
    O I am chang'd, for here, 'fore the dread power,
    In true contrition I do dedicate
    My breath to solitary holiness,
    My lips to prayer, and my breast's care shall be
    Restoring Altofront to regency.
Malevole. Thy vows are heard, and we accept thy faith.

    Enter Ferneze *and* Celso.   *Undisguiseth himself.*

    Banish amazement: come, we four must stand
    Full shock of fortune: be not so wonder-stricken.
Pietro. Doth Ferneze live?
Ferneze. For your pardon.   130
Pietro. Pardon and love: give leave to recollect
    My thoughts, disperst in wild astonishment:
    My vows stand fixt in heaven, and from hence
    I crave all love and pardon.
Malevole.   Who doubts of Providence,
    That sees this change? A hearty faith to all!
    He needs must rise, who can no lower fall,
    For still impetuous vicissitude
    Touseth the world: then let no maze intrude
    Upon your spirits: wonder not I rise,
    For who can sink, that close can temporize?   140
    The time grows ripe for action, I'll detect
    My privat'st plot, lest ignorance fear suspect:
    Let's close to counsel, leave the rest to fate,
    Mature discretion is the life of state.   *Exeunt.*

ACTUS QUINTUS. SCE. PRIMA

    Enter Bilioso *and* Passarello.

Bilioso. Fool, how dost thou like my calf in a long stocking?
Passarello. An excellent calf, my Lord.
Bilioso. This calf hath been a reveller this twenty year: when Monsieur
    Gundi lay here ambassador, I could have carried a lady up and down at

138 touseth] turns upside down   138 maze] amazement   140 close] secretly
141 detect] disclose   142 suspect] suspicion   143 close] go secretly

arms' end in a platter; and I can tell you there were those at that time who, to try the strength of a man's back, and his arm, would be coster'd: I have measured calves with most of the palace, and they come nothing near me; besides, I think there be not many armours in the arsenal will fit me, especially for the headpiece. I'll tell thee——

Passarello. What, my Lord? 10

Bilioso. I can eat stew'd broath as it comes seething off the fire; or a custard, as it comes reeking out of the oven; and I think there are not many lords can do it. A good pomander, a little decayed in the scent, but six grains of musk ground with rose-water, and temper'd with a little civet shall fetch her again presently.

Passarello. O ay, as a bawd with aqua vitae.

Bilioso. And what, dost thou rail upon the ladies as thou wert wont?

Passarello. I were better roast a live cat, and might do it with more safety. I am as secret to the thieves as their painting: there's Maquerelle, oldest bawd, and a perpetual beggar. Did you never hear of her trick to be known in the city? 21

Bilioso. Never.

Passarello. Why, she gets all the picter-makers to draw her picture: when they have done, she most courtly finds fault with them one after another, and never fetcheth them: they in revenge of this execute her in pictures as they do in Germany, and hang her in their shops: by this means is she better known to the stinkards, than if she had been five times carted.

Bilioso. 'Fore God, an excellent policy.

Passarello. Are there any revels tonight, my Lord?

Bilioso. Yes. 30

Passarello. Good my Lord, give me leave to break a fellow's pate that hath abused me.

Bilioso. Whose pate?

Passarello. Young Ferrard, my Lord.

Bilioso. Take heed, he's very valiant, I have known him fight eight quarrels in five days, believe it.

Passarello. O, is he so great a quarreller? Why then, he's an arrant coward.

Bilioso. How prove you that?

Passarello. Why thus: he that quarrels seeks to fight; and he that seeks to fight, seeks to die; and he that seeks to die, seeks never to fight more; and he that will quarrel and seeks means never to answer a man more, I think he's a coward. 42

6 coster'd] wearing a coster (curtain with a heavy drape) to add to the weight in the platter; the quartos have 'coister'd', which has never been satisfactorily explained   11 broath] broth   13 pomander] a perfume ball worn usually round the neck (presumably Bilioso displays his)   15 fetch . . . presently] restore it again immediately   16 aqua vitae] strong spirits   19 secret to] intimate with ('the' does not appear in the quartos)   27 carted] Taking round in a cart was a special punishment for bawds.

Bilioso. Thou canst prove any thing.

Passarello. Any thing but a rich knave, for I can flatter no man.

Bilioso. Well, be not drunk, good fool, I shall see you anon in the presence.

Exit.

Enter Malevole *and* Maquerelle, *at several doors opposite, singing.*

Malevole. The Dutchman for a drunkard——

Maquerelle. The Dane for golden locks——

Malevole. The Irishman for usquebath——

Maquerelle. The Frenchman for the (   ).

Malevole. O, thou art a blessed creature: had I a modest woman to conceal, I would put her to thy custody, for no reasonable creature would ever suspect her to be in thy company: ha, thou art a melodious Maquerelle, thou picture of a woman, and substance of a beast! 53

Maquerelle. O fool, will ye be ready anon to go with me to the revels? the hall will be so pest'red anon.

Passarello. Ay, as the country is with attorneys.

Malevole. What hast thou there, fool?

Passarello. Wine: I have learnt to drink since I went with my lord embassador, I'll drink to the health of Madam Maquerelle.

Malevole. Why, thou wast wont to rail upon her. 60

Passarello. Ay, but since I borrow'd money of her. I'll drink to her health now as gentlemen visit brokers, or as knights send venison to the city, either to take up more money, or to procure longer forbearance.

Malevole. Give me the bowl. I drink a health to Altofront, our deposed Duke.

Passarello. I'll take it. So! Now I'll begin a health to Madam Maquarelle.

Malevole. Puh! I will not pledge her.

Passarello. Why, I pledg'd your lord.

Malevole. I care not.

Passarello. Not pledge Madam Maquerelle? Why then, will I spew up your Lord again with this fool's finger. 70

Malevole. Hold, I'll take it.

Maquerelle. Now thou hast drunk my health, fool, I am friends with thee.

Passarello. Art? art?

When Griffon saw the reconciled quean,
    Offering about his neck her arms to cast:
He threw off sword and heart's malignant stream,
    And lovely her below the loins embrac'd.
Adieu, Madam Maquerelle.   *Exit* Passarello.

48 usquebath] usquebaugh, whisky (the word is derived ultimately from *aqua vitae*) 49 (   )] So in quartos: the rhyme word is obvious.   53] The third quarto has 'Enter Passarello' here, but there seems no need for him to leave the stage.   61 since] i.e., since then   65 take] return   74 Griffon] a hero in *Orlando Furioso*: the source of the lines is unknown

Malevole. And how dost thou think o' this transformation of state now?

Maquerelle. Verily, very well, for we women always note, the falling of the one is the rising of the other: some must be fat, some must be lean, some must be fools, and some must be lords; some must be knaves, and some must be officers: some must be beggars, some must be knights: some must be cuckolds, and some must be citizens: as for example, I have two court dogs, the most fawning curs, the one called Watch, th'other Catch: now I, like lady Fortune, sometimes love this dog, sometimes raise that dog, sometimes favour Watch, most commonly fancy Catch: now that dog which I favour I feed, and he's so ravenous, that what I give he never chaws it, gulps it down whole, without any relish of what he has, but with a greedy expectation of what he shall have: the other dog, now—— 91

Malevole. No more dog, sweet Maquerelle, no more dog. And what hope hast thou of the Duchess Maria, will she stoop to the Duke's lure, will she come, think'st?

Maquerelle. Let me see, where's the sign now? ha' ye e'er a calendar? where's the sign, trow you?

Malevole. Sign! why, is there any moment in that?

Maquerelle. O! believe me, a most secret power: look ye, a Chaldean or an Assyrian, I am sure 'twas a most sweet Jew, told me, court any woman in the right sign, you shall not miss: but you must take her in the right vein then: as when the sign is in Pisces, a fishmonger's wife is very sociable; in Cancer, a precisian's wife is very flexible; in Capricorn, a merchant's wife hardly holds out; in Libra, a lawyer's wife is very tractable, especially if her husband be at the term: only in Scorpio 'tis very dangerous meddling: has the Duke sent any jewel, any rich stones?

Enter Captain.

Malevole. Ay, I think those are the best signs to take a lady in. By your favour, signor, I must discourse with the Lady Maria, Altofront's Duchess: I must enter for the Duke. 108

Captain. She here shall give you enterview: I received the guardship of this citadel from the good Altofront, and for his use I'll keep 't, till I am of no use. 111

Malevole. Wilt thou? O heavens, that a Christian should be found in a buff jerkin! Captain conscience: I love thee, Captain. We attend. (*Exit* Captain.) And what hope hast thou of this Duchess' easiness?

Maquerelle. 'Twill go hard, she was a cold creature ever, she hated monkeys, fools, jesters, and gentlemen-ushers extremely: she had the vilde trick on't, not only to be truly modestly honourable in her own conscience,

89 chaws] chews   95 sign] zodiacal sign   102 precisian] puritan   104 term] session at law

but she would avoid the least wanton carriage that might incur suspect, as, God bless me, she had almost brought bed-pressing out of fashion: I could scarce get a fine for the lease of a lady's favour once in a fortnight.

Malevole. Now in the name of immodesty, how many maidenheads hast thou brought to the block? 122

Maquerelle. Let me see: heaven forgive us our misdeeds! Here's the Duchess.

SCENA SECUNDA

Enter Maria *and* Captain.

Malevole. God bless thee, Lady.

Maria. Out of thy company.

Malevole. We have brought thee tender of a husband.

Maria. I hope I have one already.

Maquerelle. Nay, by mine honour, Madam, as good ha' ne'er a husband as a banisht husband, he's in another world now. I'll tell ye, Lady, I have heard of a sect that maintained, when the husband was asleep the wife might lawfully entertain another man: for then her husband was as dead: much more when he is banished.

Maria. Unhonest creature! 10

Maquerelle. Pish, honesty is but an art to seem so: pray ye, what's honesty? what's constancy? but fables feigned, odd old fools' chat, devis'd by jealous fools to wrong our liberty.

Malevole. Mully, he that loves thee is a Duke, Mendoza, he will maintain thee royally, love thee ardently, defend thee powerfully, marry thee sumptuously, and keep thee in despite of Rosicleer, or Donzel del Phoebo: there's jewels: if thou wilt, so; if not, so.

Maria. Captain, for God's love save poor wretchedness
From tyranny of lustful insolence:
Enforce me in the deepest dungeon dwell 20
Rather than here; here round about is hell.
O my dear'st Altofront, where'er thou breathe,
Let my soul sink into the shades beneath,
Before I stain thine honour: this thou hast:
And long as I can die, I will live chaste.

Malevole. 'Gainst him that can enforce, how vain is strife!

Maria. She that can be enforc'd has ne'er a knife.
She that through force her limbs with lust enrolls,
Wants Cleopatra's asps and Portia's coals.
God amend you. *Exit with* Captain.

---

118 carriage] behaviour 119 as] so that 119 bed-pressing] intercourse 120 fine] fee
V. ii, 14 Mully] Molly, a term of endearment 16 Rosicleer . . . Phoebo] heroes from
The Mirror of Knighthood 25 long] so long

Malevole. Now the fear of the devil for ever go with thee!——Maquerelle,
I tell thee, I have found an honest woman: 'faith, I perceive when all is
done, there is of women, as of all other things, some good, most bad:
some saints, some sinners: for as nowadays, no courtier but has his
mistress, no captain but has his cockatrice, no cuckold but has his horns,
and no fool but has his feather: even so, no woman but has her weakness
and feather too, no sex but has his: [*aside*] I can hunt the letter no furder:
O God, how loathsome this toying is to me! that a Duke should be forc'd
to fool it! Well, *Stultorum plena sunt omnia*, better play the fool lord,
than be the fool lord.——Now, where's your sleights, Madam Maquerelle?

Maquerelle. Why, are ye ignorant that 'tis said, a squeamish affected niceness
is natural to women, and that the excuse of their yielding is only (forsooth)
the difficult obtaining? You must put her to't: women are flax, and will
fire in a moment.   44

Malevole. Why, was the flax put into thy mouth, and yet thou——thou set
fire? thou inflame her?

Maquerelle. Marry, but I'll tell ye now, you were too hot.

Malevole. The fitter to have inflamed the flaxwoman.

Maquerelle. You were too boisterous, spleeny; for indeed——

Malevole. Go, go, thou art a weak pandress, now I see.   50
     Sooner earth's fire heaven it self shall waste,
     Than all with heat can melt a mind that's chaste.
     Go: thou the Duke's lime-twig? I'll make the Duke turn thee out of thine
office. What, not get one touch of hope, & had her at such advantage!

Maquerelle. Now o' my conscience, now I think in my discretion, we did not
take her in the right sign, the blood was not in the true vein, sure.   *Exit.*

     Enter Bilioso.

Bilioso. Make way there, the Duke returns from the enthronement. Malevole!

Malevole. Out, rogue!

Bilioso. Malevole!

Malevole. Hence, ye gross-jaw'd peasantly, out, go!   60

Bilioso. Nay, sweet Malevole, since my return I hear you are become the
thing I always prophesied would be, an advanced virtue, a worthily
employed faithfulness, a man o' grace, dear friend. Come; what? *Si
quoties peccant homines*——if as often as courtiers play the knaves, honest
men must be angry——Why, look ye, we must collogue sometimes,
forswear sometimes.

---

35 cockatrice] whore   36 feather] as a symbol of folly   37 hunt the letter] pursue
verbal parallels   37 furder] further   39 *Stultorum . . . omnia*] fools are everywhere
(Cicero)   41 niceness] coyness   49 spleeny] peevish   53 lime-twig] snare   60 peasantly]
peasant-like; and cf. III. iii. 30   63–4 *Si . . . homines*] 'if as often as men sin' (Ovid);
the continuation is 'Jupiter should hurl his thunderbolts, he would soon be weaponless'
65 collogue] feign agreement

Malevole. Be damn'd sometimes.

Bilioso. Right. *Nemo omnibus horis sapit*: no man can be honest at all hours. Necessity often depraves virtue.

Malevole. I will commend thee to the Duke.   70

Bilioso. Do, let us be friends, man.

Malevole. And knaves, man.

Bilioso. Right, let us prosper and purchase; our lordships shall live and our knavery be forgotten.

Malevole. He that by any ways gets riches, his means never shames him.

Bilioso. True.

Malevole. For impudency and faithlessness are the mainstays to greatness.

Bilioso. By the Lord, thou art a profound lad.

Malevole. By the Lord, thou art a perfect knave. Out, ye ancient damnation!

Bilioso. Peace, peace: and thou wilt not be a friend to me as I am a knave, be not a knave to me as I am thy friend and disclose me. Peace: cornets!

SCENA TERTIA.

Enter Prepasso *and* Ferrardo, *two* Pages *with lights*, Celso *and* Equato, Mendoza *in duke's robes, and* Guerrino.

Mendoza. On, on, leave us, leave us.   *Exeunt all saving* Malevole [*and* Stay, where is the hermit?   Mendoza].

Malevole. With Duke Pietro, with Duke Pietro.

Mendoza. Is he dead? is he poisoned?

Malevole. Dead, as the Duke is.

Mendoza. Good, excellent, he will not blab, secureness lives in secrecy: come hether, come hether.

Malevole. Thou hast a certain strong villainous scent about thee my nature cannot endure.

Mendoza. Scent, man? What returns Maria? what answer to our suit?   10

Malevole. Cold, frosty, she is obstinate.

Mendoza. Then she's but dead, 'tis resolute, she dies.
     Black deed only through black deed safely flies.

Malevole. Puh! *per scelera semper sceleribus tutum est iter.*

Mendoza. What, art thou a scholar? art a politician? sure, thou art an arrand knave!

Malevole. Who, I? I have been twice an under-sheriff, man.

Mendoza. Hast bin with Maria?

Malevole. As your scrivener to your usurer I have dealt about taking of this commodity, but she's cold, frosty. Well, I will go rail upon some great

68 *Nemo . . . sapit*] from Pliny   V. iii, 12 resolute] resolved   14 *per . . . iter*] the safe way to crimes is through crimes (Seneca): a frequently quoted tag   18–20] These lines which in the quarto are preceded by 'Enter Malevole and Mendoza' may represent the intended start of the scene, the rest of which has perhaps been improperly cancelled.

man, that I may purchase the bastinado, or else go marry some rich
Genoan lady and instantly go travel.   22

Mendoza. Travel when thou art married?

Malevole. Ay, 'tis your young Lord's fashion to do so, though he was so
lazy being a bachelor, that he would never travel so far as the university,
yet when he married her, tails off, and catzo!——for England!

Mendoza. And why for England?

Malevole. Because there is no brothelhouses there.

Mendoza. Nor courtesans.

Malevole. Neather; your whore went down with the stews, and your punk
came up with your puritan.   31

Mendoza. Canst thou empoison? canst thou empoison?

Malevole. Excellently, no Jew, potecary, or politician better: look ye, here's
a box, whom wouldst thou empoison? Here's a box, which opened, and
the fume ta'en up in conduits, thorough which the brain purges it self,
doth instantly for 12 hours' space bind up all show of life in a deep
senseless sleep: here's another, which being opened under the sleeper's
nose, chokes all the power of life, kills him suddenly.

Mendoza. I'll try experiments, 'tis good not to be deceived: so, so, catzo!

Seems to poison Malevole [*who falls*].

Who would fear that may destroy?   40
    Death hath no teeth, nor tongue,
And he that's great, to him are slaves
    Shame, murder, fame, and wrong.
Celso!

Enter Celso.

Celso. My honoured Lord.

Mendoza. The good Malevole, that plain-tongu'd man,
    Alas, is dead on sudden wondrous strangely;
    He held in our esteem good place.
Celso, see him buried, see him buried.

Celso. I shall observe ye.   50

Mendoza. And Celso, prethee let it be thy care tonight
    To have some pretty show, to solemnize
    Our high instalment, some musick, masquery:
    We'll give fair entertainment unto Maria,
    The Duchess to the banisht Altofront:
    Thou shalt conduct her from the citadel
    Unto the palace: think on some masquery.

21 bastinado] cudgelling   26 tails] slinks   30 Neather] neither   30 stews] brothels
(the Southwark brothels were put down in 1546 at the same time as Puritanism arose)
30 punk] prostitute   38 power] The first two quartos have 'pores', which may be better.
38 suddenly] instantly   50 observe ye] carry out your orders

Celso. Of what shape, sweet Lord?

Mendoza. Why, shape? why, any quick-done fiction,
　　As some brave spirits of the Genoan dukes   60
　　To come out of Elysium forsooth,
　　Led in by Mercury to gratulate
　　Our happy fortune, some such any thing,
　　Some far-fet trick, good for ladies, some stale toy or other,
　　No matter so't be of our devising.
　　Do thou prepare't, 'tis but for a fashion sake,
　　Fear not, it shall be grac'd man, it shall take.

Celso. All service.

Mendoza. All thanks:
　　Our hand shall not be close to thee: farewell.   70
　　[*Aside*] Now is my treachery secure, nor can we fall:
　　Mischief that prospers men do virtue call:
　　I'll trust no man, he that by tricks gets wreaths
　　Keeps them with steel: no man securely breathes
　　Out of deserved ranks: the crowd will mutter. Fool!
　　Who cannot bear with spite, he cannot rule:
　　The chiefest secret for a man of state
　　Is, to live senseless of a strengthless hate.   *Exit* Mendoza.

Malevole (*starts up and speaks*).
　　Death of the damn'd thief: I'll make one i'the masque:
　　Thou shalt   80
　　Ha' some brave spirits of the antique dukes.

Celso. My Lord, what strange delusion?

Malevole. Most happy, dear Celso, poison'd with an empty box! I'll give
thee all anon: my lady comes to court, there is a whirl of fate comes
tumbling on, the castle's captain stands for me, the people pray for me,
and the great leader of the just stands for me: then courage, Celso.
　　For no disastrous chance can ever move him,
　　That leaveth nothing but a God above him.   [*Exeunt.*]

[SCENA QUARTA]

Enter Prepasso *and* Bilioso, *two* Pages *before them:* Maquer: Beancha *and*
Emilia.

Bilioso. Make room there, room for the ladies: why, gentlemen, will not
ye suffer the ladies to be ent'red in the great chamber? why, gallants!
and you, sir, to drop your torch where the beauties must sit too.

64 far-fet] far-fetched, ingenious   70 close] stingy   73 wreaths] honours, here
specifically thrones   74–5 no man . . . ranks] no one is secure who has risen out of his
station   78 senseless of] indifferent to   83 give] tell

Prepasso. And there's a great fellow plays the knave, why dost not strike him?

Bilioso. Let him play the knave a' God's name; think'st thou I have no more wit than to strike a great fellow? The music! more lights, revelling, scaffolds, do you hear? let there be others enow ready at the door, swear out the devil himself. Let's leave the ladies, and go see if the lords be ready for them.   [*All save the* Ladies *depart.*]

Maquerelle. And by my troth, beauties, why do you not put you into the fashion? This is a stale cut, you must come in fashion: look ye, you must be all felt, felt and feather, a felt upon your bare hair: look ye, these tiring things are justly out of request now: and do ye hear? you must wear falling bands, you must come into the falling fashion: there is such a deal o' pinning these ruffs, when the fine clean fall is worth all: and again, if you should chance to take a nap in the afternoon, your falling band requires no poting stick to recover his form: believe me, no fashion to the falling, I say.   19

Beancha. And is not Signor Sir Andrew a gallant fellow now?

Maquerelle. By my maidenhead, la, honour and he agrees as well together, as a satten suit and woollen stockings.

Emilia. But is not Marshall Make-room my servant in reversion a proper gentleman?

Maquerelle. Yes in reversion, as he had his office, as in truth he hath all things in reversion: he has his mistress in reversion, his clothes in reversion, his wit in reversion: & indeed is a suitor to me, for my dog in reversion: but in good verity, la, he is as proper a gentleman in reversion as——and indeed, as fine a man as may be, having a red beard and a pair of warpt legs.

Beancha. But i'faith I am most monstrously in love with Count Quidlibet-in-Quodlibet, is he not a pretty dapper unidle gallant?   31

Maquerelle. He is even one of the most busy-finger'd lords, he will put the beauties to the squeak most hideously.

Enter Bilioso.

Bilioso. Room! make a lane there, the Duke is ent'ring. Stand handsomely for beauty's sake, take up the ladies there. So, cornets, cornets!

Enter Prepasso, *joins to* Bilioso, *two* Pages *with lights,* Ferrardo, Mendoza, *at the other door two* Pages *with lights, and the* Captain *leading in* Maria; *the* Duke *meets* Maria, *and closeth with her, the rest fall back.*

13 felt] for a hat   14 tiring things] headdresses   15 falling bands] flat collars fashionable in the 17th century   18 poting stick] stick for adjusting the plaits of ruffs 18 to] to compare with   23 in reversion] by right of succession   29 red . . . legs] thought to be Marston laughing at himself   30 Quidlibet-in-Quodlibet] a mocking reference to wordy philosophizing   31 unidle] The first quarto has 'windle', a possible misprint for 'wimble' (= nimble), which may be a better reading.

Mendoza. Madam, with gentle ear receive my suit,
 A kingdom's safety should o'erpeise slight rights,
 Marriage is merely nature's policy:
 Then, since, unless our royal beds be join'd,
 Danger and civil tumult frights the state,   40
 Be wise as you are fair, give way to fate.
Maria. What wouldst thou, thou affliction to our house?
 Thou ever devil, 'twas thou
 That banishedst my truly noble lord.
Mendoza. I?
Maria. Ay, by thy plots, by thy black stratagems,
 Twelve moons have suff'red change since I beheld
 The loved presence of my dearest lord.
 O thou far worse than death! he parts but soul
 From a weak body: but thou soul from soul   50
 Dissever'st, that which God's own hand did knit.
 Thou scant of honour, full of devilish wit.
Mendoza. We'll check your too intemperate lavishness:
 I can and will!
Maria. What canst?
Mendoza. Go to: in banishment thy husband dies.
Maria. He ever is at home that's ever wise.
Mendoza. You'st never meet more, reason should love control.
Maria. Not meet?
 She that dear loves, her love's still in her soul.   60
Mendoza. You are but a woman, Lady, you must yield.
Maria. O save me, thou innated bashfulness,
 Thou only ornament of woman's modesty.
Mendoza. Modesty? Death, I'll torment thee.
Maria. Do, urge all torments, all afflictions try,
 I'll die my lord's as long as I can die.
Mendoza. Thou obstinate, thou shalt die!——Captain,
 That lady's life is forfeited to justice:
 We have examin'd her,
 And we do find she hath empoisoned   70
 The reverend hermit: therefore we command
 Severest custody.——Nay, if you'll do's no good,
 You'st do's no harm: a tyrant's peace is blood.
Maria. O thou art merciful, O gracious devil,
 Rather by much let me condemned be
 For seeming murder than be damn'd for thee.

37 o'erpeise] outweigh   49 he] i.e., death   58 You'st] You must   62 bashfulness]
uprightness

I'll mourn no more, come girt my brows with flow'rs,
Revel and dance; soul now thy wish thou hast,
Die like a bride, poor heart, thou shalt die chaste.

Enter Aurelia *in mourning habit.*

Aurelia. Life is a frost of cold felicity,   80
    And death the thaw of all our vanity.
    Wast not an honest priest that wrote so?
Mendoza. Who let her in?
Bilioso. Forbear.
Prepasso. Forbear.
Aurelia. Alas, calamity is every where.
    Sad misery, despite your double doors,
    Will enter even in court.
Bilioso. Peace.
Aurelia. I ha' done: one word—take heed! I ha' done.   90

Enter Mercury *with loud music.*

Mercury. Cyllenian Mercury, the god of ghosts,
    From gloomy shades that spread the lower coasts,
    Calls four high-famed Genoan dukes to come
    And make this presence their Elysium:
    To pass away this high triumphal night,
    With song and dances, court's more soft delight.
Aurelia. Are you god of ghosts? I have a suit depending in hell betwixt me
and my conscience, I would fain have thee help me to an advocate.
Bilioso. Mercury shall be your lawyer, Lady.
Aurelia. Nay, 'faith, Mercury has too good a face to be a right lawyer.
Prepasso. Peace, forbear. Mercury presents the masque.   101

Cornets. The song to the cornets, which playing, the masque enters. Malevole,
Pietro, Ferneze, *and* Celso *in white robes, with dukes' crowns upon laurel
wreaths, pistolets and short swords under their robes.*

Mendoza. Celso, Celso, court Maria for our love; Lady, be gracious, yet
    grace.

                        Malevole *takes his wife to dance.*
Maria. With me, sir?
Malevole.   Yes, more loved than my breath.
    With you I'll dance.

91 Cyllenian] Mercury was born on Mount Cyllene.   94 presence] presence-chamber
97 ghosts] now more in the sense of spirit   101 Mercury . . . masque] This should
perhaps be a stage direction.

Maria.   Why, then you dance with death.
　　But come sir, I was ne'er more apt to mirth:
　　Death gives eternity a glorious breath:
　　O to die honour'd, who would fear to die?
Malevole. They die in fear, who live in villainy.
Mendoza. Yes, believe him, Lady, and be rul'd by him.   110
Fietro. Madam, with me?   Pietro *takes his wife* Aurelia *to dance.*
Aurelia.   Wouldst then be miserable?
Fietro. I need not wish.
Aurelia. O, yet forbear my hand, away, fly, fly,
　　O seek not her, that only seeks to die.
Fietro. Poor loved soul.
Aurelia.   What, wouldst court misery?
Fietro. Yes.
Aurelia. She'll come too soon:
　　O my griev'd heart!
Fietro.   Lady, ha' done, ha' done.
　　Come, let's dance, be once from sorrow free.
Aurelia. Art a sad man?
Fietro.   Yes, sweet.
Aurelia.   Then we'll agree.   120

　　Ferneze *takes* Maquerelle, *and* Celso Beancha: *then the cornets sound the measure, one change and rest.*

Ferneze. (*To* Beancha) Believe it, lady: shall I swear? let me enjoy you in
　　private, and I'll marry you, by my soul.
Beancha. I had rather you would swear by your body: I think that would
　　prove the more regarded oath with you.
Ferneze. I'll swear by them both to please you.
Beancha. O, damn them not both to please me, for God's sake.
Ferneze. 'Faith, sweet creature, let me enjoy you tonight, and I'll marry
　　you tomorrow fortnight, by my troth la.
Maquerelle. On his troth la! believe him not, that kind of cunnicatching is as
　　stale as Sir Oliver Anchovy's perfum'd jerkin: promise of matrimony
　　by a young gallant, to bring a virgin lady into a fool's paradise: make her a
　　great woman, and then cast her off: 'tis as common, as natural to a courtier,
　　as jealousy to a citizen, gluttony to a puritan, wisdom to an alderman,
　　pride to a tailor, or an empty handbasket to one of these sixpenny damna-
　　tions: of his troth la, believe him not: traps to catch polecats.   135

---

129 cunnicatching] coney-catching, knavery   134 sixpenny damnations] common whores
135 polecats] prostitutes

Malevole. (*To* Maria) Keep your face constant, let no sudden passion
    Speak in your eyes.
Maria.   O, my Altofront!
Pietro. (*To* Aurelia) A tyrant's jealousies
    Are very nimble, you receive it all.
Aurelia. (Aurelia *to* Pietro) My heart, though not my knees, doth humbly fall,
    Low as the earth to thee.   141
Pietro. Peace, next change, no words.
Maria. Speech to such, ay, O, what will affords!

   Cornets sound the measure over again : which danced, they unmask.

Mendoza. Malevole!   *They environ* Mendoza, *bending
                                 their pistols on him.*
Malevole. No.
Mendoza. Altofront, Duke Pietro, Ferneze, hah!
All. Duke Altofront, Duke Altofront!   *Cornets a flourish.*
Mendoza. Are we surpris'd? What strange delusions mock
    Our senses, do I dream? or have I dreamt
    This two days' space? where am I?   *They seize upon* Mendoza.
Malevole. Where an arch-villain is.   151
Mendoza. O lend me breath, till I am fit to die.
    For peace with heaven, for your own souls' sake,
    Vouchsafe me life.
Pietro. Ignoble villain, whom neither heaven nor hell,
    Goodness of God or man, could once make good!
Malevole. Base treacherous wretch, what grace canst thou expect,
    That hast grown impudent in gracelessness?
Mendoza. O life!
Malevole. Slave, take thy life.   160
    Wert thou defenced, thorough blood and wounds,
    The sternest horror of a civil fight,
    Would I achieve thee: but prostrate at my feet,
    I scorn to hurt thee: 'tis the heart of slaves,
    That deigns to triumph over peasants' graves.
    For such thou art, since birth doth ne'er enroll
    A man 'mong monarchs, but a glorious soul.
    O, I have seen strange accidents of state!——
    The flatterer like the ivy clip the oak,
    And waste it to the heart: lust so confirm'd   170
    That the black act of sin it self not sham'd
    To be term'd courtship.
    O they that are as great as be their sins,

144 s.d. *bending*] aiming   161 defenced] prepared with defences   163 achieve] kill

Let them remember that th'inconstant people
Love many princes merely for their faces,
And outward shows: and they do covet more
To have a sight of these men than of their virtues:
Yet thus much let the great ones still conceive:
When they observe not heaven's impos'd conditions,
They are no kings, but forfeit their commissions.   180

Maquerelle. O good my Lord, I have lived in the court this twenty year,
they that have been old courtiers and come to live in the city, they are
spited at and thrust to the walls like apricocks, good my Lord.

Bilioso. My Lord, I did know your Lordship in this disguise, you heard
me ever say, if Altofront did return I would stand for him: besides,
'twas your Lordship's pleasure to call me wittol and cuckold; you must
not think, but that I knew you, I would have put it up so patiently.

Malevole. (*To* Pietro *&* Aurelia) You o'erjoy'd spirits, wipe your long-wet
eyes:
Hence with this man: an eagle takes not flies.   *Kicks out* Mend.
(*To* Pietro *and* Aurelia) You to your vows: (*to* Maquerelle) and thou
unto the suburbs.   190
(*To* Bilioso) You to my worst friend I would hardly give:
Thou art a perfect old knave: all-pleased live.
(*To* Celso *and the* Captain) You two unto my breast; (*to* Maria) thou to
my heart.
The rest of idle actors idly part,
And as for me, I here assume my right,
To which I hope all's pleas'd: to all goodnight.
                              Cornets a flourish. Exeunt omnes.

FINIS

175 princes] Here and for 'kings' (l. 180), the corrected version of the third quarto has
'men'—doubtless an alteration for the sake of political safety.   178 conceive] Quartos have
'conceale'.   187 put it up] put up with it   192 all-pleased] nevertheless (?)

AN IMPERFECT ODE, BEING BUT ONE STAFF,

(*Spoken by the Prologue*)

To wrest each hurtless thought to private sense
Is the foul use of ill-bred impudence:
    Immodest censure now grows wild,
        All over-running.
Let innocence be ne'er so chaste,
        Yet at the last
        She is defil'd
With too nice-brained cunning.
O you of fairer soul,
        Control,   10
With an Herculean arm,
        This harm:
And once teach all old freedom of a pen,
Which still must write of fools, whilst writes of men.

EPILOGUS

Your modest silence, full of heedy stillness,
Makes me thus speak: a voluntary illness
Is merely senseless; but unwilling error,
Such as proceeds from too rash youthful fervour,
May well be call'd a fault but not a sin.
Rivers take names from founts where they begin.
   Then let not too severe an eye peruse
The slighter brakes of our reformed Muse,
Who could her self her self of faults detect,
But that she knows 'tis easy to correct,   10
Though some men's labour: troth, to err is fit,
As long as wisdom's not profess'd, but wit.

Ode, title, *staff*] stanza   1 hurtless] innocent   2 use] habit, way   Epilogus, 1
heedy] heedful, attentive   2 illness] flaw   3 merely] wholly   8 brakes] flaws
11 Though . . . labour] though to some men it is a labour

Then till an other's happier Muse appears,
Till his Thalia feast your learned ears,
To whose desertful lamps pleas'd fates impart
Art above nature, judgment above art,
Receive this piece, which hope, nor fear yet daunteth,
He that knows most knows most how much he wanteth.

FINIS

---

13 an other] generally assumed to be Jonson   14 Thalia] Muse of comedy   15 desertful]
deserving   15 lamps] nocturnal studies   18 wanteth] lacks

THE REVENGER'S TRAGEDY

The Revenger's Tragedy

Written about 1605; printed either in 1607 or 1608

[*Works of Cyril Tourneur*, ed. Allardyce Nicoll, London 1930. A full edition by R. A. Foakes in The Revels Plays, London 1966.]

THE
REVENGERS
TRAGÆDIE.

*As it hath beene sundry times Acted,
by the Kings Maiesties
Seruants.*

AT LONDON.
Printed by G. E L D, and are to be sold at his
house in Fleete-lane at the signe of the
Printers-Presse.
1607.

DRAMATIS PERSONAE

The Duke.
Lussurioso, the Duke's son.
Spurio, the Duke's bastard son.
Ambitioso,
Supervacuo, } the Duchess's elder sons.
Junior, the Duchess's youngest son.
Antonio,
Piero, } Nobles.
Vindice, also known as Piato,
Hippolito, also known as Carlo, } brothers.
Dondolo, servant to Castiza.

The Duchess.
Castiza, sister to Vindice and Hippolito.
Gratiana, their mother.

Nobles, Gentlemen, Judges, Officers, Guards, a Prison-Keeper, and Servants.

Enter Vindice; *the* Duke, Duchess, Lussurioso *his son*, Spurio *the bastard*, *with a train, pass over the Stage with Torch-light.*

Vindice. Duke: royal lecher; go, grey-hair'd adultery,
    And thou his son, as impious steept as he:
    And thou his bastard true-begot in evil:
    And thou his Duchess that will do with Devil,
    Four ex'lent characters—O that marrowless age
    Would stuff the hollow bones with damn'd desires,
    And 'stead of heat kindle infernal fires,
    Within the spend-thrift veins of a dry Duke,
    A parcht and juiceless luxur. O God! one
    That has scarce blood enough to live upon,   10
    And he to riot it like a son and heir?
    O the thought of that
    Turns my abused heart-strings into fret.
    Thou sallow picture of my poisoned love,
    My study's ornament, thou shell of death,
    Once the bright face of my betrothed lady,
    When life and beauty naturally fill'd out
    These ragged imperfections;
    When two heaven-pointed diamonds were set
    In those unsightly rings;—then 'twas a face   20
    So far beyond the artificial shine
    Of any woman's bought complexion
    That the uprightest man, (if such there be,
    That sin but seven times a day) broke custom
    And made up eight with looking after her.
    Oh she was able to ha' made a usurer's son
    Melt all his patrimony in a kiss,
    And what his father fifty yearès told
    To have consum'd, and yet his suit been cold:
    But oh accursed palace!   30
    Thee when thou wert apparell'd in thy flesh,
    The old Duke poison'd,
    Because thy purer part would not consent
    Unto his palsy-lust, for old men lust-full
    Do show like young men angry, eager-violent,

s.d.] Vindice carries a skull, which he addresses at l. 14.   4 do] copulate

Out-bid like their limited performances—
O 'ware an old man hot, and vicious:
'Age as in gold, in lust is covetous.'
Vengeance, thou murder's quit-rent, and whereby
Thou show'st thyself tenant to tragedy,   40
Oh keep thy day, hour, minute, I beseech,
For those thou hast determin'd: hum: whoe'er knew
Murder unpaid? faith, give revenge her due
Sh'as kept touch hitherto—be merry, merry,
Advance thee, O thou terror to fat folks,
To have their costly three-pil'd flesh worn off
As bare as this—for banquets, ease and laughter
Can make great men, as greatness goes by clay,
But wise men little are more great than they.

    Enter his brother Hippolito.

Hippolito. Still sighing o'er death's vizard.
Vindice.   Brother, welcome,   50
    What comfort bring'st thou? how go things at court?
Hippolito. In silk and silver brother: never braver.
Vindice. Puh,
    Thou play'st upon my meaning, prithee say
    Has that bald madam, opportunity,
    Yet thought upon's? speak, are we happy yet?
    Thy wrongs and mine are for one scabbard fit.
Hippolito. It may prove happiness.
Vindice.   What is't may prove?
    Give me to taste.
Hippolito.   Give me your hearing then,
    You know my place at court.
Vindice.   Ay; the Duke's chamber.   60
    But 'tis a marvel thou'rt not turn'd out yet!
Hippolito. Faith I have been shov'd at, but 'twas still my hap
    To hold by th' Duchess' skirt, you guess at that,
    Whom such a coat keeps up can ne'er fall flat.
    But to the purpose.
    Last evening predecessor unto this,
    The Duke's son warily enquir'd for me,
    Whose pleasure I attended: he began,

---

39 quit-rent] rent paid by a freeholder in lieu of service   44 kept touch] kept covenant,
been faithful   46 three-pil'd] like best-quality velvet   55 bald madam] a common
personification ('Take occasion by the forelock, for she is bald behind')

By policy to open and unhusk me
About the time and common rumour: 70
But I had so much wit to keep my thoughts
Up in their built houses, yet afforded him
An idle satisfaction without danger.
But the whole aim, and scope of his intent
Ended in this, conjuring me in private,
To seek some strange-digested fellow forth:
Of ill-contented nature, either disgrac'd
In former times, or by new grooms displac'd,
Since his stepmother's nuptials, such a blood
A man that were for evil only good;   80
To give you the true word some base-coin'd pander.
Vindice. I reach you, for I know his heat is such,
Were there as many concubines as ladies
He would not be contain'd, he must fly out:
I wonder how ill-featur'd, vilde-proportion'd
That one should be, if she were made for woman,
Whom at the insurrection of his lust
He would refuse for once; heart, I think none;
Next to a skull, tho' more unsound than one
Each face he meets he strongly dotes upon.   90
Hippolito. Brother y'ave truly spoke him.
He knows not you, but I'll swear you know him.
Vindice. And therefore I'll put on that knave for once,
And be a right man then, a man a'th' time,
For to be honest is not to be i'th' world,
Brother I'll be that strange-composed fellow.
Hippolito. And I'll prefer you brother.
Vindice.   Go to then,
The small'st advantage fattens wronged men;
It may point out occasion; if I meet her,
I'll hold her by the fore-top fast enough;   100
Or like the French mole heave up hair and all.
I have a habit that will fit it quaintly.
Here comes our mother.
Hippolito.   And sister.
Vindice.   We must quoyne.

71–2 keep . . . up] shut up secure (as in a keep)   85 vilde] vile   99 It may . . . meet
her] an obscure line, possibly meaning that Vindice's preferment may provide him with an
opportunity   100 foretop] cf. l. 55 above   101 French mole] a tumour in the head
caused by syphilis   102 habit] costume   102 quaintly] cleverly, neatly   103 quoyne]
coin, counterfeit

Women are apt you know to take false money,
But I dare stake my soul for these two creatures,
Only excuse excepted—that they'll swallow,
Because their sex is easy in belief.

Enter Gratiana *and* Castiza.

Gratiana. What news from court, son Carlo?
Hippolito.   Faith mother,
 'Tis whisper'd there the Duchess' youngest son
 Has play'd a rape on Lord Antonio's wife.   110
Gratiana. On that religious lady!
Castiza. Royal blood! Monster, he deserves to die,
 If Italy had no more hopes but he.
Vindice. Sister, y'ave sentenc'd most direct, and true,
 The law's a woman, and would she were you:
 Mother I must take leave of you.
Gratiana. Leave for what?
Vindice. I intend speedy travel.
Hippolito. That he does Madam.
Gratiana. Speedy indeed!   120
Vindice. For since my worthy father's funeral,
 My life's unnaturally to me, e'en compell'd
 As if I liv'd now when I should be dead.
Gratiana. Indeed he was a worthy gentleman
 Had his estate been fellow to his mind.
Vindice. The Duke did much deject him.
Gratiana.   Much!
Vindice.   Too much.
 And through disgrace oft smother'd in his spirit,
 When it would mount, surely I think he died
 Of discontent: the nobleman's consumption.
Gratiana. Most sure he did!
Vindice.   Did he, 'lack,—you know all,   130
 You were his midnight secretary.
Gratiana.   No.
 He was too wise to trust me with his thoughts.
Vindice. I' faith then father thou wast wise indeed,
 'Wives are but made to go to bed and feed.'
 Come mother, sister: you'll bring me onward brother?
Hippolito. I will.
Vindice.   I'll quickly turn into another.

                 Exeunt.

131 secretary] confidante

[SCENE II]

Enter the old Duke, Lussurioso *his son, the* Duchess: *the* Bastard, *the* Duchess' *two sons* Ambitioso, *and* Supervacuo, *the third her youngest brought out with* Officers *for the rape: two* Judges.

Duke. Duchess it is your youngest son, we're sorry,
    His violent act has e'en drawn blood of honour
    And stain'd our honours,
    Thrown ink upon the forehead of our state
    Which envious spirits will dip their pens into
    After our death; and blot us in our tombs.
    For that which would seem treason in our lives
    Is laughter when we're dead; who dares now whisper
    That dares not then speak out, and e'en proclaim,
    With loud words and broad pens our closest shame?   10
1. Judge. Your Grace hath spoke like to your silver years
    Full of confirmed gravity;—for what is it to have
    A flattering false insculption on a tomb:
    And in men's hearts reproach? The bowell'd corpse
    May be cer'd in, but with free tongue I speak,
    'The faults of great men through their cereclothes break.'
Duke. They do, we're sorry for't, it is our fate,
    To live in fear and die to live in hate:
    I leave him to your sentence, doom him Lords—
    The fact is great—whilst I sit by and sigh.   20
Duchess. My gracious Lord I pray be merciful,
    Although his trespass far exceed his years,
    Think him to be your own as I am yours,
    Call him not son in law: the law I fear
    Will fall too soon upon his name and him:
    Temper his fault with pity.
Lussurioso.   Good my Lord;
    Then 'twill not taste so bitter and unpleasant
    Upon the judges' palate, for offences
    Gilt o'er with mercy, show like fairest women,
    Good only for their beauties, which wash'd off,   30
    No sin is uglier.
Ambitioso.   I beseech your Grace,
    Be soft and mild, let not relentless law,
    Look with an iron forehead on our brother.

14 bowell'd] disembowelled (for embalming)   15 cer'd in] embalmed and wrapped in a winding sheet ('cerecloth')   24 son in law] stepson

Spurio. [*Aside*] He yields small comfort yet, hope he shall die,
　　　And if a bastard's wish might stand in force,
　　　Would all the court were turn'd into a corse.
Duchess. No pity yet? must I rise fruitless then,
　　　A wonder in a woman? are my knees,
　　　Of such low metal—that without respect—
1. Judge. Let the offender stand forth;　　　　　　　　　　40
　　　'Tis the Duke's pleasure that impartial doom,
　　　Shall take first hold of his unclean attempt,
　　　A rape! why 'tis the very core of lust,
　　　Double adultery.
Junior.　　　　　So sir.
2. Judge.　　　　　　　　And which was worse,
　　　Committed on the Lord Antonio's wife,
　　　That general honest lady; confess my Lord!
　　　What mov'd you to't?
Junior.　　　　　　　Why flesh and blood my Lord.
　　　What should move men unto a woman else?
Lussurioso. O do not jest thy doom, trust not an axe
　　　Or sword too far; the law is a wise serpent　　　　50
　　　And quickly can beguile thee of thy life.
　　　Tho' marriage only has made thee my brother,
　　　I love thee so far, play not with thy death.
Junior. I thank you troth, good admonitions 'faith,
　　　If I'd the grace now to make use of them.
1. Judge. That lady's name has spread such a fair wing
　　　Over all Italy; that if our tongues
　　　Were sparing toward the fact, judgment itself
　　　Would be condemn'd and suffer in men's thoughts.
Junior. Well then 'tis done, and it would please me well　60
　　　Were it to do again: sure she's a goddess,
　　　For I'd no power to see her, and to live.
　　　It falls out true in this for I must die,
　　　Her beauty was ordain'd to be my scaffold,
　　　And yet me thinks I might be easier 'sess'd,
　　　My fault being sport, let me but die in jest.
1. Judge. This be the sentence—
Duchess. O keep't upon your tongue, let it not slip,
　　　Death too soon steals out of a lawyer's lip,
　　　Be not so cruel-wise!

65 'sess'd] assessed, judged; the quarto reading is 'ceast', which suggests a pun on 'ceased',
i.e., stopped from indulging in lechery

1. Judge.   Your Grace must pardon us,   70
 'Tis but the justice of the law.
Duchess.   The law
 Is grown more subtle than a woman should be.
Spurio. [*Aside*] Now, now he dies, rid 'em away.
Duchess. [*Aside*] O what it is to have an old-cool Duke,
 To be as slack in tongue as in performance.
1. Judge. Confirm'd, this be the doom irrevocable.
Duchess. Oh!
1. Judge. Tomorrow early—
Duchess.   Pray be abed my Lord.
1. Judge. Your Grace much wrongs yourself.
Ambitioso.   No 'tis that tongue,
 Your too much right, does do us too much wrong.   80
1. Judge. Let that offender—
Duchess.   Live, and be in health.
1. Judge. Be on a scaffold—
Duke.   Hold, hold, my Lord.
Spurio. [*Aside*]   Pox on't,
 What makes my dad speak now?
Duke. We will defer the judgment till next sitting;
 In the meantime let him be kept close prisoner:
 Guard, bear him hence.
Ambitioso. [*Aside*]   Brother, this makes for thee,
 Fear not, we'll have a trick to set thee free.
Junior. [*Aside*] Brother, I will expect it from you both;
 And in that hope I rest.
Supervacuo.   Farewell, be merry.   *Exit* [Junior] *with*
               a Guard.
Spurio. [*Aside*] Delay'd, deferr'd—nay then if judgment have cold blood,
 flattery and bribes will kill it.   91
Duke. About it then my Lords with your best powers,
 More serious business calls upon our hours.
         Exeunt. Manet Duchess.
Duchess. Was't ever known step-Duchess was so mild,
 And calm as I? some now would plot his death,
 With easy doctors, those loose-living men,
 And make his wither'd Grace fall to his grave,
 And keep church better.
 Some second wife would do this, and dispatch
 Her double-loathed lord at meat and sleep.   100
 Indeed 'tis true an old man's twice a child,

80 Your too much right] your excessive insistence on the law

Mine cannot speak, one of his single words
Would quite have freed my youngest dearest son
From death or durance, and have made him walk
With a bold foot upon the thorny law,
Whose prickles should bow under him: but 'tis not,
And therefore wedlock faith shall be forgot;
I'll kill him in his forehead, hate there feed,
That wound is deepest tho' it never bleed:

Enter Spurio.

And here comes he whom my heart points unto,   110
His bastard son, but my love's true-begot;
Many a wealthy letter have I sent him,
Swell'd up with jewels, and the timorous man
Is yet but coldly kind;
That jewel's mine that quivers in his ear,
Mocking his master's chillness and vain fear.
H'as spied me now.
Spurio.   Madam? your Grace so private?
My duty on your hand.
Duchess. Upon my hand sir, troth I think you'd fear
To kiss my hand too if my lip stood there.   120
Spurio. Witness I would not Madam.   *Kisses her.*
Duchess.   'Tis a wonder,
For ceremony has made many fools;
It is as easy way unto a duchess,
As to a hatted dame, (if her love answer)
But that by timorous honours, pale respects,
Idle degrees of fear, men make their ways
Hard of themselves.—What, have you thought of me?
Spurio. Madam I ever think of you, in duty,
Regard and—
Duchess.   Puh, upon my love I mean.
Spurio. I would 'twere love, but 't'as a fouler name   130
Than lust;
You are my father's wife, your Grace may guess now
What I could call it.
Duchess.   Why, th'art his son but falsely,
'Tis a hard question whether he begot thee.
Spurio. I'faith 'tis true too; I'm an uncertain man, of more uncertain
woman; maybe his groom a'th'stable begot me, you know I know not;

108 kill . . . forehead] i.e., by cuckolding him (alluding to the cuckold's horns)   124 hatted
dame] Only lower-class women wore hats.

he could ride a horse well, a shrewd suspicion marry—he was wondrous
tall, he had his length i' faith, for peeping over half-shut holiday windows, men would desire him 'light; when he was afoot, he made a goodly
show under a penthouse,   140
    And when he rid, his hat would check the signs,
    And clatter barbers' basins.
Duchess.   Nay, set you a-horseback once,
    You'll ne'er 'light off.
Spurio.   Indeed I am a beggar.
Duchess. That's more the sign thou art great—but to our love:
    Let it stand firm both in thy thought and mind,
    That the Duke was thy father, as no doubt then
    He bid fair for't, thy injury is the more,
    For had he cut thee a right diamond,
    Thou hadst been next set in the dukedom's ring,
    When his worn self like age's easy slave,   150
    Had dropt out of the collet into th'grave;
    What wrong can equal this? canst thou be tame
    And think upon't?
Spurio.   No, mad and think upon't.
Duchess. Who would not be reveng'd of such a father,
    E'en in the worst way? I would thank that sin,
    That could most injury him, and be in league with it.
    Oh what a grief 'tis, that a man should live
    But once i'th'world, and then to live a bastard,
    The curse a'the womb, the thief of nature,
    Begot against the seventh commandment,   160
    Half-damn'd in the conception, by the justice
    Of that unbribed everlasting law.
Spurio. Oh I'd a hot-back'd devil to my father.
Duchess. Would not this mad e'en patience, make blood rough?
    Who but an eunuch would not sin, his bed
    By one false minute disinherited?
Spurio. [*Aside*] Ay, there's the vengeance that my birth was wrapt in,
    I'll be reveng'd for all, now hate begin,
    I'll call foul incest but a venial sin.
Duchess. Cold still? in vain then must a duchess woo?   170
Spurio. Madam I blush to say what I will do.

137–40] he was so tall that on horseback he could see over the top of windows with their
lower halves shuttered for holidays and would be asked to alight   140 penthouse] over-
hanging eaves   141 check the signs] knock against (shopkeepers') signs   142–3] alluding
to the proverb, 'Set a beggar on horseback, and he'll ride a gallop', with an obvious sexual
quibble as well   151 collet] socket in a ring (to hold a stone)

Duchess. Thence flew sweet comfort.—Earnest and farewell.   *Kisses him.*
Spurio. Oh one incestuous kiss picks open hell.
Duchess. Faith now old Duke; my vengeance shall reach high,
    I'll arm thy brow with woman's heraldry.   *Exit.*
Spurio. Duke, thou didst do me wrong, and by thy act
    Adultery is my nature;
    Faith if the truth were known, I was begot
    After some gluttonous dinner, some stirring dish
    Was my first father; when deep healths went round,   180
    And ladies' cheeks were painted red with wine,
    Their tongues as short and nimble as their heels
    Uttering words sweet and thick; and when they rose,
    Were merrily dispos'd to fall again,
    In such a whisp'ring and withdrawing hour,
    When base male-bawds kept sentinel at stair-head,
    Was I stol'n softly; oh—damnation met
    The sin of feasts, drunken adultery.
    I feel it swell me; my revenge is just,
    I was begot in impudent wine and lust: 190
    Step-mother I consent to thy desires,
    I love thy mischief well, but I hate thee,
    And those three cubs thy sons, wishing confusion
    Death and disgrace may be their epitaphs;
    As for my brother the Duke's only son,
    Whose birth is more beholding to report
    Than mine, and yet perhaps as falsely sown
    (Women must not be trusted with their own),
    I'll loose my days upon him, hate all I,
    Duke, on thy brow I'll draw my bastardy.   200
    For indeed a bastard by nature should make cuckolds,
because he is the son of a cuckold-maker.   *Exit.*

[SCENE III]

Enter Vindice *and* Hippolito, Vindice *in disguise to attend L.* Lussurioso
the Duke's son.

Vindice. What brother? am I far enough from myself?
Hippolito. As if another man had been sent whole
    Into the world, and none wist how he came.

172 Earnest] her kiss is earnest of more to come   175 woman's heraldry] cuckold's horns:
cf. ll. 108, 200   199 loose my days] spend my time (in working his ruin) (*Salgado*)

Vindice. It will confirm me bold: the child o'th'court.
    Let blushes dwell i'th'country. Impudence!
    Thou goddess of the palace, mistress of mistresses
    To whom the costly perfum'd people pray,
    Strike thou my forehead into dauntless marble;
    Mine eyes to steady sapphires: turn my visage,
    And if I must needs glow, let me blush inward   10
    That this immodest season may not spy
    That scholar in my cheeks, fool-bashfulness,
    That maid in the old time, whose flush of grace
    Would never suffer her to get good clothes;
    Our maids are wiser; and are less asham'd,
    Save Grace the bawd, I seldom hear grace nam'd.
Hippolito. Nay brother you reach out a'th'verge now,—'Sfoot, the Duke's
    son, settle your looks.
Vindice. Pray let me not be doubted.

    Enter Lussurioso.

Hippolito. My Lord—
Lussurioso.   Hippolito? [*To* Vindice] Be absent, leave us.   20
                                             Vindice *moves aside.*
Hippolito. My Lord after long search, wary inquiries
    And politic siftings, I made choice of yon fellow,
    Whom I guess rare for many deep employments;
    This our age swims within him; and if Time
    Had so much hair, I should take him for Time,
    He is so near kin to this present minute.
Lussurioso. 'Tis enough,
    We thank thee: yet words are but great men's blanks,
    Gold tho' it be dumb does utter the best thanks.   *Gives him money.*
Hippolito. Your plenteous honour—an ex'lent fellow my Lord.   30
Lussurioso. So, give us leave. [*Exit* Hippolito.] Welcome, be not far off, we
    must be better acquainted. Push, be bold with us, thy hand.
Vindice. With all my heart i'faith. How dost sweet musk-cat?
    When shall we lie together?
Lussurioso. [*Aside*]   Wondrous knave!
    Gather him into boldness? 'sfoot, the slave's
    Already as familiar as an ague,

---

17 you reach ... now] you go to the limit now, with a quibble on 'verge', penis
28 blanks] promises of payment (perhaps unsigned)   33 musk-cat] a fop given to using
perfume (obtained from the musk-cat)   35 Gather ... boldness?] no need to encourage
him to be bold

And shakes me at his pleasure. [*To* Vindice] Friend I can
Forget myself in private, but elsewhere,
I pray do you remember me.
Vindice. Oh very well sir—I conster myself saucy!   40
Lussurioso. What hast been, of what profession?
Vindice. A bone-setter!
Lussurioso. A bone-setter!
Vindice. A bawd my Lord,
   One that sets bones together.
Lussurioso.   Notable bluntness!
   Fit, fit for me, e'en train'd up to my hand.
   Thou hast been scrivener to much knavery then.
Vindice. Fool to abundance sir; I have been witness
   To the surrenders of a thousand virgins,
   And not so little,
   I have seen patrimonies washt apieces,   50
   Fruit-fields turn'd into bastards,
   And in a world of acres,
   Not so much dust due to the heir 'twas left to
   As would well gravel a petition!
Lussurioso. [*Aside*] Fine villain! troth I like him wonderously,
   He's e'en shap'd for my purpose. [*To* Vindice] Then thou know'st
   I'th'world strange lust.
Vindice.   O Dutch lust! fulsome lust!
   Drunken procreation, which begets so many drunkards;
   Some fathers dread not (gone to bed in wine)   60
   To slide from the mother, and cling the daughter-in-law,
   Some uncles are adulterous with their nieces,
   Brothers with brothers' wives, O hour of incest!
   Any kin now next to the rim o'th'sister
   Is man's meat in these days, and in the morning
   When they are up and drest, and their mask on,
   Who can perceive this? save that eternal eye
   That sees through flesh and all? Well:—if anything
   Be damn'd, it will be twelve o'clock at night;
   That twelve will never scape;   70
   It is the Judas of the hours; wherein,
   Honest salvation is betray'd to sin.
Lussurioso. In troth it is too; but let this talk glide,
   It is our blood to err, tho' hell gap'd loud.

---

40 conster] construe   48 Fool] accessory or voluntary dupe (*Nicoll*)   55 gravel] alluding
to the use of sand to dry ink   58 Dutch lust] The Dutch were proverbially regarded as
heavy drinkers (*Foakes*).   61 cling] embrace   64 rim] womb, with a quibble on 'limit'

  Ladies know Lucifer fell, yet still are proud!
  Now sir! wert thou as secret as thou art subtle,
  And deeply fadom'd into all estates
  I would embrace thee for a near employment,
  And thou shouldst swell in money, and be able
  To make lame beggars crouch to thee.

Vindice.   My Lord?   80
  Secret? I ne'er had that disease o'th'mother
  I praise my father: why are men made close
  But to keep thoughts in best? I grant you this,
  Tell but some woman a secret over night,
  Your doctor may find it in the urinal i'th'morning.
  But my Lord—

Lussurioso.   So, thou'rt confirmed in me
  And thus I enter thee.   *Gives him money.*

Vindice.   This Indian devil
  Will quickly enter any man but a usurer,
  He prevents that, by ent'ring the devil first.

Lussurioso. Attend me, I am past my depth in lust   90
  And I must swim or drown, all my desires
  Are levell'd at a virgin not far from court,
  To whom I have convey'd by messenger
  Many waxt lines, full of my neatest spirit,
  And jewels that were able to ravish her
  Without the help of man; all which and more
  She, foolish chaste, sent back, the messengers
  Receiving frowns for answers.

Vindice.   Possible?
  'Tis a rare Phoenix whoe'er she be;
  If your desires be such, she so repugnant,   100
  In troth my Lord I'd be reveng'd and marry her.

Lussurioso. Push; the dowry of her blood & of her fortunes,
  Are both too mean,—good enough to be bad withal—
  I'm one of that number can defend
  Marriage is good: yet rather keep a friend.
  Give me my bed by stealth—there's true delight;
  What breeds a loathing in't, but night by night?

Vindice. A very fine religion!

Lussurioso.   Therefore thus,
  I'll trust thee in the business of my heart
  Because I see thee well experienc'd   110

---

77 fadom'd] fathomed   87 Indian devil] gold from the East Indies   94 waxt] waxed,
i.e., sealed with wax   100 repugnant] reluctant   105 friend] mistress

In this luxurious day wherein we breathe:
Go thou, and with a smooth enchanting tongue
Bewitch her ears, and cozen her of all grace,
Enter upon the portion of her soul,
Her honour, which she calls her chastity
And bring it into expense, for honesty
Is like a stock of money laid to sleep,
Which ne'er so little broke, does never keep.

Vindice. You have gi'n't the tang i'faith my Lord.
  Make known the lady to me, and my brain   120
  Shall swell with strange invention: I will move it
  Till I expire with speaking, and drop down
  Without a word to save me;—but I'll work—

Lussurioso. We thank thee, and will raise thee:—receive her name, it is the
  only daughter to Madame Gratiana the late widow.

Vindice. [*Aside*] Oh, my sister, my sister!—

Lussurioso.   Why dost walk aside?

Vindice. My Lord, I was thinking how I might begin
  As thus, 'Oh Lady'—or twenty hundred devices,
  Her very bodkin will put a man in.

Lussurioso. Ay, or the wagging of her hair.   130

Vindice. No, that shall put you in my Lord.

Lussurioso. Shall't? why content, dost know the daughter then?

Vindice. O ex'lent well by sight.

Lussurioso.   That was her brother
  That did prefer thee to us.

Vindice.   My Lord I think so,
  I knew I had seen him somewhere—

Lussurioso. And therefore prethee let thy heart to him,
  Be as a virgin, close.

Vindice.   Oh me good Lord!

Lussurioso. We may laugh at that simple age within him.

Vindice. Ha, ha, ha.

Lussurioso. Himself being made the subtle instrument,   140
  To wind up a good fellow.

Vindice.   That's I my Lord.

Lussurioso. That's thou.
  To entice and work his sister.

Vindice.   A pure novice!

Lussurioso. 'Twas finely manag'd.

Vindice.   Gallantly carried;
  [*Aside*] A pretty-perfum'd villain.

116 expense] use   129 put a man in] suggest an opening   138 simple age] age of
innocence   141 wind up] advance

Lussurioso.   I've bethought me
 If she prove chaste still and immovable,
 Venture upon the mother, and with gifts
 As I will furnish thee, begin with her.
Vindice. Oh fie, fie, that's the wrong end my Lord. 'Tis mere impossible
 that a mother by any gifts should become a bawd to her own daughter!
Lussurioso. Nay then I see thou'rt but a puny in the subtle mystery of a
 woman:—why 'tis held now no dainty dish: the name   152
 Is so in league with age that nowadays
 It does eclipse three quarters of a mother.
Vindice. Does't so my Lord?
 Let me alone then to eclipse the fourth.
Lussurioso. Why well said, come I'll furnish thee, but first
 Swear to be true in all.
Vindice.   True?
Lussurioso.   Nay but swear!
Vindice. Swear?
 I hope your honour little doubts my faith.   160
Lussurioso. Yet for my humour's sake 'cause I love swearing.
Vindice. 'Cause you love swearing, 'slud I will.
Lussurioso. Why enough,
 Ere long look to be made of better stuff.
Vindice. That will do well indeed my Lord.
Lussurioso.   Attend me.   *Exit.*
Vindice. Oh.
 Now let me burst, I've eaten noble poison,
 We are made strange fellows, brother, innocent villains,
 Wilt not be angry when thou hear'st on't, think'st thou?
 I'faith thou shalt. Swear me to foul my sister!   170
 Sword, I durst make a promise of him to thee,
 Thou shalt dis-heir him, it shall be thine honour;
 And yet now angry froath is down in me,
 It would not prove the meanest policy
 In this disguise to try the faith of both,
 Another might have had the self-same office,
 Some slave that would have wrought effectually,
 Ay and perhaps o'erwrought'em, therefore I,
 Being thought travell'd, will apply myself,
 Unto the self-same form, forget my nature,   180
 As if no part about me were kin to 'em,
 So touch 'em,—tho' I durst almost for good,
 Venture my lands in heaven upon their blood.   *Exit.*

152 name] i.e., of bawd 162 'slud] by God's blood 173 froath] froth 182 touch] test

[SCENE IV]

Enter the discontented Lord Antonio, *whose wife the Duchess's youngest son ravisht; he discovering the body of her dead to certain Lords;* [Piero] *and* Hippolito.

Antonio. Draw nearer Lords and be sad witnesses
    Of a fair comely building newly fall'n,
    Being falsely undermined: violent rape
    Has play'd a glorious act, behold my Lords
    A sight that strikes man out of me.
Piero. That virtuous lady?
Antonio.   Precedent for wives!
Hippolito. The blush of many women, whose chaste presence
    Would e'en call shame up to their cheeks, and make
    Pale wanton sinners have good colours,—
Antonio.   Dead!
    Her honour first drunk poison, and her life,   10
    Being fellows in one house did pledge her honour.
Piero. O grief of many!
Antonio.   I mark'd not this before—
    A prayer-book the pillow to her cheek,
    This was her rich confection, and another
    Plac'd in her right hand, with a leaf tuckt up,
    Pointing to these words:
    Melius virtute mori, quam per dedecus vivere.
    True and effectual it is indeed.
Hippolito. My Lord since you invite us to your sorrows,
    Let's truly taste 'em, that with equal comfort,   20
    As to ourselves we may relieve your wrongs.
    We have grief too, that yet walks without tongue,
    Curae leves loquuntur, maiores stupent.
Antonio. You deal with truth my Lord.
    Lend me but your attentions, and I'll cut
    Long grief into short words: last revelling night,
    When torchlight made an artificial noon
    About the court, some courtiers in the masque,
    Putting on better faces than their own,
    Being full of fraud and flattery: amongst whom,   30
    The Duchess' youngest son (that moth to honour)
    Fill'd up a room; and with long lust to eat

6 precedent] example   14 confection] preservative   17] It is better to die in virtue than to live through dishonour (a commonplace tag of unknown origin)   23] Small cares speak out, greater ones are struck dumb (a misquotation of Seneca, *Hippolytus,* 607)

Into my wearing; amongst all the ladies,
Singled out that dear form; who ever liv'd
As cold in lust, as she is now in death;
(Which that step-duchess-monster knew too well;)
And therefore in the height of all the revels,
When music was heard loudest, courtiers busiest,
And ladies great with laughter;—O vicious minute!
Unfit but for relation to be spoke of,   40
Then with a face more impudent than his vizard
He harried her amidst a throng of panders,
That live upon damnation of both kinds,
And fed the ravenous vulture of his lust,
(O death to think on't!)—she, her honour forc'd,
Deem'd it a nobler dowry for her name,
To die with poison than to live with shame.
Hippolito. A wondrous lady; of rare fire compact,
    Sh'as made her name an empress by that act.
Piero. My Lord what judgment follows the offender?   50
Antonio. Faith none my Lord, it cools and is deferr'd.
Piero. Delay the doom for rape?
Antonio.   O you must note
    Who 'tis should die,
    The Duchess' son; she'll look to be a saver,
    'Judgment in this age is near kin to favour.'
Hippolito. Nay then step forth thou bribeless officer;   *Draws sword.*
    I bind you all in steel to bind you surely,
    Here let your oaths meet, to be kept and paid,
    Which else will stick like rust and shame the blade;
    Strengthen my vow, that if at the next sitting,   60
    Judgment speak all in gold, and spare the blood
    Of such a serpent, e'en before their seats
    To let his soul out, which long since was found
    Guilty in heaven.
All.   We swear it and will act it.
Antonio. Kind gentlemen, I thank you in mine ire.
Hippolito. 'Twere pity
    The ruins of so fair a monument,
    Should not be dipt in the defacer's blood.
Piero. Her funeral shall be wealthy, for her name
    Merits a tomb of pearl; my Lord Antonio,   70
    For this time wipe your lady from your eyes,
    No doubt our grief and yours may one day court it,
    When we are more familiar with revenge.

Antonio. That is my comfort gentlemen, and I joy
    In this one happiness above the rest,
    Which will be call'd a miracle at last,
    That being an old man I'd a wife so chaste.   *Exeunt.*

ACTUS 2. SCAE. 1

Enter Castiza *the sister.*

Castiza. How hardly shall that maiden be beset,
    Whose only fortunes are her constant thoughts,
    That has no other child's-part but her honour,
    That keeps her low and empty in estate.
    Maids and their honours are like poor beginners,
    Were not sin rich there would be fewer sinners;
    Why had not virtue a revenue? well,
    I know the cause, 'twould have impoverish'd hell.

[*Enter* Dondolo.]
    How now Dondolo?

Dondolo. Madona, there is one as they say a thing of flesh and blood, a man
    I take him by his beard, that would very desirously mouth to mouth with
    you.   12

Castiza. What's that?

Dondolo. Show his teeth in your company.

Castiza. I understand thee not.

Dondolo. Why, speak with you Madona!

Castiza. Why, say so, madman, and cut off a great deal of dirty way; had it
    not been better spoke in ordinary words that one would speak with me?

Dondolo. Ha, ha, that's as ordinary as two shillings, I would strive a little
    to show myself in my place, a gentleman-usher scorns to use the phrase
    and fancy of a servingman.   21

Castiza. Yours be your own sir, go direct him hether.   *Exit* Dondolo.
    I hope some happy tidings from my brother,
    That lately travell'd, whom my soul affects.
    Here he comes.

Enter Vindice *her brother disguised.*

Vindice. Lady the best of wishes to your sex:
    Fair skins and new gowns.

Castiza.   Oh they shall thank you sir.
    Whence this?   Vindice *gives her a letter.*

II. i, 3 child's-part] inheritance   24 affects] loves

Vindice.   Oh from a dear and worthy friend,
    Mighty!
Castiza.   From whom?
Vindice.   The Duke's son!
Castiza.   Receive that! *A box o'th'ear*
    I swore I'd put anger in my hand,   *to her brother.*
    And pass the virgin limits of myself,   31
    To him that next appear'd in that base office,
    To be his sins' attorney; bear to him
    That figure of my hate upon thy cheek
    While 'tis yet hot, and I'll reward thee for't,
    Tell him my honour shall have a rich name,
    When several harlots shall share his with shame.
    Farewell, commend me to him in my hate!   *Exit.*
Vindice. It is the sweetest box, that e'er my nose came nigh,
    The finest drawn-work cuff that e'er was worn,   40
    I'll love this blow for ever, and this cheek
    Shall still henceforward take the wall of this.
    Oh I'm above my tongue: most constant sister,
    In this thou hast right honourable shown,
    Many are call'd by their honour that have none,
    Thou art approv'd for ever in my thoughts.
    It is not in the power of words to taint thee,
    And yet for the salvation of my oath,
    As my resolve in that point, I will lay
    Hard siege unto my mother, tho' I know   50
    A siren's tongue could not bewitch her so.
    Mass, fitly here she comes. Thanks my disguise.
    [*Enter* Gratiana.]
    Madam good afternoon.
Gratiana.   You're welcome sir.
Vindice. The next of Italy commends him to you,
    Our mighty expectation, the Duke's son.
Gratiana. I think myself much honour'd, that he pleases
    To rank me in his thoughts.
Vindice.   So may you lady:
    One that is like to be our sudden duke,
    The crown gapes for him every tide, and then
    Commander o'er us all, do but think on him,   60
    How blest were they now that could pleasure him
    E'en with anything almost.

42 take the wall of] take precedence over   43 I'm above my tongue] I cannot express
(my delight)   54 next] i.e., in succession to the dukedom

Gratiana.   Ay, save their honour.
Vindice. Tut, one would let a little of that go too
        And ne'er be seen in't: ne'er be seen in't, mark you,
        I'd wink and let it go—
Gratiana.   Marry but I would not.
Vindice. Marry but I would I hope, I know you would too,
        If you'd that blood now which you gave your daughter,
        To her indeed 'tis, this wheel comes about;
        That man that must be all this, perhaps ere morning
        (For his white father does but mould away)   70
        Has long desir'd your daughter—
Gratiana. Desir'd?
Vindice.   —Nay but hear me,
        He desires now that will command hereafter,
        Therefore be wise, I speak as more a friend
        To you than him; Madam, I know y'are poor,
        And 'lack the day, there are too many poor ladies already,
        Why should you vex the number? 'tis despis'd,
        Live wealthy, rightly understand the world,
        And chide away that foolish country girl
        Keeps company with your daughter, chastity.   80
Gratiana. O fie, fie, the riches of the world cannot hire a mother to such a
    most unnatural task.
Vindice. No, but a thousand angels can,
        Men have no power, angels must work you to't,
        The world descends into such base-born evils
        That forty angels can make fourscore devils;
        There will be fools still I perceive, still fools.
        Would I be poor, dejected, scorn'd of greatness,
        Swept from the palace, and see other daughters
        Spring with the dew o'th'court, having mine own   90
        So much desir'd and lov'd—by the Duke's son?
        No, I would raise my state upon her breast
        And call her eyes my tenants, I would count
        My yearly maintenance upon her cheeks:
        Take coach upon her lip, and all her parts
        Should keep men after men, and I would ride,
        In pleasure upon pleasure:
        You took great pains for her, once when it was,
        Let her requite it now, tho' it be but some;
        You brought her forth, she may well bring you home.   100
Gratiana. O heavens! this overcomes me!

83 angels] gold coins   98 once when it was] once upon a time

Vindice. [*Aside*] Not I hope, already?

Gratiana. [*Aside*] It is too strong for me, men know that know us,
  We are so weak their words can overthrow us.
  He toucht me nearly, made my virtues bate
  When his tongue struck upon my poor estate.

Vindice. [*Aside*] I e'en quake to proceed, my spirit turns edge.
  I fear me she's unmother'd, yet I'll venture,
  'That woman is all male, whom none can enter.'
  [*To her*] What think you now lady, speak, are you wiser?   110
  What said advancement to you? thus it said:
  The daughter's fall lifts up the mother's head!
  Did it not Madam? but I'll swear it does
  In many places, tut, this age fears no man,
  ''Tis no shame to be bad, because 'tis common.'

Gratiana. Ay, that's the comfort on't.

Vindice. [*Aside*]   The comfort on't!
  —I keep the best for last, can these persuade you
  To forget heaven—and—   *Offers her money.*

Gratiana. Ay these are they—

Vindice.   Oh!

Gratiana.   —that enchant our sex,
  These are the means that govern our affections,—   120
  That woman
  Will not be troubled with the mother long,
  That sees the comfortable shine of you,
  I blush to think what for your sakes I'll do!

Vindice. [*Aside*] O suff'ring heaven, with thy invisible finger,
  E'en at this instant turn the precious side
  Of both mine eye-balls inward, not to see myself.

Gratiana. Look you sir.

Vindice.   Holla.

Gratiana.   Let this thank your pains.   [*Gives him*

Vindice. O you're a kind madam.   *money.*]

Gratiana. I'll see how I can move.

Vindice.   Your words will sting.   130

Gratiana. If she be still chaste I'll ne'er call her mine.

Vindice. [*Aside*] Spoke truer than you meant it.

Gratiana. Daughter Castiza.

  [*Enter* Castiza.]

Castiza.   Madam?

105 bate] abate   122 troubled with the mother] affected by hysteria (with of course a
quibble on the literal meaning of the word)   125 suff'ring] permissive

Vindice.   O she's yonder.
    Meet her.
    [*Aside*] Troops of celestial souldiers guard her heart.
    Yon dam has devils enough to take her part.
Castiza. Madam what makes yon evil-offic'd man,
    In presence of you?
Gratiana.   Why?
Castiza.   He lately brought
    Immodest writing sent from the Duke's son
    To tempt me to dishonourable act.   140
Gratiana. Dishonourable act?—good honourable fool,
    That wouldst be honest 'cause thou wouldst be so,
    Producing no one reason but thy will.
    And 't'as a good report, prettily commended,
    But pray by whom? mean people; ignorant people,
    The better sort I'm sure cannot abide it.
    And by what rule should we square out our lives,
    But by our betters' actions? oh if thou knew'st
    What 'twere to lose it, thou would never keep it:
    But there's a cold curse laid upon all maids,   150
    Whilst other clip the sun they clasp the shades!
    Virginity is paradise, lockt up.
    You cannot come by your selves without fee.
    And 'twas decreed that man should keep the key!
    Deny advancement, treasure, the Duke's son!
Castiza. I cry you mercy. Lady I mistook you,
    Pray did you see my mother? which way went you?
    Pray God I have not lost her.
Vindice. [*Aside*]   Prettily put by.
Gratiana. Are you as proud to me as coy to him?
    Do you not know me now?
Castiza.   Why, are you she?   160
    The world's so chang'd, one shape into another,
    It is a wise child now that knows her mother.
Vindice. [*Aside*] Most right i'faith.
Gratiana.   I owe your cheek my hand,
    For that presumption now, but I'll forget it.
    Come you shall leave those childish haviours,
    And understand your time: fortunes flow to you,
    What, will you be a girl?
    If all fear'd drowning, that spy waves ashore,
    Gold would grow rich, and all the merchants poor.
151 clip] embrace   151 shades] with a quibble on the sense of something insubstantial

Castiza. It is a pretty saying of a wicked one,   170
    But methinks now
    It does not show so well out of your mouth,
    Better in his.
Vindice. [*Aside*]   Faith, bad enough in both,
    Were I in earnest, as I'll seem no less.
    —I wonder lady your own mother's words
    Cannot be taken, nor stand in full force.
    'Tis honesty you urge; what's honesty?
    'Tis but heaven's beggar; and what woman is
    So foolish to keep honesty,
    And be not able to keep herself? No,   180
    Times are grown wiser and will keep less charge,
    A maid that has small portion now intends,
    To break up house, and live upon her friends.
    How blest are you, you have happiness alone;
    Others must fall to thousands, you to one,
    Sufficient in himself to make your forehead
    Dazzle the world with jewels, and petitionary people
    Start at your presence.
Gratiana.   Oh if I were young,
    I should be ravisht.
Castiza.   Ay, to lose your honour.
Vindice. 'Slid, how can you lose your honour   190
    To deal with my Lord's Grace?
    He'll add more honour to it by his title,
    Your mother will tell you how.
Gratiana.   That I will.
Vindice. O think upon the pleasure of the palace,
    Secured ease and state; the stirring meats
    Ready to move out of the dishes, that
    E'en now quicken when they're eaten,
    Banquets abroad by torch-light, musics, sports,
    Bare-headed vassals, that had ne'er the fortune
    To keep on their own hats, but let horns wear 'em.   200
    Nine coaches waiting—hurry, hurry, hurry.
Castiza. Ay, to the devil.
Vindice. [*Aside*] Ay, to the devil.—To the Duke by my faith.
Gratiana. Ay, to the Duke: daughter you'd scorn to think o'th'devil and you
    were there once.
Vindice. [*Aside*] True, for most there are as proud as he for his heart i'faith.

177 honesty] chastity   181 keep less charge] put up with less expense   195 stirring]
stimulating   204 and] if

—Who'd sit at home in a neglected room,
Dealing her short-liv'd beauty to the pictures,
That are as useless as old men, when those
Poorer in face and fortune than herself,   210
Walk with a hundred acres on their backs,
Fair meadows cut into green fore-parts—Oh
It was the greatest blessing ever happened to women,
When farmers' sons agreed, and met again,
To wash their hands, and come up gentlemen;
The commonwealth has flourish'd ever since;
Lands that were mete by the rod, that labour's spar'd,
Tailors ride down, and measure 'em by the yard;
Fair trees, those comely fore-tops of the field,
Are cut to maintain head-tires—much untold.   220
All thrives but Chastity, she lies a-cold.
Nay, shall I come nearer to you? mark but this:
Why are there so few honest women, but because 'tis the poorer
profession? that's accounted best, that's best followed; least in trade, least
in fashion, and that's not honesty, believe it, and do but note the low and
dejected price of it:
'Lose but a pearl, we search and cannot brook it.
But that once gone, who is so mad to look it?'
Gratiana. Troth he says true.
Castiza.   False, I defy you both:
I have endur'd you with an ear of fire,   230
Your tongues have struck hot irons on my face;
Mother, come from that poisonous woman there.
Gratiana. Where?
Castiza. Do you not see her? she's too inward then:
Slave, perish in thy office: you heavens please,
Henceforth to make the mother a disease,
Which first begins with me, yet I've outgone you.   *Exit.*
Vindice. [*Aside*] O angels clap your wings upon the skies,
And give this virgin crystal plaudities.
Gratiana. Peevish, coy, foolish—but return this answer,   240
My lord shall be most welcome, when his pleasure
Conducts him this way; I will sway mine own,
Women with women can work best alone.   *Exit.*
Vindice. Indeed I'll tell him so.
O more uncivil, more unnatural,

212 fore-parts] stomachers   220 head-tires] head-dresses (worn only by the rich)
220 much untold] either, much more could be told; or, the cost is unknown   236 mother]
quibbling on the use of the word to mean hysteria (cf. l. 122)   245 uncivil] barbarous

Than those base-titled creatures that look downward!
Why does not heaven turn black, or with a frown
Undo the world—why does not earth start up,
And strike the sins that tread upon't?—oh;
Were't not for gold and women, there would be no damnation, hell
would look like a lord's great kitchen without fire in't;   251
But 'twas decreed before the world began,
That they should be the hooks to catch at man.   *Exit.*

[SCENE II]

Enter Lussurioso, *with* Hippolito, Vindice's *brother.*

Lussurioso. I much applaud thy judgment, thou art well read in a fellow,
    And 'tis the deepest art to study man;
    I know this, which I never learnt in schools,
    The world's divided into knaves and fools.
Hippolito. [*Aside*] Knave in your face my Lord, behind your back—
Lussurioso. And I much thank thee, that thou hast preferr'd
    A fellow of discourse—well mingled,
    And whose brain time hath season'd.
Hippolito.   True my Lord,
    We shall find season once I hope; [*Aside*] O villain!
    To make such an unnatural slave of me;—but—   10
Lussurioso. Mass, here he comes.

    [*Enter* Vindice *disguised.*]

Hippolito. [*Aside*] And now shall I have free leave to depart.
Lussurioso. Your absence, leave us.
Hippolito. [*Aside*]   Are not my thoughts true?
    I must remove; but brother you may stay:
    Heart, we are both made bawds a new-found way.   *Exit.*
Lussurioso. Now, we're an even number; a third man's dangerous,
    Especially her brother; say, be free,
    Have I a pleasure toward?
Vindice.   Oh my Lord.
Lussurioso. Ravish me in thine answer, art thou rare,
    Hast thou beguil'd her of salvation,   20
    And rubb'd hell o'er with honey? is she a woman?
Vindice. In all but in desire.
Lussurioso.   Then she's in nothing,—
    I bate in courage now.

II. ii, 9 season] opportunity   23 courage] desire

Vindice.   The words I brought,
 Might well have made indifferent honest, naught;
 A right good woman in these days is chang'd
 Into white money with less labour far,
 Many a maid has turn'd to Mahomet
 With easier working; I durst undertake
 Upon the pawn and forfeit of my life
 With half those words to flat a Puritan's wife,   30
 But she is close and good;
 [*Aside*] Yet 'tis a doubt by this time; oh the mother, the mother!
Lussurioso. I never thought their sex had been a wonder,
 Until this minute; what fruit from the mother?
Vindice. [*Aside*] Now must I blister my soul, be forsworn,
 Or shame the woman that receiv'd me first.
 I will be true, thou liv'st not to proclaim;
 Spoke to a dying man, shame has no shame.
 —My Lord.
Lussurioso.   Who's that?
Vindice.   Here's none but I my Lord.
Lussurioso. What would thy haste utter?
Vindice.   Comfort.
Lussurioso.   Welcome.   40
Vindice. The maid being dull, having no mind to travel
 Into unknown lands, what did me I straight,
 But set spurs to the mother; golden spurs,
 Will put her to a false gallop in a trice.
Lussurioso. Is't possible that in this
 The mother should be damn'd before the daughter?
Vindice. Oh, that's good manners my Lord, the mother for her age must go
foremost you know.
Lussurioso. Thou'st spoke that true! but where comes in this comfort?
Vindice. In a fine place my Lord—the unnatural mother   50
 Did with her tongue so hard beset her honour,
 That the poor fool was struck to silent wonder,
 Yet still the maid like an unlighted taper,
 Was cold and chaste, save that her mother's breath,
 Did blow fire on her cheeks. The girl departed,
 But the good ancient madam half mad, threw me
 These promising words, which I took deeply note of:
 'My Lord shall be most welcome—'

---

26 white money] silver, i.e., the woman is prostituted 37 thou ... proclaim] you will
not live to publish (her shame) 43–4 spurs, will] i.e., spurs such as will

Lussurioso.   Faith I thank her.

Vindice. '—When his pleasure conducts him this way—'

Lussurioso. That shall be soon i'faith.

Vindice.   '—I will sway mine own—'   60

Lussurioso. She does the wiser, I commend her for't.

Vindice. '—Women with women can work best alone.'

Lussurioso. By this light and so they can; give 'em their due, men are not comparable to 'em.

Vindice. No that's true, for you shall have one woman knit more in an hour than any man can ravel again in seven and twenty year.

Lussurioso. Now my desires are happy, I'll make 'em free-men now;
    Thou art a precious fellow, faith I love thee,
    Be wise and make it thy revenue, beg, leg.
    What office couldst thou be ambitious for?   70

Vindice. Office my Lord? marry if I might have my wish I would have one that was never begg'd yet.

Lussurioso. Nay then thou canst have none.

Vindice. Yes my Lord I could pick out another office yet, nay and keep a horse and drab upon't.

Lussurioso. Prethee good bluntness tell me.

Vindice. Why, I would desire but this my Lord, to have all the fees behind the arras; and all the farthingales that fall plump about twelve o'clock at night upon the rushes.

Lussurioso. Thou'rt a mad apprehensive knave, dost think to make any great purchase of that?   81

Vindice. Oh 'tis an unknown thing my Lord, I wonder 'tas been miss'd so long!

Lussurioso. Well, this night I'll visit her, and 'tis till then
    A year in my desires.—Farewell, attend,
    Trust me with thy preferment.   *Exit*.

Vindice.   My lov'd Lord.
    Oh shall I kill him o'th'wrong side now? no!
    Sword thou wast never a back-biter yet;
    I'll pierce him to his face, he shall die looking upon me;
    Thy veins are swell'd with lust, this shall unfill 'em,   90
    Great men were gods, if beggars could not kill 'em.
    Forgive me heaven, to call my mother wicked,
    Oh lessen not my days upon the earth.
    I cannot honour her; by this I fear me
    Her tongue has turn'd my sister into use.

66 ravel] unravel   69 leg] kneel   75 drab] whore   77–8 fees . . arras] fees for making assignations behind wall-hangings, with a pun on 'fees' as draperies, cf. l. 130
80 apprehensive] quick-witted

I was a villain not be forsworn
To this our lecherous hope, the Duke's son;
For lawyers, merchants, some divines and all,
Count beneficial perjury a sin small;
It shall go hard yet, but I'll guard her honour   100
And keep the ports sure.

Enter Hippolito.

Hippolito.   Brother how goes the world?
I would know news of you but I have news
To tell you.
Vindice.   What in the name of knavery?
Hippolito. Knavery, faith,
This vicious old Duke's worthily abus'd,
The pen of his bastard writes him cuckold!
Vindice. His bastard?
Hippolito.   Pray believe it, he and the Duchess,
By night meet in their linen, they have been seen
By stair-foot panders!
Vindice.   Oh sin foul and deep,
Great faults are wink'd at when the Duke's asleep.   110
See, see, here comes the Spurio.
Hippolito.   Monstrous luxur!

[*Enter* Spurio *and* Servants.]

Vindice. Unbrac'd: two of his valiant bawds with him.
O there's a wicked whisper; hell is in his ear.
Stay let's observe his passage.—
Spurio. Oh but are you sure on't?
Servant. My Lord most sure on't, for 'twas spoke by one,
That is most inward with the Duke's son's lust:
That he intends within this hour to steal,
Unto Hippolito's sister, whose chaste life
The mother has corrupted for his use.   120
Spurio. Sweet word, sweet occasion. 'Faith then brother
I'll disinherit you in as short time,
As I was when I was begot in haste:
I'll damn you at your pleasure: precious deed!
After your lust, oh 'twill be fine to bleed.
Come let our passing out be soft and wary.   *Exeunt.*
Vindice. Mark, there, there, that step, now to the Duchess,
This their second meeting writes the Duke cuckold
With new additions, his horns newly reviv'd:

101 ports] gates   112 Unbrac'd] in his shirt sleeves

Night! thou that look'st like funeral heralds' fees   130
Torn down betimes i'th'morning, thou hangst fitly
To grace those sins that have no grace at all.
Now 'tis full sea a-bed over the world,
There's juggling of all sides, some that were maids
E'en at sunset are now perhaps i'th'toll-book,
This woman in immodest thin apparel
Lets in her friend by water, here a dame
Cunning, nails leather hinges to a door
To avoid proclamation,
Now cuckolds are a-quoyning, apace, apace, apace, apace!   140
And careful sisters spin that thread i'th'night
That does maintain them and their bawds i'th'day!
Hippolito. You flow well, brother!
Vindice.   Puh I'm shallow yet,
Too sparing and too modest, shall I tell thee?
If every trick were told that's dealt by night
There are few here that would not blush outright.
Hippolito. I am of that belief too.
Vindice.   Who's this comes?
   [*Enter* Lussurioso.]
The Duke's son up so late?—Brother fall back,
And you shall learn some mischief.—My good Lord.
Lussurioso. Piato, why the man I wisht for, come,   150
I do embrace this season for the fittest
To taste of that young lady.
Vindice. [*Aside*]   Heart, and hell.
Hippolito. [*Aside*] Damn'd villain.
Vindice. [*Aside*] I ha' no way now to cross it, but to kill him.
Lussurioso. Come only thou and I.
Vindice.   My Lord, my Lord.
Lussurioso. Why dost thou start us?
Vindice.   I'd almost forgot—
The bastard!
Lussurioso.   What of him?
Vindice.   This night, this hour—
This minute, now—
Lussurioso.   What? what?
Vindice.   Shadows the Duchess—
Lussurioso. Horrible word.

---

130 fees] pheaze or hangings, perhaps with a quibble on the fees charged by heralds for
appearing at great men's funerals, cf. l. 77.   135 toll-book] list of animals for sale, hence
of prostitutes   140 quoyning] coining   141 sisters] prostitutes

Vindice.   And like strong poison eats
  Into the Duke your father's forehead.
Lussurioso.   Oh.   160
Vindice. He makes horn royal.
Lussurioso.   Most ignoble slave!
Vindice. This is the fruit of two beds.
Lussurioso.   I am mad.
Vindice. That passage he trod warily.
Lussurioso.   He did!
Vindice. And hush'd his villains every step he took.
Lussurioso. His villains? I'll confound them.
Vindice. Take 'em finely, finely, now.
Lussurioso. The Duchess' chamber-door shall not control me.   *Exeunt.*
Hippolito. Good, happy, swift, there's gunpowder i'th'court,
  Wild-fire at midnight, in this heedless fury
  He may show violence to cross himself.   170
  I'll follow the event.   *Exit.*

[SCENE III]

  Enter again [Lussurioso *and* Vindice]. [Duke *and* Duchess *discovered in
bed*.]

Lussurioso. Where is that villain?
Vindice. Softly my Lord, and you may take 'em twisted.
Lussurioso. I care not how!
Vindice.   Oh 'twill be glorious,
  To kill 'em doubled, when they're heap'd; be soft my Lord.
Lussurioso. Away! my spleen is not so lazy, thus, and thus,
  I'll shake their eyelids ope, and with my sword
  Shut 'em again for ever.—Villain, strumpet—
Duke. You upper guard defend us—
Duchess. Treason, treason.
Duke.   —Oh take me not in sleep,
  I have great sins, I must have days,   10
  Nay months dear son, with penitential heaves,
  To lift 'em out, and not to die unclear,
  O thou wilt kill me both in heaven and here.
Lussurioso. I am amaz'd to death.
Duke.   Nay villain traitor,
  Worse than the foulest epithet, now I'll gripe thee
  E'en with the nerves of wrath, and throw thy head
  Among the lawyers. Guard!

II. iii, 8 upper] innermost   11 heaves] groans

Enter Nobles *and Sons* [*with* Hippolito].

1. Noble. How comes the quiet of your Grace disturb'd?
Duke. This boy that should be myself after me,
 Would be myself before me, and in heat   20
 Of that ambition bloodily rusht in
 Intending to depose me in my bed.
2. Noble. Duty and natural loyalty forfend!
Duchess. He call'd his father villain; and me strumpet,
 A word that I abhor to file my lips with.
Ambitioso. That was not so well done brother.
Lussurioso.   I am abus'd—
 I know there's no excuse can do me good.
Vindice. [*Aside*] 'Tis now good policy to be from sight;
 His vicious purpose to our sister's honour
 Is cross'd beyond our thought.
Hippolito. [*Aside*]   You little dreamt   30
 His father slept here.
Vindice. [*Aside*]   Oh 'twas far beyond me.
 But since it fell so;—without frightful word,
 Would he had kill'd him, 'twould have eas'd our swords.
         They dissemble a flight and steal away.
Duke. Be comforted our Duchess, he shall die.
Lussurioso. Where's this slave-pander now? out of mine eye,
 Guilty of this abuse.

 Enter Spurio *with his villains.*

Spurio.   Y'are villains, fablers,
 You have knaves' chins, and harlots' tongues, you lie,
 And I will damn you with one meal a day.
1. Servant. O good my Lord!
Spurio.   'Sblood, you shall never sup.
2. Servant. O I beseech you sir.
Spurio.   To let my sword   40
 Catch cold so long and miss him!
1. Servant.   Troth my Lord—
 'Twas his intent to meet there.
Spurio.   Heart he's yonder!
 Ha? what news here? is the day out o'th'socket,
 That it is noon at midnight? the court up?
 How comes the guard so saucy with his elbows?

19 myself] i.e., duke 32 fell] fell out 32 frightful] arousing their fears 36ff.] Spurio
is apart and speaks to his servants. 45 his] i.e., Lussurioso's

Lussurioso. The bastard here?
 [*Aside*] Nay then the truth of my intent shall out.
 —My Lord and father hear me.
Duke.   Bear him hence.
Lussurioso. I can with loyalty excuse—
Duke.   Excuse?
 To prison with the villain,   50
 Death shall not long lag after him.
Spurio. Good i'faith, then 'tis not much amiss.
Lussurioso. Brothers, my best release lies on your tongues,
 I pray persuade for me.
Ambitioso.   It is our duties:
 Make yourself sure of us.
Supervacuo.   We'll sweat in pleading.
Lussurioso. And I may live to thank you.   *Exeunt* Lussurioso
                  and Guards.

Ambitioso. [*Aside*]   No, thy death
 Shall thank me better.
Spurio.   He's gone: I'll after him,
 And know his trespass, seem to bear a part
 In all his ills, but with a Puritan heart.   *Exit.*
Ambitioso. Now brother, let our hate and love be woven so subtilly together,
 that in speaking one word for his life, we may make three for his death,
 The craftiest pleader gets most gold for breath.   62
Supervacuo. Set on, I'll not be far behind you brother.
Duke. Is't possible a son should be disobedient as far as the sword? it is
 the highest, he can go no farther.
Ambitioso. My gracious Lord, take pity,—
Duke.   Pity, boys?
Ambitioso. Nay we'd be loth to move your Grace too much,
 We know the trespass is unpardonable,
 Black, wicked, and unnatural—
Supervacuo. In a son, oh monstrous.
Ambitioso.   —yet my Lord,   70
 A Duke's soft hand strokes the rough head of law,
 And makes it lie smooth.
Duke.   But my hand shall ne'er do't.
Ambitioso. That as you please my Lord.
Supervacuo.   We must needs confess,
 Some father would have enter'd into hate,
 So deadly pointed, that before his eyes,

55 Make . . . us] rely on us   59 Puritan] hypocritical

He would ha' seen the execution sound,
Without corrupted favour.
Ambitioso.   But my Lord,
Your Grace may live the wonder of all times,
In pard'ning that offence which never yet
Had face to beg a pardon.
Duke. [*Aside*]   Honey? how's this?   80
Ambitioso. Forgive him good my Lord, he's your own son,
And I must needs say 'twas the vildlier done.
Supervacuo. He's the next heir—yet this true reason gathers,
None can possess that dispossess their fathers:
Be merciful;—
Duke. [*Aside*]   Here's no stepmother's wit,
I'll try 'em both upon their love and hate.
Ambitioso. Be merciful—altho'—
Duke.   You have prevail'd,
My wrath like flaming wax hath spent itself,
I know 'twas but some peevish moon in him:
Go, let him be releas'd.
Supervacuo. [*Aside*]   'Sfoot how now brother?   90
Ambitioso. Your Grace doth please to speak beside your spleen,
I would it were so happy.
Duke.   Why go, release him.
Supervacuo. O my good Lord, I know the fault's too weighty,
And full of general loathing; too inhuman,
Rather by all men's voices worthy death.
Duke. 'Tis true too;
Here then, receive this signet, doom shall pass,
Direct it to the judges, he shall die
Ere many days; make haste.
Ambitioso.   All speed that may be,
We could have wisht his burthen not so sore,   100
We knew your Grace did but delay before.   *Exeunt.*
Duke. Here's envy with a poor thin cover o'er't,
Like scarlet hid in lawn, easily spied through;
This their ambition by their mother's side,
Is dangerous, and for safety must be purg'd;
I will prevent their envies; sure it was
But some mistaken fury in our son,
Which these aspiring boys would climb upon:
He shall be releas'd suddenly.

76 sound] properly performed   80 Honey?] sweet words?   82 vildlier] vilelier
89 moon] fit of frenzy (associated with the phases of the moon)

Enter Nobles.

1. Noble. Good morning to your Grace—   110
Duke. Welcome my Lords.
2. Noble.   Our knees shall take
    Away the office of our feet for ever,
    Unless your Grace bestow a father's eye,
    Upon the clouded fortunes of your son,
    And in compassionate virtue grant him that,
    Which makes e'en mean men happy—liberty.
Duke. [*Aside*] How seriously their loves and honours woo
    For that, which I am about to pray them do,
    Which—Rise my Lords, your knees sign his release,
    We freely pardon him.   120
1. Noble. We owe your Grace much thanks, and he much duty.   *Exeunt.*
Duke. It well becomes that judge to nod at crimes,
    That does commit greater himself and lives:
    I may forgive a disobedient error,
    That expect pardon for adultery
    And in my old days am a youth in lust:
    Many a beauty have I turn'd to poison
    In the denial, covetous of all;
    Age hot is like a monster to be seen:
    My hairs are white, and yet my sins are green.   130

ACT. 3. [SCENE 1]

Enter Ambitioso, *and* Supervacuo.

Supervacuo. Brother, let my opinion sway you once,
    I speak it for the best, to have him die
    Surest and soonest; if the signet come
    Unto the judges' hands, why then his doom
    Will be deferr'd till sittings and court-days:
    Juries and further,—faiths are bought and sold,
    Oaths in these days are but the skin of gold.
Ambitioso. In troth 'tis true too!
Supervacuo.   Then let's set by the judges
    And fall to the officers; 'tis but mistaking
    The Duke our father's meaning, and where he nam'd   10
    'Ere many days', 'tis but forgetting that
    And, have him die i'th'morning.

127–8 Many . . . denial] I have poisoned (or driven to suicide) many beautiful women who
have denied me   III. i, 8 set by] bypass

Ambitioso.   Excellent,
    Then I am heir—Duke in a minute.
Supervacuo. [*Aside*]   Nay,
    And he were once pufft out, here is a pin
    Should quickly prick your bladder.
Ambitioso.   Blest occasion!
    He being pack'd, we'll have some trick and wile,
    To wind our younger brother out of prison,
    That lies in for the rape; the lady's dead,
    And people's thoughts will soon be buriéd.
Supervacuo. We may with safety do't, and live and feed,   20
    The Duchess' sons are too proud to bleed.
Ambitioso. We are i'faith to say true,—come let's not linger,
    I'll to the officers, go you before,
    And set an edge upon the executioner.
Supervacuo. Let me alone to grind him.   *Exit.*
Ambitioso.   Meet; farewell.
    I am next now, I rise just in that place,
    Where thou'rt cut off, upon thy neck kind brother.
    The falling of one head lifts up another.   *Exit.*

[SCENE II]

Enter with the Nobles, Lussurioso *from prison.*

Lussurioso. My Lords,
    I am so much indebted to your loves,
    For this, O this delivery.
1. Noble.   But our duties,
    My Lord, unto the hopes that grow in you.
Lussurioso. If ere I live to be myself I'll thank you.
    O liberty, thou sweet and heavenly dame!
    But hell for prison is too mild a name.   *Exeunt.*

[SCENE III]

Enter Ambitioso, *and* Supervacuo, *with* Officers.

Ambitioso. Officers,
    Here's the Duke's signet, your firm warrant brings
    The command of present death along with it
    Unto our brother, the Duke's son; we are sorry,

14 and] if   14 he] i.e., Lussurioso   25 Meet] fitting   III. ii, 3 But] merely (i.e., it
was simply our duty to the heir apparent)   5 myself] i.e., duke

That we are so unnaturally employ'd
In such an unkind office, fitter far
For enemies than brothers.
Supervacuo.   But you know,
The Duke's command must be obey'd.
1. Officer. It must and shall my Lord—this morning then,
So suddenly?
Ambitioso.   Ay alas, poor good soul,   10
He must break fast betimes, the executioner
Stands ready to put forth his cowardly valour.
2. Officer. Already?
Supervacuo. Already i'faith; O sir, destruction hies,
And that is least impudent, soonest dies.
1. Officer. Troth you say true my Lord; we take our leaves,
Our office shall be sound, we'll not delay
The third part of a minute.
Ambitioso.   Therein you show
Yourselves good men, and upright officers.
Pray let him die as private as he may,   20
Do him that favour, for the gaping people
Will but trouble him at his prayers,
And make him curse, and swear, and so die black.
Will you be so far kind?
1. Officer.   It shall be done my Lord.
Ambitioso. Why, we do thank you; if we live to be,
You shall have a better office.
2. Officer.   Your good Lordship.
Supervacuo. Commend us to the scaffold in our tears.
1. Officer. We'll weep and do your commendations.   *Exeunt.*
Ambitioso. Fine fools in office!
Supervacuo.   Things fall out so fit.
Ambitioso. So happily; come brother, ere next clock,   30
His head will be made serve a bigger block.   *Exeunt.*

[SCENE IV]

Enter in prison Junior *Brother.*

Junior. Keeper.
Keeper. My Lord.

15] he that soonest dies is the least impudent (i.e., shameless)   23 die black] die in sin
25 if . . . be] if I live to be duke   31 block] i.e., the executioner's, with a quibble on the
block used for hat-making

Junior. No news lately from our brothers? Are they unmindful of us?
Keeper. My Lord a messenger came newly in
    And brought this from 'em.   *Gives him a letter.*
Junior.   Nothing but paper comforts?
    I look'd for my delivery before this,
    Had they been worth their oaths—prethee be from us. *Exit* Keeper.
    Now what say you forsooth, speak out I pray.
[*Reads letter.*] 'Brother be of good cheer'—'slud, it begins like a whore with
    good cheer; 'thou shalt not long be a prisoner'—not five and thirty year
    like a banqrout, I think so; 'we have thought upon a device to get thee
    out by a trick!'—by a trick, pox o' your trick and it be so long a-playing;
    'and so rest comforted, be merry and expect it suddenly!'—be merry?
    hang merry, draw and quarter merry, I'll be mad! Is't not strange that a
    man should lie in a whole month for a woman? Well, we shall see how
    sudden our brothers will be in their promise; I must expect still a trick!
    I shall not be long a prisoner.   17

[*Enter* Keeper.]

    How now, what news?
Keeper. Bad news my Lord, I am discharg'd of you.
Junior. Slave, call'st thou that bad news? I thank you brothers.   20
Keeper. My Lord 'twill prove so; here come the officers,
    Into whose hands I must commit you.
Junior. Ha, officers? what? why?

[*Enter* Officers.]

1. Officer. You must pardon us my Lord,
    Our office must be sound, here is our warrant—
    The signet from the Duke, you must straight suffer.
Junior. Suffer? I'll suffer you to be gone, I'll suffer you to come no more,
    what would you have me suffer?
2. Officer. My Lord those words were better chang'd to prayers,
    The time's but brief with you, prepare to die.   30
Junior. Sure 'tis not so.
3. Officer.   It is too true my Lord.
Junior. I tell you 'tis not, for the Duke my father
    Deferr'd me till next sitting, and I look
    E'en every minute, threescore times an hour,
    For a release, a trick wrought by my brothers.
1. Officer. A trick my Lord? if you expect such comfort,
    Your hope's as fruitless as a barren woman:
    Your brothers were the unhappy messengers,
    That brought this powerful token for your death.

12 and it] if it   15 lie in] be confined

Junior. My brothers? no, no.

2. Officer.   'Tis most true my Lord.   40

Junior. My brothers to bring a warrant for my death?
    How strange this shows!

3. Officer.   There's no delaying time.

Junior. Desire 'em hether, call 'em up, my brothers!
    They shall deny it to your faces.

1. Officer.   My Lord,
    They're far enough by this, at least at court,
    And this most strict command they left behind 'em,
    When grief swum in their eyes, they show'd like brothers,
    Brim-full of heavy sorrow: but the Duke
    Must have his pleasure.

Junior. His pleasure?   50

1. Officer. These were their last words which my memory bears,
    'Commend us to the scaffold in our tears.'

Junior. Pox dry their tears, what should I do with tears?
    I hate 'em worse than any citizen's son
    Can hate salt water; here came a letter now,
    New-bleeding from their pens, scarce stinted yet,—
    Would I'd been torn in pieces when I tore it,—
    Look you officious whoresons, words of comfort,
    'Not long a prisoner.'

1. Officer. It says true in that sir, for you must suffer presently.   60

Junior. A villainous Duns upon the letter—knavish exposition; look you
then here sir: 'We'll get thee out by a trick', says he.

2. Officer. That may hold too sir, for you know a trick is commonly four
cards, which was meant by us four officers.

Junior. Worse and worse dealing.

1. Officer.   The hour beckons us,
    The headsman waits, lift up your eyes to heaven.

Junior. I thank you 'faith; good pretty-wholesome counsel,
    I should look up to heaven as you said,
    Whilst he behind me cozens me of my head,
    Ay, that's the trick.

3. Officer.   You delay too long my Lord.   70

Junior. Stay, good authority's bastards, since I must
    Through brothers' perjury die, O let me venom
    Their souls with curses.

1. Officer.   Come, 'tis no time to curse.

42 delaying time] putting off the time (of the execution)   45 by this] by this time
56 stinted] staunched   61 Duns] sophistical interpretation, alluding to Duns Scotus, the
scholastic theologian, whose ambiguity of thought had become proverbial

Junior. Must I bleed then, without respect of sign?
   Well—
   My fault was sweet sport, which the world approves,
   I die for that which every woman loves.   *Exeunt.*

[SCENE V]

  Enter Vindice *with* Hippolito *his brother.*

Vindice. O sweet, delectable, rare, happy, ravishing!
Hippolito. Why what's the matter brother?
Vindice.   O 'tis able
   To make a man spring up, & knock his forehead
   Against yon silver ceiling.
Hippolito.   Prethee tell me,
   Why may not I partake with you? you vow'd once
   To give me share to every tragic thought.
Vindice. By th'Mass I think I did too;
   Then I'll divide it to thee:—the old Duke
   Thinking my outward shape and inward heart
   Are cut out of one piece, (for he that prates his secrets,   10
   His heart stands o'th'outside)
   Hires me by price: to greet him with a lady,
   In some fit place veil'd from the eyes o'th'court,
   Some dark'ned blushless angle, that is guilty
   Of his forefathers' lusts, and great folks' riots,
   To which I easily (to maintain my shape)
   Consented, and did wish his impudent grace
   To meet her here in this unsunned lodge,
   Wherein 'tis night at noon, and here the rather,
   Because unto the torturing of his soul,   20
   The Bastard and the Duchess have appointed
   Their meeting too in this luxurious circle,
   Which most afflicting sight will kill his eyes
   Before we kill the rest of him.
Hippolito. 'Twill i'faith, most dreadfully digested,
   I see not how you could have miss'd me brother.
Vindice. True, but the violence of my joy forgot it.
Hippolito. Ay, but where's that lady now?

III. v, 4 silver ceiling] the painted stage canopy or 'heavens'   25 digested] contrived
26 miss'd me] left me out

Vindice.   Oh at that word,
     I'm lost again, you cannot find me yet,
     I'm in a throng of happy apprehensions.   30
     He's suited for a lady, I have took care
     For a delicious lip, a sparkling eye—
     You shall be witness brother;
     Be ready, stand with your hat off.   *Exit.*
Hippolito. Troth I wonder what lady it should be?
     Yet 'tis no wonder, now I think again,
     To have a lady stoop to a duke, that stoops unto his men;
     'Tis common to be common, through the world:
     And there's more private-common shadowing vices,
     Than those who are known both by their names and prices.   40
     'Tis part of my allegiance to stand bare
     To the Duke's concubine,—and here she comes.

Enter Vindice, *with the skull of his love drest up in Tires.*

Vindice. Madam his Grace will not be absent long.
     Secret? ne'er doubt us Madam; 'twill be worth
     Three velvet gowns to your Ladyship;—known?
     Few ladies respect that;—disgrace? a poor thin shell,
     'Tis the best grace you have to do it well.
     I'll save your hand that labour, I'll unmask you.
Hippolito. Why brother, brother.
Vindice. Art thou beguil'd now? tut, a lady can,   50
     At such, all hid, beguile a wiser man.
     Have I not fitted the old surfeiter
     With a quaint piece of beauty? Age and bare bone
     Are e'er allied in action; here's an eye,
     Able to tempt a greatman—to serve God,
     A pretty hanging lip, that has forgot now to dissemble:
     Methinks this mouth should make a swearer tremble,
     A drunkard clasp his teeth, and not undo 'em
     To suffer wet damnation to run through 'em.
     Here's a cheek keeps her colour, let the wind go whistle;   60
     Spout rain, we fear thee not, be hot or cold,
     All's one with us; and is not he absurd,
     Whose fortunes are upon their faces set,
     That fear no other God but wind and wet?

---

30 apprehensions] anticipations   31 He's . . . lady] I've found a lady to suit him
39–40] i.e., there are more who indulge secretly in common vices than there are publicly
known prostitutes   43 s.d. *Tires*] head-dress, including a mask

Hippolito. Brother y'ave spoke that right;
 Is this the form that living shone so bright?
Vindice. The very same,—
 And now methinks I could e'en chide myself,
 For doating on her beauty, tho' her death
 Shall be reveng'd after no common action;   70
 Does the silk-worm expend her yellow labours
 For thee? for thee does she undo herself?
 Are lordships sold to maintain ladyships
 For the poor benefit of a bewitching minute?
 Why does yon fellow falsify high-ways
 And put his life between the judge's lips,
 To refine such a thing, keeps horse and men
 To beat their valours for her?
 Surely, we're all mad people, and they
 Whom we think are, are not,—we mistake those,   80
 'Tis we are mad in sense, they but in clothes.
Hippolito. Faith and in clothes too we, give us our due.
Vindice. Does every proud and self-affecting dame
 Camphire her face for this? and grieve her Maker
 In sinful baths of milk,—when many an infant starves,
 For her superfluous outside, all for this?
 Who now bids twenty pound a night, prepares
 Music, perfumes, and sweetmeats? all are husht,
 Thou may'st lie chaste now! It were fine methinks,
 To have thee seen at revels, forgetful feasts,   90
 And unclean brothels; sure 'twould fright the sinner
 And make him a good coward, put a reveller
 Out of his antic amble
 And cloy an epicure with empty dishes.
 Here might a scornful and ambitious woman
 Look through and through herself;—see ladies, with false forms
 You deceive men, but cannot deceive worms.
 Now to my tragic business,—look you brother,
 I have not fashion'd this only for show
 And useless property, no, it shall bear a part   100
 E'en in its own revenge. This very skull,
 Whose mistress the Duke poisoned, with this drug
 The mortal curse of the earth, shall be reveng'd

---

73 lordships] estates 73 ladyships] i.e., in fine clothes and adornments 75 falsify
high-ways] turn highwayman 78 beat their valours] use up their strengths 82] alluding
to the disguise Vindice wears 84 Camphire] camphor (used as a perfume in soaps and
cosmetics) 100 property] i.e., stage property

    In the like strain, and kiss his lips to death;
    As much as the dumb thing can, he shall feel:
    What fails in poison, we'll supply in steel.
Hippolito. Brother I do applaud thy constant vengeance,
    The quaintness of thy malice above thought.
Vindice. [*Puts poison on the skull's lips.*] So 'tis laid on: now come and welcome,
    Duke,
    I have her for thee. I protest it brother: 110
    Methinks she makes almost as fair a sign
    As some old gentlewoman in a periwig.   *Puts a mask on the skull.*
    Hide thy face now for shame, thou hadst need have a mask now,
    'Tis vain when beauty flows, but when it fleets
    This would become graves better than the streets.
Hippolito. You have my voice in that; hark, the Duke's come.
Vindice. Peace, let's observe what company he brings,
    And how he does absent 'em, for you know
    He'll wish all private.—Brother fall you back a little
    With the bony lady.
Hippolito.   That I will.
Vindice.   So, so,—   120
    Now 9 years' vengeance crowd into a minute!

[*Enter* Duke *and* Gentlemen.]

Duke. You shall have leave to leave us, with this charge,
    Upon your lives, if we be miss'd by th'Duchess
    Or any of the nobles, to give out,
    We're privately rid forth.
Vindice. [*Aside*]   Oh happiness!
Duke. With some few honourable gentlemen you may say,
    You may name those that are away from court.
Gentleman. Your will and pleasure shall be done my Lord.   *Exeunt.*
Vindice. [*Aside*] Privately rid forth!
    He strives to make sure work on't.—Your good Grace?   130
Duke. Piato, well done; hast brought her, what lady is't?
Vindice. Faith my Lord a country lady, a little bashful at first as most of
    them are, but after the first kiss my Lord the worst is past with them;
    your Grace knows now what you have to do; sh'as somewhat a grave
    look with her—but—
Duke. I love that best; conduct her.
Vindice. [*Aside*]   Have at all.

108 quaintness] ingenuity   114 fleets] disappears, i.e., by death   115 this] i.e., the
skull   136 Have at all] On with the business (*Foakes*); Venture all (*Salgado*)

Duke. In gravest looks the greatest faults seem less,
 Give me that sin that's rob'd in holiness.

Vindice. [*Aside*] Back with the torch; brother raise the perfumes.

Duke. How sweet can a duke breathe! Age has no fault,   140
 Pleasure should meet in a perfumed mist.
 Lady, sweetly encount'red;
 I came from court, I must be bold with you.   *Kisses skull.*
 Oh, what's this? oh!

Vindice. Royal villain, white devil!

Duke. Oh!

Vindice. Brother—
 Place the torch here, that his affrighted eye-balls
 May start into those hollows. Duke, dost know
 Yon dreadful vizard? View it well, 'tis the skull   150
 Of Gloriana, whom thou poisonedst last.

Duke. Oh, 't'as poisoned me.

Vindice. Didst not know that till now?

Duke.   What are you two?

Vindice. Villains all three!—The very ragged bone
 Has been sufficiently reveng'd.

Duke. Oh, Hippolito! call treason.

Hippolito. Yes my good Lord, treason, treason, treason.

            Stamping on him.

Duke. Then I'm betray'd.

Vindice. Alas poor lecher in the hands of knaves,
 A slavish duke is baser than his slaves.   160

Duke. My teeth are eaten out.

Vindice.   Hadst any left?

Hippolito. I think but few.

Vindice.   Then those that did eat are eaten.

Duke. O my tongue!

Vindice. Your tongue? 'twill teach you to kiss closer,
 Not like a flobbering Dutchman—you have eyes still:
 Look monster, what a lady hast thou made me,
 My once betrothed wife.

Duke.   Is it thou, villain?
 Nay then—

Vindice.   'Tis I, 'tis Vindice, 'tis I.

Hippolito. And let this comfort thee: our lord and father
 Fell sick upon the infection of thy frowns,   170
 And died in sadness; be that thy hope of life.

---

143 be bold with] i.e., kiss   145 white devil] hypocrite   149 start] So in the quarto, perhaps a mistake for 'stare'.

Duke. Oh!

Vindice. He had his tongue, yet grief made him die speechless.
  Puh, 'tis but early yet, now I'll begin
  To stick thy soul with ulcers, I will make
  Thy spirit grievous sore, it shall not rest,
  But like some pestilent man toss in thy breast—
  (Mark me Duke)
  Thou'rt a renowned, high, and mighty cuckold.

Duke. Oh!   180

Vindice. Thy bastard,
  Thy bastard rides a-hunting in thy brow.

Duke. Millions of deaths!

Vindice.   Nay, to afflict thee more,
  Here in this lodge they meet for damned clips,
  Those eyes shall see the incest of their lips.

Duke. Is there a hell besides this, villains?

Vindice.   Villain?
  Nay heaven is just, scorns are the hires of scorns,
  I ne'er knew yet adulterer without horns.

Hippolito. Once ere they die 'tis quitted.

Vindice.   Hark the music,
  Their banquet is prepar'd, they're coming—   190

Duke. Oh, kill me not with that sight.

Vindice. Thou shalt not lose that sight for all thy dukedom.

Duke. Traitors, murderers!

Vindice. What? is not thy tongue eaten out yet?
  Then we'll invent a silence; brother stifle the torch.

Duke. Treason, murther!

Vindice. Nay 'faith, we'll have you husht now with thy dagger.
  Nail down his tongue, and mine shall keep possession
  About his heart, if he but gasp he dies,
  We dread not death to quittance injuries;—   200
  Brother,
  If he but wink, not brooking the foul object,
  Let our two other hands tear up his lids,
  And make his eyes like comets shine through blood;
  When the bad bleeds, then is the tragedy good.

Hippolito. Whist, brother, music's at our ear, they come.

  Enter the Bastard *meeting the* Duchess.

Spurio. Had not that kiss a taste of sin 'twere sweet.

177 pestilent] plague-bearing 184 clips] embraces 187 hires] wages 189 quitted]
requited 200 quittance] repay

Duchess. Why, there's no pleasure sweet but it is sinful.
Spurio. True, such a bitter sweetness fate hath given,
    Best side to us is the worst side to heaven.   210
Duchess. Push, come: 'tis the old Duke thy doubtful father,
    The thought of him rubs heaven in thy way,
    But I protest by yonder waxen fire,
    Forget him, or I'll poison him.
Spurio. Madam, you urge a thought which ne'er had life;
    So deadly do I loathe him for my birth,
    That if he took me hasp'd within his bed,
    I would add murther to adultery,
    And with my sword give up his years to death.
Duchess. Why now thou'rt sociable, let's in and feast;   220
    Loud'st music sound: pleasure is banquet's guest.   *Exeunt.*
Duke. I cannot brook—   *Dies.*
Vindice.   The brook is turn'd to blood.
Hippolito. Thanks to loud music.
Vindice.   'Twas our friend indeed,
    'Tis state in music for a duke to bleed:
    The dukedom wants a head, tho' yet unknown,
    As fast as they peep up, let's cut 'em down.   *Exeunt.*

[SCENE VI]

  Enter the Duchess' two sons, Ambitioso *and* Supervacuo.

Ambitioso. Was not his execution rarely plotted?
    We are the Duke's sons now.
Supervacuo.   Ay, you may thank
    My policy for that.
Ambitioso.   Your policy,
    For what?
Supervacuo.   Why, was't not my invention brother,
    To slip the judges, and in lesser compass,
    Did I not draw the model of his death,
    Advising you to sudden officers,
    And e'en extemporal execution?
Ambitioso. Heart, 'twas a thing I thought on too.
Supervacuo. You thought on't too? 'sfoot, slander not your thoughts   10
    With glorious untruth, I know 'twas from you.

213 waxen fire] presumably a torch held by an attendant   217 hasp'd] i.e., with the
Duchess   224] i.e., if a duke is to be killed, it is fitting that it be done to music   III. vi, 3
policy] stratagem or cunning   7 sudden] perhaps a verb, to move to immediate action   11
glorious] boastful   11 'twas from you] it had not occurred to you

Ambitioso. Sir,
    I say 'twas in my head.
Supervacuo.   Ay, like your brains then,
    Ne'er to come out as long as you liv'd.
Ambitioso. You'd have the honour on't forsooth, that your wit
    Led him to the scaffold.
Supervacuo.   Since it is my due,
    I'll publish't, but I'll ha't in spite of you.
Ambitioso. Methinks y'are much too bold, you should a little
    Remember us brother, next to be honest Duke.
Supervacuo. [*Aside*] Ay, it shall be as easy for you to be Duke,   20
    As to be honest, and that's never i'faith.
Ambitioso. Well, cold he is by this time, and because
    We're both ambitious, be it our amity,
    And let the glory be shar'd equally.
Supervacuo. I am content to that.
Ambitioso. This night our younger brother shall out of prison,
    I have a trick.
Supervacuo.   A trick, prethee what is't?
Ambitioso. We'll get him out by a wile.
Supervacuo.   Prethee what wile?
Ambitioso. No sir, you shall not know it, till't be done,
    For then you'd swear 'twere yours.

    [*Enter an* Officer.]

Supervacuo.   How now, what's he?   30
Ambitioso. One of the officers.
Supervacuo.   Desired news.
Ambitioso. How now my friend?
Officer. My Lords, under your pardon, I am allotted
    To that desertless office, to present you
    With the yet bleeding head.
Supervacuo. [*Aside*]   Ha, ha, excellent.
Ambitioso. [*Aside*] All's sure our own: brother, canst weep think'st thou?
    'Twould grace our flattery much; think of some dame,
    'Twill teach thee to dissemble.
Supervacuo. [*Aside*]   I have thought,—
    Now for yourself.
Ambitioso.   Our sorrows are so fluent,
    Our eyes o'erflow our tongues, words spoke in tears   40
    Are like the murmurs of the waters, the sound
    Is loudly heard, but cannot be distinguisht.

17 in spite of] to be taken literally   19 honest] by right   37 flattery] pretence

Supervacuo. How died he, pray?

Officer.   O full of rage and spleen.

Supervacuo. He died most valiantly then, we're glad to hear it.

Officer. We could not woo him once to pray.

Ambitioso. He show'd himself a gentleman in that:
    Give him his due.

Officer.   But in the stead of prayer,
    He drew forth oaths.

Supervacuo.   Then did he pray dear heart,
    Although you understood him not.

Officer.   My Lords,
    E'en at his last, with pardon be it spoke,   50
    He curst you both.

Supervacuo.   He curst us? 'las, good soul.

Ambitioso. It was not in our powers, but the Duke's pleasure.—
    [*Aside*] Finely dissembled o' both sides, sweet fate,
    O happy opportunity!

    Enter Lussurioso.

Lussurioso.   Now my Lords.

Both. Oh!—

Lussurioso. Why do you shun me brothers?
    You may come nearer now;
    The savour of the prison has forsook me,
    I thank such kind lords as yourselves, I'm free.

Ambitioso. Alive!   60

Supervacuo. In health!

Ambitioso. Releas'd!
    We were both e'en amaz'd with joy to see it.

Lussurioso. I am much to thank you.

Supervacuo.   Faith,
    We spar'd no tongue unto my Lord the Duke.

Ambitioso. I know your delivery brother
    Had not been half so sudden but for us.

Supervacuo. O how we pleaded!

Lussurioso.   Most deserving brothers,
    In my best studies I will think of it.   *Exit* Luss.

Ambitioso. O death and vengeance!   70

Supervacuo. Hell and torments!

Ambitioso. Slave, cam'st thou to delude us?

Officer. Delude you my Lords?

Supervacuo. Ay villain, where's this head now?

Officer.   Why here my Lord,
 Just after his delivery, you both came
 With warrant from the Duke to behead your brother.
Ambitioso. Ay, our brother, the Duke's son.
Officer. The Duke's son, my Lord, had his release before you came.
Ambitioso. Whose head's that then?
Officer. His whom you left command for, your own brother's. 80
Ambitioso. Our brother's? oh furies!—
Supervacuo. Plagues!
Ambitioso. Confusions!
Supervacuo. Darkness!
Ambitioso. Devils!
Supervacuo. Fell it out so accursedly?
Ambitioso. So damnedly?
Supervacuo. Villain I'll brain thee with it.
Officer. O my good Lord!   *Exit.*
Supervacuo. The devil overtake thee.   90
Ambitioso. O fatal!
Supervacuo.   O prodigious to our bloods!
Ambitioso. Did we dissemble?
Supervacuo.   Did we make our tears
 Women for thee?
Ambitioso.   Laugh and rejoice for thee?
Supervacuo. Bring warrant for thy death?
Ambitioso.   Mock off thy head?
Supervacuo. You had a trick, you had a wile forsooth.
Ambitioso. A murrain meet 'em, there's none of these wiles that ever come
 to good: I see now, there is nothing sure in mortality, but mortality;
 Well, no more words, 'shalt be reveng'd i'faith.
 Come, throw off clouds now brother, think of vengeance,
 And deeper settled hate; sirrah sit fast,   100
 We'll pull down all, but thou shalt down at last. *Exeunt.*

ACT. 4.   SCEN. I

 Enter Lussurioso *with* Hippolito.

Lussurioso. Hippolito.
Hippolito. My Lord:
 Has your good lordship aught to command me in?
Lussurioso. I prethee leave us.

91 prodigious] portentous

Hippolito.   How's this? come and leave us?
Lussurioso. Hippolito.
Hippolito. Your honour—I stand ready for any duteous employment.
Lussurioso. Heart, what mak'st thou here?
Hippolito. [*Aside*]   A pretty lordly humour:
    He bids me to be present, to depart;
    Something has stung his honour.
Lussurioso.   Be nearer, draw nearer.
    Y'are not so good methinks, I'm angry with you.   10
Hippolito. With me my Lord? I'm angry with myself for't.
Lussurioso. You did prefer a goodly fellow to me,
    'Twas wittily elected, 'twas; I thought
    H'ad been a villain, and he proves a knave;
    To me a knave.
Hippolito.   I chose him for the best my Lord,
    'Tis much my sorrow, if neglect in him
    Breed discontent in you.
Lussurioso.   Neglect? 'twas will:
    Judge of it,
    Firmly to tell of an incredible act,
    Not to be thought, less to be spoken of,   20
    'Twixt my stepmother and the Bastard, oh,
    Incestuous sweets between 'em.
Hippolito.   Fie my Lord!
Lussurioso. I in kind loyalty to my father's forehead,
    Made this a desperate arm, and in that fury,
    Committed treason on the lawful bed,
    And with my sword e'en rac'd my father's bosom,
    For which I was within a stroke of death.
Hippolito. Alack, I'm sorry. [*Aside*] 'Sfoot just upon the stroke
    Jars in my brother, 'twill be villainous music.

    Enter Vindice.

Vindice. My honour'd Lord.   30
Lussurioso. Away, prethee forsake us, hereafter we'll not know thee.
Vindice. Not know me my Lord? your Lordship cannot choose.
Lussurioso. Begone I say, thou art a false knave.
Vindice. Why, the easier to be known, my Lord.
Lussurioso. Push, I shall prove too bitter with a word,
    Make thee a perpetual prisoner and lay
    This ironage upon thee.

13 wittily elected] cleverly chosen   26 rac'd] scratched   29 Jars in] comes in dis-
cordantly   37 ironage] fetters

Vindice. [*Aside*]   Mum,
  For there's a doom would make a woman dumb.
  Missing the bastard, next him, the wind's come about,
  Now 'tis my brother's turn to stay, mine to go out.   *Exit* Vin.
Lussurioso. H'as greatly mov'd me.
Hippolito.   Much to blame i'faith.   41
Lussurioso. But I'll recover, to his ruin: 'twas told me lately,
  I know not whether falsely, that you'd a brother.
Hippolito. Who, I? yes my good Lord, I have a brother.
Lussurioso. How chance the court ne'er saw him? of what nature?
  How does he apply his hours?
Hippolito.   'Faith, to curse Fates,
  Who, as he thinks, ordain'd him to be poor;
  Keeps at home full of want and discontent.
Lussurioso. [*Aside*] There's hope in him, for discontent and want
  Is the best clay to mould a villain of.—   50
  Hippolito, wish him to repair to us,
  If there be aught in him to please our blood,
  For thy sake we'll advance him, and build fair
  His meanest fortunes: for it is in us
  To rear up towers from cottages.
Hippolito. It is so my Lord; he will attend your honour,
  But he's a man, in whom much melancholy dwells.
Lussurioso. Why, the better: bring him to court.
Hippolito. With willingness and speed.
  [*Aside*] Whom he cast off e'en now, must now succeed;   60
  Brother disguise must off,
  In thine own shape now I'll prefer thee to him:
  How strangely does himself work to undo him.   *Exit.*
Lussurioso. This fellow will come fitly, he shall kill
  That other slave, that did abuse my spleen,
  And made it swell to treason; I have put
  Much of my heart into him, he must die.
  He that knows great men's secrets, and proves slight,
  That man ne'er lives to see his beard turn white:
  Ay, he shall speed him: I'll employ thee brother;   70
  Slaves are but nails, to drive out one another.
  He being of black condition, suitable
  To want and ill content, hope of preferment
  Will grind him to an edge.

39 him] i.e., Lussurioso   68 slight] inconstant   72 black condition] melancholy
disposition

The Nobles *enter.*

1. Noble. Good days unto your honour.
Lussurioso. My kind Lords, I do return the like.
2. Noble. Saw you my Lord the Duke?
Lussurioso. My lord and father, is he from court?
1. Noble. He's sure from court,
  But where, which way, his pleasure took, we know not,   80
  Nor can we hear on't.
Lussurioso.   Here come those should tell.
 [*Enter more* Nobles.]
  Saw you my lord and father?
3. Noble. Not since two hours before noon my Lord, and then he privately
 rid forth.
Lussurioso. Oh he's rode forth.
1. Noble.   'Twas wondrous privately.
2. Noble. There's none i'th'court had any knowledge on't.
Lussurioso. His Grace is old and sudden, 'tis no treason
  To say, the Duke my father has a humour,
  Or such a toy about him; what in us
  Would appear light, in him seems virtuous.   90
3. Noble. 'Tis oracle my Lord.   *Exeunt.*

[SCENE II]

Enter Vindice *and* Hippolito, Vind. *out of his disguise.*

Hippolito. So, so, all's as it should be, y'are yourself.
Vindice. How that great villain puts me to my shifts.
Hippolito. He that did lately in disguise reject thee
  Shall now thou art thyself as much respect thee.
Vindice. 'Twill be the quainter fallacy; but brother,
  'Sfoot, what use will he put me to now, think'st thou?
Hippolito. Nay, you must pardon me in that, I know not:
  H'as some employment for you: but what 'tis
  He and his secretary the devil knows best.
Vindice. Well I must suit my tongue to his desires,   10
  What colour soe'er they be; hoping at last
  To pile up all my wishes on his breast.
Hippolito. 'Faith brother he himself shows the way.

89 toy] whim 91 oracle] absolute truth IV. ii, 5 quainter fallacy] more cunning
deception 9 secretary] confidant

Vindice. Now the Duke is dead, the realm is clad in clay:
 His death being not yet known, under his name
 The people still are govern'd; well, thou his son
 Art not long liv'd, thou shalt not joy his death:
 To kill thee then, I should most honour thee;
 For 'twould stand firm in every man's belief,
 Thou'st a kind child, and only diedst with grief.   20
Hippolito. You fetch about well, but let's talk in present,
 How will you appear in fashion different,
 As well as in apparel, to make all things possible?
 If you be but once tripp'd, we fall for ever.
 It is not the least policy to be doubtful;
 You must change tongue;—familiar was your first.
Vindice. Why, I'll bear me in some strain of melancholy,
 And string myself with heavy-sounding wire,
 Like such an instrument that speaks
 Merry things sadly.
Hippolito.   Then 'tis as I meant,   30
 I gave you out at first in discontent.
Vindice. I'll turn myself, and then—
Hippolito.   'Sfoot here he comes:
 Hast thought upon't?
Vindice.   Salute him, fear not me.

 [*Enter* Lussurioso.]

Lussurioso. Hippolito.
Hippolito.   Your Lordship.
Lussurioso.   What's he yonder?
Hippolito. 'Tis Vindice, my discontented brother,
 Whom, 'cording to your will I'ave brought to court.
Lussurioso. Is that thy brother? beshrew me, a good presence,
 I wonder h'as been from the court so long.
 Come nearer.
Hippolito. Brother, Lord Lussurioso the Duke's son.   40
     Snatches off his hat and makes legs to him.
Lussurioso. Be more near to us, welcome, nearer yet.
Vindice. How don you? God you god den.
Lussurioso.   We thank thee.

17 joy] enjoy 21 fetch about] speculate 21 in] about the 25 doubtful] suspicious,
cautious 32 turn] transform 40 s.d. *makes legs*] curtseys (Vindice or Hippolito?)
42 don] stage-rustic for 'do' 42 God . . . den] Good even to you

How strangely such a coarse-homely salute
Shows in the palace, where we greet in fire:
Nimble and desperate tongues, should we name God
In a salutation, 'twould ne'er be stood on't,—heaven!
Tell me what has made thee so melancholy.

Vindice. Why, going to law.

Lussurioso. Why, will that make a man melancholy?

Vindice. Yes, to look long upon ink and black buckram—I went me to law
in *Anno Quadragesimo secundo*, and I waded out of it in *Anno sextagesimo
tertio*.   52

Lussurioso. What, three and twenty years in law?

Vindice. I have known those that have been five and fifty, and all about
pullin and pigs.

Lussurioso. May it be possible such men should breathe,
To vex the terms so much?

Vindice. 'Tis food to some my Lord. There are old men at the present, that
are so poisoned with the affectation of law-words, (having had many
suits canvass'd), that their common talk is nothing but Barbary Latin:
they cannot so much as pray, but in law, that their sins may be remov'd,
with a writ of error, and their souls fetch'd up to heaven, with a sasarara.

Lussurioso. It seems most strange to me,   63
Yet all the world meets round in the same bent:
Where the heart's set, there goes the tongue's consent.
How dost apply thy studies, fellow?

Vindice. Study? why, to think how a great rich man lies a-dying, and a poor
cobbler tolls the bell for him; how he cannot depart the world, and sees
the great chest stand before him, when he lies speechless, how he will
point you readily to all the boxes, and when he is past all memory, as the
gossips guess, then thinks he of forfeitures and obligations, nay when
to all men's hearings he whurls and rotles in the throat he's busy threat-
'ning his poor tenants; and this would last me now some seven years'
thinking or thereabouts. But, I have a conceit a-coming in picture upon
this, I draw it myself, which i'faith, la, I'll present to your honour,
you shall not choose but like it for your lordship shall give me nothing
for it.   77

44–6 we greet . . . stood on't] if we used a traditional greeting, mentioning God, it would
not be understood   51 *Anno . . . secundo*] 42nd year   51 *Anno . . . tertio*] 63rd year (of
the sovereign's reign)   55 pullin] poultry   57 terms] legal sessions   60 Barbary]
barbarous   62 writ of error] writ brought to obtain reversal of judgment on grounds of
error   62 sasarara] writ of *certiorari* issued by a superior court to someone complaining
of lack of justice from an inferior   69 great chest] presumably one containing his gold
72 whurls and rotles] rumbles and rattles   74 conceit] witty notion   74 in picture] in
the form of a picture

Lussurioso. Nay, you mistake me then,
>For I am publisht bountiful enough,
>Let's taste of your conceit.   80
Vindice. In picture my Lord?
Lussurioso. Ay, in picture.
Vindice. Marry this it is—A usuring father to be boiling in hell, and his
son and heir with a whore dancing over him.
Hippolito. [*Aside*] H'as par'd him to the quick.
Lussurioso. The conceit's pretty i'faith,
>But take't upon my life 'twill ne'er be lik'd.
Vindice. No? why, I'm sure the whore will be lik'd well enough.
Hippolito. [*Aside*] Ay, if she were out o'th'picture he'd like her then him-
self.   90
Vindice. And as for the son and heir, he shall be an eyesore to no young
revellers, for he shall be drawn in cloth-of-gold breeches.
Lussurioso. And thou hast put my meaning in the pockets,
>And canst not draw that out; my thought was this,
>To see the picture of a usuring father
>Boiling in hell, our richmen would ne'er like it.
Vindice. O true, I cry you heart'ly mercy. I know the reason, for some of
'em had rather be damn'd indeed than damn'd in colours.
Lussurioso. [*Aside*] A parlous melancholy, has wit enough
>To murder any man, and I'll give him means.   100
>—I think thou art ill-monied.
Vindice.   Money, ho, ho,
>'T'as been my want so long, 'tis now my scoff.
>I've e'en forgot what colour silver's of.
Lussurioso. [*Aside*] It hits as I could wish.
Vindice.   I get good clothes
>Of those that dread my humour, and for table-room,
>I feed on those that cannot be rid of me.
Lussurioso. Somewhat to set thee up withal.   *Gives him gold.*
Vindice. O mine eyes!
Lussurioso.   How now man?
Vindice.   Almost struck blind;
>This bright unusual shine to me seems proud,
>I dare not look till the sun be in a cloud.   110
Lussurioso. [*Aside*] I think I shall affect his melancholy.
>—How are they now?
Vindice.   The better for your asking.
Lussurioso. You shall be better yet if you but fasten

Truly on my intent; now y'are both present
I will unbrace such a close private villain
Unto your vengeful swords, the like ne'er heard of,
Who hath disgrac'd you much and injur'd us.
Hippolito. Disgrac'd us my Lord?
Lussurioso.   Ay, Hippolito.
I kept it here till now that both your angers
Might meet him at once.
Vindice.   I'm covetous   120
To know the villain.
Lussurioso.   You know him—that slave pander,
Piato whom we threatened last
With irons in perpetual prisonment.
Vindice. [*Aside*] All this is I.
Hippolito.   Is't he my Lord?
Lussurioso.   I'll tell you,
You first preferr'd him to me.
Vindice.   Did you brother?
Hippolito. I did indeed.
Lussurioso.   And the ingrateful villain,
To quit that kindness, strongly wrought with me,
Being as you see a likely man for pleasure,
With jewels to corrupt your virgin sister.
Hippolito. Oh villain!
Vindice.   He shall surely die that did it.   130
Lussurioso. I far from thinking any virgin harm,
Especially knowing her to be as chaste
As that part which scarce suffers to be toucht,
Th'eye, would not endure him.
Vindice.   Would you not,
My Lord? 'Twas wondrous honourably done.
Lussurioso. But with some fine frowns kept him out.
Vindice.   Out slave!
Lussurioso. What did me he but in revenge of that,
Went of his own free will to make infirm
Your sister's honour, whom I honour with my soul
For chaste respect, and not prevailing there,   140
(As 'twas but desperate folly to attempt it,)
In mere spleen, by the way, waylays your mother,
Whose honour being a coward as it seems
Yielded by little force.
Vindice.   Coward indeed.

115 unbrace] disclose   120 covetuous] covetous, i.e., eager   127 quit] requite

Lussurioso. He proud of their advantage, (as he thought)
    Brought me these news for happy, but I, heaven forgive me for't—
Vindice. What did your honour?
Lussurioso In rage push'd him from me,
    Trampled beneath his throat, spurn'd him, and bruis'd:
    Indeed I was too cruel to say troth.   150
Hippolito. Most nobly manag'd.
Vindice. [*Aside*]   Has not heaven an ear?
    Is all the lightning wasted?
Lussurioso.   If I now
    Were so impatient in a modest cause,
    What should you be?
Vindice.   Full mad, he shall not live
    To see the moon change.
Lussurioso.   He's about the palace;
    Hippolito, entice him this way, that thy brother
    May take full mark of him.
Hippolito. Heart!—that shall not need my Lord,
    I can direct him so far.
Lussurioso.   Yet for my hate's sake,
    Go, wind him this way; I'll see him bleed myself.   160
Hippolito. [*Aside*] What now brother?
Vindice. [*Aside*] Nay e'en what you will—y'are put to't brother.
Hippolito. [*Aside*] An impossible task, I'll swear,
    To bring him hither, that's already here.   *Exit* Hippo.
Lussurioso. Thy name? I have forgot it.
Vindice. Vindice, my Lord.
Lussurioso. 'Tis a good name that.
Vindice. Ay, a revenger.
Lussurioso. It does betoken courage, thou shouldst be valiant,
    And kill thine enemies.
Vindice.   That's my hope my Lord.   170
Lussurioso. This slave is one.
Vindice.   I'll doom him.
Lussurioso.   Then I'll praise thee.
    Do thou observe me best, and I'll best raise thee.

    Enter Hip.

Vindice. Indeed, I thank you.
Lussurioso.   Now Hippolito,
    Where's the slave pander?

145 proud . . . advantage] proud of having got the better of them   146 for happy] as
good, i.e., thinking I should be pleased

Hippolito.   Your good Lordship
  Would have a loathsome sight of him, much offensive.
  He's not in case now to be seen my Lord,
  The worst of all the deadly sins is in him:
  That beggarly damnation, drunkenness.
Lussurioso. Then he's a double slave.
Vindice. [*Aside*]   'Twas well convey'd,
  Upon a sudden wit.
Lussurioso.   What, are you both   180
  Firmly resolv'd? I'll see him dead myself.
Vindice. Or else, let us not live.
Lussurioso.   You may direct
  Your brother to take note of him.
Hippolito.   I shall.
Lussurioso. Rise but in this, and you shall never fall.
Vindice. Your honour's vassals.
Lussurioso. [*Aside*]   This was wisely carried,
  Deep policy in us makes fools of such:
  Then must a slave die, when he knows too much.   *Exit* Luss.
Vindice. O thou almighty patience, 'tis my wonder,
  That such a fellow, impudent and wicked,
  Should not be cloven as he stood, or with   190
  A secret wind burst open!
  Is there no thunder left, or is't kept up
  In stock for heavier vengeance? [*Thunder*] There it goes!
Hippolito. Brother we lose ourselves.
Vindice.   But I have found it,
  'Twill hold, 'tis sure, thanks, thanks to any spirit,
  That mingled it 'mongst my inventions.
Hippolito. What is't?
Vindice.   'Tis sound, and good, thou shalt partake it:
  I'm hir'd to kill myself—
Hippolito.   True.
Vindice.   Pree-thee mark it:—
  And the old Duke being dead, but not convey'd,
  For he's already miss'd too, and you know   200
  Murder will peep out of the closest husk.
Hippolito. Most true.
Vindice.   What say you then to this device,
  If we drest up the body of the Duke—
Hippolito. In that disguise of yours?

193 s.d.] Not in the quarto, but implied by the text; the thunder is the sign of heavenly
judgment.

Vindice.   Y'are quick, y'ave reacht it.
Hippolito. I like it wonderously.
Vindice. And being in drink, as you have publisht him,
    To lean him on his elbow, as if sleep
    Had caught him;
    Which claims most interest in such sluggy men.
Hippolito. Good yet, but here's a doubt,   210
    We, thought by th'Duke's son to kill that pander,
    Shall when he is known be thought to kill the Duke.
Vindice. Neither, O thanks, it is substantial;
    For that disguise being on him, which I wore,
    It will be thought I, which he calls the pander, did kill the Duke, &
    fled away in his apparel, leaving him so disguis'd, to avoid swift pursuit.
Hippolito. Firmer and firmer.
Vindice.   Nay doubt not, 'tis in grain,
    I warrant it hold colour.
Hippolito.   Let's about it.
Vindice. But by the way too, now I think on't, brother,
    Let's conjure that base devil out of our mother.   *Exeunt.*

[SCENE III]

   Enter the Duchess *arm in arm with the* Bastard: *he seemeth lasciviously to
her; after them, enter* Supervacuo, *running with a rapier; his brother stops him.*

Spurio. Madam, unlock yourself, should it be seen,
    Your arm would be suspected.
Duchess. Who is't that dares suspect or this or these?   *Kisses him.*
    May we not deal our favours where we please?
Spurio. I'm confident you may.   *Exeunt.*
Ambitioso.   'Sfoot brother, hold.
Supervacuo. Woult let the bastard shame us?
Ambitioso.   Hold, hold, brother;
    There's fitter time than now.
Supervacuo.   Now, when I see it.
Ambitioso. 'Tis too much seen already.
Supervacuo.   Seen and known;
    The nobler she's, the baser is she grown.

---

209 sluggy] sluggish   213] Neither will be thought, the plan is sound (the thanks presumably to heaven)   217 in grain] short for 'dyed in [the] grain', i.e., fast dyed
IV. iii, 3 or this or these] either this [linking arms] or these [kisses]

Ambitioso. If she were bent lasciviously, the fault   10
    Of mighty women, that sleep soft,—O death,
    Must she needs choose such an unequal sinner,
    To make all worse?
Supervacuo.   A bastard, the Duke's bastard!
    Shame heapt on shame!
Ambitioso.   O our disgrace!
    Most women have small waist the world throughout,
    But their desires are thousand miles about.
Supervacuo. Come stay not here, let's after, and prevent,
    Or else they'll sin faster than we'll repent.   *Exeunt.*

[SCENE IV]

Enter Vindice *and* Hippolito, *bringing out their Mother, one by one shoulder, and the other by the other, with daggers in their hands.*

Vindice. O thou, for whom no name is bad enough!
Gratiana. What means my sons? what, will you murder me?
Vindice. Wicked, unnatural parent!
Hippolito.   Fiend of women!
Gratiana. Oh! are sons turn'd monsters? Help!
Vindice.   In vain.
Gratiana. Are you so barbarous to set iron nipples
    Upon the breast that gave you suck?
Vindice.   That breast
    Is turn'd to quarled poison.
Gratiana. Cut not your days for't, am not I your mother?
Vindice. Thou dost usurp that title now by fraud,
    For in that shell of mother breeds a bawd.   10
Gratiana. A bawd? O name far loathsomer than hell!
Hippolito. It should be so, knew'st thou thy office well.
Gratiana. I hate it.
Vindice. Ah, is't possible? thou only? You powers on high,
    That women should dissemble when they die!
Gratiana. Dissemble?
Vindice.   Did not the Duke's son direct
    A fellow, of the world's condition, hither,
    That did corrupt all that was good in thee,
    Made thee uncivilly forget thyself,
    And work our sister to his lust?

IV. iv, 7 quarled] curdled   8 Cut] cut short (by being executed for murder)   12 office] duty

Gratiana.   Who, I?   20
    That had been monstrous! I defy that man
    For any such intent; none lives so pure,
    But shall be soil'd with slander:
    Good son believe it not.
Vindice. [*Aside*]   Oh I'm in doubt,
    Whether I'm myself, or no.
    —Stay, let me look again upon this face.
    Who shall be sav'd when mothers have no grace?
Hippolito. 'Twould make one half despair.
Vindice.   I was the man:
    Defy me now! let's see, do't modestly.
Gratiana. O hell unto my soul!
Vindice.   In that disguise,   30
    I, sent from the Duke's son,
    Tried you, and found you base metal,
    As any villain might have done.
Gratiana.   O no,
    No tongue but yours could have bewitcht me so.
Vindice. O nimble in damnation, quick in tune,
    There is no devil could strike fire so soon:
    I am confuted in a word.
Gratiana.   Oh sons,
    Forgive me; to myself I'll prove more true;
    You that should honour me, I kneel to you.
Vindice. A mother to give aim to her own daughter!   40
Hippolito. True brother, how far beyond nature 'tis,
    Tho' many mothers do't.   *She weeps.*
Vindice. Nay, and you draw tears once, go you to bed,
    Wet will make iron blush and change to red:
    Brother it rains, 'twill spoil your dagger, house it.
Hippolito. 'Tis done.
Vindice. I'faith 'tis a sweet shower, it does much good;
    The fruitful grounds and meadows of her soul
    Has been long dry: pour down thou blessed dew;
    Rise Mother, troth this shower has made you higher.   50
Gratiana. O you heavens!
    Take this infectious spot out of my soul;
    I'll rence it in seven waters of mine eyes.
    Make my tears salt enough to taste of grace:

---

40 give aim to] guide the aim of, or perhaps simply aim at   43 and] if   43 you] i.e.,
his dagger—hence the image in the following line   53 rence] rinse

To weep is to our sex naturally given:
But to weep truly, that's a gift from heaven.
Vindice. Nay, I'll kiss you now: kiss her brother.
    Let's marry her to our souls, wherein's no lust,
    And honourably love her.
Hippolito.   Let it be.
Vindice. For honest women are so sild and rare,   60
    'Tis good to cherish those poor few that are.
    Oh you of easy wax, do but imagine
    Now the disease has left you, how leprously
    That office would have cling'd unto your forehead;
    All mothers that had any graceful hue
    Would have worn masks to hide their face at you:
    It would have grown to this, at your foul name
    Green-colour'd maids would have turn'd red with shame.
Hippolito. And then our sister full of hire, and baseness!
Vindice. There had been boiling lead again: 70
    The Duke's son's great concubine:
    A drab of state, a cloth-o'-silver slut,
    To have her train borne up, and her soul trail
    I'th'dirt—great!
Hippolito. To be miserably great, rich to be eternally wretched.
Vindice. O common madness:
    Ask but the thriving'st harlot in cold blood,
    She'd give the world to make her honour good;
    Perhaps you'll say, but only to the Duke's son,
    In private; why, she first begins with one,   80
    Who afterward to thousand proves a whore:
    'Break ice in one place, it will crack in more.'
Gratiana. Most certainly applied.
Hippolito. Oh brother, you forgot our business.
Vindice. And well rememb'red; joy's a subtle elf,
    I think man's happiest, when he forgets himself.
    Farewell once dry'd, now holy-wat'red mead,
    Our hearts wear feathers, that before wore lead.
Gratiana. I'll give you this: that one I never knew
    Plead better for, and 'gainst, the devil than you.   90
Vindice. You make me proud on't.
Hippolito. Commend us in all virtue to our sister.
Vindice. Ay for the love of heaven, to that true maid.

---

60 sild] seldom found   62 of easy wax] easily moulded   75 To . . . great] Hippolito completes Vindice's exclamation and caps it with another (note the similarity in sound between 'rich' and 'wretched').

Gratiana. With my best words.
Vindice.   Why, that was motherly said.   *Exeunt.*
Gratiana. I wonder now what fury did transport me?
    I feel good thoughts begin to settle in me.
    Oh with what forehead can I look on her,
    Whose honour I've so impiously beset?
    And here she comes.

    [*Enter* Castiza.]

Castiza. Now mother, you have wrought with me so strongly,   100
    That what for my advancement, as to calm
    The trouble of your tongue, I am content.
Gratiana. Content, to what?
Castiza.   To do as you have wisht me,
    To prostitute my breast to the Duke's son:
    And put myself to common usury.
Gratiana. I hope you will not so.
Castiza.   Hope you I will not?
    That's not the hope you look to be sav'd in.
Gratiana. Truth, but it is.
Castiza.   Do not deceive yourself;
    I am as you, e'en out of marble wrought.
    What would you now, are ye not pleas'd yet with me?   110
    You shall not wish me to be more lascivious
    Than I intend to be.
Gratiana.   Strike not me cold.
Castiza. How often have you charg'd me on your blessing
    To be a cursed woman?—When you knew
    Your blessing had no force to make me lewd,
    You laid your curse upon me: that did more;
    The mother's curse is heavy: where that fights,
    Suns set in storm, and daughters lose their lights.
Gratiana. Good child, dear maid, if there be any spark
    Of heavenly intellectual fire within thee,   120
    Oh let my breath revive it to a flame:
    Put not all out, with woman's wilful follies.
    I am recover'd of that foul disease
    That haunts too many mothers; kind forgive me,
    Make me not sick in health. If then
    My words prevail'd when they were wickedness,
    How much more now when they are just and good!

97 forehead] As elsewhere in the play the word carries overtones of loyalty and honour as well as more obvious sexual ones.   120 intellectual] spiritual   124 kind] either 'kind child' or 'kindly', doubtless with a quibble on 'kin'

Castiza. I wonder what you mean; are not you she
 For whose infect persuasions I could scarce
 Kneel out my prayers, and had much ado   130
 In three hours' reading, to untwist so much
 Of the black serpent, as you wound about me?
Gratiana. 'Tis unfruitful, held tedious to repeat
 What's past; I'm now your present mother.
Castiza.   Push,
 Now 'tis too late.
Gratiana. Bethink again, thou know'st not what thou say'st.
Castiza. No?
 Deny advancement, treasure, the Duke's son?
Gratiana. O see,
 I spoke those words, and now they poison me: 140
 What will the deed do then?
 Advancement, true: as high as shame can pitch.
 For treasure, whoe'er knew a harlot rich,
 Or could build by the purchase of her sin,
 An hospital to keep their bastards in?
 The Duke's son?—oh when women are young courtiers,
 They are sure to be old beggars;
 To know the miseries most harlots taste,
 Thou'dst wish thyself unborn, when thou art unchaste.
Castiza. O mother let me twine about your neck,   150
 And kiss you till my soul melt on your lips,
 I did but this to try you.
Gratiana.   O speak truth.
Castiza. Indeed I did not, for no tongue has force
 To alter me from honest.
 If maidens would, men's words could have no power;
 A virgin honour is a crystal tower,
 Which being weak is guarded with good spirits,
 Until she basely yields no ill inherits.
Gratiana. O happy child! faith and thy birth hath sav'd me;
 'Mongst thousand daughters happiest of all others, 160
 Be thou a glass for maids, and I for mothers.   *Exeunt.*

145 hospital] orphanage 155 would] i.e., be honest 158 inherits] takes possession

[ACT 5.   SCENE 1]

Enter Vindice *and* Hippolito [*with the Duke's corpse*].

Vindice. So, so, he leans well, take heed you wake him not brother.
Hippolito. I warrant you my life for yours.
Vindice. That's a good lay, for I must kill myself.
　Brother, that's I: that sits for me: do you mark it; and I must stand ready
　here to make away myself yonder—I must sit to be kill'd, and stand to
　kill myself; I could vary it not so little as thrice over again, 't'as some
　eight returns, like Michaelmas term.
Hippolito. That's enow, o'conscience.
Vindice. But sirrah, does the Duke's son come single?
Hippolito. No, there's the hell on't, his faith's too feeble to go alone; he
　brings flesh-flies after him, that will buzz against supper time, and hum
　for his coming out.   12
Vindice. Ah the fly-flop of vengeance beat 'em to pieces! here was the sweetest
　occasion, the fittest hour, to have made my revenge familiar with him,
　show him the body of the Duke his father, and how quaintly he died, like
　a politician, in hugger-mugger, made no man acquainted with it, and in
　catastrophe slain him over his father's breast; and oh I'm mad to lose such
　a sweet opportunity.
Hippolito. Nay push, pree-thee be content! there's no remedy present: may
　not hereafter times open in as fair faces as this?   20
Vindice. They may if they can paint so well.
Hippolito. Come, now to avoid all suspicion, let's forsake this room, and be
　going to meet the Duke's son.
Vindice. Content, I'm for any weather. Heart, step close, here he comes.

Enter Lussurioso.

Hippolito. My honour'd Lord?
Lussurioso. Oh me; you both present?
Vindice. E'en newly my Lord, just as your Lordship enter'd now; about
　this place we had notice given he should be, but in some loathsome plight
　or other.
Hippolito. Came your Honour private?   30
Lussurioso. Private enough for this: only a few
　Attend my coming out.
Hippolito. [*Aside*]   Death rot those few!

---

7 returns] reports (for which eight days were set aside during Michaelmas term), here used
of ways to describe the same thing   14 familiar] intimate(ly)   16 politician] intriguer
16 hugger-mugger] secret   17 catastrophe] conclusion

Lussurioso. Stay, yonder's the slave.

Vindice. Mass, there's the slave indeed my Lord.

    [*Aside*] 'Tis a good child, he calls his father slave.

Lussurioso. Ay, that's the villain, the damn'd villain: softly,

    Tread easy.

Vindice.   Puh, I warrant you my Lord,

    We'll stifle in our breaths.

Lussurioso.   That will do well.

    Base rogue, thou sleep'st thy last. [*Aside*] 'Tis policy

    To have him kill'd in's sleep, for if he wak'd   40

    He would betray all to them.

Vindice.   But my Lord—

Lussurioso. Ha, what say'st?

Vindice. Shall we kill him now he's drunk?

Lussurioso. Ay, best of all.

Vindice. Why then, he will ne'er live to be sober.

Lussurioso. No matter, let him reel to hell.

Vindice. But being so full of liquor, I fear he will put out all the fire.

Lussurioso. Thou art a mad beast.

Vindice. [*Aside*] And leave none to warm your Lordship's gols withal;

    —For he that dies drunk falls into hell-fire like a bucket o' water, qush,

    qush.   51

Lussurioso. Come be ready, nake your swords,

    Think of your wrongs, this slave has injur'd you.

Vindice. [*Aside*] Troth so he has, and he has paid well for't.

Lussurioso. Meet with him now.

Vindice.   You'll bear us out my Lord?

Lussurioso. Puh, am I a lord for nothing think you? Quickly, now.

Vindice. Sa, sa, sa: thump, there he lies.   *Stabs the corpse.*

Lussurioso. Nimbly done. Ha! oh, villains, murderers,

    'Tis the old Duke my father.

Vindice.   That's a jest.

Lussurioso. What, stiff and cold already?   60

    O pardon me to call you from your names:

    'Tis none of your deed,—that villain Piato

    Whom you thought now to kill, has murder'd him,

    And left him thus disguis'd.

Hippolito.   And not unlikely.

Vindice. O rascal, was he not asham'd

    To put the Duke into a greasy doublet?

---

49 gols] hands   52 nake] unsheathe (make naked)   57 sa, sa, sa] said to be a trans-
literation of French *ça*, used in fencing   61 from your names] by names far from what
you deserve

Lussurioso. He has been cold and stiff, who knows how long?

Vindice. [*Aside*] Marry, that do I.

Lussurioso. No words I pray, of any thing intended.

Vindice. Oh my Lord.   70

Hippolito. I would fain have your Lordship think that we have small reason
   to prate.

Lussurioso. Faith, thou say'st true. I'll forthwith send to court,
   For all the nobles, Bastard, Duchess, all;
   How here by miracle we found him dead,
   And in his raiment that foul villain fled.

Vindice. That will be the best way my Lord, to clear us all: let's cast about
   to be clear.

Lussurioso. Ho, Nencio, Sordido, and the rest!

   Enter all.

1. Servant. My Lord.   80

2. Servant. My Lord.

Lussurioso. Be witnesses of a strange spectacle:
   Choosing for private conference that sad room,
   We found the Duke my father geal'd in blood.

1. Servant. My Lord the Duke!—run, hie thee Nencio,
   Startle the court by signifying so much.   *Exit* Nencio.

Vindice. [*Aside*] Thus much by wit a deep revenger can,
   When murder's known, to be the clearest man.
   We're fordest off, and with as bold an eye,
   Survey his body as the standers-by.   90

Lussurioso. My royal father, too basely let blood,
   By a malevolent slave.

Hippolito. [*Aside*]   Hark,
   He calls thee slave again.

Vindice. [*Aside*]   H'as lost, he may.

Lussurioso. Oh sight, look hether, see, his lips are gnawn
   With poison.

Vindice.   How—his lips? by th' mass they be.

Lussurioso. O villain—O rogue—O slave—O rascal!

Hippolito. [*Aside*] O good deceit, he quits him with like terms.

   [*Enter* Nobles, *with* Ambitioso *and* Supervacuo, *the* Duchess *and* Spurio.]

1. Noble. Where?

2. Noble. Which way?

Ambitioso. Over what roof hangs this prodigious comet   100
   In deadly fire?

---

84 geal'd] congealed   87 deep] cunning   88 clearest] furthest from suspicion
89 fordest] furthest   97 quits] repays   100 prodigious] ominous

Lussurioso.   Behold, behold my Lords,
    The Duke my father's murder'd by a vassal,
    That owes this habit, and here left disguis'd.
Duchess. My lord and husband!
2. Noble.   Reverend Majesty!
1. Noble. I have seen these clothes often attending on him.
Vindice. [*Aside*] That nobleman
    Has been i'th' country, for he does not lie.
Supervacuo. [*Aside*] Learn of our mother, let's dissemble too:
    I am glad he's vanisht; so I hope are you.
Ambitioso. [*Aside*] Ay, you may take my word for't.
Spurio. [*Aside*]   Old dad dead?   110
    I, one of his cast sins, will send the Fates
    Most hearty commendations by his own son,
    I'll tug in the new stream, till strength be done.
Lussurioso. Where be those two, that did affirm to us
    My Lord the Duke was privately rid forth?
1. Noble. O pardon us my Lords, he gave that charge
    Upon our lives, if he were miss'd at court
    To answer so; he rode not anywhere,
    We left him private with that fellow here.
Vindice. [*Aside*] Confirm'd.
Lussurioso.   O heavens, that false charge was his death.   120
    Impudent beggars, durst you to our face
    Maintain such a false answer? Bear him straight
    To execution.
1. Noble.   My Lord!
Lussurioso.   Urge me no more.
    In this the excuse may be call'd half the murther.
Vindice. You've sentenc'd well.
Lussurioso.   Away, see it be done.

                                 Exit Noble, *guarded.*

Vindice. [*Aside*] Could you not stick? see what confession doth!
    Who would not lie when men are hang'd for truth?
Hippolito. [*Aside*] Brother,
    How happy is our vengeance!
Vindice. [*Aside*]   Why, it hits,
    Past the apprehension of indifferent wits.   130
Lussurioso. My Lord let post-horse be sent
    Into all places to entrap the villain.
Vindice. [*Aside*] Post-horse, ha, ha!

103 owes] owns   113 tug ... stream] i.e., swim with the tide   126 stick] hold your
tongue

Noble. My Lord, we're something bold to know our duty.
Your father's accidentally departed,
The titles that were due to him meet you.
Lussurioso. Meet me? I'm not at leisure my good Lord,
I've many griefs to dispatch out o'th' way.
[*Aside*] Welcome sweet titles.—Talk to me my Lords,
Of sepulchres, and mighty emperors' bones,   140
That's thought for me.
Vindice. [*Aside*]   So, one may see by this,
How foreign markets go:
Courtiers have feet o'th' nines, and tongues o'th' twelves,
They flatter dukes and dukes flatter themselves.
Noble. My Lord it is your shine must comfort us.
Lussurioso. Alas I shine in tears like the sun in April.
Noble. You're now my Lord's Grace.
Lussurioso. My Lord's Grace? I perceive you'll have it so.
Noble. 'Tis but your own.
Lussurioso. Then heavens give me grace to be so.   150
Vindice. [*Aside*] He prays well for himself.
Noble.   Madam [*to Duchess*] all sorrows
Must run their circles into joys; no doubt but time
Will make the murderer bring forth himself.
Vindice. [*Aside*] He were an ass then i'faith.
Noble.   In the mean season,
Let us bethink the latest funeral honours
Due to the Duke's cold body,—and withal,
Calling to memory our new happiness,
Spread in his royal son;—lords, gentlemen,
Prepare for revels.
Vindice. [*Aside*] Revels?
Noble.   Time hath several falls;   160
Griefs lift up joys, feasts put down funerals.
Lussurioso. Come then my Lords, my favours to you all.
[*Aside*] The Duchess is suspected foully bent,
I'll begin dukedom with her banishment.   *Exeunt* Duke, Nobles
Hippolito. [*Aside*] Revels!   *and* Duchess.
Vindice. [*Aside*]   Ay, that's the word, we are firm yet,
Strike one strain more, and then we crown our wit.
                                                Exeunt Brothers.

---

142 foreign markets] an obscure phrase perhaps referring to extraordinary sizes and
measures as in the next sentence   143] 'Their feet are of size 9, but their flattering
tongues are 3 sizes larger' (*Nicoll*)   160 time ... falls] things turn about

Spurio. [*Aside*] Well, have at the fairest mark,—(so said the Duke
    When he begot me,)
    And if I miss his heart or near about,
    Then have at any; a bastard scorns to be out.   *Exit.*
Supervacuo. Not'st thou that Spurio, brother?   171
Ambitioso. Yes, I note him to our shame.
Supervacuo. He shall not live, his hair shall not grow much longer: in this
    time of revels tricks may be set afoot. Seest thou yon new moon? it shall
    outlive the new Duke by much, this hand shall dispossess him, then
    we're mighty.
    A mask is treason's licence, that build upon;
    'Tis murder's best face when a vizard's on.   *Exit.*
Ambitioso. Is't so? 'tis very good;
    And do you think to be Duke then, kind brother?   180
    I'll see fair play, drop one, and there lies t'other.   *Exit.*

[SCENE II]

    Enter Vindice *&* Hippolito, *with* Piero *and other* Lords.

Vindice. My Lords: be all of music, strike old griefs into other countries
    That flow in too much milk, and have faint livers,
    Not daring to stab home their discontents:
    Let our hid flames break out, as fire, as lightning,
    To blast this villainous dukedom vext with sin;
    Wind up your souls to their full height again.
Piero. How?
1. Lord.   Which way?
3. Lord.   Any way: our wrongs are such,
    We cannot justly be reveng'd too much.
Vindice. You shall have all enough:—revels are toward,
    And those few nobles that have long suppress'd you,   10
    Are busied to the furnishing of a masque,
    And do affect to make a pleasant tale on't;
    The masquing suits are fashioning, now comes in
    That which must glad us all—we too take pattern
    Of all those suits, the colour, trimming, fashion,
    E'en to an undistinguisht hair almost:
    Then ent'ring first, observing the true form,

---

170 have at any] strike at any part   170 out] put out, or out of office or position
171ff.] Nicoll reverses the speakers in this final dialogue; but the two are hardly to be dis-
tinguished.   V. ii, 12 affect] pretend   16 undistinguisht] unnoticeable   17 form]
i.e., of the dance

Within a strain or two we shall find leisure
To steal our swords out handsomely,
And when they think their pleasure sweet and good,   20
In midst of all their joys, they shall sigh blood.
Piero. Weightily, effectually.
3. Lord. Before the t'other masquers come—
Vindice. We're gone, all done and past.
Piero. But how for the Duke's guard?
Vindice.   Let that alone,
By one and one their strengths shall be drunk down.
Hippolito. There are five hundred gentlemen in the action,
That will apply themselves, and not stand idle.
Piero. Oh let us hug your bosoms.
Vindice.   Come my Lords,
Prepare for deeds, let other times have words.   *Exeunt.*

[SCENE III]

In a dumb show, the possessing of the young Duke, *with all his* Nobles: *then
sounding music. A furnisht table is brought forth: then enters the* Duke & *his*
Nobles *to the banquet. A blazing star appeareth.*

1. Noble. Many harmonious hours, and choicest pleasures,
Fill up the royal numbers of your years.
Lussurioso. My Lords, we're pleas'd to thank you,—[*Aside*] tho' we know,
'Tis but your duty now to wish it so.
1. Noble. That shine makes us all happy.
3. Noble.   His Grace frowns.
2. Noble. Yet we must say he smiles.
1. Noble.   I think we must.
Lussurioso. [*Aside*] That foul incontinent Duchess we have banisht,
The Bastard shall not live: after these revels
I'll begin strange ones; he and the stepsons
Shall pay their lives for the first subsidies;   10
We must not frown so soon, else 't'ad been now.
1. Noble. My gracious Lord, please you prepare for pleasure,
The masque is not far off.
Lussurioso.   We are for pleasure.
Beshrew thee, what art thou mad'st me start?
Thou hast committed treason,—a blazing star!

---

18 strain] i.e., of music   V. iii, s.d. *possessing*] coronation   s.d. *furnisht*] i.e., for a
banquet   s.d. *blazing star*] a comet (as previous references have hinted)   10 subsidies]
instalments on my vengeance   15 treason] The comet was held to forebode death.

1. Noble. A blazing star, O where my Lord?
Lussurioso.   Spy out.
2. Noble. See, see, my Lords, a wondrous-dreadful one.
Lussurioso. I am not pleas'd at that ill-knotted fire,
    That bushing-flaring star:—am not I duke?
    It should not quake me now: had it appear'd   20
    Before, it I might then have justly fear'd.
    But yet, they say, whom art and learning weds,
    When stars wear locks, they threaten great men's heads.
    Is it so? you are read, my Lords.
1. Noble.   May it please your Grace,
    It shows great anger.
Lussurioso.   That does not please our Grace.
2. Noble. Yet here's the comfort my Lord, many times
    When it seems most, it threatens fardest off.
Lussurioso. 'Faith, and I think so too.
1. Noble.   Beside, my Lord,
    You're gracefully establisht with the loves
    Of all your subjects: and for natural death,   30
    I hope it will be threescore years a-coming.
Lussurioso. True? no more but threescore years?
1. Noble. Fourscore I hope, my Lord.
2. Noble.   And fivescore, I.
3. Noble. But 'tis my hope my Lord, you shall ne'er die.
Lussurioso. Give me thy hand, these others I rebuke;
    He that hopes so is fittest for a duke:
    Thou shalt sit next me; take your places Lords,
    We're ready now for sports, let 'em set on.
    You thing? we shall forget you quite anon!
3. Noble. I hear 'em coming my Lord.

Enter the Masque of Revengers, the two Brothers, and two Lords more.

Lussurioso.   Ah, 'tis well.   40
    [*Aside*] Brothers, and Bastard, you dance next in hell.

*The Revengers dance. At the end, steal out their swords, and these four kill
the four at the Table, in their Chairs. It thunders.*

Vindice. Mark, thunder! dost know thy cue, thou big-voic'd crier?
    Duke's groans are thunder's watch-words.

19 bushing] descriptive of the comet's tail   24 read] learned   27 fardest] farthest
36 fittest] i.e., fittest companion   39 You thing] i.e., the blazing star   43 watch-words]
stage calls or cues

Hippolito.   So my Lords,
   You have enough.
Vindice.   Come let's away, no ling'ring.
Hippolito. Follow, go.   *Exeunt.*
Vindice. No power is angry when the lustful die;
   When thunder claps, heaven likes the tragedy.   *Exit Vin.*
Lussurioso. Oh, oh.

*Enter the other Masque of intended murderers: Stepsons; Bastard; and a
fourth man, coming in dancing. The Duke recovers a little in voice, and groans,—
calls, 'A guard! treason!'*

*At which they all start out of their measure, and turning towards the Table,
they find them all to be murdered.*

Spurio. Whose groan was that?
Lussurioso. Treason, a guard!
Ambitioso.   How now? all murder'd!
Supervacuo.   Murder'd!   50
4. Noble. And those his nobles?
Ambitioso.   Here's a labour sav'd,
   I thought to have sped him. 'Sblood, how came this?
Supervacuo. Then I proclaim myself, now I am Duke.
Ambitioso. Thou Duke! Brother thou liest.   [*Stabs* Supervacuo.]
Spurio.   Slave, so dost thou!
                                    [*Stabs* Ambitioso.]
4. Noble. Base villain, hast thou slain my lord and master? [*Stabs* Spurio.]

Enter the first men.

Vindice. Pistols! treason! murder! help, guard my Lord
   The Duke.
Hippolito.   Lay hold upon this traitor!
Lussurioso.   Oh.
Vindice. Alas, the Duke is murder'd.
Hippolito.   And the nobles.
Vindice. Surgeons, surgeons! [*Aside*] Heart, does he breathe so long?
Antonio. A piteous tragedy, able to make   60
   An old man's eyes bloodshot.
Lussurioso. Oh.

52 sped] killed   53ff.] The quarto gives this line to Spurio, and has no s.d. in the
following lines; the text may be a little confused, but the version given sorts things out
and is followed by most modern editors.   55 s.d.] i.e., Vindice and the other revengers
60 *Antonio*] He cannot have been one of the 'first men', and there should perhaps be an
additional entry for him.

Vindice. Look to
    My Lord the Duke—[*Aside*]—a vengeance throttle him.
    —Confess, thou murd'rous and unhallowed man,
    Didst thou kill all these?
4. Noble.   None but the Bastard I.
Vindice. How came the Duke slain then?
4. Noble.   We found him so.
Lussurioso. O villain.
Vindice. Hark.
Lussurioso. Those in the masque did murder us.   70
Vindice. Law you now sir.
    O marble impudence! will you confess now?
4. Noble. 'Sblood, 'tis all false.
Antonio.   Away with that foul monster,
    Dipp'd in a Prince's blood.
4. Noble.   Heart, 'tis a lie.
Antonio. Let him have bitter execution.   [*Exit 4. Noble, guarded.*]
Vindice. [*Aside*] New marrow! no, I cannot be express'd.
    —How fares my Lord the Duke?
Lussurioso.   Farewell to all,
    He that climbs highest has the greatest fall,
    My tongue is out of office.
Vindice.   Air, gentlemen, air!
    [*Aside*] Now thou'lt not prate on't, 'twas Vindice murd'red thee,— 80
Lussurioso. Oh.
Vindice.   —Murd'red thy father,—
Lussurioso.   Oh.
Vindice.   —And I am he—
    Tell nobody. [*Luss. dies.*] —So so, the Duke's departed.
Antonio. It was a deadly hand that wounded him.
    The rest, ambitious who should rule and sway,
    After his death were so made all away.
Vindice. My Lord was unlikely.
Hippolito.   Now the hope
    Of Italy lies in your reverend years.
Vindice. Your hair will make the silver age again,
    When there was fewer but more honest men.
Antonio. The burden's weighty and will press age down,   90
    May I so rule that heaven may keep the crown!

---

76 New marrow] new food for my revenge   76 express'd] squeezed out, i.e., he cannot
get his feelings out   86 unlikely] unsuitable (to be Duke); but a syllable is missing from
the line, and the word may be a misreading

Vindice. The rape of your good lady has been quited,
    With death on death.

Antonio.   Just is the law above.
    But of all things it puts me most to wonder
    How the old Duke came murd'red.

Vindice.   Oh, my Lord.

Antonio. It was the strangeliest carried, I not heard of the like.

Hippolito. 'Twas all done for the best my Lord.

Vindice. All for your Grace's good; we may be bold to speak it now,
    'Twas somewhat witty carried tho' we say it.
    'Twas we two murd'red him.   100

Antonio. You two?

Vindice. None else i'faith my Lord, nay 'twas well manag'd.

Antonio. Lay hands upon those villains.

Vindice.   How? on us?

Antonio. Bear 'em to speedy execution.

Vindice. Heart, was't not for your good my Lord?

Antonio.   My good!
    Away with 'em; such an old man as he,
    You that would murder him would murder me.

Vindice. Is't come about?

Hippolito.   'Sfoot brother, you begun.

Vindice. May not we set as well as the Duke's son?
    Thou hast no conscience, are we not reveng'd?   110
    Is there one enemy left alive amongst those?
    'Tis time to die, when we are ourselves our foes.
    When murders shut deeds close, this curse does seal 'em,
    If none disclose 'em they themselves reveal 'em!
    This murder might have slept in tongueless brass
    But for ourselves, and the world died an ass;
    Now I remember too, here was Piato
    Brought forth a knavish sentence once—no doubt
    (Said he) but time
    Will make the murderer bring forth himself.   120
    'Tis well he died, he was a witch.
    And now my Lord, since we are in for ever,
    This work was ours which else might have been slipp'd,
    And if we list, we could have nobles clipp'd

---

92 quited] requited   99 witty] ingeniously   109 set] i.e., die, with a quibble on son/sun
110 conscience] sense of fitness   113 murders] So in the quarto, but often amended to
'murd'rers'.   115 brass] i.e., in a memorial slab   121 witch] for having foreseen later
events   123 slipp'd] passed over

And go for less than beggars, but we hate
To bleed so cowardly; we have enough,
I'faith we're well, our mother turn'd, our sister true,
We die after a nest of Dukes. Adieu.

Exeunt Vindice *&* Hippolito, *guarded.*

Antonio. How subtilly was that murder clos'd! Bear up
Those tragic bodies, 'tis a heavy season: 130
Pray heaven their blood may wash away all treason.

Exeunt Omnes.

FINIS.

THE ATHEIST'S TRAGEDY
OR,
THE HONEST MAN'S REVENGE

by

CYRIL TOURNEUR

CYRIL TOURNEUR (c. 1570/80–1626)

The Atheist's Tragedy

Probably written in 1610 or 1611; printed in 1611

[*Works*, ed. Allardyce Nicoll, London 1930. A full edition by Irving Ribner in The Revels Plays, London 1964.]

THE ATHEISTS TRAGEDIE:
OR
The honest Man's Reuenge.

As in diuers places it hath often beene Acted.

WRITTEN
By *Cyril Tourneur.*

AT LONDON,
Printed for *Iohn Stepneth,* and *Richard Redmer,* and are to
be sold at their Shops at the West end of Paules.
1 6 1 1.

THE NAMES AND QUALITIES OF THE ACTORS

Montferrers, a baron.
Belforest, a baron.
D'Amville, brother to Montferrers.
Levidulcia, Lady to Belforest.
Castabella, daughter to Belforest.
Charlemont, son to Montferrers.
Rousard, elder son to D'Amville.
Sebastian, younger son to D'Amville.
Languebeau Snuffe, a Puritain; Chaplain to Belforest.
Borachio, D'Amville's instrument.
Cataplasma, a maker of periwigs and attires.
Soquette, a seeming gentlewoman to Cataplasma.
Fresco, servant to Cataplasma.
Other servants.
Sergeant in war.
Soldiers.
Watchmen.
Officers.
Judges.
[Doctor.]
[Keeper of the prison.]
[Executioner.]

Enter D'Amville, Borachio, *attended.*

D'Amville. I saw my nephew Charlemont but now
 Part from his father. Tell him I desire
 To speak with him.   *Exit* Servant.
      Borachio, thou art read
 In Nature and her large philosophy.
 Observ'st thou not the very self same course
 Of revolution both in man and beast?
Borachio. The same: for birth, growth, state, decay and death:
 Only, a man's beholding to his Nature
 For th' better composition o'the two.
D'Amville. But where that favour of his Nature is   10
 Not full and free, you see a man becomes
 A fool, as little-knowing as a beast.
Borachio. That shows there's nothing in a man, above
 His Nature; if there were, consid'ring 'tis
 His being's excellency, 'twould not yield
 To Nature's weakness.
D'Amville.   Then if death casts up
 Our total sum of joy and happiness,
 Let me have all my senses feasted in
 Th'abundant fulness of delight at once,
 And with a sweet insensible increase   20
 Of pleasing surfeit melt into my dust.
Borachio. That revolution is too short me thinks.
 If this life comprehends our happiness,
 How foolish to desire to die so soon!
 And if our time runs home unto the length
 Of Nature, how improvident it were
 To spend our substance on a minute's pleasure,
 And after live an age in misery!
D'Amville. So thou conclud'st that pleasure only flows
 Upon the stream of riches.
Borachio.   Wealth is Lord   30
 Of all felicity.
D'Amville. 'Tis oracle.
 For what's a man that's honest without wealth?

31 oracle] the Gospel truth

Borachio. Both miserable and contemptible.
D'Amville. He's worse Borachio. For if charity
    Be an essential part of honesty,
    And should be practis'd first upon our selves,
    Which must be granted, then your honest man
    That's poor, is most dishonest, for he is
    Uncharitable to the man, whom he
    Should most respect. But what doth this touch me,   40
    That seem to have enough? Thanks industry.
    'Tis true. Had not my body spread it self
    Into posterity, perhaps I should
    Desire no more increase of substance, than
    Would hold proportion with mine own dimensions.
    Yet even in that sufficiency of state,
    A man has reason to provide and add.
    For what is he hath such a present eye,
    And so prepar'd a strength, that can foresee,
    And fortify his substance and himself,   50
    Against those accidents, the least whereof
    May rob him of an age's husbandry?
    And for my children: they are as near to me,
    As branches to the tree whereon they grow;
    And may as numerously be multiply'd.
    As they increase, so should my providence;
    For from my substance they receive the sap,
    Whereby they live and flourish.
Borachio.   Sir enough,
    I understand the mark whereat you aim.

   Enter Charlemont.

D'Amville. Silence. W'are interrupted. Charlemont!   60
Charlemont. Good morrow Uncle.
D'Amville.   Noble Charlemont;
    Good morrow. Is not this the honour'd day
    You purpos'd to set forward to the war?
Charlemont. My inclination did intend it so.
D'Amville. And not your resolution?
Charlemont.   Yes my Lord;
    Had not my father contradicted it.
D'Amville. O noble war! Thou first original
    Of all man's honour. How dejectedly

---

48 present] ready   56 providence] foresightful management

The baser spirit of our present time
Hath cast it self below the ancient worth   70
Of our forefathers! From whose noble deeds
Ignobly we derive our pedigrees.
Charlemont. Sir; tax not me for his unwillingness.
By the command of his authority,
My disposition's forc'd against it self.
D'Amville. Nephew, you are the honour of our blood.
The troop of gentry, whose inferior worth
Should second your example, are become
Your leaders: and the scorn of their discourse
Turns smiling back upon your backwardness.   80
Charlemont. You need not urge my spirit by disgrace,
'Tis free enough. My father hinders it.
To curb me, he denies me maintenance
To put me in the habit of my rank.
Unbind me from that strong necessity,
And call me coward if I stay behind.
D'Amville. For want of means? Borachio! Where's the gold?
I'd disinherit my posterity
To purchase honour. 'Tis an interest
I prize above the principal of wealth.   90
I'm glad I had th'occasion to make known
How readily my substance shall unlock
It self to serve you. Here's a thousand crowns.
Charlemont. My worthy uncle; in exchange for this,
I leave my bond. So I am doubly bound:
By that for the repayment of this gold,
And by this gold to satisfy your love.
D'Amville. Sir; 'tis a witness (only) of my love;
And love doth always satisfy it self.
Now to your father; labour his consent.   100
My importunity shall second yours.
We will obtain it.
Charlemont.   If entreaty fail,
The force of reputation shall prevail.   *Exit.*
D'Amville. Go call my sons, that they may take their leaves
Of noble Charlemont. Now, my Borachio!
Borachio. The substance of our former argument
Was wealth.
D'Amville.   The question how to compass it.
Borachio. Young Charlemont is going to the war.

84 habit] equipment   85 Unbind ... necessity] repair that lack

D'Amville. O, thou begin'st to take me.
Borachio.   Mark me then.
    Me thinks, the pregnant wit of man might make   110
    The happy absence of this Charlemont
    A subject for commodious providence.
    He has a wealthy father, ready ev'n
    To drop into his grave. And no man's power
    When Charlemont is gone, can interpose
    'Twixt you and him.
D'Amville.   Th'ast apprehended; both
    My meaning and my love. Now let thy trust,
    For undertaking and for secrecy,
    Hold measure with thy amplitude of wit;
    And thy reward shall parallel thy worth.   120
Borachio. My resolution has already bound
    Me to your service.
D'Amville.   And my heart to thee.

    Enter Rousard *and* Sebastian.

    Here are my sons.—
    There's my eternity. My life in them
    And their succession shall for ever live.
    And in my reason dwells the providence,
    To add to life as much of happiness.
    Let all men lose, so I increase my gain,
    I have no feeling of another's pain.   *Exeunt.*

[SCENE II]

    Enter old Montferrers *and* Charlemont.

Montferrers. I prithee let this current of my tears
    Divert thy inclination from the war.
    For of my children thou art only left,
    To promise a succession to my house.
    And all the honour thou canst get by arms
    Will give but vain addition to thy name,
    Since from thy ancestors thou dost derive
    A dignity sufficient, and as great
    As thou hast substance to maintain and bear.
    I prithee stay at home.

128 so] so long as

Charlemont.   My noble Father,   10
  The weakest sigh you breathe hath power to turn
  My strongest purpose; and your softest tear
  To melt my resolution to as soft
  Obedience. But my affection to the war
  Is as hereditary as my blood,
  To ev'ry life of all my ancestry.
  Your predecessors were your precedents;
  And you are my example. Shall I serve
  For nothing but a vain parenthesis
  I'th'honour'd story of your family?   20
  Or hang but like an empty scutcheon,
  Between the trophies of my predecessors,
  And the rich arms of my posterity?
  There's not a Frenchman of good blood and youth,
  But either out of spirit or example
  Is turn'd a soldier. Only Charlemont
  Must be reputed that same heartless thing,
  That cowards will be bold to play upon.

    Enter D'Amville, Rousard *and* Sebastian.

D'Amville. Good morrow my Lord.
Montferrers. Morrow good Brother.   30
Charlemont. Good morrow Uncle.
D'Amville. Morrow kind Nephew.
  What? ha'you wash'd your eyes wi'tears this morning?
  Come: by my soul his purpose does deserve
  Your free consent. Your tenderness dissuades him.
  What to the father of a gentleman,
  Should be more tender than the maintenance
  And the increase of honour to his house?
  My Lord; here are my boys. I should be proud
  That either this were able, or that inclin'd   40
  To be my nephew's brave competitor.
Montferrers. Your importunities have overcome.
  Pray God my forc'd grant prove not ominous.
D'Amville. [*Aside*] We have obtain'd it.—Ominous? in what?
  It cannot be in any thing but death.
  And I am of a confident belief,
  That ev'n the time, place, manner of our deaths
  Do follow fate with that necessity,

14 affection for] inclination towards   15 as . . ancestry] as much my inheritance as my
blood   28 play upon] mock   41 competitor] rival

That makes us sure to die. And in a thing
Ordain'd so certainly unalterable,   50
What can the use of providence prevail?

[Enter] Belforest, Levidulcia, Castabella, *attended.*

Belforest. Morrow my Lord Montferrers, Lord D'Amville.
   Good morrow gentlemen. Cousin Charlemont!
   Kindly good morrow. Troth I was afear'd
   I should ha' come too late, to tell you that
   I wish your undertakings a success
   That may deserve the measure of their worth.
Charlemont. My Lord; my duty would not let me go,
   Without receiving your commandements.
Belforest. Accompliments are more for ornament,   60
   Than use. We should employ no time in them,
   But what our serious business will admit.
Montferrers. Your favour had by his duty been prevented,
   If we had not withheld him in the way.
D'Amville. He was a-coming to present his service.
   But now no more. The cook invites to breakfast.
   Will't please your Lordship enter.—Noble Lady.   *Exeunt.*

   Manent Charlemont *and* Castabella.

Charlemont. My noble mistress! this accompliment
   Is like an elegant and moving speech,
   Compos'd of many sweet persuasive points,   70
   Which second one another, with a fluent
   Increase, and confirmation of their force,
   Reserving still the best until the last,
   To crown the strong impulsion of the rest
   With a full conquest of the hearer's sense:
   Because th'impression of the last we speak
   Doth always longest and most constantly
   Possess the entertainment of remembrance.
   So all that now salute my taking leave
   Have added numerously to the love,   80
   Wherewith I did receive their courtesy.
   But you (dear mistress) being the last and best
   That speaks my farewell, like th'imperious close
   Of a most sweet oration, wholly have

57 deserve] reward according to   59 commandements] The first *e* is necessary for
scansion.   63] i.e., your kindness would have been thwarted by his already having left

Possess'd my liking, and shall ever live
Within the soul of my true memory.
So (mistress) with this kiss I take my leave.
Castabella. My worthy servant! you mistake th'intent
Of kissing. 'Twas not meant to separate
A pair of lovers; but to be the seal 90
Of love; importing by the joining of
Our mutual and incorporated breaths,
That we should breathe but one contracted life.
Or stay at home, or let me go with you.
Charlemont. My Castabella! for my self to stay,
Or you to go, would either tax my youth
With a dishonourable weakness, or
Your loving purpose with immodesty.

Enter Languebeau Snuffe.

And for the satisfaction of your love,
Here comes a man whose knowledge I have made 100
A witness to the contract of our vows,
Which my return by marriage shall confirm.
Languebeau. I salute you both with the spirit of copulation, I am already informed of your matrimonial purposes, and will be a testimony to the integrity of your promises.
Castabella. O the sad trouble of my fearful soul!
My faithful servant! did you never hear,
That when a certain great man went to th'war,
The lovely face of Heav'n was mask'd with sorrow,
The sighing winds did move the breast of earth, 110
The heavy clouds hung down their mourning heads,
And wept sad showers the day that he went hence,
As if that day presag'd some ill success,
That fatally should kill his happiness;
And so it came to pass. Methinks my eyes
(Sweet Heav'n forbid) are like those weeping clouds,
And as their showers presag'd so do my tears,
Some sad event will follow my sad fears.
Charlemont. Fie, superstitious? is it bad to kiss?
Castabella. May all my fears hurt me no more than this. [*They kiss.*]
Languebeau. Fie, fie, fie, these carnal kisses do stir up the concupiscences of the flesh. 122

Enter Belforest *and* Levidulcia.

Levidulcia. O! here's your daughter under her servant's lips.

Charlemont. Madam, there is no cause you should mistrust
    The kiss I gave, 'twas but a parting one.
Levidulcia. A lusty blood! Now by the lip of love
    Were I to choose, your joining one for me.
Belforest. Your father stays to bring you on the way.
    Farewell. The great commander of the war
    Prosper the course you undertake. Farewell.   130
Charlemont. My Lord! I humbly take my leave.—Madam!
    I kiss your hand.—And your sweet lip.—Farewell.   *Exeunt.*

   Manent Charlemont *and* Languebeau.

    Her power to speak is perish'd in her tears.
    Something within me would persuade me stay,
    But reputation will not yield unto't.
    Dear sir, you are the man whose honest trust
    My confidence hath chosen for my friend.
    I fear my absence will discomfort her.
    You have the power and opportunity
    To moderate her passion. Let her grief   140
    Receive that friendship from you; and your love
    Shall not repent it self of courtesy.
Languebeau. Sir, I want words and protestation to insinuate into your credit;
   but in plainness and truth, I will qualify her grief with the spirit of
   consolation.
Charlemont. Sir, I will take your friendship up at use.
    And fear not that your profit shall be small;
    Your interest shall exceed your principal.   *Exit.*

   Enter D'Amville *and* Borachio.

D'Amville. Monsieur Languebeau! Happily encount'red. The honesty of
   your conversation makes me request more int'rest in your familiarity.
Languebeau. If your Lordship will be pleased to salute me without ceremony,
   I shall be willing to exchange my service for your favour; but this wor-
   shipping kind of entertainment is a superstitious vanity; in plainness and
   truth I love it not.   154
D'Amville. I embrace your disposition; and desire to give you as liberal
   assurance of my love, as my Lord Belforest your deserved favourer.

---

127 joining] This is an adjective, in apposition to, but contrasted with, 'parting' in l. 125.
129 The great . . . war] i.e., God   146 take . . . use] i.e., borrow it as I should money,
paying interest   150 more . . . familiarity] a closer connexion with you   155 I . . . dis-
position] I agree with you (D'Amville is using the same jargon)   156 deserved] worthy

Languebeau. His Lordship is pleased with my plainness and truth of conversation.

D'Amville. It cannot displease him. In the behaviour of his noble daughter Castabella, a man may read her worth and your instruction.   160

Languebeau. That gentlewoman is most sweetly modest, fair, honest, handsome, wise, well-born, and rich.

D'Amville. You have given me her picture in small.

Languebeau. She's like your diamond; a temptation in every man's eye, yet not yielding to any light impression her self.

D'Amville. The praise is hers; but the comparison your own.

> *Gives him the ring.*

Languebeau. You shall forgive me that, sir.

D'Amville. I will not do so much at your request as forgive you it. I will only give you it sir. By——You will make me swear.

Languebeau. O! by no means. Profane not your lips with the foulness of that sin. I will rather take it. To save your oath, you shall lose your ring.— Verily my Lord, my praise came short of her worth. She exceeds a jewel. This is but only for ornament; she both for ornament and use.   173

D'Amville. Yet unprofitably kept without use. She deserves a worthy husband, sir. I have often wish'd a match between my elder son and her. The marriage would join the houses of Belforest and D'Amville into a noble alliance.

Languebeau. And the unity of families is a work of love and charity.

D'Amville. And that work an employment well becoming the goodness of your disposition.   180

Languebeau. If your Lordship please to impose it upon me, I will carry it without any second end, the surest way to satisfy your wish.

D'Amville. Most joyfully accepted.—Rousard! Here are letters to my Lord Belforest touching my desire to that purpose.

Enter Rousard *sickly.*

Rousard! I send you a suitor to Castabella. To this gentleman's discretion I commit the managing of your suit. His good success shall be most thankful to your trust. Follow his instructions, he will be your leader.

Languebeau. In plainness and truth.

Rousard. My leader? does your Lordship think me too weak to give the on-set my self?   191

Languebeau. I will only assist your proceedings.

Rousard. To say true, so I think you had need, for a sick man can hardly get a woman's good will without help.

---

182 any second end] any ulterior motive, or perhaps, any other purpose to distract me
187 thankful . . . trust] assured if you trust him

Languebeau. [*Aside*] Charlemont! thy gratuity and my promises were both
    but words;
        And both like words shall vanish into air.—
        For thy poor empty hand I must be mute:
        This gives me feeling of a better suit.
                        Exeunt Languebeau *and* Rousard.
D'Amville. Borachio! didst precisely note this man?   200
Borachio. His own profession would report him pure.
D'Amville. And seems to know if any benefit
    Arises of religion after death;
    Yet but compare's profession with his life;
    They so directly contradict themselves,
    As if the end of his instructions were
    But to divert the world from sin, that he
    More easily might engross it to himself.
    By that I am confirm'd an atheist.
    Well! Charlemont is gone. And here thou seest,   210
    His absence the foundation of my plot.
Borachio. He is the man whom Castabella loves.
D'Amville. That was the reason I propounded him
    Employment fix'd upon a foreign place,
    To draw his inclination out o'th'way.
Borachio. 'T has left the passage of our practice free.
D'Amville. This Castabella is a wealthy heir,
    And by her marriage with my elder son,
    My house is honour'd, and my state increas'd.
    This work alone deserves my industry: 220
    But if it prosper, thou shalt see my brain
    Make this but an induction to a point
    So full of profitable policy
    That it would make the soul of honesty
    Ambitious to turn villain.
Borachio.   I bespeak
    Employment in't. I'll be an instrument
    To grace performance with dexterity.
D'Amville. Thou shalt. No man shall rob thee of the honour.
    Go presently and buy a crimson scarf,
    Like Charlemont's. Prepare thee a disguise,   230
    I'th'habit of a soldier, hurt and lame;

---

195 gratuity] kindness   198–9] empty hand . . . suit] a quibble on card-playing and
courting   201 profession] vocation, with a quibble on what he professes   208 engross]
collect from all quarters   222 induction . . . point] preliminary to a plan

And then be ready at the wedding feast,
Where thou shalt have employment in a work
Will please thy disposition.
Borachio.   As I vow'd;
Your instrument shall make your project proud.
D'Amville. This marriage will bring wealth. If that succeed,
I will increase it though my brother bleed.   *Exeunt.*

[SCENE III]

Enter Castabella *avoiding the importunity of* Rousard.

Castabella. Nay good sir; in troth if you knew how little it pleases me, you
would forbear it.
Rousard. I will not leave thee, till th'ast entertain'd me for thy servant.
Castabella. My servant? You are sick you say. You would tax me of indiscre-
tion to entertain one that is not able to do me service.
Rousard. The service of a gentlewoman consists most in chamber work, and
sick men are fittest for the chamber. I prithee give me a favour.
Castabella. Me thinks you have a very sweet favour of your own.
Rousard. I lack but your black eye.
Castabella. If you go to buffets among the boys, they'll give you one.   10
Rousard. Nay if you grow bitter, I'll dispraise your black eye. The grey-
eyed morning makes the fairest day.
Castabella. Now that you dissemble not, I could be willing to give you a
favour. What favour would you have?
Rousard. Any toy: any light thing.
Castabella. Fie. Will you be so uncivil to ask a light thing at a gentlewoman's
hand?
Rousard. Wilt give me a bracelet o' thy hair then?
Castabella. Do you want hair sir?
Rousard. No faith, I'll want no hair, so long as I can have it for money.
Castabella. What would you do with my hair then?   21
Rousard. Wear it for thy sake, sweet heart.
Castabella. Do you think I love to have my hair worn off?
Rousard. Come, you are so witty now, and so sensible.   *Kisses her.*
Castabella. Tush. I would I wanted one o' my senses now.
Rousard. Bitter again? What's that? Smelling?
Castabella. No, no, no. Why now y'are satisfied I hope. I have given you a
favour.

235 proud] perfect   I. iii, 8 favour] face   9 black eye] slang for vagina   15 light]
trifling, but Castabella takes it in the sense of wanton   19 want] lack   20 hair]
punning on 'hare' (prostitute)   23 worn off] i.e., off (away from) my head

Rousard. What favour? a kiss? I prithee give me another.

Castabella. Show me that I gave you then.   30

Rousard. How should I show it?

Castabella. You are unworthy of a favour if you will not bestow the keeping of it one minute.

Rousard. Well in plain terms, dost love me? That's the purpose of my coming.

Castabella. Love you? Yes. Very well.

Rousard. Give me thy hand upon't.

Castabella. Nay, you mistake me. If I love you very well, I must not love you now. For now you are not very well, y'are sick.

Rousard. This equivocation is for the jest now.   40

Castabella. I speak't as 'tis now in fashion, in earnest. But I shall not be in quiet for you I perceive, till I have given you a favour. Do you love me?

Rousard. With all my heart.

Castabella. Then with all my heart, I'll give you a jewel to hang in your ear. —Hark ye—I can never love you.   *Exit.*

Rousard. Call you this a jewel to hang in mine ear? 'Tis no light favour, for I'll be sworn it comes somewhat heavily to me. Well, I will not leave her for all this. Me thinks it animates a man to stand to't, when a woman desires to be rid of him at the first sight.   *Exit.*

[SCENE IV]

Enter Belforest *and* Languebeau Snuffe.

Belforest. I entertain the offer of this match,
　　With purpose to confirm it presently.
　　I have already mov'd it to my daughter;
　　Her soft excuses savour'd at the first
　　(Methought) but of a modest innocence
　　Of blood; whose unmov'd stream was never drawn
　　Into the current of affection. But when I
　　Reply'd with more familiar arguments,
　　Thinking to make her apprehension bold,
　　Her modest blush fell to a pale dislike,
　　And she refus'd it with such confidence,   10
　　As if she had been prompted by a love
　　Inclining firmly to some other man,
　　And in that obstinacy she remains.

---

41 in quiet for] free from trouble from　　48 stand to't] persist　　I. iv, 8 familiar]
intimate　　9 apprehension] understanding　　9 bold] confident

Languebeau. Verily that disobedience doth not become a child. It proceedeth
from an unsanctified liberty. You will be accessory to your own dishonour
if you suffer it.

Belforest. Your honest wisdom has advis'd me well.
    Once more I'll move her by persuasive means.
    If she resist, all mildness set apart,   20
    I will make use of my authority.

Languebeau. And instantly, lest fearing your constraint, her contrary affection
teach her some devise that may prevent you.

Belforest. To cut off ev'ry opportunity
    Procrastination may assist her with,
    This instant night she shall be marry'd.

Languebeau.   Best.

   Enter Castabella.

Castabella. Please it your Lordship, my mother attends i'th'gallery, and
    desires your conference.   *Exit* Belforest.
    This means I us'd to bring me to your ear.
    Time cuts off circumstance; I must be brief.   30
    To your integrity did Charlemont
    Commit the contract of his love and mine,
    Which now so strong a hand seeks to divide:
    That if your grave advice assist me not,
    I shall be forc'd to violate my faith.

Languebeau. Since Charlemont's absence, I have weighed his love with the
spirit of consideration; and in sincerity I find it to be frivolous and vain.
Withdraw your respect; his affection deserveth it not.

Castabella. Good sir; I know your heart cannot profane
    The holiness you make profession of,   40
    With such a vicious purpose as to break
    The vow your own consent did help to make.

Languebeau. Can he deserve your love, who in neglect of your delightful
conversation, and in obstinate contempt of all your prayers and tears,
absents himself so far from your sweet fellowship, and with a purpose so
contracted to that absence, that you see he purchases your separation with
the hazard of his blood and life, fearing to want pretence to part your
companies?—

---

22 contrary affection] love turned in another direction   30 Time . . . circumstance]
shortage of time forces me to cut out details   43–8] Most modern editors print these
lines as verse, though the quarto has prose for the whole speech, which is in truth a mixture
between the two, containing some blank verse lines.   47–8 pretence . . . companies]
an excuse to part from you

   'Tis rather hate that doth division move;
   Love still desires the presence of his love.—   50
   Verily,
   He is not of the Family of Love.
Castabella. O do not wrong him. 'Tis a generous mind
   That led his disposition to the war:
   For gentle love and noble courage are
   So near ally'd, that one begets another:
   Or, love is sister, and courage is the brother.
   Could I affect him better than before,
   His soldier's heart would make me love him more.
Languebeau. But Castabella——

  Enter Levidulcia.

Levidulcia. Tush, you mistake the way into a woman,   60
   The passage lies not through her reason, but
   Her blood.   *Exit* Languebeau, Castabella *about to follow.*
      Nay, stay! How wouldst thou call the child,
   That being rais'd with cost and tenderness,
   To full hability of body and means,
   Denies relief unto the parents, who
   Bestow'd that bringing up?
Castabella.   Unnatural.
Levidulcia. Then Castabella is unnatural.
   Nature, the loving mother of us all,
   Brought forth a woman for her own relief,
   By generation to revive her age;   70
   Which, now thou hast hability and means
   Presented, most unkindly dost deny.
Castabella. Believe me Mother; I do love a man.
Levidulcia. Prefer'st th' affection of an absent love,
   Before the sweet possession of a man;
   The barren mind before the fruitful body;
   Where our creation has no reference
   To man but in his body, being made
   Only for generation, which (unless
   Our children can be gotten by conceit)   80
   Must from the body come? If reason were
   Our counsellor, we would neglect the work

---

51 Family of Love] a religious sect often ridiculed and attacked for promiscuity
57 affect] love 72 unkindly] with a quibble on 'unnaturally' 80 conceit] imagination

Of generation, for the prodigal
Expense it draws us to, of that which is
The wealth of life. Wise Nature (therefore) hath
Reserv'd for an inducement to our sense,
Our greatest pleasure in that greatest work.
Which being offer'd thee, thy ignorance
Refuses for th'imaginary joy
Of an unsatisfy'd affection to   90
An absent man, whose blood once spent i'th'war,
Then he'll come home, sick, lame and impotent,
And wed thee to a torment, like the pain
Of Tantalus, continuing thy desire
With fruitless presentation of the thing
It loves; still mov'd and still unsatisfy'd.

Enter Belforest, D'Amville, Rousard, Sebastian, Languebeau, *&c.*

Belforest. Now Levidulcia! Hast thou yet prepar'd
My daughter's love to entertain this man,
Her husband here?
Levidulcia.　　　　　　I'm but her mother i' law;
Yet if she were my very flesh and blood,   100
I could advise no better for her good.
Rousard. Sweet wife! Thy joyful husband thus salutes
Thy cheek.
Castabella.　　My husband? O! I am betray'd.—
Dear friend of Charlemont! your purity
Professes a divine contempt o'th'world;
O be not brib'd by that you so neglect,
In being the world's hated instrument,
To bring a just neglect upon yourself!—　　*Kneel from one to another.*
Dear Father! let me but examine my
Affection.—Sir, your prudent judgment can   110
Persuade your son that 'tis improvident
To marry one whose disposition he
Did ne'er observe.—Good sir, I may be of
A nature so unpleasing to your mind,
Perhaps you'll curse the fatal hour wherein
You rashly marry'd me.
D'Amville.　　　　　My Lord Belforest!
I would not have her forc'd against her choice.

83–5 prodigal . . . life] It was commonly believed that life was shortened by sexual intercourse.　　106 neglect] despise　　108 s.d.] instruction to kneel in turn to B., D.'A., R.

Belforest. Passion o'me, thou peevish girl! I charge
    Thee by my blessing, and th'authority
    I have to claim th'obedience; marry him.   120
Castabella. Now Charlemont! O my presaging tears!
    This sad event hath follow'd my sad fears.
Sebastian. A rape, a rape, a rape!
Belforest.   How now?
D'Amville.   What's that?
Sebastian. Why what is't but a rape to force a wench
    To marry, since it forces her to lie
    With him she would not?
Languebeau. Verily, his tongue is an unsanctified member.
Sebastian. Verily,
    Your gravity becomes your perish'd soul,
    As hoary mouldiness does rotten fruit.   130
Belforest. Cousin, y'are both uncivil and profane.
D'Amville. Thou disobedient villain; get thee out of my sight. Now by my
    soul I'll plague thee for this rudeness.
Belforest. Come; set forward to the church.   *Exeunt.*

Manet Sebastian.

Sebastian. And verify the proverb—the nearer the church, the further from
    God.—Poor wench. For thy sake, may his hability die in his appetite,
    that thou beest not troubled with him thou lovest not. May his appetite
    move thy desire to another man: so he shall help to make himself cuckold.
    And let that man be one that he pays wages to: so thou shalt profit by
    him thou hatest. Let the chambers be matted, the hinges oil'd, the curtain
    rings silenced, and the chamber-maid hold her peace at his own request,
    that he may sleep the quietlier. And in that sleep let him be soundly
    cuckolded. And when he knows it, and seeks to sue a divorce, let him
    have no other satisfaction than this: *He lay by and slept: the law will
    take no hold of her, because he wink'd at it.*   *Exit.*

ACTUS SECUNDI SCENA PRIMA

Music. A banquet. In the night.

Enter D'Amville, Belforest, Levidulcia, Rousard, Castabella, Languebeau
Snuffe, *at one door. At the other door*, Cataplasma *and* Soquette, *usher'd by*
Fresco.

136 hability] sexual potency   145 wink'd] turned his back on   II. i, s.d. *Music, &c.*]
These unusual stage directions are, as W. J. Lawrence points out, prompter's notes:
D'Amville does not call for the music until l. 16.

Levidulcia. Mistress Cataplasma! I expected you an hour since.

Cataplasma. Certain ladies at my house (Madam) detain'd me; otherwise I
had attended your Ladyship sooner.

Levidulcia. We are beholding to you for your company. My Lord; I pray
you bid these gentlewomen welcome: th'are my invited friends.

D'Amville. Gentlewomen, y'are welcome, pray sit down.

Levidulcia. Fresco! by my Lord D'Amville's leave I prithee go into the
butt'ry. Thou sha't find some o' my men there; if they bid thee not
welcome, they are very loggerheads.

Fresco. If your loggerheads will not, your hogsheads shall Madam, if I get
into the butt'ry   *Exit.*

D'Amville. That fellow's disposition to mirth should be our present example.
Let's be grave and meditate, when our affairs require our seriousness.
'Tis out of season to be heavily disposed.   14

Levidulcia. We should be all wound up into the key of mirth.

D'Amville. The music there!

Belforest. Where's my Lord Montferrers? Tell him here's a room attends
him.

   Enter Montferrers.

Montferrers. Heaven give your marriage that I am depriv'd of, joy.

D'Amville. My Lord Belforest! Castabella's health.   *D'Amville drinks.*
Set ope the cellar doors, and let this health   21
Go freely round the house.—Another to
Your son, my Lord; to noble Charlemont.
He is a soldier. Let the instruments
Of war congratulate his memory.—   *Drums and trumpets.*

   Enter a Servant.

Servant. My Lord, here's one i'th'habit of a soldier says he is newly return'd
from Ostend, and has some business of import to speak.

D'Amville. Ostend! let him come in. My soul foretells
He brings the news will make our music full.
My brother's joy would do't: and here comes he   30
Will raise it.

   Enter Borachio *disguised.*

Montferrers.   O my spirit, it does dissuade
My tongue to question him, as if it knew
His answer would displease.

D'Amville.   Soldier! what news?
We heard a rumour of a blow you gave
The enemy.

9 loggerheads] blockheads   17 room] place

Borachio.   'Tis very true my Lord.
Belforest. Canst thou relate it?
Borachio.   Yes.
D'Amville.   I prithee do.
Borachio. The enemy, defeated of a fair
    Advantage by a flatt'ring stratagem,
    Plants all th'artillery against the town,
    Whose thunder and lightning made our bulwarks shake;   40
    And threat'ned in that terrible report
    The storm wherewith they meant to second it.
    Th'assault was general. But for the place
    That promis'd most advantage to be forc'd,
    The pride of all their army was drawn forth,
    And equally divided into front
    And rear. They march'd. And coming to a stand,
    Ready to pass our channel at an ebb,
    W'advis'd it for our safest course, to draw
    Our sluices up and make't unpassable.   50
    Our governor oppos'd; and suffer'd 'em
    To charge us home e'en to the rampier's foot,
    But when their front was forcing up our breach,
    At push o'pike, then did his policy
    Let go the sluices, and tripp'd up the heels
    Of the whole body of their troop, that stood
    Within the violent current of the stream.
    Their front beleaguer'd 'twixt the water and
    The town, seeing the flood was grown too deep
    To promise them a safe retreat, expos'd   60
    The force of all their spirits, (like the last
    Expiring gasp of a strong-hearted man)
    Upon the hazard of one charge; but were
    Oppress'd and fell. The rest that could not swim
    Were only drown'd; but those that thought to scape
    By swimming were, by murtherers that flanker'd
    The level of the flood, both drown'd and slain.
D'Amville. Now by my soul (soldier) a brave service.
Montferrers. O what became of my dear Charlemont?
Borachio. Walking next day upon the fatal shore,   70
    Among the slaughter'd bodies of their men,
    Which the full-stomach'd sea had cast upon

38 flatt'ring] deceptive   42 second it] follow it up   48 at an ebb] The river of course
is tidal.   52 rampier] rampart   54 at push o'pike] in hand-to-hand combat
66–7 flanker'd . . . flood] spread along the banks

     The sands, it was m'unhappy chance to light
     Upon a face, whose favour when it liv'd
     My astonish'd mind inform'd me I had seen.
     He lay in's armour, as if that had been
     His coffin; and the weeping sea, (like one
     Whose milder temper doth lament the death
     Of him whom in his rage he slew) runs up
     The shore; embraces him; kisses his cheek,   80
     Goes back again and forces up the sands
     To bury him; and ev'ry time it parts,
     Sheds tears upon him; till at last (as if
     It could no longer endure to see the man
     Whom it had slain, yet loath to leave him;) with
     A kind of unresolv'd unwilling pace,
     Winding her waves one in another, like
     A man that folds his arms, or wrings his hands
     For grief; ebb'd from the body and descends:
     As if it would sink down into the earth,   90
     And hide it self for shame of such a deed.
D'Amville. And souldier, who was this?
Montferrers.   O Charlemont!
Borachio. Your fear hath told you that whereof my grief
     Was loath to be the messenger.
Castabella.   O God.   *Exit* Castabella.
D'Amville. Charlemont drown'd? Why how could that be, since
     It was the adverse party that receiv'd
     The overthrow?
Borachio. His forward spirit press'd into the front;
     And being engag'd within the enemy,
     When they retreated through the rising stream,   100
     I'the violent confusion of the throng
     Was overborn and perish'd in the flood.
     And here's the sad remembrance of his life,   *—The scarf.*
     Which for his sake I will for ever wear.
Montferrers. Torment me not with witnesses of that,
     Which I desire, not to believe; yet must.
D'Amville. Thou art a screech-owl; and dost come i'night
     To be the cursed messenger of death.
     Away. Depart my house; or (by my soul)

103 *The scarf*] This again is clearly a prompter's memorandum.   105–6] The punctuation here is awkward to a modern reader: the point is that Montferrers does not merely not want to believe it, he wants to disbelieve.

You'll find me a more fatal enemy,   110
    Than ever was Ostend. Be gone. Dispatch.
Borachio. Sir 'twas my love.
D'Amville.   Your love to vex my heart
    With that I hate? Hark, do you hear? you knave——
    [*Aside to* Borachio] O th'art a most delicate sweet eloquent villain!
Borachio. [*Aside to* D'Amville] Was't not well counterfeited?
D'Amville. [*Aside to* Borachio] Rarely.—Be gone. I will not hear reply.
Borachio. Why then farewell: I will not trouble you.   *Exit.*
D'Amville. [*Aside*] So. The foundation's laid. Now by degrees,
    The work will rise and soon be perfected.
    —O this uncertain state of mortal man!   120
Belforest. What then? it is th'inevitable fate
    Of all things underneath the moon.
D'Amville.   'Tis true.
    Brother for health's sake overcome your grief.
Montferrers. I cannot sir. I am uncapable
    Of comfort. My turn will be next. I feel
    My self not well.
D'Amville.   You yield too much to grief.
Languebeau. All men are mortal. The hour of death is uncertain. Age makes
    sickness the more dangerous. And grief is subject to distraction. You
    know not how soon you may be depriv'd of the benefit of sense. In my
    understanding (therefore) you shall do well if you be sick to set your
    state in present order. Make your will.   131
D'Amville. [*Aside*] I have my wish.
    ——Lights for my brother.
Montferrers.   I'll withdraw a while;
    And crave the honest counsel of this man.
Belforest. With all my heart. I pray attend him sir.
                    Exeunt Montferrers *and* Snuffe.
    This next room, please your Lordship.
D'Amville.   Where you will.
                    Exeunt Belforest *and* D'Amville.
Levidulcia. My daughter's gone. Come son. Mistress Cataplasma, come;
    we'll up into her chamber. I'd fain see how she entertains the expectation
    of her husband's bedfellowship.
Rousard. 'Faith howsoever she entertains it, I   140
    Shall hardly please her; therefore let her rest.
Levidulcia. Nay, please her hardly and you please her best.   *Exeunt*

---

128 subject to] likely to be an occasion of

[SCENE II]

Enter 3 Servants *drunk, drawing in* Fresco.

1 Servant. Boy! fill some drink boy.

Fresco. Enough good sir; not a drop more by this light.

2 Servant. Not by this light? Why then, put out the candles and we'll drink i'the dark and t'wut old boy.

Fresco. No, no, no, no, no.

3 Servant. Why then, take thy liquor. A health Fresco.   *Kneel.*

Fresco. Your health will make me sick sir.

1 Servant. Then 'twill bring you o' your knees I hope sir.

Fresco. May I not stand and pledge it sir?

2 Servant. I hope you will do as we do.   10

Fresco. Nay then indeed I must not stand, for you cannot.

3 Servant. Well said old boy.

Fresco. Old boy! you'll make me a young child anon: for if I continue this, I shall scarce be able to go alone.

1 Servant. My body is as weak as water, Fresco.

Fresco. Good reason sir, the beer has sent all the malt up into your brain, and left nothing but the water in your body.

Enter D'Amville *and* Borachio *closely observing their drunkenness.*

D'Amville. Borachio! seest those fellows?

Borachio.   Yes my Lord.

D'Amville. Their drunkenness that seems ridiculous
　　Shall be a serious instrument, to bring   20
　　Our sober purposes to their success.

Borachio. I am prepar'd for th' execution, sir.

D'Amville. Cast off this habit, and about it straight.

Borachio. Let them drink healths, & drown their brains i'the flood;
　　I'll promise them they shall be pledg'd in blood.   *Exit.*

1 Servant. You ha' left a damnable snuff here.

2 Servant. Do you take that in snuff sir?

1 Servant. You are a damnable rogue then.   *—Together by th'ears.*

D'Amville. Fortune I honour thee. My plot still rises,
　　According to the model of mine own desires.   30
　　—Lights for my brother. What, ha' you drunk your selves mad, you knaves?

4 and t'wut] i.e., 'an thou wilt' (if you will)   6 *Kneel*] It was customary to kneel to drink toasts to a lady.   8 o' your knees] i.e., in order to drink a further toast   26 snuff] remnant of drink left in a glass   27 take that in snuff] take offence at that   28 s.d.] i.e., they attack one another

1 Servant. My Lord, the jacks abus'd me.

D'Amville. I think they are the jacks indeed that have abus'd thee. Dost
hear? that fellow is a proud knave. He has abus'd thee. As thou goest over
the fields by and by, in lighting my brother home, I'll tell thee what
sha't do: knock him over the pate with thy torch, I'll bear thee out in't.

1 Servant. I will singe the goose by this torch.   *Exit.*

D'Amville. Dost hear, fellow? Seest thou that proud knave? I have given
him a lesson for his sauciness. H'as wrong'd thee. I'll tell thee what
sha't do: as we go over the fields by and by, clap him suddenly o'er the
coxcomb with thy torch, I'll bear thee out in't.   42

2 Servant. I will make him understand as much.   *Exit.*

    Enter Languebeau Snuffe.

D'Amville. Now Monsieur Snuffe! What has my brother done?

Languebeau. Made his will; and by that will made you his heir; with this
proviso, that as occasion shall hereafter move him, he may revoke or
alter it when he pleases.

D'Amville. Yes. Let him if he can.—I'll make it sure
  From his revoking.   *Aside.*

    Enter Montferrers *and* Belforest, *attended with lights.*

Montferrers.   Brother now good night.

D'Amville. The sky is dark, we'll bring you o'er the fields.   50
  [*Aside*] Who can but strike wants wisdom to maintain:
  He that strikes safe and sure has heart and brain.   *Exeunt.*

               [SCENE III]

    Enter Castabella *alone.*

Castabella. O love! thou chaste affection of the soul,
  Without th'adult'rate mixture of the blood;
  That virtue which to goodness addeth good:
  The minion of Heaven's heart. Heaven! is't my fate
  For loving that thou lov'st to get thy hate?
  Or was my Charlemont thy chosen love?
  And therefore hast receiv'd him to thy self?
  Then I confess thy anger's not unjust.

---

33 jacks] knaves   34 jacks] large drinking vessels   49 *Aside*] The only occasion in the
two plays attributed to Tourneur in which the quarto prints this direction, though of course
many speeches are asides (e.g., contrast ll. 51-2 below).   51 maintain] persevere
II. iii, 4 minion] darling

    I was thy rival. Yet to be divorc'd
    From love has been a punishment enough,   10
    (Sweet Heaven) without being marry'd unto hate,
    Hadst thou been pleas'd: O double misery!
    Yet since thy pleasure hath inflicted it,
    If not my heart, my duty shall submit.

Enter Levidulcia, Rousard, Cataplasma, Soquette, *and* Fresco *with a lanthorn.*

Levidulcia. Mistress Cataplasma, good night. I pray when your man has brought you home, let him return and light me to my house.

Cataplasma. He shall instantly wait on your Ladyship.

Levidulcia. Good Mistress Cataplasma! For my servants are all drunk; I cannot be beholding to 'em for their attendance.
                        Exeunt Cataplasma, Soquette, *and* Fresco.
    O here's your bride.

Rousard.   And melancholic too,   20
    Me thinks.

Levidulcia.   How can she choose? your sickness will
    Distaste th'expected sweetness o' the night.
    That makes her heavy.

Rousard.   That should make her light.

Levidulcia. Look you to that.

Castabella.   What sweetness speak you of?
    The sweetness of the night consists in rest.

Rousard. With that sweetness thou shalt be surely blest,
    Unless my groaning wake thee. Do not moan.

Levidulcia. Sh'ad rather you would wake, and make her groan.

Rousard. Nay 'troth sweet heart, I will not trouble thee.
    Thou shalt not lose thy maidenhead tonight.   30

Castabella. [*Aside*] O might that weakness ever be in force;
    I never would desire to sue divorce!

Rousard. Wilt go to bed?

Castabella.   I will attend you, sir.

Rousard. Mother, good night.

Levidulcia.   Pleasure be your bedfellow.
                      Exeunt Rousard *and* Castabella.
    Why sure their generation was asleep,
    When she begot those dormice, that she made
    Them up so weakly and imperfectly.

---

19 beholding] obliged, i.e., it's no use expecting their attendance   22 distaste] spoil 35–6 their generation . . . dormice] their parents must have been asleep when they were conceived, they are so sleepy

One wants desire; the t'other hability—
When my affection even with their cold bloods
(As snow rubb'd through an active hand does make   40
The flesh to burn) by agitation is
Inflam'd. I could unbrace, and entertain
The air to cool it.

Enter Sebastian.

Sebastian.   That but mitigates
    The heat; rather embrace and entertain
    A younger brother; he can quench the fire.
Levidulcia. Can you so, sir? Now I beshrew your ear.
    Why bold Sebastian, how dare you approach
    So near the presence of your displeas'd father?
Sebastian. Under the protection of his present absence.
Levidulcia. Belike you knew he was abroad then.
Sebastian.   Yes.   50
    Let me encounter you so: I'll persuade
    Your means to reconcile me to his love.
Levidulcia. Is that the way? I understand you not.
    But for your reconcilement, meet m'at home;
    I'll satisfy your suit.
Sebastian.   Within this half
    Hour?   *Exit* Sebastian.
Levidulcia. Or within this whole hour. When you will.—
    A lusty blood! has both the presence and
    The spirit of a man. I like the freedom
    Of his behaviour.—Ho—Sebastian! Gone?—
    Has set my blood a-boiling i' my veins.   60
    And now (like water pour'd upon the ground,
    That mixes it self with ev'ry moisture it meets)
    I could clasp with any man.

Enter Fresco *with a lanthorn.*

    O Fresco! art thou come?
    If t'other fail, then thou art entertain'd.
    Lust is a spirit, which whosoe'er doth raise,
    The next man that encounters boldly lays.   *Exeunt.*

---

39 affection] passion   42 unbrace] undress   46 beshrew] curse   51-2 I'll ... means]
I'll persuade you to use your powers   67 boldly] This qualifies 'encounters' rather
than 'lays'.

[SCENE IV]

Enter Borachio *warily and hastily over the stage, with a stone in either hand.*

Borachio. Such stones men use to raise a house upon;
    But with these stones I go to ruin one.   *Descends.*

Enter two Servants *drunk, fighting with their torches,* D'Amville,
Montferrers, Belforest, *and* Languebeau Snuffe.

Belforest. Passion o' me you drunken knaves, you'll put
    The lights out.
D'Amville.   No my Lord; th'are but in jest.
1 Servant. Mine's out.
D'Amville. Then light it at his head, that's light enough.—
    'Fore God, th'are out. You drunken rascals, back
    And light 'em.
Belforest.   'Tis exceeding dark.   *Exeunt* Servants.
D'Amville.   No matter:
    I am acquainted with the way. Your hand.
    Let's easily walk. I'll lead you till they come.   10
Montferrers. My soul's opprest with grief. 'T lies heavy at
    My heart. O my departed son! ere long
    I shall be with thee.   *D'Amville thrusts him down into the gravel pit.*
D'Amville.   Marry, God forbid!
Montferrers. O, o, o.
D'Amville.   Now all the host
    Of Heaven forbid. Knaves, rogues!
Belforest.   Pray God he be
    Not hurt! He's fall'n into the gravel pit.
D'Amville. Brother! dear brother! Rascals, villains, knaves!

Enter the Servants *with lights.*

    Eternal darkness damn you; come away.
    Go round about into the gravel pit,
    And help my brother up. Why what a strange   20
    Unlucky night is this! Is't not, my Lord?
    I think that dog that howl'd the news of grief,
    That fatal screech-owl, usher'd on this mischief.

Enter with the murd'red body.

Languebeau. Mischief indeed my Lord. Your brother's dead.
Belforest. He's dead?

22–3 dog . . . screech-owl] i.e., the disguised Borachio

Servant.   He's dead.

D'Amville.   Dead be your tongues. Drop out
  Mine eye-balls, and let envious fortune play
  At tennis with 'em. Have I liv'd to this?
  Malicious Nature! hadst thou borne me blind,
  Th'adst yet been something favourable to me.
  No breath? No motion? Prithee tell me Heaven!   30
  Hast shut thine eye to wink at murther; or
  Hast put this sable garment on, to mourn
  At's death?
  Not one poor spark in the whole spacious sky
  Of all that endless number would vouchsafe
  To shine? You viceroys to the King of Nature!
  Whose constellations govern mortal births,
  Where is that fatal planet rul'd at his
  Nativity? That might ha' pleas'd to light
  Him out, as well as into th'world; unless   40
  It be asham'd t'have been the instrument
  Of such a good man's cursed destiny.—

Belforest. Passions transport you. Recollect your self.
  Lament him not. Whether our deaths be good
  Or bad, it is not death but life that tries;
  He liv'd well, (therefore) questionless, well dies.

D'Amville. Ay—'tis an easy thing for him that has
  No pain to talk of patience. Do you think
  That Nature has no feeling?

Belforest.   Feeling? Yes.
  But has she purpos'd any thing for nothing?   50
  What good receives this body by your grief?
  Whether is't more unnatural not to grieve
  For him you cannot help with it; or hurt
  Your self with grieving and yet grieve in vain?

D'Amville. Indeed had he been taken from me like
  A piece o' dead flesh, I should neither ha' felt it,
  Nor griev'd for't. But come hether, 'pray look here.
  Behold the lively tincture of his blood!
  Neither the dropsy nor the jaundice in't,
  But the true freshness of a sanguine red,   60
  For all the fog of this black murd'rous night
  Has mix'd with it. For any thing I know,
  He might ha' liv'd till doomsday, and ha' done
  More good than either you or I. O brother!
  He was a man of such a native goodness,

    As if regeneration had been given
    Him in his mother's womb; so harmless,
    That rather than ha' trod upon a worm,
    He would ha' shunn'd the way; so dearly pitiful,
    That ere the poor could ask his charity   70
    With dry eyes, he gave 'em relief wi' tears—
    With tears—yes faith, with tears.
Belforest.   Take up the corpse.
    For wisdom's sake let reason fortify
    This weakness.
D'Amville.   Why, what would you ha' me do?
    Foolish Nature will have her course in spite o'wisdom. But I have e'en
done. All these words were but a great wind, and now
    This shower of tears has laid it, I am calm
    Again. You may set forward when you will.
    I'll follow you, like one that must and would not.
Languebeau. Our opposition will but trouble him.   80
Belforest. The grief that melts to tears by it self is spent,
    Passion resisted grows more violent.   *Exeunt*.

    Manet D'Amville. Borachio *ascends*.

D'Amville. Here's a sweet comedy. 'T begins with *O*
    Dolentis, and concludes with ha, ha, he.
Borachio. Ha, ha, he.
D'Amville.   O my echo! I could stand
    Reverberating this sweet musical air
    Of joy, till I had perish'd my sound lungs
    With violent laughter. Lovely night-raven!
    Th'ast seiz'd a carcass.
Borachio.   Put him out on's pain.
    I lay so fitly underneath the bank   90
    From whence he fell, that ere his falt'ring tongue
    Could utter double Oo, I knock'd out's brains
    With this fair ruby; and had another stone
    Just of this form and bigness ready: that
    I laid i'the broken skull upo' the ground
    For's pillow; against the which they thought he fell
    And perish'd.

---

66 regeneration] rebirth, i.e., resurrection   67 harmless] Three syllables are needed
here (though this whole passage appears in prose in the quarto).   93 this fair ruby] i.e.,
the stone covered in blood

D'Amville. Upon this ground I'll build my manor-house;
    And this shall be the chiefest corner stone.
Borachio. 'T has crown'd the most judicious murder that   100
    The brain of man was e'er deliver'd of.
D'Amville. Ay. Mark the plot. Not any circumstance
    That stood within the reach of the design,
    Of persons, dispositions, matter, time
    Or place, but by this brain of mine was made
    An instrumental help; yet nothing from
    Th'induction to th'accomplishment seem'd forc'd,
    Or done o' purpose, but by accident.
Borachio. First, my report that Charlemont was dead,
    Though false, yet cover'd with a mask of truth.   110
D'Amville. Ay, and deliver'd in as fit a time,
    When all our minds so wholly were possess'd
    With one affair, that no man would suspect
    A thought employ'd for any second end.
Borachio. Then the precisian to be ready, when
    Your brother spake of death, to move his will.
D'Amville. His business call'd him thither; and it fell
    Within his office, unrequested to't.
    From him it came religiously, and sav'd
    Our project from suspicion, which if I   120
    Had mov'd had been endanger'd.
Borachio.   Then your healths,
    Though seeming but the ordinary rites,
    And ceremonies due to festivals——
D'Amville. Yet us'd by me to make the servants drunk,
    An instrument the plot could not have miss'd.
    'Twas easy to set drunkards by the ears:
    Th'ad nothing but their torches to fight with:
    And when those lights were out——
Borachio.   Then darkness did
    Protect the execution of the work,
    Both from prevention and discovery.   130
D'Amville. Here was a murther bravely carry'd through
    The eye of observation, unobserv'd.
Borachio. And those that saw the passage of it made
    The instruments yet knew not what they did.
D'Amville. That power of rule philosophers ascribe
    To him they call the supreme of the stars,

115 precisian] Puritan   125 miss'd] gone without   131–2 through . . . observation]
with witnesses present

Making their influences governors
Of sublunary creatures, when their selves
Are senseless of their operations——   *Thunder and lightning.*
                What!
Dost start at thunder? Credit my belief,   140
'Tis a mere effect of nature:
An ezhalation hot and dry, involv'd
Within a wat'ry vapour i'the middle
Region of the air, whose coldness
Congealing that thick moisture to a cloud,
The angry exhalation shut within
A prison of contrary quality
Strives to be free; and with the violent
Eruption through the grossness of that cloud,
Makes this noise we hear.   150
Borachio. 'Tis a fearful noise.
D'Amville. 'Tis a brave noise; and me thinks graces our accomplish'd
   project, as a peal of ordnance does a triumph. It speaks
Encouragement. Now Nature shows thee how
It favour'd our performance: to forbear
This noise when we set forth, because it should
Not terrify my brother's going home,
Which would have dash'd our purpose; to forbear
This lightning in our passage, lest it should
Ha' warn'd him o' the pitfall.   160
Then propitious Nature wink'd
At our proceedings; now it doth express
How that forbearance favour'd our success.
Borachio. You have confirm'd me. For it follows well
That Nature (since her self decay doth hate)
Should favour those that strengthen their estate.
D'Amville. Our next endeavour is (since on the false
Report that Charlemont is dead depends
The fabric of the work) to credit that
With all the countenance we can.
Borachio.   Faith sir,   170
Even let his own inheritance, whereof
Y'ave dispossess'd him, countenance the act.
Spare so much out of that, to give him a
Solempnity of funeral. 'Twill quit
The cost; and make your apprehension of
His death appear more confident and true.

156 because] so that   164 confirm'd] convinced   174 quit] repay

D'Amville. I'll take thy counsel. Now farewell black night,
    Thou beauteous mistress of a murderer:
    To honour thee, that hast accomplish'd all,
    I'll wear thy colours at his funeral.   *Exeunt.*

[SCENE V]

Enter Levidulcia *into her chamber, mann'd by* Fresco.

Levidulcia. Th'art welcome into my chamber, Fresco. Prithee shut the door.
    —Nay thou mistakest me. Come in and shut it.
Fresco. 'Tis somewhat late Madam.
Levidulcia. No matter. I have somewhat to say to thee. What? is not thy
    mistress towards a husband yet?
Fresco. Faith Madam, she has suitors. But they will not suit her me thinks.
    They will not come off lustily it seems.
Levidulcia. They will not come on lustily, thou wouldst say.
Fresco. I mean (Madam) they are not rich enough.
Levidulcia. But ay (Fresco) they are not bold enough. Thy mistress is of a
    lively attractive blood, Fresco. And in troth she's o' my mind for that. A
    poor spirit is poorer than a poor purse. Give me a fellow that brings not
    only temptation with him, but has the activity of wit, and audacity of
    spirit to apply every word and gesture of a woman's speech and behaviour
    to his own desire, and make her believe she's the suitor her self, never
    give back till he has made her yield to it.   16
Fresco. Indeed among our equals Madam; but otherwise we shall be put
    horribly out o' countenance.
Levidulcia. Thou art deceiv'd, Fresco. Ladies are as courteous as yeomen's
    wives, and me thinks they should be more gentle. Hot diet and soft ease
    makes 'em (like wax always kept warm) more easy to take impression.—
    Prithee untie my shoe.—What? art thou shamefac'd too? Go roundly
    to work man. My leg is not gouty: 'twill endure the feeling, I warrant thee.
    Come hither Fresco; thine ear.—'S dainty, I mistook the place. I
    miss'd thine ear and hit thy lip.   25
Fresco. Your Ladyship has made me blush.
Levidulcia. That shows th'art full o' lusty blood, and thou knowest not how
    to use it. Let me see thy hand. Thou shouldst not be shamefac'd by thy
    hand, Fresco. Here's a brawny flesh and a hairy skin: both signs of an able
    body. I do not like these phlegmatic, smooth-skinn'd, soft-flesh'd fellows.
    They are like candied suckets when they begin to perish; which I would

II. v, s.d. *mann'd*] accompanied   24 'S dainty] God's dignity   31 suckets] sweet-
meats

always empty my closet of, and give 'em my chambermaid.—I have
some skill in palmistry: by this line that stands directly against me, thou
shouldst be near a good fortune, Fresco, if thou hadst the grace to entertain
it.   35

Fresco. O what is that Madam, I pray?

Levidulcia. No less than the love of a fair lady, if thou dost not lose her with
faint-heartedness.

Fresco. A lady, Madam? alas, a lady is a great thing, I cannot compass her.

Levidulcia. No? Why? I am a lady. Am I so great I cannot be compassed?
Clasp my waist and try.   41

Fresco. I could find i' my heart Madam.

                                                     Sebastian *knocks within.*

Levidulcia. 'Ud's body, my husband! Faint-hearted fool! I think thou wert
begotten between the North Pole and the congeal'd passage. Now like an
ambitious coward that betrays himself with fearful delay, you must suffer
for the treason you never committed. Go hide thy self behind yond'arras,
instantly.   Fresco *hides himself.*

Enter Sebastian.

Sebastian! What do you here so late?

Sebastian. Nothing yet; but I hope I shall.——   *Kisses her.*

Levidulcia. Y'are very bold.   50

Sebastian. And you very valiant; for you met me at full career.

Levidulcia. You come to ha' me move your father's reconciliation. I'll write
a word or two i' your behalf.

Sebastian. A word or two, Madam? That you do for me will not be contain'd
in less than the compass of two sheets. But in plain terms, shall we take
the opportunity of privateness?

Levidulcia. What to do?

Sebastian. To dance the beginning of the world after the English manner.

Levidulcia. Why not after the French or Italian?

Sebastian. Fie. They dance it preposterously: backward.   60

Levidulcia. Are you so active to dance?

Sebastian. I can shake my heels.

Levidulcia. Y'are well made for't.

Sebastian. Measure me from top to toe; you shall not find me differ much
from the true standard of proportion.

                                                     Belforest *knocks within.*

43 'Ud's] God's   44 congeal'd] frozen: a reference to Arctic voyages   45 fearful]
frightened   51 at full career] at full speed (an image from jousting)   58 dance . . .
manner] have sexual intercourse; 'The Beginning of the World' was a popular dance also
known as Sellenger's Round (*Ribner*)   60 They . . . backward] a reference to perversions
supposed characteristic of France and Italy

Levidulcia. I think I am accurs'd. Sebastian! There's one at the door has beaten opportunity away from us. In brief, I love thee. And it shall not be long before I give thee a testimony of it. To save thee now from suspicion, do no more but draw thy rapier; chafe thy self; and when he comes in, rush by without taking notice of him. Only seem to be angry, and let me alone for the rest.   71

Enter Belforest.

Sebastian. Now by the hand of Mercury——   *Exit* Sebastian.
Belforest. What's the matter wife?
Levidulcia. Ooh, ooh, husband!
Belforest. Prithee what ail'st thou woman?
Levidulcia. O feel my pulse. It beats, I warrant you. Be patient a little, sweet husband; tarry but till my breath come to me again, and I'll satisfy you.
Belforest. What ails Sebastian, he looks so distractedly?
Levidulcia. The poor gentleman's almost out on's wits I think. You remember the displeasure his father took against him about the liberty of speech he us'd even now when your daughter went to be married.   81
Belforest. Yes, what of that?
Levidulcia. 'T has craz'd him sure: he met a poor man i' the street even now. Upon what quarrel I know not: but he pursued him so violently, that if my house had not been his rescue, he had surely kill'd him.
Belforest. What a strange desperate young man is that!
Levidulcia. Nay husband, he grew so in rage when he saw the man was conveyed from him, that he was ready even to have drawn his naked weapon upon me. And had not your knocking at the door prevented him, surely h'ad done something to me.   90
Belforest. Where's the man?
Levidulcia. Alas here. I warrant you the poor fearful soul is scarce come to himself again yet. [*Aside*] If the fool have any wit he will apprehend me.—Do you hear sir? You may be bold to come forth; the fury that haunted you is gone.

                  Fresco *peeps fearfully forth from behind the arras.*
Fresco. Are you sure he is gone?
Belforest. He's gone; he's gone, I warrant thee.
Fresco. I would I were gone too. Has shook me almost into a dead palsy.
Belforest. How fell the difference between you?
Fresco. I would I were out at the back door.   100
Belforest. Th'art safe enough. Prithee tell's the falling out.
Fresco. Yes sir, when I have recovered my spirits. My memory is almost frighted from me.—Oh, so, so, so.—Why sir, as I came along the street

69 chafe thy self] make yourself appear angry   75 what ail'st thou?] a curious form, possibly a slip for 'what ails thee?'   88 naked weapon] with an obvious sexual quibble

sir;—this same gentleman came stumbling after me, and trod o' my heel,—
I cried O. Do you cry sirrah? says he. Let me see your heel; if it be not
hurt, I'll make you cry for something. So he claps my head between his
legs, and pulls of my shoe. I having shifted no socks in a sennight, the
gentleman cried foh; and said my feet were base and cowardly feet, they
stunk for fear. Then he knock'd my shoe about my pate, and I cried O,
once more. In the mean time comes a shag-hair'd dog by, and rubs
against his shins. The gentleman took the dog in shag-hair to be some
watchman in a rug gown; and swore he would hang me up at the next
door with my lanthorn in my hand, that passengers might see their way
as they went, without rubbing against gentlemen's shins. So, for want of a
cord, he took his own garters off; and as he was going to make a nooze,
I watch'd my time and ran away. And as I ran (indeed) I bid him hang
himself in his own garters. So he in choler pursued me hither as you see.

Belforest. Why this savours of distraction.

Levidulcia. Of mere distraction.

Fresco. [*Aside*] Howsoever it savours, I am sure it smells like a lie.   120

Belforest. Thou may'st go forth at the back door (honest fellow), the way is
    private and safe.

Fresco. So had it need, for your fore-door (here) is both common and
    dangerous.   *Exit* Belforest.

Levidulcia. Good night honest Fresco.

Fresco. Good night Madam; if you get me kissing o' ladies again——
                                               Exit Fresco.

Levidulcia. This falls out handsomely.
    But yet the matter does not well succeed,
    Till I have brought it to the very deed.   *Exit.*

[SCENE VI]

Enter Charlemont *in arms, a* Musketeer, *and a* Sergeant.

Charlemont. Sergeant! what hour o' the night is't?

Sergeant. About one.

Charlemont. I would you would relieve me; for I am
    So heavy that I shall ha' much ado
    To stand out my perdu.   *Thunder and lightning.*

Sergeant.   I'll e'en but walk
    The round (sir) and then presently return.

Soldier. For God's sake Sergeant, relieve me. Above five hours together in
    so foul a stormy night as this?

107 having . . . sennight] not having changed my socks for a week   123 common] free to
all (like that of a brothel)   II. vi, 5 perdu] an exposed and dangerous sentry post or watch

Sergeant. Why 'tis a music Soldier. Heaven and earth are now in consort,
　　when the thunder and the canon play one to another.　　　　　　10

　　　　　　　　　　　　　　　　　　　　　　　　　Exit Sergeant.

Charlemont. I know not why I should be thus inclin'd
　　To sleep, I feel my disposition press'd
　　With a necessity of heaviness.
　　Soldier! if thou hast any better eyes,
　　I prithee wake me when the Sergeant comes.
Soldier. Sir, 'tis so dark and stormy that I shall
　　Scarce either see or hear him ere he comes
　　Upon me.
Charlemont.　　I cannot force my self to wake.　　　　　　—*Sleeps.*

　　Enter the ghost of Montferrers.

Montferrers. Return to France; for thy old father's dead;
　　And thou by murther disinherited.　　　　　　　　　　20
　　Attend with patience the success of things;
　　But leave revenge unto the King of kings.　　　　　　*Exit.*

　　　　　　　　　　　　　　Charlemont *starts and wakes.*

Charlemont. O my affrighted soul! what fearful dream
　　Was this that wak'd me? Dreams are but the rais'd
　　Impressions of premeditated things,
　　By serious apprehensions left upon
　　Our minds, or else th'imaginary shapes
　　Of objects proper to th'complexion, or
　　The dispositions of our bodies. These
　　Can neither of them be the cause, why I　　　　　　　30
　　Should dream thus; for my mind has not been mov'd
　　With any one conception of a thought
　　To such a purpose; nor my nature wont
　　To trouble me with fantasies of terror.
　　It must be something that my genius would
　　Inform me of. Now gracious Heaven forbid!
　　O! let my spirit be depriv'd of all
　　Foresight and knowledge, ere it understand
　　That vision acted; or divine that act
　　To come. Why should I think so? Left I not　　　　　40
　　My worthy father i'the kind regard
　　Of a most loving uncle? Soldier! sawst
　　No apparition of a man?

---

21 patience] in the religious sense of suffering　　21 success] outcome　　35 genius]
tutelary spirit　　37–9 let my . . . acted] let my spirit be without foresight rather than the
vision be true in fact

Soldier.   You dream
   Sir; I saw nothing.
Charlemont.   Tush. These idle dreams
   Are fabulous. Our boiling fantasies
   Like troubled waters falsify the shapes
   Of things retain'd in them; and make 'em seem
   Confounded, when they are distinguish'd. So
   My actions daily conversant with war
   (The argument of blood and death) had left   50
   (Perhaps) th'imaginary presence of
   Some bloody accident upon my mind;
   Which mix'd confusedly with other thoughts,
   (Whereof th'remembrance of my father might
   Be one) presented all together, seem
   Incorporate; as if his body were
   The owner of that blood, the subject of
   That death, when he's at Paris, and that blood
   Shed here. It may be thus. I would not leave
   The war, for reputation's sake, upon   60
   An idle apprehension, a vain dream.

Enter the Ghost.

Soldier. Stand. Stand, I say. No? Why then have at thee.
   Sir, if you will not stand, I'll make you fall.
   Nor stand, nor fall? Nay then the Devil's dam
   Has broke her husband's head: for sure it is a spirit,
   I shot it through, and yet it will not fall.   *Exit.*
              The Ghost approaches Charlemont.
                   He fearfully avoids it.

Charlemont. O pardon me! my doubtful heart was slow
   To credit that which I did fear to know.   *Exeunt.*

ACTUS TERTIJ SCENA PRIMA

Enter the Funeral of Montferrers.

D'Amville. Set down the body. Pay earth what she lent,
   But she shall bear a living monument,
   To let succeeding ages truly know
   That she is satisfy'd what he did owe:

45 fabulous] untrue (as in a fable)   56 Incorporate] compounded into a body
III. i, 4 is satisfy'd] has been repaid

Both principal and use; because his worth
Was better at his death than at his birth.

A dead march. Enter the Funeral of Charlemont *as a Soldier.*

And with his body, place that memory
Of noble Charlemont his worthy son.
And give their graves the rites that do belong
To soldiers. They were soldiers both. The father   10
Held open war with sin; the son with blood:
This in a war more gallant; that more good.

The first volley.

There place their arms; and here their epitaphs.
And may these lines survive the last of graves.

THE EPITAPH OF *MONTFERRERS*.

Here lie the ashes of that earth and fire,
        whose heat and fruit did feed and warm the poor:
And they (as if they would in sighs expire,
        and into tears dissolve) his death deplore.
He did that good freely, for goodness' sake,
        unforc'd: for gen'rousness he held so dear,   20
That he fear'd none but him that did him make;
        and yet he serv'd him more for love than fear.
                So's life provided, that though he did die
                A sudden death, yet died not suddenly.

THE EPITAPH OF *CHARLEMONT*.

His body lies interr'd within this mould;
Who died a young man, yet departed old;
And in all strength of youth that man can have
Was ready still to drop into his grave.
For ag'd in virtue, with a youthful eye
He welcom'd it, being still prepar'd to die;   30
And living so, though young depriv'd of breath,
He did not suffer an untimely death.
But we may say of his brave bless'd decease:
He died in war; and yet he died in peace.

The second volley.

5 use] interest   7 memory] some substitute obtained to take the place of Charlemont's
body   15ff.] The epitaphs are evidently to be read out by D'Amville.   24 *suddenly*]
unprepared   30 *still*] always

O might that fire revive the ashes of
This phoenix! Yet the wonder would not be
So great as he was good; and wond'red at
For that. His live's example was so true
A practique of religion's theory,
That her divinity seem'd rather the   40
Description than th'instruction of his life.
And of his goodness was his virtuous son
A worthy imitator. So that on
These two Herculean pillars, where their arms
Are plac'd, there may be writ, *Non ultra*. For
Beyond their lives as well for youth as age,
Nor young nor old, in merit or in name,
Shall e'er exceed their virtues or their fame.

The third volley.

'Tis done. [*Aside*] Thus fair accompliments make foul
Deeds gracious. Charlemont! come now when t'wut,   50
I've bury'd under these two marble stones
Thy living hopes, and thy dead father's bones.

Exeunt.

Enter Castabella *mourning to the monument of* Charlemont.

Castabella. O thou that know'st me justly Charlemont's,
Though in the forc'd possession of another;
Since from thine own free spirit we receive it,
That our affections cannot be compell'd,
Though our actions may, be not displeas'd, if on
The altar of his tomb I sacrifice
My tears. They are the jewels of my love
Dissolved into grief, and fall upon   60
His blasted spring, as April dew upon
A sweet young blossom shak'd before the time.

Enter Charlemont *with a* Servant.

Charlemont. Go see my trunks dispos'd of. I'll but walk
A turn or two i'th'church and follow you.   *Exit* Servant.
O! here's the fatal monument of my
Dead father first presented to mine eye.
What's here? in memory of Charlemont?
Some false relation has abus'd belief.

39 a practique . . . theory] a putting of religious theory into practice   44–5 These . . .
ultra] two pillars set up like the Pillars of Hercules to prevent passing beyond   47 name]
reputation   50 t'wut] thou wilt   68 relation] narration (just possibly with a quibble on
D'Amville's being his relation)

I am deluded. But I thank thee Heaven.
For ever let me be deluded thus.   70
My Castabella mourning o'er my hearse?
Sweet Castabella rise, I am not dead.
Castabella. O Heaven defend me.   *Falls in a swoon.*
Charlemont.   I beshrew my rash
And inconsid'rate passion.—Castabella!—
That could not think—my Castabella!—that
My sudden presence might affright her sense.—
I prithee (my affection) pardon me.   *She rises.*
Reduce thy understanding to thine eye.
Within this habit which thy misinform'd
Conceit takes only for a shape, live both   80
The soul and body of thy Charlemont.
Castabella. I feel a substance, warm, and soft, and moist,
Subject to the capacity of sense.
Charlemont. Which spirits are not; for their essence is
Above the nature and the order of
Those elements whereof our senses are
Created. Touch my lip. Why turn'st thou from me?
Castabella. Grief above griefs. That which should woe relieve,
Wish'd and obtain'd, gives greater cause to grieve.
Charlemont. Can Castabella think it cause of grief   90
That the relation of my death proves false?
Castabella. The presence of the person we affect
(Being hopeless to enjoy him) makes our grief
More passionate than if we saw him not.
Charlemont. Why not enjoy? has absence chang'd thee?
Castabella.   Yes.
From maid to wife.
Charlemont.   Art marry'd?
Castabella.   O I am.
Charlemont. Marry'd! Had not my mother been a woman,
I should protest against the chastity
Of all thy sex. How can the merchant,
Or the mariner, absent whole years (from wives   100
Experienc'd in the satisfaction of
Desire) promise themselves to find their sheets
Unspotted with adultery, at their
Return, when you that never had the sense

69 deluded] misrepresented   77 my affection] my love   78 Reduce . . . eye] believe
your eyes, nothing else   80 Conceit] imagination   80 shape] phantom   92 affect] love

    Of actual temptation, could not stay
    A few short months?
Castabella.   O do but hear me speak.
Charlemont. But thou wert wise: and didst consider that
    A soldier might be maim'd, and so (perhaps)
    Lose his hability to please thee.
Castabella.   No.
    That weakness pleases me in him I have.   110
Charlemont. What? marry'd to a man unable too?
    O strange incontinence! Why? was thy blood
    Increas'd to such a pleurisy of lust,
    That of necessity there must a vein
    Be open'd, though by one that had no skill
    To do't?
Castabella.   Sir, I beseech you hear me.
Charlemont.   Speak.
Castabella. Heav'n knows I am unguilty of this act.
Charlemont. Why? wert thou forc'd to do't?
Castabella.   Heav'n knows I was.
Charlemont. What villain did it?
Castabella.   Your uncle D'Amville.
    And he that dispossess'd my love of you   120
    Hath disinherited you of possession.
Charlemont. Disinherited? wherein have I deserv'd
    To be depriv'd of my dear father's love?
Castabella. Both of his love and him. His soul's at rest.
    But here your injur'd patience may behold
    The signs of his lamented memory.
                       Charlemont *finds his father's monument.*
    H'as found it. When I took him for a ghost,
    I could endure the torment of my fear
    More eas'ly than I can his sorrows hear.   *Exit.*
Charlemont. Of all men's griefs must mine be singular?   130
    Without example? Here I met my grave.
    And all men's woes are bury'd i' their graves
    But mine. In mine my miseries are born.
    I prithee sorrow, leave a little room,
    In my confounded and tormented mind,
    For understanding to deliberate
    The cause or author of this accident.—
    A close advantage of my absence made,
    To dispossess me both of land and wife:

113 pleurisy] superabundance   130 singular] unique, perhaps also to be endured alone

And all the profit does arise to him,   140
By whom my absence was first mov'd and urg'd.
These circumstances (Uncle) tell me, you
Are the suspected author of those wrongs;
Whereof the lightest is more heavy than
The strongest patience can endure to bear.   *Exit.*

[SCENE II]

Enter D'Amville, Sebastian, *and* Languebeau.

D'Amville. Now sir! your business?
Sebastian.   My annuity.
D'Amville. Not a denier.
Sebastian.   How would you ha' me live?
D'Amville. Why, turn crier. Cannot you turn crier?
Sebastian. Yes.
D'Amville.   Then do so, y'ave a good voice for't.
    Y'are excellent at crying of a rape.
Sebastian. Sir, I confess in particular respect to your self, I was somewhat
    forgetful. Gen'ral honesty possess'd me.
D'Amville. Go, th'art the base corruption of my blood;
    And like a tetter grow'st unto my flesh.
Sebastian. Inflict any punishment upon me. The severity shall not discourage
    me, if it be not shameful, so you'll but put money i' my purse. The want
    of money makes a free spirit more mad than the possession does an
    usurer.   13
D'Amville. Not a farthing.
Sebastian. Would you ha' me turn purse-taker? 'Tis the next way to do't.
    For want is like the rack; it draws a man to endanger himself to the
    gallows rather than endure it.

Enter Charlemont, D'Amville *counterfeits to take him for a ghost.*

D'Amville. What art thou? Stay. Assist my troubled sense.
    My apprehension will distract me. Stay.
                              Languebeau Snuffe *avoids him fearfully.*
Sebastian. What art thou? speak.
Charlemont.   The spirit of Charlemont.   20
D'Amville. O stay! compose me. I dissolve.
Languebeau. No. 'Tis profane. Spirits are invisible. 'Tis the fiend i' the
    likeness of Charlemont. I will have no conversation with Satan.
                                                          Exit Snuffe.

III. ii, 7 Gen'ral honesty] concern for honour (or chastity) in general   9 tetter] skin
disease

Sebastian. The spirit of Charlemont? I'll try that.

                                                            Strike, and the blow return'd.

'Fore God thou sayest true, th'art all spirit.

D'Amville. Go call the officers.   *Exit* D'Amville.

Charlemont. Th'art a villain; and the son of a villain.

Sebastian. You lie.   *Fight.*

                                                            Sebastian *is down.*

Charlemont. Have at thee.

  Enter the Ghost of Montferrers.

  Revenge to thee I'll dedicate this work.   30

Montferrers. Hold Charlemont!

  Let him revenge my murder, and thy wrongs,

  To whom the justice of revenge belongs.   *Exit.*

Charlemont. You torture me between the passion of

  My blood, and the religion of my soul.   Sebastian *rises.*

Sebastian. A good honest fellow.

  Enter D'Amville *with* Officers.

D'Amville. What? wounded? Apprehend him. Sir; is this

  Your salutation for the courtesy

  I did you when we parted last? You ha'

  Forgot I lent you a thousand crowns. First, let   40

  Him answer for this riot. When the law

  Is satisfy'd for that, an action for

  His debt shall clap him up again. I took

  You for a spirit; and I'll conjure you

  Before I ha' done.

Charlemont.   No. I'll turn conjurer.

  Devil!

  Within this circle, in the midst of all

  Thy force and malice I conjure thee do

  Thy worst.

D'Amville.   Away with him.   *Exeunt* Officers *with* Charlemont.

Sebastian.   Sir, I have got

  A scratch or two here for your sake. I hope   50

  You'll give me money to pay the surgeon.

D'Amville. Borachio! fetch me a thousand crowns. I am

  Content to countenance the freedom of

  Your spirit when 'tis worthily employ'd.

  A' God's name give behaviour the full scope

  Of gen'rous liberty; but let it not

  Disperse and spend it self in courses of

  Unbounded license. Here, pay for your hurts.   *Exit* D'Amville.

24 try] test, prove   44 conjure] exorcise

Sebastian. I thank you sir.—Gen'rous liberty,—that is to say, freely
to bestow my habilities to honest purposes. Me thinks I should not follow
that instruction now, if having the means to do an honest office for an
honest fellow, I should neglect it. Charlemont lies in prison for a thousand
crowns. And here I have a thousand crowns. Honesty tells me 'twere
well done to release Charlemont. But discretion says I had much ado to
come by this; and when this shall be gone I know not where to finger
any more: especially if I employ it to this use, which is like to endanger
me into my father's perpetual displeasure. And then I may go hang
my self, or be forc'd to do that, will make another save me the labour.
No matter. Charlemont! Thou gav'st me my life and that's somewhat of a
purer earth than gold, as fine as it is. 'Tis no courtesy I do thee but
thankfulness. I owe thee it and I'll pay it. He fought bravely, but the
officers dragg'd him villainously. Arrant knaves! for using him so dis-
courteously, may the sins o' the poor people be so few that you sha' not
be able to spare so much out o' your gettings as will pay for the hire of a
lame starv'd hackney to ride to an execution, but go afoot to the gallows,
and be hang'd. May elder brothers turn good husbands, and younger
brothers get good wives, that there be no need of debt-books, nor use of
sergeants. May there be all peace but i' the war, and all charity but i' the
Devil; so that prisons may be turn'd to hospitals, though the officers
live o' the benevolence. If this curse might come to pass, the world would
say, *Blessed be he that curseth.*   *Exit.*

[SCENE III]

Enter Charlemont *in prison.*

Charlemont. I grant thee Heaven, thy goodness doth command
　　　　Our punishments: but yet no further than
　　　　The measure of our sins. How should they else
　　　　Be just? Or how should that good purpose of
　　　　Thy justice take effect, by bounding men
　　　　Within the confines of humanity,
　　　　When our afflictions do exceed our crimes?
　　　　Then they do rather teach the barb'rous world
　　　　Examples that extend her cruelties
　　　　Beyond their own dimensions; and instruct   10
　　　　Our actions to be more, more barbarous.

68 to do . . . labour] i.e., to commit such a crime as I shall be hanged for   75 hackney]
horse used for general or rough duties   78 sergeants] sheriff's officers employed to make
arrests for debt   79 hospitals] almshouses   79–80 though . . . benevolence] even though
the officers live off the alms from it

O my afflicted soul! How torment swells
Thy apprehension with profane conceit,
Against the sacred justice of my God!
Our own constructions are the authors of
Our misery. We never measure our
Conditions but with men above us in
Estate. So while our spirits labour to
Be higher than our fortunes th'are more base.
Since all those attributes, which make men seem   20
Superior to us, are man's subjects, and
Were made to serve him, the repining man
Is of a servile spirit to deject
The value of himself below their estimation.

Enter Sebastian *with the* Keeper.

Sebastian. Here. Take my sword.—How now my wild swagg'rer! y'are
tame enough now; are you not? The penury of a prison is like a soft
consumption. 'Twill humble the pride o' your mortality, and arm your
soul in complete patience to endure the weight of affliction without
feeling it. What? Hast no music in thee? Th' hast trebles and basses
enough. Treble injury; and base usage. But trebles and basses make
poor music without means. Thou want'st means, dost? What? dost
droop? art dejected?   32

Charlemont. No sir. I have a heart above the reach
Of thy most violent maliciousness;
A fortitude in scorn of thy contempt
(Since Fate is pleas'd to have me suffer it)
That can bear more than thou hast power t'inflict.
I was a baron. That thy father has
Depriv'd me of. Instead of that, I am
Created king. I've lost a signory,   40
That was confin'd within a piece of earth;
A wart upon the body of the world.
But now I am an emp'ror of a world,
This little world of man. My passions are
My subjects; and I can command them laugh,
Whilst thou dost tickle 'em to death with misery.

Sebastian. 'Tis bravely spoken; and I love thee for't. Thou liest here for a
thousand crowns. Here are a thousand to redeem thee. Not for the ransom
o' my life thou gav'st me—that I value not at one crown. 'Tis none o' my
deed. Thank my father for't. 'Tis his goodness. Yet he looks not for thanks.

23 deject] lower   24 their estimation] i.e., the rank at which apparently superior men are
rated   26 soft] easily endured   31 means] the middle part   40 signory] lordship

For he does it underhand, out of a reserv'd disposition to do thee good
without ostentation.—Out o' great heart you'll refuse't now, will you?

Charlemont. No. Since I must submit my self to Fate,   53
    I never will neglect the offer of
    One benefit; but entertain them as
    Her favours, and th' inductions to some end
    Of better fortune, as whose instrument
    I thank thy courtesy.

Sebastian.   Well, come along.   *Exeunt.*

[SCENE IV]

Enter D'Amville *and* Castabella.

D'Amville. Daughter you do not well to urge me. I
    Ha' done no more than justice. Charlemont
    Shall die and rot in prison; and 'tis just.

Castabella. O Father! Mercy is an attribute
    As high as justice; an essential part
    Of his unbounded goodness, whose divine
    Impression, form, and image man should bear.
    And (me thinks) man should love to imitate
    His mercy, since the only countenance
    Of justice were destruction, if the sweet   10
    And loving favour of his mercy did
    Not mediate between it and our weakness.

D'Amville. Forbear. You will displease me. He shall rot.

Castabella. Dear sir! Since, by your greatness, you
    Are nearer Heav'n in place, be nearer it
    In goodness. Rich men should transcend the poor,
    As clouds the earth; rais'd by the comfort of
    The sun, to water dry and barren grounds.
    If neither the impression in your soul
    Of goodness, nor the duty of your place   20
    As goodness' substitute, can move you, then
    Let Nature, which in savages, in beasts,
    Can stir to pity, tell you that he is
    Your kinsman.——

56 inductions] prelude   III. iv, 10 justice] i.e., eternal justice   11 favour] with a
quibble on the sense of 'face' as in 'countenance', l. 9   20–21 place . . . substitute]
(magistrate's) position as the agent of God's goodness

D'Amville.   You expose your honesty
    To strange construction: why should you so urge
    Release for Charlemont? Come, you profess
    More nearness to him than your modesty
    Can answer. You have tempted my suspicion.
    I tell thee he shall starve, and die, and rot.

   Enter Charlemont *and* Sebastian.

Charlemont. Uncle, I thank you.
D'Amville. [*Aside*]   Much good do it you.—   30
    Who did release him?
Sebastian.   I.   *Exit* Castabella.
D'Amville.   You are a villain.
Sebastian. Y'are my father.   *Exit* Sebastian.
D'Amville. [*Aside*]   I must temporize.
    —Nephew! had not his open freedom made
    My disposition known, I would ha' borne
    The course and inclination of my love
    According to the motion of the sun,
    Invisibly enjoy'd and understood.
Charlemont. That shows your good works are directed to
    No other end than goodness. I was rash,
    I must confess. But——
D'Amville.   I will excuse you.   40
    To lose a father, and (as you may think)
    Be disinherited (it must be granted)
    Are motives to impatience. But for death,
    Who can avoid it? And for his estate,
    In the uncertainty of both your lives,
    'Twas done discreetly, to confer't upon
    A known successor, being the next in blood,
    And one (dear Nephew) whom in time to come
    You shall have cause to thank. I will not be
    Your dispossessor, but your guardian.   50
    I will supply your father's vacant place,
    To guide your green improvidence of youth,
    And make you ripe for your inheritance.
Charlemont. Sir, I embrace your gen'rous promises.

   Enter Rousard *sick, and* Castabella.

Rousard. Embracing? I behold the object that
    Mine eye affects. Dear cousin Charlemont!

24 honesty] chastity   25 construction] interpretation   28 tempted] aroused   33 open
freedom] frankness

D'Amville. My elder son! He meets you happily.
　　For with the hand of our whole family
　　We interchange th'indenture of our loves.
Charlemont. And I accept it. Yet not joyfully　　　　　60
　　Because y'are sick.
D'Amville.　　　　　　　　Sir, his affection's sound,
　　Though he be sick in body.
Rousard.　　　　　　　　　　Sick indeed.
　　A gen'ral weakness did surprise my health
　　The very day I marry'd Castabella,
　　As if my sickness were a punishment,
　　That did arrest me for some injury
　　I then committed. Credit me (my love)
　　I pity thy ill fortune to be match'd
　　With such a weak unpleasing bedfellow.
Castabella. Believe me sir; it never troubles me.　　　70
　　I am as much respectless to enjoy
　　Such pleasure as ignorant what it is.
Charlemont. Thy sex's wonder. Unhappy Charlemont.
D'Amville. Come, let's to supper. There we will confirm
　　The eternal bond of our concluded love.　　　　*Exeunt.*

ACTUS QUARTI SCENA PRIMA

Enter Cataplasma *and* Soquette *with needlework.*

Cataplasma. Come Soquette; your work! let's examine your work. What's
　　here? A medlar with a plum-tree growing hard by it; the leaves o' the
　　plum-tree falling off; the gum issuing out o' the perish'd joints; and the
　　branches some of 'em dead, and some rotten; and yet but a young plum-
　　tree. In good sooth, very pretty.
Soquette. The plum-tree (forsooth) grows so near the medlar, that the medlar
　　sucks and draws all the sap from it, and the natural strength o' the ground,
　　so that it cannot prosper.
Cataplasma. How conceited you are! But here th'ast made a tree to bear no
　　fruit. Why's that?　　　　　　　　　　　　　　　　　　　10
Soquette. There grows a savin-tree next it, forsooth.
Cataplasma. Forsooth you are a little too witty in that.

Enter Sebastian.

59 indenture] formal bond　　71 respectless] careless, indifferent　　IV. i, 2 medlar . . .
plum-tree] both used as sexual symbols: the entire scene is riddled with half-hidden
sexual references　　9 conceited] fanciful　　11 savin] The juice of the savin berry
(*Juniperus Sabina*) was frequently used to induce abortions.

Sebastian. But this honeysuckle winds about this whitethorn very prettily and lovingly. Sweet Mistress Cataplasma!

Cataplasma. Monsieur Sebastian! in good sooth very uprightly welcome this evening.

Sebastian. What? moralizing upon this gentlewoman's needlework? let's see.

Cataplasma. No sir. Only examining whether it be done to the true nature and life o' the thing.

Sebastian. Here y'have set a medlar with a bachelor's-button o' one side, and a snail o' th' t'other. The bachelor's-button should have held his head up more pertly towards the medlar; the snail o' th' t'other side should ha' been wrought with an artificial laziness, doubling his tail, and putting out his horn but half the length; and then the medlar falling (as it were) from the lazy snail, and inclining towards the pert bachelor's-button; their branches spreading and winding one within another as if they did embrace. But here's a moral. A poppring pear-tree growing upon the bank of a river, seeming continually to look downwards into the water, as if it were enamour'd of it, and ever as the fruit ripens, lets it fall for love (as it were) into her lap; which the wanton stream, like a strumpet, no sooner receives, but she carries it away, and bestows it upon some other creature she maintains, still seeming to play and dally under the poppring, so long that it has almost wash'd away the earth from the root; and now the poor tree stands as if it were ready to fall and perish by that whereon it spent all the substance it had. 35

Cataplasma. Moral for you that love those wanton running waters.

Sebastian. But is not my lady Levidulcia come yet?

Cataplasma. Her purpose promis'd us her company ere this. *Lirie*! your lute and your book.

Sebastian. Well said. A lesson o' th' lute to entertain the time with till she comes. 41

Cataplasma. Sol, fa, mi, la.—Mi, mi, mi.—Precious! Dost not see *mi* between the two crotchets? Strike me full there.—So—forward.— This is a sweet strain, and thou finger'st it beastly. *Mi* is a large there; and the prick that stands before *mi*, a long; always half your note.—— Now—run your division pleasingly with those quavers. Observe all your graces i' the touch.—Here's a sweet close—strike it full, it sets off your music delicately.

---

20 bachelor's button] *chrysanthemum parthenium* or feverfew; this and the snail were symbols of sexual potency   27 poppring] Poperinghe, the town in Flanders whose pear was held to resemble the phallus   38 *Lirie*!] Unexplained.   42–8] A sexual *double entente* runs through the whole of this speech.   44 large] the longest written musical note, equivalent to four breves   45 prick] the dot increasing the length of the note by half   45 long] note twice the length of a breve (the syntax is obscure here: 'a long' possibly should be 'along', i.e., alongside)

Enter Languebeau Snuffe *and* Levidulcia.

Languebeau. Purity be in this house.

Cataplasma. 'Tis now enter'd; and welcome with your good Ladyship.

Sebastian. Cease that music. Here's a sweeter instrument.   51

                                                 [Goes to embrace her.]

Levidulcia. Restrain your liberty. See you not Snuffe?

Sebastian. What does the stinkard here? Put Snuffe out. He's offensive.

Levidulcia. No. The credit of his company defends my being abroad from the eye of suspicion.

Cataplasma. Will 't please your Ladyship go up into the closet? There are those falls and tires I told you of.

Levidulcia. Monsieur Snuffe, I shall request your patience. My stay will not be long.   *Exit cum* Sebast.

Languebeau. My duty Madam.—Falls and tires? I begin to suspect what falls and tires you mean. My Lady and Sebastian the fall and the tire, and I the shadow. I perceive the purity of my conversation is us'd but for a property to cover the uncleanness of their purposes. The very contemplation o' the thing makes the spirit of the flesh begin to wriggle in my blood. And here my desire has met with an object already. This gentlewoman (me thinks) should be swayed with the motion, living in a house where moving example is so common. Temptation has prevail'd over me; and I will attempt to make it overcome her.—Mistress Cataplasma! My Lady (it seems) has some business that requires her stay. The fairness o' the evening invites me into the air; will it please you give this gentlewoman leave to leave her work, and walk a turn or two with me for honest recreation?   72

Cataplasma. With all my heart sir. Go Soquette; give ear to his instructions; you may get understanding by his company I can tell you.

Languebeau. In the way of holiness, Mistress Cataplasma.

Cataplasma. Good Monsieur Snuffe!—I will attend your return.

Languebeau. Your hand, gentlewoman.—

    [Aside] The flesh is humble till the spirit move it;

    But when 'tis rais'd it will command above it.   *Exeunt.*

[SCENE II]

Enter D'Amville, Charlemont, *and* Borachio.

D'Amville. Your sadness and the sickness of my son

    Have made our company and conference

    Less free and pleasing than I purpos'd it.

---

57 falls and tires] women's headgear

Charlemont. Sir; for the present I am much unfit
  For conversation or society.
  With pardon I will rudely take my leave.
D'Amville. Good night, dear Nephew.—   *Exit* Charlemont.
                                  Seest thou that same man?
Borachio. Your meaning sir?
D'Amville.   That fellow's life, Borachio,
  Like a superfluous letter in the law,
  Endangers our assurance.
Borachio.   Scrape him out.   10
D'Amville. Wu't do't?
Borachio.   Give me your purpose, I will do't.
D'Amville. Sad melancholy has drawn Charlemont,
  With meditation on his father's death,
  Into the solitary walk behind the church.
Borachio. The churchyard? This the fittest place for death.
  Perhaps he's praying. Then he's fit to die.
  We'll send him charitably to his grave.
D'Amville. No matter how thou tak'st him. First take this.—   *Pistol.*
  Thou knowest the place. Observe his passages;
  And with the most advantage make a stand,   20
  That favour'd by the darkness of the night,
  His breast may fall upon thee at so near
  A distance, that he sha' not shun the blow.
  The deed once done, thou may'st retire with safety.
  The place is unfrequented; and his death
  Will be imputed to th' attempt of thieves.
Borachio. Be careless. Let your mind be free and clear.
  This pistol shall discharge you of your fear.   *Exit.*
D'Amville. But let me call my projects to accompt,
  For what effect and end I have engag'd   30
  My self in all this blood: to leave a state
  To the succession of my proper blood.
  But how shall that succession be continu'd?
  Not in my elder son, I fear. Disease
  And weakness have disabled him for issue.
  For th' t'other, his loose humour will endure
  No bond of marriage. And I doubt his life;
  His spirit is so boldly dangerous.
  O pity that the profitable end
  Of such a prosp'rous murther should be lost!   40

9 superfluous . . . law] an error of one letter might nullify a deed   18 *Pistol*] a stage
direction   27 Be careless] have no care   31 state] estate

Nature forbid. I hope I have a body,
That will not suffer me to lose my labour
For want of issue yet. But then 't must be
A bastard.—Tush; they only father bastards,
That father other men's begettings. Daughter!
Be it mine own, let it come whence it will.
I am resolv'd.
Daughter!

Enter Servant.

Servant.   My Lord.
D'Amville.   I prithee call my daughter.

Enter Castabella.

Castabella. Your pleasure sir?
D'Amville. Is thy husband i' bed?   50
Castabella. Yes my Lord.
D'Amville. The evening's fair. I prithee walk a turn or two.
Castabella. Come, Jaspar.
D'Amville. No.
   We'll walk but to the corner o' the church;
   And I have something to speak privately.
Castabella. No matter, stay.   *Exit* Servant
D'Amville.   This falls out happily.   *Exeunt.*

[SCENE III]

Enter Charlemont, Borachio *dogging him in the Churchyard. The clock
strikes twelve.*

Charlemont. Twelve.
Borachio. [*Aside*]   'Tis a good hour, 'twill strike one anon.
Charlemont. How fit a place for contemplation is this dead of night, among
   the dwellings of the dead.—This grave.—Perhaps th'inhabitant was
   in his lifetime the possessor of his own desires. Yet in the midst of all
   his greatness and his wealth, he was less rich and less contented than in
   this poor piece of earth, lower and lesser than a cottage. For here he neither
   wants nor cares.
   Now that his body savours of corruption,
   He enjoys a sweeter rest than e'er he did
   Amongst the sweetest pleasures of this life.   10

IV. iii, 2–7 There are signs of verse in this speech, but it is impossible to arrange it all
satisfactorily as verse.

For here, there's nothing troubles him.—And there.—
In that grave lies another. He (perhaps)
Was in his life as full of misery
As this of happiness. And here's an end
Of both. Now both their states are equal. O
That man with so much labour should aspire
To worldly height, when in the humble earth,
The world's condition's at the best! Or scorn
Inferior men; since to be lower than
A worm is to be higher than a king!   20

Borachio. Then fall and rise.   *Discharges.—Gives false fire.*
Charlemont.   What villain's hand was that?
Save thee or thou shalt perish.   *They fight.*
Borachio.   Zownes, unsav'd
I think.   *Fall.*
Charlemont. What? Have I kill'd him? Whatsoe'er thou beest
I would thy hand had prosper'd. For I was
Unfit to live, and well prepar'd to die.
What shall I do? Accuse my self. Submit
Me to the law, and that will quickly end
This violent increase of misery.
But 'tis a murther to be accessory
To mine own death. I will not. I will take   30
This opportunity to 'scape. It may
Be Heav'n reserves me to some better end.   *Exit* Charlemont.

Enter [Languebeau] Snuffe *and* Soquette *into the Churchyard.*

Soquette. Nay good sir; I dare not. In good sooth I come of a generation
   both by Father and Mother, that were all as fruitful as costard-mongers'
   wives.
Languebeau. Tush then, a tympany is the greatest danger can be fear'd.
   Their fruitfulness turns but to a certain kind of phlegmatic windy disease.
Soquette. I must put my understanding to your trust sir. I would be loth
   to be deceiv'd.
Languebeau. No, conceive thou sha't not. Yet thou shalt profit by my
   instruction too. My body is not every day drawn dry, wench.   41
Soquette. Yet me thinks sir, your want of use should rather make your
   body like a well; the lesser 'tis drawn, the sooner it grows dry.
Languebeau. Thou shalt try that instantly.
Soquette. But we want place and opportunity.
Languebeau. We have both. This is the back side of the house which the

36 tympany] a swelling or tumour

superstitious call Saint Winifred's Church; and is verily a convenient
unfrequented place,—
   Where under the close curtains of the night——
Soquette. You purpose i' the dark to make me light.   50
                    [Languebeau] *pulls out a sheet, a hair, and a beard.*
But what ha' you there?
Languebeau. This disguise is for security sake, wench. There's a talk, thou
   know'st, that the ghost of old Montferrers walks. In this church he was
   buried. Now if any stranger fall upon us before our business be ended,
   in this disguise I shall be taken for that ghost, and never be call'd to
   examination I warrant thee. Thus we shall 'scape both prevention and
   discovery. How do I look in this habit, wench?
Soquette. So like a ghost, that notwithstanding I have some fore-knowledge
   of you, you make my hair stand almost on end.
Languebeau. I will try how I can kiss in this beard.—O fie, fie, fie. I will put
   it off; and then kiss; and then put it on. I can do the rest without kissing.

Enter Charlemont *doubtfully with his sword drawn, is upon them before
they are aware. They run out divers ways, and leave the disguise.*

Charlemont. What ha' we here? a sheet? a hair? a beard?   62
   What end was this disguise intended for?
   No matter what. I'll not expostulate
   The purpose of a friendly accident.
   Perhaps it may accommodate my 'scape.—
   I fear I am pursu'd. For more assurance,
   I'll hide me here i' th' charnel house,
   This convocation-house of dead men's skulls.—
                    *To get into the charnel house, he takes hold of a
                    death's head; it slips and staggers him.*
   Death's head! deceiv'st my hold?   70
   Such is the trust to all mortality.   *Hides himself in the charnel house.*

Enter D'Amville *and* Castabella.

Castabella. My Lord! The night grows late. Your Lordship spake
   Of something you desir'd to move in private.
D'Amville. Yes. Now I'll speak it. Th' argument is love.
   The smallest ornament of thy sweet form
   (That abstract of all pleasure) can command
   The senses into passion; and thy entire
   Perfection is my object; yet I love
   Thee with the freedom of my reason. I
   Can give thee reason for my love.

50 light] wanton   51 s.d. *hair*] wig

Castabella.   Love me,   80
    My Lord? I do believe it, for I am
    The wife of him you love.
D'Amville.   'Tis true. By my
    Persuasion thou wert forc'd to marry one,
    Unable to perform the office of
    A husband. I was author of the wrong.
    My conscience suffers under't; and I would
    Disburthen it by satisfaction.
Castabella.   How?
D'Amville. I will supply that pleasure to thee which
    He cannot.
Castabella.   Are y' a devil or a man?
D'Amville. A man; and such a man, as can return   90
    Thy entertainment with as prodigal
    A body, as the covetous desire
    Of woman ever was delighted with.
    So, that besides the full performance of
    Thy empty husband's duty, thou shalt have
    The joy of children to continue the
    Succession of thy blood. For the appetite
    That steals her pleasure draws the forces of
    The body to an united strength; and puts
    'Em altogether into action;   100
    Never fails of procreation.
    All the purposes
    Of man aim but at one of these two ends,
    Pleasure or profit: and in this one sweet
    Conjunction of our loves, they both will meet.
    Would it
    Not grieve thee, that a stranger to thy blood
    Should lay the first foundation of his house
    Upon the ruins of thy family?
Castabella. Now Heav'n defend me! May my memory   110
    Be utterly extinguish'd; and the heir
    Of him that was my father's enemy
    Raise his eternal monument upon
    Our ruins, ere the greatest pleasure or
    The greatest profit ever tempt me to
    Continue it by incest.
D'Amville.   Incest? Tush.
    These distances affinity observes
    Are articles of bondage cast upon

Our freedoms by our own subjections.
Nature allows a gen'ral liberty   120
Of generation to all creatures else.
Shall man to whose command and use
All creatures were made subject be less free
Than they?
Castabella.   O God! is thy unlimited
And infinite omnipotence less free
Because thou dost no ill? Or if
You argue merely out of Nature, do
You not degenerate from that, and are
You not unworthy the prerogative
Of Nature's masterpiece, when basely you   130
Prescribe your self authority and law
From their examples whom you should command?
I could confute you; but the horror of
The argument confounds my understanding.—
Sir, I know
You do but try me in your son's behalf;
Suspecting that my strength and youth of blood
Cannot contain themselves with impotence.—
Believe me (sir)
I never wrong'd him. If it be your lust,   140
O quench it on their prostituted flesh,
Whose trade of sin can please desire with more
Delight, and less offence.—
The poison of your breath,
Evaporated from so foul a soul,
Infects the air more than the damps that rise
From bodies but half rotten in their graves.
D'Amville. Kiss me. I warrant thee my breath is sweet.
These dead men's bones lie here of purpose to
Invite us to supply the number of   150
The living. Come; we'll get young bones and do't.
I will enjoy thee. No? Nay then invoke
Your great suppos'd protector; I will do't.
Castabella. Suppos'd protector? Are y' an atheist? Then,
I know my prayers and tears are spent in vain.
O patient Heav'n! Why dost thou not express
Thy wrath in thunderbolts, to tear the frame
Of man in pieces? How can earth endure
The burden of this wickedness without

150 supply] make up   151 get] beget

An earthquake? Or the angry face of Heav'n   160
Be not enflam'd with lightning?
D'Amville.   Conjure up
The Devil and his dam; cry to the graves;
The dead can hear thee; invocate their help.
Castabella. O would this grave might open, and my body
Were bound to the dead carcass of a man
For ever, ere it entertain the lust
Of this detested villain.
D'Amville.   Tereus-like,
Thus will I force my passage to——
Charlemont.   The Devil.

Charlemont *rises in the disguise and frights* D'Amville *away.*

Now Lady! with the hand of Charlemont,
I thus redeem you from the arm of lust.—   170
My Castabella!
Castabella.   My dear Charlemont!
Charlemont. For all my wrongs I thank thee gracious Heav'n;
Th'ast made me satisfaction to reserve
Me for this blessed purpose. Now sweet Death,
I'll bid thee welcome. Come. I'll guard thee home;
And then I'll cast my self into the arms
Of apprehension, that the law may make
This worthy work the crown of all my actions,
Being the best and last.
Castabella.   The last? The law?
Now Heav'n forbid! what ha' you done?
Charlemont.   Why, I have kill'd   180
A man; not murder'd him, my Castabella;
He would ha' murder'd me.
Castabella.   Then Charlemont,
The hand of Heav'n directed thy defence.
That wicked atheist, I suspect his plot.
Charlemont. My life he seeks. I would he had it since
He has depriv'd me of those blessings that
Should make me love it. Come; I'll give it him.
Castabella. You sha' not. I will first expose my self
To certain danger, than for my defence
Destroy the man that sav'd me from destruction.   190

167 Tereus] the ravisher of Philomela   177 apprehension] arrest

Charlemont. Thou canst not satisfy me better, than
    To be the instrument of my release
    From misery.
Castabella.   Then work it by escape.
    Leave me to this protection that still guards
    The innocent; or I
    Will be a partner in your destiny.
Charlemont. My soul is heavy. Come; lie down to rest;
    These are the pillows whereon men sleep best.

> *They lie down with either of them a death's head for a pillow.*

Enter [Languebeau] Snuffe *seeking* Soquette.

Languebeau. Soquette! Soquette! Soquette! O art thou there?—
                He mistakes the body of Borachio *for* Soquette.
Verily thou liest in a fine premeditate readiness for the purpose. Come kiss
me sweet Soquette.—Now purity defend me from the sin of Sodom.—
This is a creature of the masculine gender.—Verily the man is blasted.—
Yea? cold and stiff?—Murder, murder, murder.   *Exit.*

Enter D'Amville *distractedly; starts at the sight of a death's head.*

D'Amville. Why dost thou stare upon me? Thou art not   204
    The skull of him I murder'd. What has thou
    To do to vex my conscience? Sure thou wert
    The head of a most dogged usurer,
    Th'art so uncharitable. And that bawd,
    The sky, there; she could shut the windows and
    The doors of this great chamber of the world;   210
    And draw the curtains of the clouds between
    Those lights and me about this bed of earth,
    When that same strumpet murder & my self
    Committed sin together. Then she could
    Leave us i' the dark, till the close deed was done:
    But now, that I begin
    To feel the loathsome horror of my sin;
    And (like a lecher empty'd of his lust)
desire to bury my face under my eyebrows, and would steal from my shame
unseen; she meets me i' the face with all her light corrupted eyes,
    To challenge payment o' me.—O behold!   221
    Yonder's the ghost of old Montferrers in
    A long white sheet, climbing yond' lofty mountain
    To complain to Heav'n of me.—Montferrers!

212 Those lights] i.e., the stars; cf. l. 220

'Pox o' fearfulness. 'Tis nothing but
A fair white cloud. Why, was I born a coward?
He lies that says so. Yet the count'nance of
A bloodless worm might ha' the courage now
To turn my blood to water.
The trembling motion of an aspen leaf   230
Would make me like the shadow of that leaf,
Lie shaking under 't. I could now commit
A murder, were it but to drink the fresh
Warm blood of him I murder'd; to supply
The want and weakness o' mine own; 'tis grown
So cold and phlegmatic.
Languebeau. Murder, murder, murder.   *Within.*
D'Amville. Mountains o'erwhelm me, the ghost of old Montferrers haunts me.
Languebeau. Murder, murder, murder.
D'Amville. O were my body circumvolv'd   240
Within that cloud; that when the thunder tears
His passage open, it might scatter me
To nothing in the air!

Enter Languebeau Snuffe *with the* Watch.

Languebeau.   Here you shall find
The murder'd body.
D'Amville.   Black Beelzebub.
And all his hell-hounds come to apprehend me?
Languebeau. No my good Lord. We come to apprehend
The murderer.
D'Amville.   The ghost (great Pluto) was
A fool; unfit to be employ'd
In any serious business for the state
Of hell. Why, could not he ha' suffer'd me   250
To raise the mountain o' my sins with one
As damnable as all the rest; and then
Ha' tumbled me to ruin? But apprehend
Me e'en between the purpose and the act,
Before it was committed!
Watch. Is this the murderer? He speaks suspiciously.
Languebeau. No verily. This is my Lord D'Amville. And his distraction (I
think) grows out of his grief for the loss of a faithful servant. For surely
I take him to be Borachio that is slain.
D'Amville. Haah! Borachio slain? Thou look'st like Snuffe, dost not?   260
Languebeau. Yes in sincerity my Lord.
D'Amville. Hark thee!—Sawest thou not a ghost?

Languebeau. A ghost? Where, my Lord?—I smell a fox.

D'Amville. Here i' the churchyard.

Languebeau. Tush, tush; their walking spirits are mere imaginary fables. There's no such thing in *rerum natura*. Here is a man slain. And with the spirit of consideration, I rather think him to be the murderer got into that disguise, than any such fantastic toy.

D'Amville. My brains begin to put themselves in order. I apprehend thee now.—'Tis e'en so.—Borachio! I will search the centre but I'll find the murderer.   271

Watch. Here, here, here.—

D'Amville. Stay. Asleep? so soundly? and so sweetly upon death's heads? and in a place so full of fear and horror? Sure there is some other happiness within the freedom of the conscience, than my knowledge e'er attain'd to.—Ho, ho, ho!

Charlemont. Y'are welcome Uncle. Had you sooner come,
    You had been sooner welcome. I'm the man
    You seek. You sha' not need examine me.

D'Amville. My Nephew! and my daughter! O my dear   280
    Lamented blood! what fate has cast you thus
    Unhappily upon this accident?

Charlemont. You know sir, she's as clear as chastity.

D'Amville. As her own chastity. The time, the place,
    All circumstances argue that unclear.

Castabella. Sir, I confess it; and repentantly
    Will undergo the selfsame punishment,
    That justice shall inflict on Charlemont.

Charlemont. Unjustly she betrays her innocence.

Watch. But sir, she's taken with you; and she must   290
    To prison with you.

D'Amville.   There's no remedy.
    Yet were it not my son's bed she abus'd,
    My land should fly but both should be excus'd.   *Exeunt.*

[SCENE IV]

Enter Belforest *and a* Servant.

Belforest. Is not my wife come in yet?

Servant.   No my Lord.

Belforest. Me thinks she's very affectedly inclin'd,
    To young Sebastian's company o' late.

266 *rerum natura*] Ribner suggests an allusion to Lucretius, 'regarded by Tourneur's contemporaries as a virtual handbook of atheism'.   270 centre] i.e., of the earth

But jealousy is such a torment, that
I am afraid to entertain it. Yet
The more I shun by circumstance to meet
Directly with it, the more ground I find
To circumvent my apprehension. First,
I know sh'as a perpetual appetite;
Which being so oft encounter'd with a man   10
Of such a bold luxurious freedom as
Sebastian is; and of so promising
A body: her own blood, corrupted, will
Betray her to temptation.——

Enter Fresco *closely.*

Fresco. [*Aside*] 'Precious! I was sent by his lady to see if her lord were in
bed; I should ha' done't slily without discovery; and now I am blurted
upon 'em before I was aware.   *Exit.*

Belforest. Know not you the gentlewoman my wife brought home?

Servant. By sight my Lord. Her man was here but now.

Belforest. Her man? I prithee run and call him quickly. [*Exit* Servant.]—
This villain, I suspect him ever since I found him hid behind the tapestry.—

Enter Fresco *and* Servant.

Fresco! th'art welcome Fresco.—Leave us. [*Exit* Servant.] Dost hear
Fresco? is not my wife at thy mistress's?   23

Fresco. I know not my Lord.

Belforest. I prithee tell me Fresco; we are private; tell me. Is not thy mistress
a good wench?

Fresco. How means your Lordship that? A wench o' the trade?

Belforest. Yes faith, Fresco; e'en a wench o' the trade.

Fresco. O no my Lord. Those falling diseases cause baldness, and my mistress recovers the loss of hair, for she is a periwig-maker.   30

Belforest. And nothing else?

Fresco. Sells falls and tires, and bodies for ladies; or so.

Belforest. So sir: and she helps my Lady to falls and bodies now and then;
does she not?

Fresco. At her Ladyship's pleasure; my Lord.

Belforest. Her pleasure, you rogue? You are the pandar to her pleasure,
you varlet, are you not? You know the conveyances between Sebastian
and my wife. Tell me the truth; or by this hand I'll nail thy bosom to
the earth. Stir not, you dog; but quickly tell the truth.

6 by circumstance] by being indirect   11 luxurious] lecherous   14 s.d. *closely*] trying
to avoid being seen   29 falling diseases] epilepsy, but also those caused by lying down,
i.e., chiefly syphilis, believed to cause baldness   32 bodies] bodices, with an obvious
quibble

Fresco. O yes!   *—Speak like a crier.*
Belforest. Is not thy mistress a bawd to my wife?   41
Fresco. O yes!
Belforest. And acquainted with her tricks, and her plots, and her devises?
Fresco. O yes! If any man, 'court, city or country, has found my lady
  Levidulcia in bed, but my lord Belforest, it is Sebastian.
Belforest. What, dost thou proclaim it? Dost thou cry it, thou villain?
Fresco. Can you laugh it, my Lord? I thought you meant to proclaim your
  self cuckold.

Enter the Watch.

Belforest. The Watch! Met with my wish. I must request th' assistance
  of your offices.   *Fresco runs away.*
  'Sdeath; stay that villain; pursue him.   *Exeunt.*

[SCENE V]

Enter [Languebeau] Snuffe *importuning* Soquette.

Soquette. Nay, if you get me any more into the churchyard——
Languebeau. Why, Soquette, I never got thee there yet.
Soquette. Got me there? No. Not with child.
Languebeau. I promis'd thee I would not; and I was as good as my word.
Soquette. Yet your word was better than your deed. But, steal up into the
  little matted chamber o' the left hand.
Languebeau. I prithee let it be the right hand; thou left'st me before and I
  did not like that.
Soquette. 'Precious quickly; so soon as my mistress shall be in bed I'll
  come to you.   *Exit Snuffe.*

Enter Sebastian, Levidulcia *and* Cataplasma.

Cataplasma. I wonder Fresco stays so long.   11
Sebastian. Mistress Soquette, a word with you.   *—Whisper.*
Levidulcia. If he brings word my husband is i' bed,
          I will adventure one night's liberty
          To lie abroad.—
          My strange affection to this man!—'Tis like
          That natural sympathy which e'en among
          The senseless creatures of the earth commands
          A mutual inclination and consent;
          For though it seems to be the free effect   20
          Of mine own voluntary love; yet I
          Can neither restrain it, nor give reason for't.

40 O yes!] Fresco imitates a town crier.

But now 'tis done; and in your power it lies
To save my honour; or dishonour me.
Cataplasma. Enjoy your pleasure (Madam) without fear.
I never will betray the trust you have
Committed to me. And you wrong your self,
To let consideration of the sin
Molest your conscience. Me thinks 'tis unjust,
That a reproach should be inflicted on   30
A woman for offending but with one;
When 'tis a light offence in husbands to
Commit with many.
Levidulcia.   So it seems to me.—
Why how now Sebastian? making love to that gentlewoman? how many
mistresses ha' you i' faith?
Sebastian. In faith none. For I think none of 'em are faithful, but otherwise,
as many as clean shirts. The love of a woman is like a mushroom; it
grows in one night, and will serve somewhat pleasingly, next morning to
breakfast: but afterwards waxes fulsome and unwholesome.
Cataplasma. Nay by Saint Winifred; a woman's love lasts as long as winter
fruit.   41
Sebastian. 'Tis true. Till new come in. By my experience no longer.

Enter Fresco *running.*

Fresco. Some body's doing has undone us; and we are like pay dearly for't.
Sebastian. Pay dear? for what?
Fresco. Will't not be a chargeable reckoning, think you, when here are half
a dozen fellows coming to call us to accompt, with ev'ry man a several
bill in his hand, that we are not able to discharge?
                                                —*Knock at the door.*
Cataplasma. Passion o' me. What bouncing's that? Madam! withdraw your
self.
Levidulcia. Sebastian if you love me, save my honour.   —*Exeunt.*

[*Manet* Sebastian.]

Sebastian. What violence is this? What seek you? Zownes! you shall not pass.

Enter Belforest *and the* Watch.

Belforest. Pursue the strumpet. Villain, give me way;   52
Or I will make my passage through thy blood.
Sebastian. My blood will make it slippery, my Lord.
'Twere better you would take another way.
You may hap fall else.
                    They fight. Both slain. Sebastian *falls first.*
          I ha't i' faith.   —*Dies.*

While Belforest *is staggering, enter* Levidulcia.

Levidulcia. O God! my husband! my Sebastian! husband!
    Neither can speak; yet both report my shame.
    Is this the saving of my honour? when
    Their blood runs out in rivers; and my lust   60
    The fountain whence it flows? Dear husband! let
    Not thy departed spirit be displeas'd,
    If with adult'rate lips I kiss thy cheek.
    Here I behold the hatefulness of lust,
    Which brings me kneeling to embrace him dead,
    Whose body living I did loathe to touch.
    Now I can weep. But what can tears do good,
    When I weep only water, they weep blood?
    But could I make an ocean with my tears,
    That on the flood this broken vessel of   70
    My body, laden heavy with light lust
    Might suffer shipwrack, and so drown my shame:
    Then weeping were to purpose; but alas!
    The sea wants water enough to wash away
    The foulness of my name. O! in their wounds,
    I feel my honour wounded to the death.
    Shall I outlive my honour? Must my life
    Be made the world's example? Since it must,
    Then thus in detestation of my deed,
    To make th' example move more forceably   80
    To virtue, thus I seal it with a death
    As full of horror as my life of sin.   *—Stabs herself.*

Enter the Watch *with* Cataplasma, Fresco, [Languebeau] Snuffe, *and*
Soquette.

Watch. Hold Madam! Lord, what a strange night is this.
Languebeau. May not Snuffe be suffer'd to go out of himself?
Watch. Nor you; nor any. All must go with us.
    O with what virtue lust should be withstood,
    Since 'tis a fire quench'd seldom without blood.   *Exeunt.*

ACTUS QUINTI SCENA PRIMA

Music. A closet discover'd. A Servant *sleeping with lights and money before him.*

Enter D'Amville.

D'Amville. What, sleep'st thou?
Servant.   No my Lord. Nor sleep; nor wake:
    But in a slumber troublesome to both.
D'Amville. Whence comes this gold?
Servant.   'Tis part of the revenue,
    Due to your Lordship since your brother's death.
D'Amville. To bed. Leave me my gold.
Servant.   And me my rest:
    Two things wherewith one man is seldom blest.   *Exit.*
D'Amville. Cease that harsh music. W'are not pleas'd with it.
                                        He handles the gold.
    Here sounds a music whose melodious touch,
    Like angels' voices ravishes the sense.
    Behold thou ignorant astronomer,   10
    Whose wand'ring speculation seeks among
    The planets for men's fortunes! with amazement,
    Behold thine error and be planet-struck.
    These are the stars whose operations make
    The fortunes and the destinies of men.
    Yond' lesser eyes of Heav'n, (like subjects rais'd
    Into their lofty houses, when their prince
    Rides underneath th'ambition of their loves)
    Are mounted only to behold the face
    Of your more rich imperious eminence,   20
    With unprevented sight. Unmask fair queen;   *Unpurses the gold.*
    Vouchsafe their expectations may enjoy
    The gracious favour they admire to see.
    These are the stars, the ministers of Fate;
    And man's high wisdom the superior power,
    To which their forces are subordinate.   *—Sleeps.*

Enter the Ghost of Montferrers.

16–18] the subjects watch the prince ride by from the upper storeys of their houses
18 ambition] ostentation   21 unprevented] unimpeded   22–3] Vouchsafe that their
expectations may be fulfilled by enjoying the favour they wonder at

Montferrers. D'Amville! With all thy wisdom th'art a fool.
  Not like those fools that we term innocents;
  But a most wretched miserable fool:
  Which instantly, to the confusion of   30
  Thy projects, with despair thou shalt behold.   *Exit Ghost.*
                                         D'Amville *starts up.*
D'Amville. What foolish dream dares interrupt my rest,
  To my confusion? How can that be, since
  My purposes have hitherto been borne
  With prosp'rous judgment to secure success?
  Which nothing lives to dispossess me of,
  But apprehended Charlemont. And him
  This brain has made the happy instrument
  To free suspicion; to annihilate
  All interest and title of his own;   40
  To seal up my assurance; and confirm
  My absolute possession by the law.
  Thus while the simple honest worshipper
  Of a fantastic providence groans under
  The burthen of neglected misery,
  My real wisdom has rais'd up a state,
  That shall eternize my posterity.

  Enter Servants *with the body of* Sebastian.

  What's that?
Servant.   The body of your younger son
  Slain by the lord Belforest.
D'Amville.   Slain? you lie.—
  Sebastian. Speak, Sebastian! H'as lost   50
  His hearing. A physician presently!
  Go call a surgeon.
Rousard.   Ooh.   —*Within.*
D'Amville.   What groan was that?
  How does my elder son? the sound came from
  His chamber.
Servant.   He went sick to bed my Lord.
Rousard. Ooh.   —*Within.*
D'Amville. The cries of mandrakes never touch'd the ear,
  With more sad horror than that voice does mine.

  Enter a Servant *running.*

56 mandrakes] These plants were thought to shriek when pulled from the ground (a
recurrent image in Elizabethan poetry).

Servant. If ever you will see your son alive——
D'Amville. Nature forbid I e'er should see him dead.

 A bed drawn forth with Rousard.

  Withdraw the curtains. O how does my son?   60
Servant. Me thinks, he's ready to give up the ghost.
D'Amville. Destruction take thee and thy fatal tongue.
  Death, where's the doctor?—Art not thou the face
  Of that prodigious apparition stared upon
  Me in my dream?
Servant.   The doctor's come, my Lord.

 Enter Doctor.

D'Amville. Doctor! Behold two patients, in whose cure
  Thy skill may purchase an eternal fame.
  If thou hast any reading in Hippocrates,
  Galen, or Avicen; if herbs, or drugs,
  Or minerals have any power to save;   70
  Now let thy practice and their sovereign use
  Raise thee to wealth and honour.
Doctor. If any root of life remains within 'em capable of physic, fear' em not,
 my Lord.
Rousard. Ooh.
D'Amville. His gasping sighs are like the falling noise
  Of some great building when the groundwork breaks.
  On these two pillars stood the stately frame,
  And architecture of my lofty house.
  An earthquake shakes 'em. The foundation shrinks. 80
  Dear Nature! in whose honour I have rais'd
  A work of glory to posterity;
  O bury not the pride of that great action,
  Under the fall and ruin of it self.
Doctor. My Lord. These bodies are depriv'd of all
  The radical ability of Nature.
  The heat of life is utterly extinguish'd.
  Nothing remains within the power of man
  That can restore them.
D'Amville.   Take this gold; extract
  The spirit of it, and inspire new life   90
  Into their bodies.
Doctor.   Nothing can, my Lord.

68–9 Hippocrates, Galen, Avicen] the three medical authorities most highly regarded during
the Middle Ages

D'Amville. You ha' not yet examin'd the true state
         And constitution of their bodies. Sure,
         You ha' not. I'll reserve their waters till
         The morning. Questionless, their urines will
         Inform you better.
Doctor.   Ha, ha, ha.
D'Amville.   Dost laugh,
         Thou villain? must my wisdom that has been
         The object of men's admiration, now
         Become the subject of thy laughter?
Rousard.   Ooh.   —*Dies.*
All. He's dead.
D'Amville.   O there expires the date   100
         Of my posterity! Can Nature be
         So simple or malicious to destroy
         The reputation of her proper memory?
         She cannot. Sure there is some power above
         Her that controls her force.
Doctor.   A power above Nature?
         Doubt you that, my Lord? Consider but
         Whence man receives his body and his form.
         Not from corruption like some worms and flies;
         But only from the generation of
         A man. For Nature never did bring forth   110
         A man without a man; nor could the first
         Man, being but the passive subject not
         The active mover, be the maker of
         Himself; so of necessity there must
         Be a superior power to Nature.
D'Amville. Now to my self I am ridiculous.
         Nature thou are a traitor to my soul.
         Thou hast abus'd my trust. I will complain
         To a superior court, to right my wrong.
         I'll prove thee a forger of false assurances.   120
         In yond' Star Chamber thou shalt answer it.
         Withdraw the bodies. O the sense of death
         Begins to trouble my distracted soul.   *Exeunt.*

---

100 date] term of life   121 Star Chamber] the Tudor High Court, with an obvious play
on words

[SCENE II]

Enter Judges *and* Officers.

1. Judge. Bring forth the malefactors to the bar.

Enter Cataplasma, Soquette, *and* Fresco.

    Are you the gentlewoman in whose house
    The murders were committed?
Cataplasma.   Yes my Lord.
1. Judge. That worthy attribute of gentry, which
    Your habit draws from ignorant respect,
    Your name deserves not: nor your self the name
    Of woman, since you are the poison that
    Infects the honour of all womanhood.
Cataplasma. My Lord; I am a gentlewoman: yet
    I must confess my poverty compels   10
    My life to a condition lower than
    My birth or breeding.
2. Judge.   Tush, we know your birth.
1. Judge. But under colour to profess the sale
    Of tires and toys for gentlewomen's pride,
    You draw a frequentation of men's wives
    To your licentious house; and there abuse
    Their husbands.—
Fresco.   Good my Lord, her rent is great.
    The good gentlewoman has no other thing
    To live by but her lodgings: so, she's forc'd
    To let her fore-rooms out to others, and   20
    Her self contented to lie backwards.
2. Judge.   So.
1. Judge. Here is no evidence accuses you,
    For accessaries to the murder; yet
    Since from the spring of lust which you preserv'd,
    And nourish'd, ran th' effusion of that blood,
    Your punishment shall come as near to death,
    As life can bear it. Law cannot inflict
    Too much severity upon the cause
    Of such abhorr'd effects.
2. Judge.   Receive your sentence.
    Your goods (since they were gotten by that means,   30
    Which brings diseases;) shall be turn'd to th' use
    Of hospitals; you carted through the streets,

According to the common shame of strumpets,
Your bodies whipp'd till with the loss of blood,
You faint under the hand of punishment.
Then that the necessary force of want
May not provoke you to your former life,
You shall be set to painful labour; whose
Penurious gains shall only give you food
To hold up Nature; mortify your flesh;   40
And make you fit for a repentant end.
All. O good my Lord!
1. Judge.   No more; away with 'em.   *Exeunt.*

Enter Languebeau Snuffe.

2. Judge. Now Monsieur Snuffe! A man of your profession,
    Found in a place of such impiety?
Languebeau. I grant you the place is full of impurity. So much the more need
    of instruction and reformation. The purpose that carried me thither was
    with the spirit of conversion to purify their uncleanness; and I hope your
    Lordship will say, the law cannot take hold o' me for that.
1. Judge. No sir; it cannot: but yet give me leave
    To tell you, that I hold your wary answer,   50
    Rather premeditated for excuse,
    Than spoken out of a religious purpose.
    Where took you your degrees of scholarship?
Languebeau. I am no scholar my Lord. To speak the sincere truth, I am
    Snuffe the tallow-chandler.
2. Judge. How comes your habit to be alter'd thus?
Languebeau. My Lord Belforest, taking a delight in the cleanness of my
    conversation, withdrew me from that unclean life, and put me in a
    garment fit for his society and my present profession.
1. Judge. His Lordship did but paint a rotten post;   60
    Or cover foulness fairly. Monsieur Snuffe!
    Back to your candle-making. You may give
    The world more light with that, than either with
    Instruction or th'example of your life.
Languebeau. Thus the Snuffe is put out.   *Exit* Snuffe.

Enter D'Amville *distractedly with the hearses of his two sons borne after him.*

D'Amville. Judgment; judgment!
2. Judge.   Judgment my Lord? in what?
D'Amville. Your judgments must resolve me in a case.
    Bring in the bodies. Nay; I will ha't tried.
    This is the case my Lord. My providence,

Ev'n in a moment, by the only hurt   70
Of one, or two, or three at most—and those
Put quickly out o' pain too, mark me; I
Had wisely rais'd a competent estate
To my posterity. And is there not
More wisdom and more charity in that,
Than for your Lordship, or your father, or
Your grandsire, to prolong the torment, and
The rack of rent from age to age, upon
Your poor penurious tenants, yet (perhaps)
Without a penny profit to your heir?   80
Is't not more wise? more charitable? Speak.
1. Judge. He is distracted.
D'Amville.   How? distracted? Then
You ha' no judgment. I can give you sense
And solid reason for the very least
Distinguishable syllable I speak.
Since my thrift was more charitable, more judicious than your grandsire's;
why, I would fain know why your Lordship lives to make
A second generation from your father;
And the whole fry of my posterity
Extinguish'd in a moment: not a brat   90
Left to succeed me.—I would fain know that.
2. Judge. Grief for his children's death distempers him.
1. Judge. My Lord; we will resolve you of your question.
In the mean time vouchsafe your place with us.
D'Amville. I am contented, so you will resolve me.   *—Ascends.*

Enter Charlemont *and* Castabella.

2. Judge. Now Monsieur Charlemont. You are accus'd
Of having murder'd one Borachio, that
Was servant to my Lord D'Amville. How can
You clear your self? Guilty? or not guilty?
Charlemont. Guilty of killing him; but not of murder.   100
My Lords; I have no purpose to desire
Remission for my self.—   *D'Amville descends to* Charl.
D'Amville.   Uncivil boy!
Thou want'st humanity to smile at grief.
Why dost thou cast a cheerful eye upon
The object of my sorrow, my dead sons?

78 rack of rent] Rack-rent was a rent equal (or nearly) to the annual value of the land.

1. Judge. O good my Lord! Let charity forbear
    To vex the spirit of a dying man.
    A cheerful eye upon the face of death
    Is the true count'nance of a noble mind.
    For honour's sake (my Lord) molest it not.   110
D'Amville. Y'are all uncivil. O! is't not enough
    That he unjustly hath conspir'd with Fate,
    To cut off my posterity for him
    To be the heir of my possessions; but
    He must pursue me with his presence;
    And in the ostentation of his joy,
    Laugh in my face, and glory in my grief?
Charlemont. D'Amville! to show thee with what light respect
    I value death and thy insulting pride;
    Thus like a warlike navy on the sea,   120
    Bound for the conquest of some wealthy land,
    Pass'd through the stormy troubles of this life,
    And now arriv'd upon the armed coast,
    In expectation of the victory,
    Whose honour lies beyond this exigent,
    Through mortal danger with an active spirit,
    Thus I aspire to undergo my death.   *Leaps up the scaffold.*
                                           Castabella *leaps after him.*

Castabella. And thus I second thy brave enterprise.
    Be cheerful Charlemont. Our lives cut off
    In our young prime of years are like green herbs,   130
    Wherewith we strow the hearses of our friends.
    For as their virtue gather'd when th'are green,
    Before they wither or corrupt, is best;
    So we in virtue are the best for death,
    While yet we have not liv'd to such an age,
    That the increasing canker of our sins
    Hath spread too far upon us.—
D'Amville.   A boon, my Lords.
    I beg a boon.
1. Judge. What's that my Lord?
D'Amville.   His body when 'tis dead
    For an anatomy.
2. Judge.   For what my Lord?   140

---

125 exigent] extremity (i.e., death)   140 anatomy] dissection, but the word was used
colloquially for a skeleton, as perhaps at l. 149

D'Amville. Your understanding still comes short o' mine.
 I would find out by his anatomy,
 What thing there is in Nature more exact,
 Than in the constitution of my self.
 Me thinks my parts, and my dimensions, are
 As many, as large, as well compos'd as his;
 And yet in me the resolution wants,
 To die with that assurance as he does.
 The cause of that, in his anatomy
 I would find out.—

1. Judge.   Be patient and you shall.   150
D'Amville. I have bethought me of a better way.—
 Nephew; we must confer.—Sir; I am grown
 A wond'rous studient now o' late. My wit
 Has reach'd beyond the scope of Nature; yet
 For all my learning I am still to seek,
 From whence the peace of conscience should proceed.
Charlemont. The peace of conscience rises in it self.
D'Amville. Whether it be thy art or Nature, I
 Admire thee Charlemont. Why; thou hast taught
 A woman to be valiant. I will beg   160
 Thy life.—My Lords! I beg my nephew's life.—
 I'll make thee my physician. Thou shalt read
 Philosophy to me. I will find out
 Th' efficient cause of a contented mind.
 But if I cannot profit in't, then 'tis
 No more being my physician, but infuse
 A little poison in a potion when
 Thou giv'st me physic; unawares to me.
 So I shall steal into my grave without
 The understanding or the fear of death.   170
 And that's the end I aim at. For the thought
 Of death is a most fearful torment; is't not?
2. Judge. Your Lordship interrupts the course of law.
1. Judge. Prepare to die.
Charlemont.   My resolution's made.
 But ere I die; before this honour'd bench,
 With the free voice of a departing soul,
 I here protest this gentlewoman clear
 Of all offence the law condemns her for.

143 exact] perfect   147 wants] is lacking

Castabella. I have accus'd my self. The law wants power
    To clear me. My dear Charlemont; with thee   180
    I will partake of all thy punishments.
Charlemont. Uncle; for all the wealthy benefits
    My death advances you, grant me but this:
    Your mediation for the guiltless life
    Of Castabella; whom your conscience knows
    As justly clear as harmless innocence.
D'Amville. Freely. My mediation for her life;
    And all my int'rest in the world to boot,
    Let her but in exchange possess me of
    The resolution that she dies withal.—   190
    The price of things is best known in their want.
    Had I her courage, so I value it,
    The Indies should not buy 't out o' my hands.
Charlemont. Give me a glass of water.
D'Amville.   Me, of wine.—
    This argument of death congeals my blood.
    Cold fear, with apprehension of thy end,
    Hath frozen up the rivers of my veins.   —*A glass of wine.*
    I must drink wine to warm me, and dissolve
    The obstruction, or an apoplexy will
    Possess me.—Why, thou uncharitable knave;   200
    Dost bring me blood to drink? The very glass
    Looks pale and trembles at it.
Servant.   'Tis your hand
    My Lord.
D'Amville.   Canst blame me to be fearful, bearing
    Still the presence of a murderer
    About me?
Charlemont.   Is this water?
Servant.   Water sir.   —*A glass of water.*
Charlemont. Come thou clear emblem of cool temperance.
    Be thou my witness, that I use no art
    To force my courage; nor have need of helps,
    To raise my spirits like those weaker men,
    Who mix their blood with wine, and out of that   210
    Adulterate conjunction do beget
    A bastard valour. Native courage, thanks.
    Thou lead'st me soberly to undertake
    This great hard work of magnanimity.

203–4] An example of Tourneur's use of long rhythmical units which make suitable
lineation difficult; the ideal division rhythmically would be in the middle of 'bearing'.

D'Amville. Brave Charlemont! at the reflexion of
    Thy courage my cold fearful blood takes fire,
    And I begin to emulate thy death.—   [Executioner *comes forward.*]
    Is that thy executioner? My Lords;
    You wrong the honour of so high a blood,
    To let him suffer by so base a hand.   220
Judges. He suffers by the form of law my Lord.
D'Amville. I will reform it. Down, you shag-hair'd cur.
    The instrument that strikes my nephew's blood
    Shall be as noble as his blood. I'll be
    Thy executioner my self.
1. Judge. Restrain his fury. Good my Lord, forbear.
D'Amville. I'll butcher out the passage of his soul,
    That dares attempt to interrupt the blow.
2. Judge. My Lord; the office will impress a mark
    Of scandal and dishonour on your name.   230
Charlemont. The office fits him; hinder not his hand.
    But let him crown my resolution, with
    An unexampled dignity of death.
    Strike home. Thus I submit me.   —*Ready for execution.*
Castabella.   So do I.
    In scorn of death thus hand in hand we die.
D'Amville. I ha' the trick on't, Nephew. You shall see
    How eas'ly I can put you out of pain.—
    Ooh.   *As he raises up the axe, strikes out his own*
                     brains. Staggers off the scaffold.
Executioner. In lifting up the axe I think h'as knock'd
    His brains out.—
D'Amville.   What murderer was he   240
    That lifted up my hand against my head?
Judge. None but your self my Lord.
D'Amville.   I thought he was
    A murderer that did it.
Judge.   God forbid.
D'Amville. Forbid? You lie, Judge. He commanded it,
    To tell thee that man's wisdom is a fool.
    I came to thee for judgment; and thou think'st
    Thy self a wise man. I outreach'd thy wit;
    And made thy justice murder's instrument,
    In Castabella's death and Charlemont's,
    To crown my murder of Montferrers with   250
    A safe possession of his wealthy state.—
Charlemont. I claim the just advantage of his words.

Judge. Descend the scaffold and attend the rest.
D'Amville. There was the strength of natural understanding.
  But Nature is a fool. There is a power
  Above her that hath overthrown the pride
  Of all my projects and posterity
  (For whose surviving blood, I had erected
  A proud monument) and struck 'em dead
  Before me; for whose deaths, I call'd to thee   260
  For judgment. Thou didst want discretion for
  The sentence. But yond' power that struck me knew
  The judgment I deserv'd; and gave it.—O!
  The lust of death commits a rape upon
  Me as I would ha' done on Castabella.——   —*Dies.*
Judge. Strange is his death and judgment. With the hands
  Of joy and justice I thus set you free.
  The power of that eternal providence,
  Which overthrew his projects in their pride,
  Hath made your griefs the instruments to raise   270
  Your blessings to a greater height than ever.
Charlemont. Only to Heav'n I attribute the work,
  Whose gracious motives made me still forbear
  To be mine own revenger. Now I see
  That *patience is the honest man's revenge.*
Judge. Instead of Charlemont that but e'en now
  Stood ready to be dispossess'd of all;
  I now salute you with more titles, both
  Of wealth and dignity than you were born to.
  And you (sweet Madam) Lady of Belforest,   280
  You have that title by your father's death.
Castabella. With all the titles due to me, increase
  The wealth and honour of my Charlemont.
  Lord of Montferrers; Lord D'Amville; Belforest.
  And for a close to make up all the rest,   —*Embrace.*
  The lord of Castabella. Now at last
  Enjoy the full possession of my love,
  As clear and pure as my first chastity.
Charlemont. The crown of all my blessings!—I will tempt
  My stars no longer; nor protract my time   290
  Of marriage. When those nuptial rites are done,
  I will perform my kinsmen's funerals.

253 attend] wait for   258-9] Cf. note onll. 203-4 *ante.*   261 discretion] discernment
273 motives] motions

Judge. The drums and trumpets! Interchange the sounds
  Of death and triumph; for these honour'd lives,
  Succeeding their deserved tragedies.
Charlemont. Thus by the work of Heav'n, the men that thought
  To follow our dead bodies without tears
  Are dead themselves, and now we follow theirs.   *Exeunt.*

FINIS.

295 their] i.e., Charlemont's kinsmen's

THE CHANGELING

by

THOMAS MIDDLETON and WILLIAM ROWLEY

THOMAS MIDDLETON (1580–1627) and
WILLIAM ROWLEY (d. 1626)

The Changeling

Written in 1621 or 1622; printed in 1653

[*Works of Thomas Middleton*, ed. Alexander Dyce, 1840; ed. A. H. Bullen, 1885. A full edition by N. W. Bawcutt in The Revels Plays, London 1958, revised 1961; a shorter edition by Patricia Thomson in The New Mermaid Series, London 1964.]

THE
CHANGELING:

As it was Acted (with great Applause)
at the Privat house in D r u r y L a n e,
and *Salisbury Court.*

Written by {THOMAS MIDLETON,
and
WILLIAM ROWLEY.} Gent'.

Never Printed before.

DRAMATIS PERSONAE

Vermandero,	Father to Beatrice.
Tomazo de Piracquo,	A noble lord.
Alonzo de Piracquo,	His brother, suitor to Beatrice.
Alsemero,	A nobleman, afterwards married to Beatrice.
Jasperino,	His friend.
Alibius,	A jealous doctor.
Lollio,	His man.
Pedro,	Friend to Antonio.
Antonio,	The Changeling.
Franciscus,	The counterfeit madman.
Deflores,	Servant to Vermandero.
Madmen,	
Servants.	
Beatrice,	Daughter to Vermandero.
Diaphanta,	Her waiting-woman.
Isabella,	Wife to Alibius.

The Scene: *Allegant.*

Beatrice] In the text she is called indifferently Beatrice or Joanna, or occasionally Beatrice-Joanna.   *Allegant*] Alicante, a Valencian sea-port on the east coast of Spain

ACTUS PRIMUS

[SCENE I]

Enter Alsemero.

Alsemero. 'Twas in the temple where I first beheld her,
And now again the same, what omen yet
Follows of that? None but imaginary,
Why should my hopes or fate be timorous?
The place is holy, so is my intent:
I love her beauties to the holy purpose,
And that (me thinks) admits comparison
With man's first creation, the place blest,
And is his right home back (if he achieve it).
The church hath first begun our interview   10
And that's the place must join us into one,
So there's beginning and perfection too.

Enter Jasperino.

Jasperino. O sir, are you here? Come, the wind's fair with you,
Y'are like to have a swift and pleasant passage.
Alsemero. Sure y'are deceived friend, 'tis contrary
In my best judgment.
Jasperino.   What, for Malta?
If you could buy a gale amongst the witches,
They could not serve you such a lucky pennyworth
As comes a' God's name.
Alsemero.   Even now I observ'd
The temple's vane to turn full in my face,   20
I know 'tis against me.
Jasperino.   Against you?
Then you know not where you are.
Alsemero.   Not well indeed.
Jasperino. Are you not well sir?
Alsemero.   Yes, Jasperino.
Unless there be some hidden malady
Within me, that I understand not.

6 holy purpose] matrimony   8 place blest] Paradise   19 a' God's name] free, **for**
nothing

Jasperino.   And that
   I begin to doubt sir, I never knew
   Your inclinations to travels at a pause
   With any cause to hinder it till now.
   Ashore you were wont to call your servants up,
   And help to trap your horses for the speed.   30
   At sea I have seen you weigh the anchor with 'em,
   Hoist sails for fear to lose the foremost breath,
   Be in continual prayers for fair winds,
   And have you chang'd your orisons?
Alsemero.   No, friend,
   I keep the same church, same devotion.
Jasperino. Lover I'm sure y'are none, the stoic
   Was found in you long ago, your mother
   Nor best friends, who have set snares of beauty, (ay
   And choice ones too) could never trap you that way.
   What might be the cause?
Alsemero.   Lord, how violent   40
   Thou art; I was but meditating of
   Somewhat I heard within the temple.
Jasperino. Is this violence? 'tis but idleness
   Compar'd with your haste yesterday.
Alsemero. I'm all this while a-going, man.

   Enter Servants.

Jasperino. Backwards, I think, sir. Look, your servants.
1. Servant. The sea-men call, shall we board your trunks?
Alsemero. No, not to-day.
Jasperino. 'Tis the critical day, it seems, and the sign in Aquarius.
2. Servant. [*Aside*] We must not to sea to-day, this smoke will bring forth fire.
Alsemero. Keep all on shore, I do not know the end   51
   (Which needs I must do) of an affair in hand
   Ere I can go to sea.
1. Servant. Well, your pleasure.
2. Servant. [*Aside*] Let him e'en take his leisure too, we are safer on land.
                                            Exeunt Serv.

   Enter Beatrice-Joanna, Diaphanta, *and* Servants. [Alsemero *greets* Beatrice
   and kisses her.]

Jasperino. [*Aside*] How now! The laws of the Medes are chang'd sure, salute
   a woman? He kisses too: wonderful! Where learnt he this? & does it

30 trap . . . speed] harness your horses to hasten things along   49 critical] crucial
49 sign in Aquarius] i.e., a propitious time for sea travel

perfectly too; in my conscience he ne'er rehearst it before. Nay, go on,
this will be stranger and better news at Valencia, than if he had ransom'd
half Greece from the Turk.   60

Beatrice. You are a scholar, sir.

Alsemero. A weak one, Lady.

Beatrice. Which of the sciences is this love you speak of?

Alsemero. From your tongue I take it to be music.

Beatrice. You are skilful in't, can sing at first sight.

Alsemero. And I have show'd you all my skill at once.
  I want more words to express me further,
  And must be forc'd to repetition:
  I love you dearly.

Beatrice.   Be better advis'd, sir:
  Our eyes are sentinels unto our judgments,   70
  And should give certain judgment what they see;
  But they are rash sometimes, and tell us wonders
  Of common things, which when our judgments find,
  They can then check the eyes, and call them blind.

Alsemero. But I am further, Lady; yesterday
  Was mine eyes' employment, and hither now
  They brought my judgment, where are both agreed.
  Both houses then consenting, 'tis agreed,
  Only there wants the confirmation
  By the hand royal, that's your part, Lady.   80

Beatrice. Oh there's one above me, sir. [*Aside*] For five days past
  To be recall'd! Sure, mine eyes were mistaken,
  This was the man was meant me, that he should come
  So near his time, and miss it!

Jasperino. We might have come by the carriers from Valencia, I see, and
sav'd all our sea-provision: we are at farthest sure; methinks I should
do something too, I meant to be a venturer in this voyage. Yonder's
another vessel, I'll board her, if she be lawful prize, down goes her top-
sail.   [*Greets* Diaphanta.]

Enter Deflores.

Deflores. Lady, your father——

Beatrice.   Is in health, I hope.   90

Deflores. Your eye shall instantly instruct you, Lady.
  He's coming hitherward.

---

58 in my conscience] upon my word, or perhaps, to my knowledge   78–9] both Houses
of Parliament having passed the bill, only the royal signature is needed

Beatrice.   What needed then
     Your duteous preface? I had rather
     He had come unexpected, you must stall
     A good presence with unnecessary blabbing:
     And how welcome for your part you are,
     I'm sure you know.
Deflores. [*Aside*]   Wilt never mend this scorn
     One side nor other? Must I be enjoin'd
     To follow still whilst she flies from me? Well,
     Fates do your worst, I'll please my self with sight   100
     Of her, at all opportunities,
     If but to spite her anger, I know she had
     Rather see me dead than living, and yet
     She knows no cause for't, but a peevish will.
Alsemero. You seem displeas'd Lady, on the sudden.
Beatrice. Your pardon Sir, 'tis my infirmity,
     Nor can I other reason render you,
     Than his or hers, or some particular thing
     They must abandon as a deadly poison,
     Which to a thousand other tastes were wholesome;   110
     Such to mine eyes is that same fellow there,
     The same that report speaks of the basilisk.
Alsemero. This is a frequent frailty in our nature,
     There's scarce a man amongst a thousand sound,
     But hath his imperfection: one distastes
     The scent of roses, which to infinites
     Most pleasing is, and odoriferous:
     One oil, the enemy of poison,
     Another wine, the cheerer of the heart,
     And lively refresher of the countenance.   120
     Indeed this fault (if so it be) is general,
     There's scarce a thing but is both lov'd and loath'd,
     My self (I must confess) have the same frailty.
Beatrice. And what may be your poison Sir? I am bold with you.
Alsemero. And what might be your desire perhaps, a cherry.
Beatrice. I am no enemy to any creature
     My memory has, but yon gentleman.
Alsemero. He does ill to tempt your sight, if he knew it.
Beatrice. He cannot be ignorant of that Sir,

---

94 stall] forestall (though possibly with a subsidiary meaning of satiate)   112 basilisk] a
mythical beast held to kill with its glance   125] 'And', omitted in most editions, may be
a piece of dittography, but may suggest Alsemero as echoing Beatrice's form of words.

    I have not spar'd to tell him so, and I want   130
    To help my self, since he's a gentleman
    In good respect with my father, and follows him.
Alsemero. He's out of his place then now.   *[They talk apart.]*
Jasperino. I am a mad wag, wench.
Diaphanta. So me thinks; but for your comfort I can tell you, we have a
    doctor in the city that undertakes the cure of such.
Jasperino. Tush, I know what physic is best for the state of mine own body.
Diaphanta. 'Tis scarce a well-govern'd state, I believe.
Jasperino. I could show thee such a thing with an ingredian that we two
    would compound together, and if it did not tame the maddest blood i'
    th' town for two hours after, I'll ne'er profess physic again.   141
Diaphanta. A little poppy Sir, were good to cause you sleep.
Jasperino. Poppy? I'll give thee a pop i' th' lips for that first, and begin there:
    [kisses her] poppy is one simple indeed, and cuckoo (what you call't)
    another: I'll discover no more now, another time I'll show thee all.
Beatrice. My father, Sir.

    Enter Vermandero *and* Servants.

Vermandero. Oh Joanna, I came to meet thee; your devotion's ended?
Beatrice. For this time, Sir.
    [Aside] I shall change my saint, I fear me, I find
    A giddy turning in me;—Sir, this while   150
    I am beholding to this gentleman
    Who left his own way to keep me company,
    And in discourse I find him much desirous
    To see your castle: he hath deserv'd it, Sir,
    If ye please to grant it.
Vermandero.   With all my heart, Sir.
    Yet there's an article between, I must know
    Your country; we use not to give survey
    Of our chief strengths to strangers, our citadels
    Are plac'd conspicuous to outward view,
    On promonts' tops; but within are secrets.   160
Alsemero. A Valencian, Sir.
Vermandero.   A Valencian?
    That's native, Sir; of what name, I beseech you?
Alsemero. Alsemero, Sir.
Vermandero.   Alsemero; not the son
    Of John de Alsemero?
Alsemero.   The same Sir.

130-31 I want . . . my self] I am unable to do anything about it   144 simple] medicinal
herb   144 cuckoo] i.e., cuckoo-pintle, or wild arum, here used as a euphemism for the
male sexual organ   156 an article between] a condition to be settled first

Vermandero. My best love bids you welcome.

Beatrice. [*Aside*]   He was wont
     To call me so, and then he speaks a most
     Unfeigned truth.

Vermandero.   Oh Sir, I knew your father,
     We two were in acquaintance long ago
     Before our chins were worth Iulan down,
     And so continued till the stamp of time   170
     Had coin'd us into silver: well, he's gone,
     A good soldier went with him.

Alsemero. You went together in that, Sir.

Vermandero. No by Saint Jacques, I came behind him. Yet
     I have done somewhat too. An unhappy day
     Swallowed him at last at Gibraltar
     In fight with those rebellious Hollanders,
     Was it not so?

Alsemero.   Whose death I had reveng'd,
     Or followed him in fate, had not the late league
     Prevented me.

Vermandero.   Ay, ay, 'twas time to breathe: 180
     Oh Joanna, I should ha' told thee news,
     I saw Piracquo lately.

Beatrice. [*Aside*]   That's ill news.

Vermandero. He's hot preparing for this day of triumph,
     Thou must be a bride within this sevennight.

Alsemero. [*Aside*]   Ha!

Beatrice. Nay good Sir, be not so violent, with speed
     I cannot render satisfaction
     Unto the dear companion of my soul,
     Virginity (whom I thus long have liv'd with),
     And part with it so rude and suddenly;
     Can such friends divide, never to meet again,   190
     Without a solemn farewell?

Vermandero.   Tush, tush, there's a toy.

Alsemero. [*Aside*] I must now part, and never meet again
     With any joy on earth.—Sir, your pardon,
     My affairs call on me.

Vermandero.   How Sir? by no means,
     Not chang'd so soon, I hope, you must see my castle,
     And her best entertainment ere we part,

---

169 Iulan down] first growth of the beard   174 Saint Jacques] St. James the Greater
176 Gibraltar] the battle (25 April 1607) in which the Dutch fleet decisively beat a larger
Spanish fleet)   179 league] armistice   191 there's a toy] you are trifling

I shall think my self unkindly us'd else.
Come, come, let's on, I had good hope your stay
Had been a while with us in Alligant;
I might have bid you to my daughter's wedding.   200
Alsemero. [*Aside*] He means to feast me, & poisons me before hand.
  —I should be dearly glad to be there, sir,
  Did my occasions suit as I could wish.
Beatrice. I shall be sorry if you be not there
  When it is done sir;—but not so suddenly.
Vermandero. I tell you, sir, the gentleman's complete,
  A courtier and a gallant, enricht
  With many fair and noble ornaments,
  I would not change him for a son-in-law,
  For any he in Spain, the proudest he,   210
  And we have great ones, that you know.
Alsemero.   He's much
  Bound to you, sir.
Vermandero.   He shall be bound to me,
  As fast as this tie can hold him, I'll want
  My will else.
Beatrice. [*Aside*]   I shall want mine if you do it.
Vermandero. But come, by the way, I'll tell you more of him.
Alsemero. [*Aside*] How shall I dare to venture in his castle,
  When he discharges murderers at the gate?
  But I must on, for back I cannot go.
Beatrice. [*Aside*] Not this serpent gone yet? [*Drops a glove.*]
Vermandero. Look girl, thy glove's fall'n;—stay, stay, Deflores, help a little.
Deflores. Here, Lady.   221
Beatrice. Mischief on your officious forwardness,
  Who bade you stoop? they touch my hand no more:
  There, for t'other's sake I part with this, [*Throws down the other glove.*]
  Take 'em and draw thine own skin off with 'em.
                              Exeunt [*all except* Deflores.]
Deflores. Here's a favour come; with a mischief: now I know
  She had rather wear my pelt tann'd in a pair
  Of dancing pumps, than I should thrust my fingers
  Into her sockets here: I know she hates me,
  Yet cannot choose but love her: no matter,   230
  If but to vex her, I'll haunt her still,
  Though I get nothing else, I'll have my will.   *Exit.*

213-4 want my will] be thwarted   217 murderers] small cannon, i.e., which shatter my
hopes   220] Though the quarto is silent here, all editions have 'Exeunt Vermandero' etc.
at this point; evidently Beatrice's speech to Deflores is not overheard.

[SCENE II]

Enter Alibius *and* Lollio.

Alibius. Lollio, I must trust thee with a secret,
    But thou must keep it.
Lollio. I was ever close to a secret, sir.
Alibius. The diligence that I have found in thee,
    The care and industry already past,
    Assures me of thy good continuance.
    Lollio, I have a wife.
Lollio. Fie sir, 'tis too late to keep her secret, she's known to be married all
the town and country over.
Alibius. Thou goest too fast my Lollio, that knowledge   10
    I allow no man can be barr'd it;
    But there is a knowledge which is nearer,
    Deeper and sweeter, Lollio.
Lollio. Well sir, let us handle that between you and I.
Alibius. 'Tis that I go about, man; Lollio,
    My wife is young.
Lollio. So much the worse to be kept secret, sir.
Alibius. Why now thou meet'st the substance of the point,
    I am old, Lollio.
Lollio. No sir, 'tis I am old Lollio.   20
Alibius. Yet why may not this concord and sympathize?
    Old trees and young plants often grow together,
    Well enough agreeing.
Lollio. Ay sir, but the old trees raise themselves higher and broader than
the young plants.
Alibius. Shrewd application: there's the fear, man,
    I would wear my ring on my own finger;
    Whilst it is borrowed it is none of mine,
    But his that useth it.
Lollio. You must keep it on still then; if it but lie by,   30
    One or other will be thrusting into't.
Alibius. Thou conceiv'st me Lollio; here thy watchful eye
    Must have employment, I cannot always be
    At home.
Lollio. I dare swear you cannot.
Alibius.   I must look out.
Lollio. I know't, you must look out, 'tis every man's case.

24–5 Ay sir, . . . plants] i.e., the 'tree' will be higher than the 'plant' by the extent of a
cuckold's horns

Alibius. Here I do say must thy employment be,
    To watch her treadings, and in my absence
    Supply my place.
Lollio. I'll do my best, sir, yet surely I cannot see   40
    Who you should have cause to be jealous of.
Alibius. Thy reason for that, Lollio? 'tis a comfortable question.
Lollio. We have but two sorts of people in the house, and both under the
    whip, that's fools and madmen; the one has not wit enough to be knaves,
    and the other not knavery enough to be fools.
Alibius. Ay, those are all my patients, Lollio.
    I do profess the cure of either sort:
    My trade, my living 'tis, I thrive by it;
    But here's the care that mixes with my thrift:
    The daily visitants, that come to see   50
    My brainsick patients, I would not have
    To see my wife: gallants I do observe
    Of quick enticing eyes, rich in habits,
    Of stature and proportion very comely:
    These are most shrewd temptations, Lollio.
Lollio. They may be easily answered, sir; if they come to see the fools and
    madmen, you and I may serve the turn, and let my mistress alone, she's
    of neither sort.
Alibius. 'Tis a good ward, indeed come they to see
    Our madmen or our fools, let 'em see no more   60
    Than what they come for; by that consequent
    They must not see her, I'm sure she's no fool.
Lollio. And I'm sure she's no madman.
Alibius. Hold that buckler fast, Lollio my trust
    Is on thee, and I account it firm and strong.
    What hour is't Lollio?
Lollio. Towards belly-hour sir.
Alibius. Dinner time? Thou mean'st twelve o'clock.
Lollio. Yes sir, for every part has his hour, we wake at six and look about us,
    that's eye-hour; at seven we should pray, that's knee-hour; at eight
    walk, that's leg-hour; at nine gather flowers, and pluck a rose, that's nose-
    hour; at ten we drink, that's mouth-hour; at eleven lay about us for
    victuals, that's hand-hour; at twelve go to dinner, that's belly-hour.
Alibius. Profoundly, Lollio! It will be long   74
    Ere all thy scholars learn this lesson, and
    I did look to have a new one ent'red—stay,
    I think my expectation is come home.

55 shrewd] mischievous   59 a good ward] a sound defence   71 pluck a rose] pass
water

Enter Pedro *and* Antonio *like an idiot.*

Pedro. Save you sir, my business speaks it self,
    This sight takes off the labour of my tongue.
Alibius. Ay, ay, sir,   80
    'Tis plain enough, you mean him for my patient.
Pedro. And if your pains prove but commodious, to give but some little
    strength to his sick and weak part of Nature in him, these [*gives money*]
    are but patterns to show you of the whole pieces that will follow to you,
    beside the charge of diet, washing, and other necessaries fully defrayed.
Alibius. Believe it, sir, there shall no care be wanting.
Lollio. Sir, an officer in this place may deserve something, the trouble will
    pass through my hands.
Pedro. 'Tis fit something should come to your hands then, sir.
Lollio. Yes, sir, 'tis I must keep him sweet, and read to him. What is his
    name?   91
Pedro. His name is Antonio; marry, we use but half to him, only Tony.
Lollio. Tony, Tony, 'tis enough, and a very good name for a fool. What's
    your name, Tony?
Antonio. He, he, he, well I thank you cousin, he, he, he.
Lollio. Good boy, hold up your head: he can laugh, I perceive by that he
    is no beast.
Pedro. Well sir,
    If you can raise him but to any height,
    Any degree of wit, might he attain   100
    (As I might say) to creep but on all four,
    Towards the chair of wit, or walk on crutches,
    'Twould add an honour to your worthy pains,
    And a great family might pray for you,
    To which he should be heir, had he discretion
    To claim and guide his own; assure you sir,
    He is a gentleman.
Lollio. Nay, there's no body doubted that, at first sight I knew him for a
    gentleman, he looks no other yet.
Pedro. Let him have good attendance and sweet lodging.   110
Lollio. As good as my mistress lies in sir, and as you allow us time and means,
    we can raise him to the higher degree of discretion.
Pedro. Nay, there shall no cost want sir.
Lollio. He will hardly be stretcht up to the wit of a magnifico.
Pedro. Oh no, that's not to be expected, far shorter will be enough.

90 and 110 sweet] clean   92 Tony] In the 17th century the word was sometimes used for
'simpleton', and the OED suggests it may come from *The Changeling*.   96-7 he can . . .
beast] Laughter was held to distinguish men from beasts.

Lollio. I'll (warrant you) make him fit to bear office in five weeks, I'll undertake to wind him up to the wit of constable.

Pedro. If it be lower than that it might serve turn.

Lollio. No fie, to level him with a headborough, beadle, or watchman, were but little better than he is; constable I'll able him: if he do come to be a justice afterwards, let him thank the keeper. Or I'll go further with you, say I do bring him up to my own pitch, say I make him as wise as my self.

Pedro. Why there I would have it. 123

Lollio. Well, go to, either I'll be as errant a fool as he, or he shall be as wise as I, and then I think 'twill serve his turn.

Pedro. Nay, I do like thy wit passing well.

Lollio. Yes, you may, yet if I had not been a fool, I had had more wit than I have too, remember what state you find me in.

Pedro. I will, and so leave you: your best cares I beseech you. *Exit* Ped.

Alibius. Take you none with you, leave 'em all with us. 130

Antonio. Oh my cousin's gone, cousin, cousin, oh!

Lollio. Peace, peace Tony, you must not cry child, you must be whipt if you do, your cousin is here still, I am your cousin, Tony.

Antonio. He, he, then I'll not cry, if thou be'st my cousin, he, he, he.

Lollio. I were best try his wit a little, that I may know what form to place him in.

Alibius. Ay, do Lollio, do.

Lollio. I must ask him easy questions at first; Tony, how many true fingers has a tailor on his right hand?

Antonio. As many as on his left, cousin. 140

Lollio. Good, and how many on both?

Antonio. Two less than a deuce, cousin.

Lollio. Very well answered; I come to you again, cousin Tony, how many fools goes to a wise man?

Antonio. Forty in a day sometimes, cousin.

Lollio. Forty in a day? How prove you that?

Antonio. All that fall out amongst themselves, and go to a lawyer to be made friends.

Lollio. A parlous fool, he must sit in the fourth form at least, I perceive that: I come again Tony, how many knaves make an honest man? 150

Antonio. I know not that cousin.

Lollio. No, the question is too hard for you: I'll tell you cousin, there's three knaves may make an honest man, a sergeant, a gaoler, and a beadle;

117 constable] Constables had a low reputation for intelligence on the Elizabethan stage (cf. Dogberry in *Much Ado*). 119 headborough] petty constable (cf. Verges in *Much Ado*) 124 errant] arrant, but with a pun on the sense of erring, i.e., witless 128 state] position 138-9 how many . . . hand?] Tailors were proverbially dishonest. 149 parlous] shrewd, mischievous

the sergeant catches him, the gaoler holds him, and the beadle lashes him;
and if he be not honest then, the hangman must cure him.

Antonio. Ha, ha, ha, that's fine sport cousin.

Alibius. This was too deep a question for the fool Lollio.

Lollio. Yes, this might have serv'd your self, tho' I say't; once more, and
you shall go play Tony.

Antonio. Ay, play at push-pin cousin, ha, he.   160

Lollio. So thou shalt, say how many fools are here.

Antonio. Two, cousin, thou and I.

Lollio. Nay, y'are too forward there, Tony, mark my question, how many
fools and knaves are here? a fool before a knave, a fool behind a knave,
between every two fools a knave, how many fools, how many knaves?

Antonio. I never learnt so far cousin.

Alibius. Thou putt'st too hard questions to him, Lollio.

Lollio. I'll make him understand it easily; cousin stand there.

Antonio. Ay, cousin.

Lollio. Master, stand you next the fool.   170

Alibius. Well, Lollio.

Lollio. Here's my place: mark now Tony, there a fool before a knave.

Antonio. That's I, cousin.

Lollio. Here's a fool behind a knave, that's I, and between us two fools
there is a knave, that's my master, 'tis but we three, that's all.

Antonio. We three, we three, cousin.   *Madmen within.*

1 Within. Put's head i'th'pillory, the bread's too little.

2 Within. Fly, fly, and he catches the swallow.

3 Within. Give her more onion, or the devil put the rope about her crag.

Lollio. You may hear what time of day it is, the chimes of Bedlam goes.

Alibius. Peace, peace, or the wire comes.   181

3 Within. Cat whore, cat whore, her permasant, her permasant.

Alibius. Peace, I say; their hour's come, they must be fed, Lollio.

Lollio. There's no hope of recovery of that Welsh madman, was undone by
a mouse, that spoil'd him a permasant, lost his wit's for't.

Alibius. Go to your charge, Lollio, I'll to mine.

Lollio. Go to your madmen's ward, let me alone with your fools.

Alibius. And remember my last charge, Lollio.   *Exit.*

Lollio. Of which your patients do you think I am? Come Tony, you must
among your schoolfellows now, there's pretty scholars amongst 'em, I
can tell you there's some of 'em at *stultus, stulta, stultum.*   191

Antonio. I would see the madmen, cousin, if they would not bite me.

158 serv'd] i.e., tested   160 push-pin] a very simple children's game, but doubtless here
with sexual overtones   170 next] i.e., behind   179 crag] neck   181 wire] whip
182 permasant] parmesan   182 her] stage-Welsh for 'my'   191 there's ... *stultum*] i.e.,
some of them can decline the Latin for 'foolish'

Lollio. No, they shall not bite thee, Tony.

Antonio. They bite when they are at dinner, do they not, coz?

Lollio. They bite at dinner indeed, Tony; well, I hope to get credit by thee,
I like thee the best of all the scholars that ever I brought up, and thou
shalt prove a wise man, or I'll prove a fool my self.   *Exeunt.*

ACTUS SECUNDUS

[SCENE I]

Enter Beatrice *and* Jasperino *severally.*

Beatrice. Oh sir, I'm ready now for that fair service,
    Which makes the name of friend sit glorious on you.
    Good angels and this conduct be your guide,   *[Gives a paper]*
    Fitness of time and place is there set down, sir.

Jasperino. The joy I shall return rewards my service.   *Exit.*

Beatrice. How wise is Alsemero in his friend!
    It is a sign he makes his choice with judgment.
    Then I appear in nothing more approv'd,
    Than making choice of him;
    For 'tis a principle, he that can choose   10
    That bosom well, who of his thoughts partakes,
    Proves most discreet in every choice he makes.
    Me thinks I love now with the eyes of judgment,
    And see the way to merit, clearly see it.
    A true deserver like a diamond sparkles,
    In darkness you may see him, that's in absence,
    Which is the greatest darkness falls on love,
    Yet is he best discern'd then
    With intellectual eyesight; what's Piracquo
    My father spends his breath for? and his blessing   20
    Is only mine, as I regard his name,
    Else it goes from me, and turns head against me,
    Transform'd into a curse: some speedy way
    Must be rememb'red, he's so forward too,
    So urgent that way, scarce allows me breath
    To speak to my new comforts.

Enter Deflores.

II. i, 8 approv'd] prov'd (right)   16 In darkness . . . him] Diamonds were supposed to be
luminous.   20–21 his blessing . . . name] I only have my father's blessing so long as I keep
up the family name (by marrying well)

Deflores. [*Aside*]   Yonder's she.
    Whatever ails me, now alate especially,
    I can as well be hang'd as refrain seeing her;
    Some twenty times a day, nay not so little,
    Do I force errands, frame ways and excuses   30
    To come into her sight, and I have
    Small reason for't, and less encouragement;
    For she baits me still
    Every time worse than other, does profess herself
    The cruellest enemy to my face in town,
    At no hand can abide the sight of me,
    As if danger, or ill luck hung in my looks.
    I must confess my face is bad enough,
    But I know far worse has better fortune,
    And not endur'd alone, but doted on,   40
    And yet such pick-hair'd faces, chins like witches',
    Here and there five hairs, whispering in a corner,
    As if they grew in fear one of another,
    Wrinkles like troughs, where swine deformity swills
    The tears of perjury that lie there like wash,
    Fallen from the slimy and dishonest eye,—
    Yet such a one pluck'd sweets without restraint,
    And has the grace of beauty to his sweet.
    Though my hard fate has thrust me out to servitude,
    I tumbled into th'world a gentleman.   50
    She turns her blessed eye upon me now,
    And I'll endure all storms before I part with't.
Beatrice. [*Aside*] Again—
    This ominous ill-fac'd fellow more disturbs me,
    Than all my other passions.
Deflores. [*Aside*]   Now't begins again,
    I'll stand this storm of hail though the stones pelt me.
Beatrice. Thy business? What's thy business?
Deflores. [*Aside*]   Soft and fair,
    I cannot part so soon now.
Beatrice. [*Aside*]   The villain's fixt.
    —Thou standing toadpool.
Deflores. [*Aside*]   The show'r falls amain now.
Beatrice. Who sent thee? What's thy errand? leave my sight.   60
Deflores. My lord your father charg'd me to deliver
    A message to you.

---

27 alate] of late   40 alone] only   48 to his sweet] for his sweetheart

Beatrice.   What, another since?
     Do't and be hang'd then, let me be rid of thee.
Deflores. True service merits mercy.
Beatrice.   What's thy message?
Deflores. Let beauty settle but in patience,
     You shall hear all.
Beatrice.   A dallying trifling torment!
Deflores. Signor Alonzo de Piracquo, Lady,
     Sole brother to Tomazo de Piracquo——
Beatrice. Slave, when wilt make an end?
Deflores. [*Aside*]   Too soon I shall.
Beatrice. What all this while of him?
Deflores.   The said Alonzo,   70
     With the foresaid Tomazo——
Beatrice.   Yet again?
Deflores. Is new alighted.
Beatrice.   Vengeance strike the news!
     Thou thing most loath'd, what cause was there in this
     To bring thee to my sight?
Deflores.   My lord your father
     Charg'd me to seek you out.
Beatrice.   Is there no other
     To send his errand by?
Deflores.   It seems 'tis my luck
     To be i'th'way still.
Beatrice.   Get thee from me.
Deflores.   So.—
     [*Aside*] Why, am not I an ass to devise ways
     Thus to be rail'd at? I must see her still,
     I shall have a mad qualm within this hour again,   80
     I know't, and like a common Garden-bull,
     I do but take breath to be lugg'd again.
     What this may bode I know not, I'll despair
     The less, because there's daily precedents
     Of bad faces belov'd beyond all reason;
     These foul chops may
     Come into favour one day 'mongst his fellows:
     Wrangling has prov'd the mistress of good pastime;
     As children cry themselves asleep, I ha' seen
     Women have chid themselves abed to men.   *Exit* Def.

62 another since] yet another   66 A dallying . . . torment] Beatrice is tormented by his
artificial manner of speech.   81 Garden-bull] Bulls were baited at Paris Garden on
Bankside.   82 lugg'd] dragged by the ears

Beatrice. I never see this fellow, but I think   91
 Of some harm towards me, danger's in my mind still,
 I scarce leave trembling of an hour after.
 The next good mood I find my father in,
 I'll get him quite discarded: oh I was
 Lost in this small disturbance and forgot
 Affliction's fiercer torrent that now comes,
 To bear down all my comforts.

 Enter Vermandero, Alonzo, Tomazo.

Vermandero.   Y'are both welcome,
 But an especial one belongs to you, sir,
 To whose most noble name our love presents   100
 The addition of a son, our son Alonzo.
Alonzo. The treasury of honour cannot bring forth
 A title I should more rejoice in, sir.
Vermandero. You have improv'd it well; daughter prepare,
 The day will steal upon thee suddenly.
Beatrice. [*Aside*] Howe'er, I will be sure to keep the night,
 If it should come so near me. [Beatrice *and* Vermandero *talk apart.*]
Tomazo.   Alonzo.
Alonzo.   Brother.
Tomazo. In troth I see small welcome in her eye.
Alonzo. Fie, you are too severe a censurer
 Of love in all its points, there's no bringing on you;   110
 If lovers should mark everything a fault,
 Affection would be like an ill-set book,
 Whose faults might prove as big as half the volume.
Beatrice. That's all I do entreat.
Vermandero.   It is but reasonable,
 I'll see what my son says to't: son Alonzo,
 Here's a motion made but to reprieve
 A maidenhead three days longer; the request
 Is not far out of reason, for indeed
 The former time is pinching.
Alonzo.   Though my joys
 Be set back so much time as I could wish   120
 They had been forward, yet since she desires it,
 The time is set as pleasing as before,
 I find no gladness wanting.

106 keep the night] avoid that day, not see it dawn 110 there's no . . . you] probably, I
can't bring you to see reason

Vermandero.   May I ever
   Meet it in that point still: y'are nobly welcome, sirs.

                                   Exeunt Ver. *and* Bea.

Tomazo. So, did you mark the dulness of her parting now?

Alonzo. What dulness? Thou are so exceptious still.

Tomazo. Why, let it go then, I am but a fool
   To mark your harms so heedfully.

Alonzo.   Where's the oversight?

Tomazo. Come, your faith's cozened in her, strongly cozened,
   Unsettle your affection with all speed   130
   Wisdom can bring it to, your peace is ruin'd else.
   Think what a torment 'tis to marry one
   Whose heart is leapt into another's bosom:
   If ever pleasure she receive from thee,
   It comes not in thy name, or of thy gift,
   She lies but with another in thine arms,
   He the half-father unto all thy children
   In the conception; if he get 'em not,
   She helps to get 'em for him, in his passions,
   And how dangerous   140
   And shameful her restraint may go in time to,
   It is not to be thought on without sufferings.

Alonzo. You speak as if she lov'd some other then.

Tomazo. Do you apprehend so slowly?

Alonzo.   Nay, and that
   Be your fear only, I am safe enough;
   Preserve your friendship and your counsel, brother,
   For times of more distress; I should depart
   An enemy, a dangerous, deadly one
   To any but thy self, that should but think
   She knew the meaning of inconstancy,   150
   Much less the use and practice; yet w'are friends,
   Pray let no more be urg'd, I can endure
   Much, till I meet an injury to her,
   Then I am not my self. Farewell sweet brother,
   How much w'are bound to heaven to depart lovingly.   *Exit.*

Tomazo. Why, here is love's tame madness, thus a man
   Quickly steals into his vexation.   *Exit.*

---

139 in his passions] An obscure phrase which most editors omit: presumably the lover's
passions inspire the woman to beget children (though by her husband).   140–41] if she is
restrained, the consequences will be dangerous and shameful   144 and] an

[SCENE II]

Enter Diaphanta *and* Alsemero.

Diaphanta. The place is my charge, you have kept your hour,
        And the reward of a just meeting bless you.
        I hear my lady coming; complete gentleman,
        I dare not be too busy with my praises,
        Th'are dangerous things to deal with.   *Exit.*
Alsemero.   This goes well,
        These women are the ladies' cabinets,
        Things of most precious trust are lock'd into 'em.

    Enter Beatrice.

Beatrice. I have within mine eye, all my desires,
        Requests that holy prayers ascend heaven for,
        And brings 'em down to furnish our defects,   10
        Come not more sweet to our necessities,
        Than thou unto my wishes.
Alsemero.   W'are so like
        In our expressions, Lady, that unless I borrow
        The same words, I shall never find their equals.   [*Kisses her.*]
Beatrice. How happy were this meeting, this embrace,
        If it were free from envy! This poor kiss,
        It has an enemy, a hateful one,
        That wishes poison to't: how well were I now
        If there were none such name known as Piracquo,
        Nor no such tie as the command of parents!   20
        I should be but too much blessed.
Alsemero.   One good service
        Would strike off both your fears, and I'll go near it too,
        Since you are so distrest; remove the cause,
        The command ceases, so there's two fears blown out
        With one and the same blast.
Beatrice.   Pray let me find you sir.
        What might that service be, so strangely happy?
Alsemero. The honourablest piece 'bout man, valour.
        I'll send a challenge to Piracquo instantly.
Beatrice. How? Call you that extinguishing of fear
        When 'tis the only way to keep it flaming?   30
        Are you not ventured in the action,

4–5] if Beatrice overhears Diaphanta praising Alsemero, she will be suspicious

That's all my joys and comforts? Pray no more, sir.
Say you prevail'd, y'are danger's and not mine then;
The law would claim you from me, or obscurity
Be made the grave to bury you alive.
I'm glad these thoughts come forth, O keep not one
Of this condition sir; here was a course
Found to bring sorrow on her way to death:
The tears would ne'er ha' dried, till dust had chok'd 'em.
Blood-guiltiness becomes a fouler visage.   40
[*Aside*] And now I think on one——I was to blame,
I ha' marr'd so good a market with my scorn;
'T had been done questionless; the ugliest creature
Creation fram'd for some use, yet to see
I could not mark so much where it should be!
Alsemero. Lady——
Beatrice. [*Aside*]   Why, men of art make much of poison,
    Keep one to expel another, where was my art?
Alsemero. Lady, you hear not me.
Beatrice.   I do especially sir,
    The present times are not so sure of our side
    As those hereafter may be, we must use 'em then   50
    As thrifty folks their wealth, sparingly now,
    Till the time opens.
Alsemero.   You teach wisdom, Lady.
Beatrice. Within there, Diaphanta!

    Enter Diaphanta.

Diaphanta.   Do you call, Madam?
Beatrice. Perfect your service, and conduct this gentleman
    The private way you brought him.
Diaphanta.   I shall, Madam.
Alsemero. My love's as firm as love e'er built upon.   *Ex. Dia. and* Als.

    Enter Deflores.

Deflores. [*Aside*] I have watcht this meeting, and do wonder much
    What shall become of t'other, I'm sure both
    Cannot be serv'd unless she transgress; happily
    Then I'll put in for one: for if a woman   60
    Fly from one point, from him she makes a husband,
    She spreads and mounts then like arithmetic,
    1, 10, 100, 1000, 10000,

44-5 to see . . . be] to think I could not notice the use Deflores was created for

    Proves in time sutler to an army royal.
    Now do I look to be most richly rail'd at,
      Yet I must see her.
Beatrice. [*Aside*]   Why, put case I loath'd him
    As much as youth and beauty hates a sepulchre,
    Must I needs show it? Cannot I keep that secret,
    And serve my turn upon him?—See, he's here.
    —Deflores.
Deflores. [*Aside*] Ha, I shall run mad with joy,   70
    She call'd me fairly by my name Deflores,
    And neither rogue nor rascal.
Beatrice. What ha' you done to your face
    A-late? y'ave met with some good physician,
    Y'ave prun'd your self me thinks, you were not wont
    To look so amorously.
Deflores. [*Aside*]   Not I, 'tis
    The same physnomy to a hair and pimple,
    Which she call'd scurvy scarce an hour ago:
    How is this?
Beatrice.   Come hither, nearer, man.
Deflores. [*Aside*] I'm up to the chin in heaven.
Beatrice.   Turn, let me see,   80
    Vauh! 'tis but the heat of the liver, I perceiv't.
    I thought it had been worse.
Deflores. [*Aside*]   Her fingers toucht me,
    She smells all amber.
Beatrice. I'll make a water for you shall cleanse this
    Within a fortnight.
Deflores.   With your own hands, Lady?
Beatrice. Yes, mine own sir; in a work of cure,
    I'll trust no other.
Deflores. [*Aside*]   'Tis half an act of pleasure
    To hear her talk thus to me.
Beatrice.   When w'are us'd
    To a hard face, 'tis not so unpleasing,
    It mends still in opinion, hourly mends,   90
    I see it by experience.
Deflores. [*Aside*]   I was blest
    To light upon this minute, I'll make use on't.
Beatrice. Hardness becomes the visage of a man well,
    It argues service, resolution,
    Manhood, if cause were of employment.

77 physnomy] physiognomy

Deflores. 'Twould be soon seen, if e'er your Ladyship
    Had cause to use it.
    I would but wish the honour of a service
    So happy as that mounts to.
Beatrice.   We shall try you——
    Oh my Deflores!
Deflores. [*Aside*]   How's that?   100
    She calls me hers already, my Deflores.
    —You were about to sigh out somewhat, Madam.
Beatrice. No, was I? I forgot—Oh!
Deflores.   There 'tis again——
    The very fellow on't.
Beatrice.   You are too quick, sir.
Deflores. There's no excuse for't, now I heard it twice,
    Madam, that sigh would fain have utterance,
    Take pity on't, and lend it a free word;
    'Las how it labours
    For liberty, I hear the murmur yet
    Beat at your bosom.
Beatrice.   Would Creation——   110
Deflores. Ay, well said, that's it.
Beatrice.   ——Had form'd me man.
Deflores. Nay, that's not it.
Beatrice.   Oh 'tis the soul of freedom,
    I should not then be forc'd to marry one
    I hate beyond all depths, I should have power
    Then to oppose my loathings, nay remove 'em
    For ever from my sight.
Deflores. [*Aside*]   Oh blest occasion!
    —Without change to your sex, you have your wishes.
    Claim so much man in me.
Beatrice. In thee Deflores? There's small cause for that.
Deflores. Put it not from me, it's a service that   120
    I kneel for to you.   [*Kneels.*]
Beatrice. You are too violent to mean faithfully,
    There's horror in my service, blood and danger,
    Can those be things to sue for?
Deflores.   If you knew
    How sweet it were to me to be employed
    In any act of yours, you would say then
    I fail'd, and use not reverence enough
    When I receive the charge on't.

Beatrice. [*Aside*]   This is much methinks,
 Belike his wants are greedy, & to such
 Gold tastes like angels' food.—Rise   130
Deflores. I'll have the work first.
Beatrice. [*Aside*]   Possible his need
 Is strong upon him; [*gives him money*]—there's to encourage thee:
 As thou art forward and thy service dangerous,
 Thy reward shall be precious.
Deflores.   That I have thought on,
 I have assur'd my self of that beforehand,
 And know it will be precious, the thought ravishes.
Beatrice. Then take him to thy fury.
Deflores.   I thirst for him.
Beatrice. Alonzo de Piracquo.
Deflores.   His end's upon him,
 He shall be seen no more.
Beatrice.   How lovely now
 Dost thou appear to me! Never was man   140
 Dearlier rewarded.
Deflores.   I do think of that.
Beatrice. Be wondrous careful in the execution.
Deflores. Why, are not both our lives upon the cast?
Beatrice. Then I throw all my fears upon thy service.
Deflores. They ne'er shall rise to hurt you.
Beatrice.   When the deed's done,
 I'll furnish thee with all things for thy flight,
 Thou may'st live bravely in another country.
Deflores. Ay, ay, we'll talk of that hereafter.
Beatrice. [*Aside*] I shall rid my self
 Of two inveterate loathings at one time,   150
 Piracquo and his Dog-face.   *Exit.*
Deflores.   Oh my blood,
 Methinks I feel her in mine arms already,
 Her wanton fingers combing out this beard,
 And being pleased, praising this bad face.
 Hunger and pleasure they'll commend sometimes
 Slovenly dishes, and feed heartily on 'em,
 Nay, which is stranger, refuse daintier for 'em.
 Some women are odd feeders—I'm too loud:
 Here comes the man goes supperless to bed,
 Yet shall not rise tomorrow to his dinner.   160

 Enter Alonzo.

Alonzo. Deflores.

Deflores. My kind honourable Lord.

Alonzo. I am glad I ha' met with thee.

Deflores. Sir.

Alonzo. Thou canst show me the full strength of the castle?

Deflores. That I can sir.

Alonzo. I much desire it.

Deflores. And if the ways & straits of some of the passages be not too tedious
   for you, I will assure you worth your time and sight, my Lord.

Alonzo. Puh, that shall be no hinderance.   170

Deflores. I'm your servant then: 'tis now near dinner time; 'gainst your
   Lordship's rising I'll have the keys about me.

Alonzo. Thanks, kind Deflores.

Deflores. [*Aside*] He's safely thrust upon me beyond hopes.   *Exeunt.*

ACTUS TERTIUS

[SCENE I]

Enter Alonzo *and* Deflores.

(*In the act-time* Deflores *hides a naked rapier*.)

Deflores. Yes, here are all the keys; I was afraid, my Lord,
   I'd wanted for the postern, this is it.
   I've all, I've all, my Lord: this for the sconce.

Alonzo. 'Tis a most spacious and impregnable fort.

Deflores. You'll tell me more my Lord: this descent
   Is somewhat narrow, we shall never pass
   Well with our weapons, they'll but trouble us.

Alonzo. Thou say'st true.

Deflores. Pray let me help your Lordship.

Alonzo.   'Tis done.
   Thanks kind Deflores.

Deflores.   Here are hooks my Lord,   10
   To hang such things on purpose.   [*Hangs up the swords.*]

Alonzo.   Lead, I'll follow thee.
                    Exeunt at one door & enter at the other.

Deflores. All this is nothing, you shall see anon
   A place you little dream on.

Alonzo.   I am glad
   I have this leisure: all your master's house
   Imagine I ha' taken a gondola.

III. i, s.d. *act-time*] entr'acte   3 sconce] small fort

Deflores. All but my self, sir,—[*Aside*] which makes up my safety.
    —My Lord, I'll place you at a casement here,
    Will show you the full strength of all the castle.
    Look, spend your eye a while upon that object.
Alonzo. Here's rich variety, Deflores.
Deflores.   Yes, sir.   20
Alonzo. Goodly munition.
Deflores.   Ay, there's ordnance sir,
    No bastard metal, will ring you a peal like bells
    At great men's funerals; keep your eye straight, my Lord,
    Take special notice of that sconce before you,
    There you may dwell awhile.
Alonzo.   I am upon't.
Deflores. And so am I.   [*Stabs him.*]
Alonzo.   Deflores, oh Deflores,
    Whose malice hast thou put on?
Deflores.   Do you question
    A work of secrecy? I must silence you.   [*Stabs him.*]
Alonzo. Oh, oh, oh.
Deflores.   I must silence you.   [*Stabs him.*]
    So, here's an undertaking well accomplish'd.   30
    This vault serves to good use now—ha! what's that
    Threw sparkles in my eye?—oh 'tis a diamond
    He wears upon his finger: it was well found,
    This will approve the work. What, so fast on?
    Not part in death? I'll take a speedy course then,
    Finger and all shall off. So, now I'll clear
    The passages from all suspect or fear.   *Exit with body.*

[SCENE II]

Enter Isabella *and* Lollio.

Isabella. Why sirrah? Whence have you commission
    To fetter the doors against me? If you
    Keep me in a cage, pray whistle to me,
    Let me be doing something.
Lollio. You shall be doing, if it please you, I'll whistle to you if you'll pipe
    after.

34 approve] prove

Isabella. Is it your master's pleasure, or your own,
    To keep me in this pinfold?

Lollio. 'Tis for my master's pleasure, lest being taken in another man's corn,
    you might be pounded in another place.   10

Isabella. 'Tis very well, and he'll prove very wise.

Lollio. He says you have company enough in the house, if you please to be
    sociable, of all sorts of people.

Isabella. Of all sorts? Why, here's none but fools and madmen.

Lollio. Very well: and where will you find any other, if you should go abroad?
    There's my master and I, to boot too.

Isabella. Of either sort one, a madman and a fool.

Lollio. I would ev'n participate of both then if I were as you, I know y'are
    half mad already; be half foolish too.

Isabella. Y'are a brave saucy rascal, come on sir,   20
    Afford me then the pleasure of your bedlam;
    You were commending once today to me
    Your last-come lunatic, what a proper
    Body there was without brains to guide it,
    And what a pitiful delight appear'd
    In that defect, as if your wisdom had found
    A mirth in madness; pray sir, let me partake
    If there be such a pleasure.

Lollio. If I do not show you the handsomest, discreetest madman, one that
    I may call the understanding madman; then say I am a fool.   30

Isabella. Well, a match, I will say so.

Lollio. When you have a taste of the madman, you shall (if you please)
    see Fools' College, o'th'side; I seldom lock there, 'tis but shooting a
    bolt or two, and you are amongst 'em.   *Exit. Enter presently.*
    Come on sir, let me see how handsomely you'll behave your self now.

Enter Franciscus.

Franciscus. How sweetly she looks! Oh but there's a wrinkle in her brow as
    deep as philosophy; Anacreon, drink to my mistress' health, I'll pledge it:
    stay, stay, there's a spider in the cup: no, 'tis but a grape-stone, swallow it,
    fear nothing, poet; so, so, lift higher.

Isabella. Alack, alack, 'tis too full of pity   40
    To be laught at; how fell he mad? Canst thou tell?

Lollio. For love, Mistress; he was a pretty poet too, and that set him forwards
    first; the Muses then forsook him, he ran mad for a chambermaid, yet
    she was but a dwarf neither.

37–8] Anacreon choked to death on a grape-stone while drinking a cup of wine.
38 spider] Spiders were thought to be poisonous.

Franciscus. Hail bright Titania,
    Why stand'st thou idle on these flow'ry banks?
    Oberon is dancing with his Dryades,
    I'll gather daisies, primrose, violets,
    And bind them in a verse of poesy.
Lollio. Not too near, you see your danger.   [*Shows the whip.*]
Franciscus. Oh hold thy hand, great Diomed,   51
    Thou feed'st thy horses well, they shall obey thee;
    Get up, Bucephalus kneels.
Lollio. You see how I awe my flock, a shepherd has not his dog at more
    obedience.
Isabella. His conscience is unquiet, sure that was
    The cause of this. A proper gentleman.
Franciscus. Come hither, Aesculapius, hide the poison.
Lollio. Well, 'tis hid.
Franciscus.   Didst thou never hear
    Of one Tiresias, a famous poet?   60
Lollio. Yes, that kept tame wild-geese.
Franciscus. That's he, I am the man.
Lollio. No!
Franciscus. Yes, but make no words on't, I was a man seven years ago.
Lollio. A stripling I think you might.
Franciscus. Now I'm a woman, all feminine.
Lollio. I would I might see that.
Franciscus. Juno struck me blind.
Lollio. I'll ne'er believe that; for a woman, they say, has an eye more than a man.
Franciscus. I say she struck me blind.   70
Lollio. And Luna made you mad, you have two trades to beg with.
Franciscus. Luna is now big-bellied, and there's room
    For both of us to ride with Hecate;
    I'll drag thee up into her silver sphere,
    And there we'll kick the dog, and beat the bush
    That barks against the witches of the night,
    The swift lycanthropi that walks the round,

47 Oberon . . . Dryades] Presumably Oberon is Alibius who is now out enjoying himself.
51 Diomed] Diomedes, king of Thrace, son of Ares, who fed his horses on human flesh
53 Bucephalus] the great horse of Alexander, whom no one else could ride; evidently
Franciscus gets on all fours   58 Aesculapius] god of healing   58 poison] i.e., the whip
60 Tiresias] the Theban prophet who had been both man and woman, and was struck blind
by Juno for revealing that women get more pleasure than men from the act of love
69 a woman . . . a man] a low sexual joke   72 Luna . . . big-bellied] it is full moon (a
proverbial cause of madness)   73 Hecate] goddess of witchcraft, but frequently used for
the moon   75–6] The dog and the bush belong in legend to the Man in the Moon.
77 lycanthropi] those suffering from lycanthropia, a derangement in which the sufferer
believes himself to be a wolf

We'll tear their wolvish skins, and save the sheep.   [*Attacks* Lollio.]
Lollio. Is't come to this? nay then my poison comes forth again; mad slave
    indeed, abuse your keeper!   80
Isabella. I prithee hence with him, now he grows dangerous.
Franciscus. Sings.
              Sweet love pity me,
              Give me leave to lie with thee.
Lollio. No, I'll see you wiser first: to your own kennel.
Franciscus. No noise, she sleeps, draw all the curtains round,
    Let no soft sound molest the pretty soul,
    But love, and love creeps in at a mouse-hole.
Lollio. I wo'd you wo'd get into your hole.   *Exit* Fra.
    Now Mistress, I will bring you another sort, you shall be fool'd another
    while; Tony, come hither Tony, look who's yonder Tony.   90

    Enter Antonio.

Antonio. Cousin, is it not my aunt?
Lollio. Yes, 'tis one of 'em, Tony.
Antonio. He, he, how do you, Uncle?
Lollio. Fear him not, Mistress, 'tis a gentle nigget, you may play with him,
    as safely with him as with his bauble.
Isabella. How long hast thou been a fool?
Antonio. Ever since I came hither, Cousin.
Isabella. Cousin? I'm none of thy cousins, fool.
Lollio. Oh Mistress, fools have always so much wit as to claim their kindred.
Madman within. Bounce, bounce, he falls, he falls.   100
Isabella. Hark you, your scholars in the upper room
    Are out of order.
Lollio. Must I come amongst you there? Keep you the fool, Mistress, I'll
    go up, & play left-handed Orlando amongst the madmen.   *Exit.*
Isabella. Well, sir.
Antonio. 'Tis opportuneful now, sweet Lady! Nay,
    Cast no amazing eye upon this change.
Isabella. Ha!
Antonio. This shape of folly shrouds your dearest love,
    The truest servant to your powerful beauties,   110
    Whose magic had this force thus to transform me.
Isabella. You are a fine fool indeed.
Antonio.   Oh 'tis not strange:

91 aunt] prostitute   94 nigget] fool   104 left-handed Orlando] the crazed hero of
Orlando Furioso; perhaps Lollio will be left-handed because he will be a false madman
107 amazing] amazed

> Love has an intellect that runs through all
> The scrutinous sciences; and like
> A cunning poet, catches a quantity
> Of every knowledge, yet brings all home
> Into one mystery, into one secret
> That he proceeds in.

Isabella.   Y'are a parlous fool.

Antonio. No danger in me: I bring nought but love,
> And his soft-wounding shafts to strike you with: 120
> Try but one arrow; if it hurt you,
> I'll stand you twenty back in recompense.   [*Kisses her.*]

Isabella. A forward fool too.

Antonio.   This was love's teaching:
> A thousand ways she fashion'd out my way,
> And this I found the safest and nearest
> To tread the Gallaxia to my star.

Isabella. Profound, withal. Certain, you dream'd of this;
> Love never taught it waking.

Antonio.   Take no acquaintance
> Of these outward follies; there is within
> A gentleman that loves you.

Isabella.   When I see him,   130
> I'll speak with him; so in the mean time keep
> Your habit, it becomes you well enough:
> As you are a gentleman, I'll not discover you;
> That's all the favour that you must expect:
> When you are weary, you may leave the school,
> For all this while you have but play'd the fool.

Enter Lollio.

Antonio. And must again.—He, he, I thank you cousin,
> I'll be your valentine tomorrow morning.

Lollio. How do you like the fool, Mistress?

Isabella. Passing well, sir.   140

Lollio. Is he not witty, pretty well for a fool?

Isabella. If he hold on as he begins, he is like to come to something.

Lollio. Ay, thank a good tutor: you may put him to't; he begins to answer
pretty hard questions. Tony, how many is five times six?

Antonio. Five times six, is six times five.

Lollio. What arithmetician could have answer'd better? How many is one
hundred and seven?

118 parlous] dangerous   126 Gallaxia] Milky Way

Antonio. One hundred and seven, is seven hundred and one, cousin.

Lollio. This is no wit to speak on; will you be rid of the fool now?

Isabella. By no means, let him stay a little.   150

Madman within. Catch there, catch the last couple in hell.

Lollio. Again, must I come amongst you? Would my master were come
    home! I am not able to govern both these wards together.   *Exit.*

Antonio. Why should a minute of love's hour be lost?

Isabella. Fie, out again! I had rather you kept
    Your other posture: you become not your tongue,
    When you speak from your clothes.

Antonio.   How can he freeze,
    Lives near so sweet a warmth? shall I alone
    Walk through the orchard of the Hesperides,
    And cowardly not dare to pull an apple?   160
    This with the red cheeks I must venter for.   [*Tries to kiss her.*]

    Enter Lol. *above.*

Isabella. Take heed, there's giants keep 'em.

Lollio. [*Aside*] How now fool, are you good at that? have you read Lipsius?
    He's past *Ars Amandi*; I believe I must put harder questions to him, I
    perceive that——

Isabella. You are bold without fear too.

Antonio.   What should I fear,
    Having all joys about me? Do you smile,
    And love shall play the wanton on your lip,
    Meet and retire, retire and meet again:
    Look you but cheerfully, and in your eyes   170
    I shall behold mine own deformity,
    And dress my self up fairer; I know this shape
    Becomes me not, but in those bright mirrors
    I shall array me handsomely.

Lollio. [*Aside*] Cuckoo, cuckoo——   *Exit.*

    Madmen above, some as birds, others as beasts.

---

151 catch . . . hell] an allusion to the children's game of barley-brake (or last-couple-in-
hell), in which a couple in the middle section ('hell') of a marked ground had to catch other
couples running through   157 from your clothes] i.e., seriously, not as a fool
159 Hesperides] who guarded the golden apples given by Earth to Hera, which grew on a
tree protected by a dragon (cf. l. 162)   161 venter] venture   163 Lipsius] the great
scholar's name introduced only for the play on the first syllable   164 *Ars Amandi*] Ovid's
Art of Love: Antonio is clearly no novice   167 Do you smile] an imperative
175 Cuckoo] i.e., Alibius is about to be cuckolded

Antonio. What are these?
Isabella.   Of fear enough to part us,
    Yet are they but our schools of lunatics,
    That act their fantasies in any shapes
    Suiting their present thoughts; if sad, they cry;
    If mirth be their conceit, they laugh again;   180
    Sometimes they imitate the beasts and birds,
    Singing, or howling, braying, barking; all
    As their wild fancies prompt 'em.

    Enter Lollio.

Antonio.   These are no fears.
Isabella. But here's a large one, my man.
Antonio. Ha, he, that's fine sport indeed, cousin.
Lollio. I would my master were come home, 'tis too much for one shepherd
    to govern two of these flocks; nor can I believe that one churchman can
    instruct two benefices at once, there will be some incurable mad of the
    one side, and very fools on the other. Come, Tony.
Antonio. Prithee cousin, let me stay here still.   190
Lollio. No, you must to your book now you have play'd sufficiently.
Isabella. Your fool is grown wondrous witty.
Lollio. Well, I'll say nothing; but I do not think but he will put you down
    one of these days.   *Exeunt*. Lol. *and* Ant.
Isabella. Here the restrained current might make breach,
    Spite of the watchful bankers; would a woman stray,
    She need not gad abroad to seek her sin,
    It would be brought home one ways or other:
    The needle's point will to the fixed north,
    Such drawing artics women's beauties are.   200

    Enter Lollio.

Lollio. How dost thou, sweet rogue?
Isabella. How now?
Lollio. Come, there are degrees, one fool may be better than another.
Isabella. What's the matter?
Lollio. Nay, if thou giv'st thy mind to fool's-flesh, have at thee!
        [Tries to kiss her.]
Isabella. You bold slave, you!
Lollio. I could follow now as t'other fool did:
    What should I fear,
    Having all joys about me? Do you but smile,

196 bankers] dike-builders   200 artics] arctics

    And love shall play the wanton on your lip,   210
    Meet and retire, retire and meet again:
    Look you but cheerfully, and in your eyes,
    I shall behold my own deformity,
    And dress my self up fairer; I know this shape
Becomes me not—and so as it follows; but is not this the more foolish
way? Come sweet rogue, kiss me my little Lacedemonian. Let me feel
how thy pulses beat; thou hast a thing about thee, would do a man pleasure,
I'll lay my hand on't.

Isabella. Sirrah, no more, I see you have discovered
    This love's knight-arrant, who hath made adventure   220
    For purchase of my love; be silent, mute,
    Mute as a statue, or his injunction
    For me enjoying, shall be to cut thy throat:
    I'll do it, though for no other purpose,
    And be sure he'll not refuse it.

Lollio. My share, that's all, I'll have my fool's part with you.

Isabella. No more, your master.

    Enter Alibius.

Alibius.   Sweet, how dost thou?

Isabella. Your bounden servant, sir.

Alibius.   Fie, fie, sweet heart,
    No more of that.

Isabella.   You were best lock me up.

Alibius. In my arms and bosom, my sweet Isabella,   230
    I'll lock thee up most nearly. Lollio,
    We have employment, we have task in hand;
    At noble Vermandero's, our castle captain,
    There is a nuptial to be solemniz'd,
    Beatrice Joanna his fair daughter bride,
    For which the gentleman hath bespoke our pains,
    A mixture of our madmen and our fools,
    To finish (as it were) and make the fag
    Of all the revels, the third night from the first,
    Only an unexpected passage over,   240
    To make a frightful pleasure, that is all,
    But not the all I aim at; could we so act it,
    To teach it in a wild distracted measure,

---

216 Lacedemonian] presumably one who speaks tersely, though perhaps with a quibble on
'laced-mutton', a cant term for prostitute   238 fag] end   240] The madmen are
simply to rush in unexpectedly.   242ff.] Presumably Alibius aims to use the occasion
for some advertisement, though the plan is obscure.

Though out of form and figure, breaking time's head,
It were no matter, 'twould be heal'd again
In one age or other, if not in this,
This, this, Lollio, there's a good reward begun,
And will beget a bounty be it known.

Lollio. This is easy, sir, I'll warrant you: you have about you fools and madmen that can dance very well, and 'tis no wonder, your best dancers are
not the wisest men; the reason is, with often jumping they jolt their brains
down into their feet, and their wits lie more in their heels than in their
heads.   253

Alibius. Honest Lollio, thou giv'st me a good reason, and a comfort in it.

Isabella. Y'ave a fine trade on't, madmen and fools are a staple-commodity.

Alibius. Oh wife, we must eat, wear clothes, and live;
Just at the lawyers' haven we arrive,
By madmen and by fools we both do thrive.   *Exeunt.*

[SCENE III]

Enter Vermandero, Alsemero, Jasperino, *and* Beatrice.

Vermandero. Valencia speaks so nobly of you, sir,
I wish I had a daughter now for you.

Alsemero. The fellow of this creature were a partner
For a king's love.

Vermandero.   I had her fellow once, sir,
But heaven has married her to joys eternal,
'Twere sin to wish her in this vale again.
Come sir, your friend and you shall see the pleasures
Which my health chiefly joys in.

Alsemero. I hear the beauty of this seat largely.

Vermandero. It falls much short of that.   *Exeunt. Manet* Beatrice.

Beatrice.   So, here's one step   10
Into my father's favour, time will fix him,
I have got him now the liberty of the house,
So wisdom by degrees works out her freedom;
And if that eye be dark'ned that offends me,
I wait but that eclipse; this gentleman
Shall soon shine glorious in my father's liking,
Through the refulgent virtue of my love.

Enter Deflores.

Deflores. [*Aside*] My thoughts are at a banquet; for the deed
I feel no weight in't, 'tis but light and cheap
For the sweet recompense, that I set down for't.   20

257 lawyers' haven] implying that lawyers' clients were always fools

Beatrice. Deflores.

Deflores.   Lady.

Beatrice.   Thy looks promise cheerfully.

Deflores. All things are answerable, time, circumstance,
  Your wishes and my service.

Beatrice.   Is it done then?

Deflores. Piracquo is no more.

Beatrice. My joys start at mine eyes, our sweet'st delights
  Are evermore born weeping.

Deflores. I've a token for you.

Beatrice. For me?

Deflores. But it was sent somewhat unwillingly,
  I could not get the ring without the finger.   30

                                        [*Shows the finger.*]

Beatrice. Bless me! what hast thou done?

Deflores.   Why, is that more
  Than killing the whole man? I cut his heart-strings.
  A greedy hand thrust in a dish at court
  In a mistake, hath had as much as this.

Beatrice. 'Tis the first token my father made me send him.

Deflores. And I made him send it back again
  For his last token, I was loath to leave it,
  And I'm sure dead men have no use of jewels;
  He was as loath to part with't, for it stuck,
  As if the flesh and it were both one substance.   40

Beatrice. At the stag's fall the keeper has his fees:
  'Tis soon apply'd, all dead men's fees are yours, sir;
  I pray, bury the finger, but the stone
  You may make use on shortly, the true value,
  Tak't of my truth, is near three hundred ducats.

Deflores. 'Twill hardly buy a capcase for one's conscience, tho',
  To keep it from the worm, as fine as 'tis.
  Well, being my fees I'll take it,
  Great men have taught me that, or else my merit
  Would scorn the way on't.

Beatrice.   It might justly, sir: 50
  Why, thou mistak'st Deflores, 'tis not given
  In state of recompense.

Deflores.   No, I hope so, Lady,
  You should soon witness my contempt to't then.

---

46 capcase] travelling-bag

Beatrice. Prithee, thou look'st as if thou wert offended.

Deflores. That were strange, Lady, 'tis not possible
    My service should draw such a cause from you.
    Offended? Could you think so? That were much
    For one of my performance, and so warm
    Yet in my service.

Beatrice. 'Twere misery in me to give you cause, sir.   60

Deflores. I know so much, it were so, misery
    In her most sharp condition.

Beatrice.   'Tis resolv'd then;
    Look you sir, here's 3000 golden florins,
    I have not meanly thought upon thy merit.

Deflores. What, salary? Now you move me.

Beatrice.   How, Deflores?

Deflores. Do you place me in the rank of verminous fellows,
    To destroy things for wages? offer gold?
    The life blood of man! Is any thing
    Valued too precious for my recompense?

Beatrice. I understand thee not.

Deflores.   I could ha' hir'd   70
    A journeyman in murder at this rate,
    And mine own conscience might have, and have had
    The work brought home.

Beatrice. [*Aside*]   I'm in a labyrinth;
    What will content him? I would fain be rid of him.
    —I'll double the sum, sir.

Deflores.   You take a course
    To double my vexation, that's the good you do.

Beatrice. [*Aside*] Bless me! I am now in worse plight than I was,
    I know not what will please him.—For my fears' sake
    I prithee make away with all speed possible.
    And if thou be'st so modest not to name   80
    The sum that will content thee, paper blushes not,
    Send thy demand in writing, it shall follow thee,
    But prithee take thy flight.

Deflores.   You must fly too then.

Beatrice. I?

Deflores.   I'll not stir a foot else.

Beatrice.   What's your meaning?

58 For . . . performance] for what I have done   72-3 might have] I might have retained
unharmed: the quarto ends the line at 'might have' and all editors have followed Dilke in
adding the words 'slept at ease'; but though the quarto lineation suggests that something
may have been omitted, the quarto reading seems acceptable.

Deflores. Why, are not you as guilty, in, I'm sure,
　　As deep as I? and we should stick together.
　　Come, your fears counsel you but ill, my absence
　　Would draw suspect upon you instantly,
　　There were no rescue for you.
Beatrice. [*Aside*]　　　　　　　He speaks home.
Deflores. Nor is it fit we two, engag'd so jointly,　　　　　90
　　Should part and live asunder.　　　　　[*Tries to kiss her.*]
Beatrice.　　　　　　　　How now sir?
　　This shows not well.
Deflores.　　　　　　What makes your lip so strange?
　　This must not be betwixt us.
Beatrice. [*Aside*]　　　　　　The man talks wildly.
Deflores. Come kiss me with a zeal now.
Beatrice. [*Aside*]　　　　　　Heaven, I doubt him.
Deflores. I will not stand so long to beg 'em shortly.
Beatrice. Take heed Deflores of forgetfulness,
　　'Twill soon betray us.
Deflores.　　　　　　Take you heed first;
　　Faith, y'are grown much forgetful, y'are to blame in't.
Beatrice. [*Aside*] He's bold, and I am blam'd for't.
Deflores.　　　　　　　　　　I have eas'd
　　You of your trouble, think on't, I'm in pain,　　　　　100
　　And must be eas'd of you; 'tis a charity,
　　Justice invites your blood to understand me.
Beatrice. I dare not.
Deflores.　　　　　Quickly.
Beatrice.　　　　　　　Oh I never shall,
　　Speak it yet further off that I may lose
　　What has been spoken, and no sound remain on't.
　　I would not hear so much offence again
　　For such another deed.
Deflores.　　　　　　Soft, Lady, soft;
　　The last is not yet paid for. Oh this act
　　Has put me into spirit; I was greedy on't
　　As the parcht earth of moisture, when the clouds weep.　　110
　　Did not you mark, I wrought my self into't,
　　Nay, sued and kneel'd for't: why was all that pains took?
　　You see I have thrown contempt upon your gold,
　　Not that I want it not, for I do piteously:
　　In order I will come unto't, and make use on't,
　　But 'twas not held so precious to begin with;

115 in order] i.e., after what is more important

For I place wealth after the heels of pleasure,
And were I not resolv'd in my belief
That thy virginity were perfect in thee,
I should but take my recompense with grudging,   120
As if I had but half my hopes I agreed for.
Beatrice. Why, 'tis impossible thou canst be so wicked,
Or shelter such a cunning cruelty,
To make his death the murderer of my honour.
Thy language is so bold and vicious,
I cannot see which way I can forgive it
With any modesty.
Deflores.   Push, you forget your self—
A woman dipt in blood, and talk of modesty?
Beatrice. O misery of sin! would I had been bound
Perpetually unto my living hate   130
In that Piracquo, than to hear these words.
Think but upon the distance that Creation
Set 'twixt thy blood and mine, and keep thee there.
Deflores. Look but into your conscience, read me there,
'Tis a true book, you'll find me there your equal:
Push, fly not to your birth, but settle you
In what the act has made you, y'are no more now;
You must forget your parentage to me,
Y'are the deed's creature, by that name you lost
Your first condition, and I challenge you,   140
As peace and innocency has turn'd you out,
And made you one with me.
Beatrice.   With thee, foul villain?
Deflores. Yes, my fair murd'ress; do you urge me?
Though thou writ'st maid, thou whore in thy affection,
'Twas chang'd from thy first love, and that's a kind
Of whoredom in thy heart, and he's chang'd now,
To bring thy second on, thy Alsemero,
Whom (by all sweets that ever darkness tasted),
If I enjoy thee not, thou ne'er enjoy'st;
I'll blast the hopes and joys of marriage,   150
I'll confess all, my life I rate at nothing.
Beatrice. Deflores!
Deflores. I shall rest from all lovers' plagues then;
I live in pain now: that shooting eye
Will burn my heart to cinders.
Beatrice.   O sir, hear me.

138 to] in favour of   140 challenge] claim   146 he's] i.e., Alonzo

Deflores. She that in life and love refuses me,
  In death and shame my partner she shall be.
Beatrice. Stay, hear me once for all, I make thee master
  Of all the wealth I have in gold and jewels,
  Let me go poor unto my bed with honour,   160
  And I am rich in all things.
Deflores.   Let this silence thee:
  The wealth of all Valencia shall not buy
  My pleasure from me.
  Can you weep Fate from its determin'd purpose?
  So soon may you weep me.
Beatrice.   Vengeance begins;
  Murder I see is followed by more sins.
  Was my creation in the womb so curst,
  It must engender with a viper first?
Deflores. Come, rise, and shroud your blushes in my bosom,
  Silence is one of pleasure's best receipts: 170
  Thy peace is wrought for ever in this yielding.
  'Las, how the turtle pants! Thou'lt love anon
  What thou so fear'st, and faint'st to venture on.   *Exeunt.*

ACTUS QUARTUS

Enter Gentlemen, Vermandero *meeting them with action of wonderment at the flight of* Piracquo. *Enter* Alsemero, *with* Jasperino, *and* Gallants; Vermandero *points to him, the* Gentlemen *seeming to applaud the choice.* [*Exeunt*] Alsemero, Jasperino, *and* Gentlemen; Beatrice *the bride following in great state accompanied with* Diaphanta, Isabella, *and other* Gentlewomen: Deflores *after all, smiling at the accident*; Alonzo's *ghost appears to* Deflores *in the midst of his smile, startles him, showing him the hand whose finger he had cut off. They pass over in great solemnity.*

[SCENE I]

Enter Beatrice.

Beatrice. This fellow has undone me endlessly,
  Never was bride so fearfully distrest;
  The more I think upon th'ensuing night,

---

168 first] i.e., before mating with a natural man   IV, s.d.] A dumb show to pass over
action quickly.   s.d. 6 *accident*] incident   1 endlessly] perhaps with a hint of 'to eternity'

And whom I am to cope with in embraces,
One both ennobled both in blood and mind,
So clear in understanding (that's my plague now),
Before whose judgment will my fault appear
Like malefactors' crimes before tribunals:
There is no hiding on't, the more I dive
Into my own distress; how a wise man   10
Stands for a great calamity. There's no venturing
Into his bed, what course soe'er I light upon,
Without my shame, which may grow up to danger;
He cannot but in justice strangle me
As I lie by him, as a cheater use me;
'Tis a precious craft to play with a false die
Before a cunning gamester. Here's his closet,
The key left in't, and he abroad i'th'park;
Sure 'twas forgot, I'll be so bold as look in't.
Bless me! A right physician's closet 'tis,   20
Set round with vials, every one her mark too.
Sure he does practise physic for his own use,
Which may be safely call'd your great man's wisdom.
What manuscript lies here? The Book of Experiment,
Call'd *Secrets in Nature*: so 'tis, 'tis so.
'How to know whether a woman be with child or no.'
I hope I am not yet; if he should try though!
Let me see, folio 45. Here 'tis;
The leaf tuckt down upon't, the place suspicious.
'If you would know   30
Whether a woman be with child, or not,
give her two spoonfuls of the white water in Glass C.'—
Where's that Glass C? O yonder, I see't now,—
'And if she be with child,
She sleeps full twelve hours after, if not, not.'
None of that water comes into my belly.
I'll know you from a hundred, I could break
You now or turn you into milk, and so
Beguile the master of the mystery,
But I'll look to you. Ha! that which is next,   40

5] The first 'both' may be a piece of compositor's dittography.   10–11 how . . . calamity]
how the man's cleverness is bound to mean calamity for me   23 wisdom] shrewdness
(i.e., in taking precautions against his own danger)   25 *Secrets in Nature*] *De Arcanis
Naturae* by Antonius Mizaldus (1520–78) does not contain these recipes; but another book
of his has similar ones for pregnancy and virginity.

Is ten times worse. 'How to know whether
A woman be a maid, or not'; if that
Should be apply'd, what would become of me?
Belike he has a strong faith of my purity,
That never yet made proof; but this he calls
'A merry sleight, but true experiment,
the author Antonius Mizaldus. Give the party you suspect the quantity
of a spoonful of the water in the glass M, which upon her that is a maid,
makes three several effects: 'twill make her incontinently gape, then
fall into a sudden sneezing, last into a violent laughing, else dull, heavy
and lumpish.'   51
Where had I been?
I fear it, yet 'tis seven hours to bed time.

Enter Diaphanta.

Diaphanta. Cuds, madam, are you here?
Beatrice. [*Aside*]   Seeing that wench now
A trick comes in my mind; 'tis a nice piece
Gold cannot purchase.—I come hither wench,
To look my lord.
Diaphanta. [*Aside*]   Would I had such a cause
To look him too.—Why, he's i'th'park, madam.
Beatrice. There let him be.
Diaphanta.   Ay, madam, let him compass
Whole parks and forests, as great rangers do,   60
At roosting time a little lodge can hold 'em.
Earth-conquering Alexander, that thought the world
Too narrow for him, in the end had but his pit-hole.
Beatrice. I fear thou art not modest, Diaphanta.
Diaphanta. Your thoughts are so unwilling to be known, madam,
'Tis ever the bride's fashion towards bed-time,
To set light by her joys, as if she ow'd 'em not.
Beatrice. Her joys? her fears thou would'st say.
Diaphanta.   Fear of what?
Beatrice. Art thou a maid, and talk'st so to a maid?
You leave a blushing business behind,   70
Beshrew your heart for't.

44–5] The implication appears to be that those who have most faith do not put it to the
proof.   46 sleight] The quarto has 'slight', but the spellings were often interchanged.
49 gape] probably in the sense of yawn   52 Where . . . been] i.e., if I had not found this
54 Cuds] exclamation; deformation of 'God's'   55–6 'tis . . . purchase] it's a scrupulous
girl that can't be bought   63 pit-hole] implying the grave, but with a sexual suggestion
67 ow'd] owned

Diaphanta.   Do you mean good sooth, madam?
Beatrice. Well, if I'd thought upon the fear at first,
    Man should have been unknown.
Diaphanta.   Is't possible?
Beatrice. I will give a thousand ducats to that woman
    Would try what my fear were, and tell me true
    Tomorrow, when she gets from't: as she likes
    I might perhaps be drawn to't.
Diaphanta.   Are you in earnest?
Beatrice. Do you get the woman, then challenge me,
    And see if I'll fly from't; but I must tell you
    This by the way, she must be a true maid,   80
    Else there's no trial, my fears are not hers else.
Diaphanta. Nay, she that I would put into your hands, madam,
    Shall be a maid.
Beatrice.   You know I should be sham'd else,
    Because she lies for me.
Diaphanta.   'Tis a strange humour:
    But are you serious still? Would you resign
    Your first night's pleasure, and give money too?
Beatrice. As willingly as live; [*Aside*] alas, the gold
    Is but a by-bet to wedge in the honour.
Diaphanta. I do not know how the world goes abroad
    For faith or honesty, there's both requir'd in this.   90
    Madam, what say you to me, and stray no further?
    I've a good mind in troth to earn your money.
Beatrice. Y'are too quick, I fear, to be a maid.
Diaphanta. How? not a maid? nay then you urge me, madam,
    Your honourable self is not a truer
    With all your fears upon you——
Beatrice. [*Aside*]   Bad enough then.
Diaphanta. Than I with all my lightsome joys about me.
Beatrice. I'm glad to hear't then; you dare put your honesty
    Upon an easy trial?
Diaphanta.   Easy?—anything.
Beatrice. I'll come to you straight.   [*Goes to closet.*]
Diaphanta. [*Aside*]   She will not search me? will she?   100
    Like the forewoman of a female jury?

73 Man ... unknown] I should have remained a virgin   88 by-bet] A much-disputed
phrase; the sense appears to be that this is an extra assurance to make her honour safe.
101] Perhaps an allusion to the Countess of Essex's divorce trial (in 1613), where she was
examined by a panel of matrons.

Beatrice. Glass M. Ay, this is it; look Diaphanta,
    You take no worse than I do.   [*Drinks.*]
Diaphanta.   And in so doing,
    I will not question what 'tis, but take it.   [*Drinks.*]
Beatrice. [*Aside*]   Now if
    The experiment be true, 'twill praise it self,
    And give me noble ease:—begins already,   [Diaphanta *gapes.*]
    There's the first symptom; and what haste it makes
    To fall into the second, there by this time!   [Diaphanta *sneezes.*]
    Most admirable secret. On the contrary
    It stirs not me a whit, which most concerns it.   110
Diaphanta. Ha, ha, ha.
Beatrice. [*Aside*]   Just in all things, and in order,
    As if 'twere circumscrib'd, one accident
    Gives way unto another.
Diaphanta.   Ha, ha, ha.
Beatrice. How now wench?
Diaphanta.   Ha, ha, ha, I am so so light
    At heart, ha, ha, ha, so pleasurable.
    But one swig more, sweet madam.
Beatrice.   Ay, tomorrow,
    We shall have time to sit by't.
Diaphanta.   Now I'm sad
    Again.
Beatrice. [*Aside*] It lays it self so gently too.
    —Come wench, most honest Diaphanta
    I dare call thee now.   120
Diaphanta. Pray tell me, madam, what trick call you this?
Beatrice. I'll tell thee all hereafter; we must study
    The carriage of this business.
Diaphanta.   I shall carry't well,
    Because I love the burthen.
Beatrice.   About midnight
    You must not fail to steal forth gently,
    That I may use the place.
Diaphanta.   Oh fear not, madam,
    I shall be cool by that time: the bride's place,
    And with a thousand ducats! I'm for a justice now,
    I bring a portion with me, I scorn small fools.   *Exeunt.*

110 which . . . it] whom it most concerns   126 use] occupy

[SCENE II]

Enter Vermandero *and* Servant.

Vermandero. I tell thee knave, mine honour is in question,
    A thing till now free from suspicion,
    Nor ever was there cause;
who of my gentlemen are absent? Tell me and truly how many, and who.
Servant. Antonio, sir, and Franciscus.
Vermandero. When did they leave the castle?
Servant. Some ten days since, sir, the one intending to Briamata, th'other
    for Valencia.
Vermandero. The time accuses 'em, a charge of murder
    Is brought within my castle gate, Piracquo's murder,   10
    I dare not answer faithfully their absence:
    A strict command of apprehension
    Shall pursue 'em suddenly, and either wipe
    The stain off clear, or openly discover it.
    Provide me winged warrants for the purpose.   *Exit* Servant.
    See, I am set on again.

    Enter Tomazo.

Tomazo. I claim a brother of you.
Vermandero.   Y'are too hot,
    Seek him not here.
Tomazo.   Yes, 'mongst your dearest bloods,
    If my peace find no fairer satisfaction,
    This is the place must yield account for him,   20
    For here I left him, and the hasty tie
    Of this snatcht marriage gives strong testimony
    Of his most certain ruin.
Vermandero.   Certain falsehood;
    This is the place indeed, his breach of faith
    Has too much marr'd both my abused love,
    The honourable love I reserv'd for him,
    And mockt my daughter's joy; the prepar'd morning
    Blusht at his infidelity, he left
    Contempt and scorn to throw upon those friends
    Whose belief hurt 'em: oh 'twas most ignoble   30
    To take his flight so unexpectedly,
    And throw such public wrongs on those that lov'd him.

---

11 faithfully] in good faith   30 whose belief hurt 'em] who were pained at having to believe what they saw

Tomazo. Then this is all your answer?

Vermandero.   'Tis too fair
    For one of his alliance; and I warn you
    That this place no more see you.   *Exit.*

    Enter Deflores.

Tomazo.   The best is,
    There is more ground to meet a man's revenge on.
    Honest Deflores.

Deflores.   That's my name indeed.
    Saw you the bride? Good sweet sir, which way took she?

Tomazo. I have blest mine eyes from seeing such a false one.

Deflores. [*Aside*] I'd fain get off, this man's not for my company,   40
    I smell his brother's blood when I come near him.

Tomazo. Come hither kind and true one; I remember
    My brother lov'd thee well.

Deflores.   O purely, dear sir.
    [*Aside*] Me thinks I am now again a-killing on him,
    He brings it so fresh to me.

Tomazo.   Thou canst guess, sirrah,
    (One honest friend has an instinct of jealousy)
    At some foul guilty person?

Deflores. 'Las sir, I am so charitable, I think none
    Worse than my self.—You did not see the bride then?

Tomazo. I prithee name her not. Is she not wicked?   50

Deflores. No, no, a pretty easy round-packt sinner,
    As your most ladies are, else you might think
    I flatter'd her; but sir, at no hand wicked,
    Till th'are so old their sins and vices meet,
    And they salute witches. I am call'd, I think sir:
    [*Aside*] His company ev'n o'erlays my conscience.   *Exit.*

Tomazo. That Deflores has a wondrous honest heart.
    He'll bring it out in time, I'm assur'd on't.
    O here's the glorious master of the day's joy.
    I will not be long till he and I do reckon.   60

    Enter Alsemero.

    Sir.

Alsemero. You are most welcome.

Tomazo.   You may call that word back,
    I do not think I am, nor wish to be.

46 jealousy] suspicion   54 sins and vices] Most editors accept Dyce's emendation to
'chins and noses', which goes well with 'witches' and is stronger than the quarto reading,
though that does make fair sense.

Alsemero. 'Tis strange you found the way to this house then.

Tomazo. Would I'd ne'er known the cause, I'm none of those sir,
　　That come to give you joy, and swill your wine,
　　'Tis a more precious liquor that must lay
　　The fiery thirst I bring.

Alsemero.　　　　　　　　　Your words and you
　　Appear to me great strangers.

Tomazo.　　　　　　　　　Time and our swords
　　May make us more acquainted; this the business:
　　I should have a brother in your place;　　　　　　　　　70
　　How treachery and malice have dispos'd of him,
　　I'm bound to enquire of him which holds his right:
　　Which never could come fairly.

Alsemero.　　　　　　　　　You must look
　　To answer for that word, sir.

Tomazo.　　　　　　　　　Fear you not,
　　I'll have it ready drawn at our next meeting.
　　Keep your day solemn. Farewell, I disturb it not,
　　I'll bear the smart with patience for a time.　　　　*Exit.*

Alsemero. 'Tis somewhat ominous this, a quarrel ent'red
　　Upon this day; my innocence relieves me,

　Enter Jasperino.

　I should be wondrous sad else.—Jasperino,　　　　　　80
　　I have news to tell thee, strange news.

Jasperino.　　　　　　　　　I ha' some too,
　　I think as strange as yours; would I might keep
　　Mine, so my faith and friendship might be kept in't.
　　Faith sir, dispense a little with my zeal,
　　And let it cool in this.

Alsemero.　　　　　　　This puts me on,
　　And blames thee for thy slowness.

Jasperino.　　　　　　　　All may prove nothing,
　　Only a friendly fear that leapt from me, sir.

Alsemero. No question it may prove nothing; let's partake it though.

Jasperino. 'Twas Diaphanta's chance, for to that wench
　　I pretend honest love, and she deserves it,　　　　　90
　　To leave me in a back part of the house,
　　A place we chose for private conference;

84-5 dispense . . . this] let me be less zealous than usual and keep back my news　85 puts
me on] alerts my interest　　90 pretend] offer

> She was no sooner gone, but instantly
> I heard your bride's voice in the next room to me;
> And lending more attention, found Deflores
> Louder than she.

Alsemero.   Deflores? Thou art out now.

Jasperino. You'll tell me more anon.

Alsemero.   Still I'll prevent thee,
> The very sight of him is poison to her.

Jasperino. That made me stagger too, but Diaphanta
> At her return confirm'd it.

Alsemero.   Diaphanta!   100

Jasperino. Then fell we both to listen, and words pass'd
> Like those that challenge interest in a woman.

Alsemero. Peace, quench thy zeal, 'tis dangerous to thy bosom.

Jasperino. Then truth is full of peril.

Alsemero.   Such truths are.
> O were she the sole glory of the earth,
> Had eyes that could shoot fire into kings' breasts,
> And toucht, she sleeps not here; yet I have time
> Though night be near, to be resolv'd hereof;
> And prithee do not weigh me by my passions.

Jasperino. I never weigh'd friend so.

Alsemero.   Done charitably.   110
> That key will lead thee to a pretty secret,   [*Gives key.*]
> By a Chaldean taught me, and I've made
> My study upon some; bring from my closet
> A glass inscrib'd there with the letter M.
> And question not my purpose.

Jasperino.   It shall be done sir.   *Exit.*

Alsemero. How can this hang together? Not an hour since,
> Her woman came pleading her lady's fears,
> Deliver'd her for the most timorous virgin
> That ever shrank at man's name, and so modest,
> She charg'd her weep out her request to me,   120
> That she might come obscurely to my bosom.

Enter Beatrice.

Beatrice. [*Aside*] All things go well, my woman's preparing yonder
> For her sweet voyage, which grieves me to lose;
> Necessity compels it; I lose all else.

---

96 out] out of your mind   107 and toucht] and yet were tainted   107 here] i.e., with
Alsemero   121 obscurely] in darkness

Alsemero. [*Aside*] Push, modesty's shrine is set in yonder forehead.
    I cannot be too sure tho'.—My Joanna!
Beatrice. Sir, I was bold to weep a message to you,
    Pardon my modest fears.
Alsemero. [*Aside*]   The dove's not meeker.
    She's abus'd, questionless.—Oh are you come, sir?

    Enter Jasperino.

Beatrice. [*Aside*] The glass upon my life; I see the letter.   130
Jasperino. Sir, this is M.
Alsemero.   'Tis it.
Beatrice. [*Aside*]   I am suspected.
Alsemero. How fitly our bride comes to partake with us!
Beatrice. What is't, my Lord?
Alsemero.   No hurt.
Beatrice.   Sir, pardon me,
    I seldom taste of any composition.
Alsemero. But this
    Upon my warrant you shall venture on.
Beatrice. I fear 'twill make me ill.
Alsemero.   Heaven forbid that.
Beatrice. [*Aside*] I'm put now to my cunning, th'effects I know,
    If I can now but feign 'em handsomely.   [*Drinks.*]
Alsemero. [*Aside to* Jasperino] It has that secret virtue, it ne'er miss'd, sir,
    Upon a virgin.   141
Jasperino.   Treble qualitied?   [Beatrice *gapes and sneezes.*]
Alsemero. By all that's virtuous it takes there, proceeds!
Jasperino. This is the strangest trick to know a maid by.
Beatrice. Ha, ha, ha,
    You have given me joy of heart to drink, my Lord.
Alsemero. No, thou hast given me such joy of heart,
    That never can be blasted.
Beatrice.   What's the matter sir?
Alsemero. [*Aside*] See now 'tis settled in a melancholy,
    Keeps both the time and method.—My Joanna,
    Chaste as the breath of heaven, or morning's womb,   150
    That brings the day forth, thus my love encloses thee.   *Exeunt.*

[SCENE III]

Enter Isabella *and* Lollio.

Isabella. Oh heaven! is this the waiting moon?
Does love turn fool, run mad, and all at once?
Sirrah, here's a madman, akin to the fool too,
A lunatic lover.

Lollio. No, no, not he I brought the letter from?

Isabella. Compare his inside with his out, and tell me.   [*Gives him letter.*]

Lollio. The out's mad, I'm sure of that, I had a taste on't.
[*Reads.*] 'To the bright Andromeda, chief chambermaid to the knight
of the sun, at the sign of Scorpio, in the middle region, sent by the
bellows-mender of Aeolus. Pay the post.'   10
This is stark madness.

Isabella.   Now mark the inside.
[*Reads.*] 'Sweet lady, having now cast off this counterfeit cover of a
madman, I appear to your best judgment
A true and faithful lover of your beauty.'

Lollio. He is mad still.

Isabella.   'If any fault you find,
Chide those perfections in you, which have made
Me imperfect; 'tis the same sun
That causeth to grow, and enforceth to wither,—'

Lollio. Oh rogue!

Isabella. '—Shapes and transshapes, destroys and builds again;   20
I come in winter to you,
Dismantled of my proper ornaments;
By the sweet splendour of your cheerful smiles,
I spring and live a lover.'

Lollio.   Mad rascal still.

Isabella. 'Tread him not under foot, that shall appear
An honour to your bounties. I remain——
Mad till I speak with you, from whom I expect
My cure. Yours all, or one beside himself,
Franciscus.'

Lollio. You are like to have a fine time on't, my master and I may give over
our professions, I do not think but you can cure fools and madmen faster
than we, with little pains too.   32

Isabella. Very likely.

1 waiting moon] perhaps, the lunatic in attendance on me (with play on 'waning moon')
8–10] This gibberish would doubtless have meant more to Jacobean audiences than to us;
Franciscus is playing the part of Perseus rescuing Andromeda; Scorpio governs the privy
parts of the body; so 'middle region' contains an obscene pun.

Lollio. One thing I must tell you, Mistress: you perceive, that I am privy
to your skill; if I find you minister once and set up the trade, I put in
for my thirds, I shall be mad or fool else.

Isabella. The first place is thine, believe it, Lollio,
    If I do fall.

Lollio.   I fall upon you.

Isabella.   So.

Lollio. Well, I stand to my venture.

Isabella. But thy counsel now, how shall I deal with 'em?   40

Lollio. Why, do you mean to deal with 'em?

Isabella. Nay, the fair understanding, how to use 'em.

Lollio. Abuse 'em, that's the way to mad the fool,
    and make a fool of the madman, and then you use 'em kindly.

Isabella. 'Tis easy, I'll practise, do thou observe it;
    The key of thy wordrobe.

Lollio. There fit your self for 'em, and I'll fit 'em both for you.
                               [Gives her the key.]

Isabella. Take thou no further notice than the outside.   *Exit.*

Lollio. Not an inch, I'll put you to the inside.

    Enter Alibius.

Alibius. Lollio, art there?   50
    Will all be perfect, think'st thou? Tomorrow night,
    As if to close up the solemnity,
    Vermandero expects us.

Lollio.   I mistrust
    The madmen most, the fools will do well enough:
    I have taken pains with them.

Alibius.   Tush,
    They cannot miss; the more absurdity,
    The more commends it, so no rough behaviours
    Affright the ladies; they are nice things thou know'st.

Lollio. You need not fear, sir, so long as we are there with our commanding
    peesles, they'll be as tame as the ladies themselves.   60

Alibius. I will see them once more rehearse before they go.

Lollio. I was about it, sir; look you to the madmen's morris, and let me
    alone with the other; there is one or two that I mistrust their fooling;
    I'll instruct them, and then they shall rehearse the whole measure.

Alibius. Do so, I'll see the music prepar'd: but Lollio,
    By the way, how does my wife brook her restraint?
    Does she not grudge at it?

36 thirds] A third of the proceeds of captures were due to the king.   42 fair under-
standing] understand me in the sense in which I spoke   57 so] so long as   60 peesles]
pizzles, i.e., whips made from bulls' penises

Lollio. So, so, she takes some pleasure in the house, she would abroad else; you must allow her a little more length, she's kept too short.

Alibius. She shall along to Vermandero's with us,   70
    That will serve her for a month's liberty.

Lollio. What's that on your face, sir?

Alibius. Where, Lollio? I see nothing.

Lollio. Cry you mercy, sir, 'tis your nose, it show'd like the trunk of a young elephant.

Alibius. Away, rascal: I'll prepare the music, Lollio.   *Ex.* Ali.

Lollio. Do, sir; and I'll dance the whilst; Tony, where art thou Tony?

Enter Antonio.

Antonio. Here cousin, where art thou?

Lollio. Come, Tony, the footmanship I taught you.

Antonio. I had rather ride, cousin.   80

Lollio. Ay, a whip take you; but I'll keep you out,
    Vault in; look you, Tony, fa, la la, la la.   [*Dances.*]

Antonio. Fa, la la, la la.   [*Dances.*]

Lollio. There, an honour.

Antonio. Is this an honour, coz?   [*Bows.*]

Lollio. Yes, and it please your worship.

Antonio. Does honour bend in the hams, coz?

Lollio. Marry does it, as low as worship, squireship, nay yeomandry it self sometimes, from whence it first stiffened; there, rise a caper.

Antonio. Caper after an honour, coz?   90

Lollio. Very proper, for honour is but a caper, rise as fast and high, has a knee or two, and falls to the ground again; you can remember your figure, Tony?   *Exit.*

Antonio. Yes, cousin, when I see thy figure, I can remember mine.

Enter Isabella [*like a madwoman*].

Isabella. Hey, how he treads the air, shough, shough, t'other way,
    He burns his wings else, here's wax enough below,
    Icarus, more
    Than will be cancelled these eighteen moons;
    He's down, he's down, what a terrible fall he had!

74–5] the long nose, perhaps because Alibius is being led by the nose   80 ride] with a sexual pun; cf. l. 142   81 keep you out] i.e., from Isabella   84 honour] curtsy in a dance   86 and] an   91 rise] rises   92–4 figure] in the senses of (1) dance measure, (2) face   95 shough] shoo (exclamation of impatience)   96 wax] that with which the wings of Icarus were attached to his body   98] The wax image now refers to wax seals.

Stand up, thou son of Cretan Dedalus,   100
And let us tread the lower labyrinth;
I'll bring thee to the clue.
Antonio. Prethee, coz, let me alone.
Isabella.   Art thou not drown'd?
Above thy head I saw a heap of clouds,
Wrapt like a Turkish turbant; on thy back,
A crookt chamelion-colour'd rainbow hung
Like a tiara down unto thy hams.
Let me suck out those billows in thy belly;
Hark how they roar and rumble in the straits!
Bless thee from the pirates.   110
Antonio. Pox upon you, let me alone.
Isabella. Why shouldst thou mount so high as Mercury,
Unless thou hadst reversion of his place?
Stay in the moon with me, Endymion,
And we will rule these wild rebellious waves,
That would have drown'd my love.
Antonio. I'll kick thee if again thou touch me,
Thou wild unshapen antic; I am no fool,
You bedlam.
Isabella.   But you are as sure as I am, mad.
Have I put on this habit of a frantic,   120
With love as full of fury to beguile
The nimble eye of watchful jealousy,
And am I thus rewarded?   [*Reveals herself.*]
Antonio.   Ha, dearest beauty!
Isabella. No, I have no beauty now,
Nor never had, but what was in my garments.
You a quick-sighted lover? come not near me.
Keep your caparisons, y'are aptly clad,
I came a feigner to return stark mad.   *Exit.*

  Enter Lollio.

Antonio. Stay, or I shall change condition,
And become as you are.   130
Lollio. Why Tony, whither now? why, fool!
Antonio. Whose fool, usher of idiots? You coxcomb! I have fool'd too much.
Lollio. You were best be mad another while then.

101-2] a reference to the thread given by Ariadne to Theseus so that he could find his
way out of the labyrinth   113 reversion] right of succession   114] Luna (the moon)
fell in love with Endymion.

Antonio. So I am, stark mad, I have cause enough,
    And I could throw the full effects on thee,
    And beat thee like a fury.

Lollio. Do not, do not; I shall not forbear the gentleman under the fool,
if you do; alas, I saw through your fox-skin before now: come, I can give
you comfort, my mistress loves you, and there is as arrant a madman
i'th'house, as you are a fool; your rival, whom she loves not; if after the
masque we can rid her of him, you earn her love she says, and the fool
shall ride her.   142

Antonio. May I believe thee?

Lollio. Yes, or you may choose whether you will or no.

Antonio. She's eas'd of him, I have a good quarrel on't.

Lollio. Well, keep your old station yet, and be quiet.

Antonio. Tell her I will deserve her love.   *Exit.*

Lollio. And you are like to have your desire.

  Enter Franciscus.

Franciscus. Down, down, down a-down a-down, and then with a horse-trick
    To kick Latona's forehead, and break her bowstring.   150

Lollio. [*Aside*] This is t'other counterfeit, I'll put him out of his humour.
[*Takes out letter & reads.*] 'Sweet Lady, having now cast this counterfeit
cover of a madman, I appear to your best judgment a true and faithful
lover of your beauty.' This is pretty well for a madman.

Franciscus. Ha! what's that?

Lollio. 'Chide those perfections in you which made me imperfect.'

Franciscus. I am discover'd to the fool.

Lollio. I hope to discover the fool in you, ere I have done with you. 'Yours
all, or one beside himself, Franciscus.' This madman will mend sure.

Franciscus. What do you read sirrah?   160

Lollio. Your destiny sir, you'll be hang'd for this trick, and another that I
know.

Franciscus. Art thou of counsel with thy mistress?

Lollio. Next her apron strings.

Franciscus. Give me thy hand.

Lollio. Stay, let me put yours in my pocket first: your hand is true, is it not?
It will not pick? I partly fear it, because I think it does lie.

Franciscus. Not in a syllable.

Lollio. So, if you love my mistress so well as you have handled the matter
here, you are like to be cur'd of your madness.   170

Franciscus. And none but she can cure it.

150 Latona] the mother of Apollo and Artemis, possibly confused with Artemis herself
166 yours] i.e., your hand[-writing], the letter   166–7 it . . . pick?] it (his real hand) will
not steal; the letter does not lie

Lollio. Well, I'll give you over then, and she shall cast your water next.

Franciscus. Take for thy pains past.   [*Gives him money.*]

Lollio. I shall deserve more, sir, I hope; my mistress loves you, but must have some proof of your love to her.

Franciscus. There I meet my wishes.

Lollio. That will not serve, you must meet her enemy and yours.

Franciscus. He's dead already.

Lollio. Will you tell me that, and I parted but now with him?

Franciscus. Show me the man.   180

Lollio. Ay, that's a right course now, see him before you kill him in any case, and yet it needs not go so far neither; 'tis but a fool that haunts the house and my mistress in the shape of an idiot; bang but his fool's coat well-favouredly, and 'tis well.

Franciscus. Soundly, soundly.

Lollio. Only reserve him till the masque be past; and if you find him not now in the dance your self, I'll show you. In, in! My master!

Franciscus. He handles him like a feather. Hey!   *Exit.*

   Enter Alibius.

Alibius. Well said; in a readiness, Lollio?

Lollio. Yes, sir.   190

Alibius. Away then, and guide them in Lollio,
   Entreat your mistress to see this sight.
   Hark, is there not one incurable fool
   That might be begg'd? I have friends.

Lollio. I have him for you, one that shall deserve it too.   *Exit.*

Alibius. Good boy, Lollio.

   [*Enter* Isabella, *then* Lollio, *with* Madmen *and* Fools.] *The* Madmen *and* Fools *dance.*

     'Tis perfect; well fit but once these strains,
     We shall have coin and credit for our pains.   *Exeunt.*

---

172 cast your water] diagnose your disease   189 Well said] a common phrase for 'well done'   193-4 one incurable . . . begg'd] 'To beg a fool was to seek appointment as his guardian and thus enjoy his estate' (*Schelling*); Lollio's answer perhaps refers to Isabella or to Alibius himself.

ACTUS QUINTUS

[SCENE I]

Enter Beatrice. *A clock strikes one.*

Beatrice. One struck, and yet she lies by't—oh my fears,
      This strumpet serves her own ends, 'tis apparent now,
      Devours the pleasure with a greedy appetite,
      And never minds my honour or my peace,
      Makes havoc of my right; but she pays dearly for't,
      No trusting of her life with such a secret,
      That cannot rule her blood to keep her promise.
      Beside,
      I have some suspicion of her faith to me,
      Because I was suspected of my lord,   10
      And it must come from her.—Hark, by my horrors,
      Another clock strikes two.   *Strike two.*

   Enter Deflores.

Deflores.   Pist, where are you?
Beatrice. Deflores!
Deflores.   Ay—is she not come from him yet?
Beatrice. As I am a living soul, not.
Deflores.   Sure the devil
      Hath sow'd his itch within her; who'd trust
      A waiting-woman?
Beatrice.   I must trust some body.
Deflores. Push, they are tarmagants.
      Especially when they fall upon their masters
      And have their ladies' first-fruits, th'are mad whelps,
      You cannot stave 'em off from game royal; then   20
      You are so harsh and hardy, ask no counsel,
      And I could have helpt you to an apothecary's daughter would have
      fall'n off before eleven, and thank you too.
Beatrice. O me, not yet? this whore forgets her self.
Deflores. The rascal fares so well, look y'are undone,
      The day-star by this hand, see Phosphorus plain yonder.
Beatrice. Advise me now to fall upon some ruin,
      There is no counsel safe else.

20 stave . . . royal] keep them from going after royalty (but 'game royal' can also mean final
victory in a contest)   26 Phosphorus] the morning star   27 fall . . . ruin] devise some
catastrophe

Deflores.   Peace, I ha't now,
For we must force a rising, there's no remedy.
Beatrice. How? take heed of that.   30
Deflores. Tush, be you quiet, or else give over all.
Beatrice. Prithee, I ha' done then.
Deflores.   This is my reach, I'll set
Some part a-fire of Diaphanta's chamber.
Beatrice. How? fire sir? that may endanger the whole house.
Deflores. You talk of danger when your fame's on fire?
Beatrice. That's true, do what thou wilt now.
Deflores.   Push, I aim
At a most rich success, strikes all dead sure:
The chimney being a-fire, and some light parcels
Of the least danger in her chamber only,
If Diaphanta should be met by chance then,   40
Far from her lodging (which is now suspicious),
It would be thought her fears and affrights then,
Drove her to seek for succour; if not seen
Or met at all, as that's the likeliest,
For her own shame she'll hasten towards her lodging,
I will be ready with a piece high-charg'd,
As 'twere to cleanse the chimney: there 'tis proper now,
But she shall be the mark.
Beatrice.   I'm forc'd to love thee now,
'Cause thou provid'st so carefully for my honour.
Deflores. 'Slid, it concerns the safety of us both,   50
Our pleasure and continuance.
Beatrice.   One word
Now prithee, how for the servants?
Deflores.   I'll dispatch them
Some one way, some another in the hurry,
For buckets, hooks, ladders; fear not you;
The deed shall find its time, and I've thought since
Upon a safe conveyance for the body too.
How this fire purifies wit! Watch you your minute.
Beatrice. Fear keeps my soul upon't, I cannot stray from't.

   Enter Alonzo's *Ghost.*

Deflores. Ha! What art thou that tak'st away the light
'Twixt that star and me? I dread thee not,   60
'Twas but a mist of conscience—all's clear again.   *Exit.*

46 piece] fowling-piece   47 proper] suitable, but with a quibble on 'clean'   50 'Slid]
God's eyelid

Beatrice. Who's that, Deflores? Bless me! it slides by,   [*Exit* Ghost.]
　　　Some ill thing haunts the house, 't has left behind it
　　　A shivering sweat upon me; I'm afraid now:
　　　This night hath been so tedious; oh this strumpet!
　　　Had she a thousand lives, he should not leave her
　　　Till he had destroy'd the last—List, oh my terrors,
　　　Three struck by St. Sebastian's.   *Struck 3 o'clock.*
Within. Fire, fire, fire.
Beatrice. Already! How rare is that man's speed!   70
　　　How heartily he serves me! his face loathes one,
　　　But look upon his care, who would not love him?
　　　The east is not more beauteous than his service.
Within. Fire, fire, fire.

　　Enter Deflores; Servants *pass over, ring a bell.*

Deflores. Away, dispatch, hooks, buckets, ladders; that's well said,
　　　The fire-bell rings, the chimney works—my charge;
　　　The piece is ready.   *Exit.*

　　Enter Diaphanta.

Beatrice.   Here's a man worth loving——
　　　Oh y'are a jewel.
Diaphanta.   Pardon frailty, madam,
　　　In troth I was so well, I ev'n forgot my self.
Beatrice. Y'have made trim work.
Diaphanta.   What?
Beatrice.   Hie quickly to your chamber,   80
　　　Your reward follows you.
Diaphanta.   I never made
　　　So sweet a bargain.   *Exit.*

　　Enter Alsemero.

Alsemero.   Oh my dear Joanna,
　　　Alas, art thou risen too? I was coming,
　　　My absolute treasure.
Beatrice.   When I miss'd you,
　　　I could not choose but follow.
Alsemero.   Th'art all sweetness.
　　　The fire is not so dangerous.
Beatrice.   Think you so sir?
Alsemero. I prithee tremble not: believe me, 'tis not.

　　Enter Vermandero, Jasperino.

71 loathes one] is loathsome

Vermandero. Oh bless my house and me.

Alsemero.   My Lord your father.

    Enter Deflores *with a piece.*

Vermandero. Knave, whither goes that piece?

Deflores. To scour the chimney.   *Exit.*

Vermandero.   Oh well said, well said;   90
    That fellow's good on all occasions.

Beatrice. A wondrous necessary man, my Lord.

Vermandero. He hath a ready wit, he's worth 'em all, sir;
    Dog at a house of fire, I ha' seen him sing'd ere now.
    Ha, there he goes.   *The piece goes off.*

Beatrice. [*Aside*]   'Tis done.

Alsemero.   Come sweet, to bed now;
    Alas, thou wilt get cold.

Beatrice.   Alas, the fear keeps that out;
    My heart will find no quiet till I hear
    How Diaphanta my poor woman fares;
    It is her chamber sir, her lodging chamber.

Vermandero. How should the fire come there?   100

Beatrice. As good a soul as ever lady countenanc'd,
    But in her chamber negligent and heavy.
    She scap'd a mine twice.

Vermandero.   Twice?

Beatrice.   Strangely twice, sir.

Vermandero. Those sleepy sluts are dangerous in a house,
    And they be ne'er so good.

    Enter Deflores.

Deflores.   Oh poor virginity!
    Thou hast paid dearly for't.

Vermandero.   Bless us! What's that?

Deflores. [*Aside*] A thing you all knew once.—Diaphanta's burnt.

Beatrice. My woman, oh my woman!

Deflores.   Now the flames are
    Greedy of her, burnt, burnt, burnt to death sir.

Beatrice. Oh my presaging soul!

Alsemero.   Not a tear more,   110
    I charge you by the last embrace I gave you
    In bed before this rais'd us.

Beatrice.   Now you tie me,

94 Dog at] adept at a case of   103 mine] danger; presumably Beatrice is thinking of her
test and Diaphanta's deception of Alsemero   105 And] an, if   107 a thing] i.e.,
virginity

Were it my sister now she gets no more.

Enter Servant.

Vermandero. How now?
Servant.   All danger's past, you may now take
    Your rests, my Lords, the fire is throughly quencht;
    Ah poor gentlewoman, how soon was she stifled!
Beatrice. Deflores, what is left of her inter,
    And we as mourners all will follow her:
    I will entreat that honour to my servant,
    Ev'n of my lord himself.
Alsemero.   Command it, sweetness.
Beatrice. Which of you spied the fire first?
Deflores.   'Twas I, Madam.   120
Beatrice. And took such pains in't too? a double goodness!
    'Twere well he were rewarded.
Vermandero.   He shall be;
    Deflores, call upon me.
Alsemero.   And upon me, sir.   *Exeunt.* [*Manet* Def.]
Deflores. Rewarded? Precious, here's a trick beyond me;
    I see in all bouts both of sport and wit,
    Always a woman strives for the last hit.   *Exit.*

[SCENE II]

Enter Tomazo.

Tomazo. I cannot taste the benefits of life
    With the same relish I was wont to do.
    Man I grow weary of, and hold his fellowship
    A treacherous bloody friendship, and because
    I am ignorant in whom my wrath should settle,
    I must think all men villains; and the next
    I meet, who e'er he be, the murderer
    Of my most worthy brother——Ha! What's he?

Enter Deflores, *passes over the stage.*

    Oh, the fellow that some call honest Deflores;
    But me thinks honesty were hard bested   10
    To come there for a lodging, as if a queen
    Should make her palace of a pest-house.

V. ii, 12 pest-house] hospital for infectious diseases

I find a contrariety in nature
Betwixt that face and me, the least occasion
Would give me game upon him; yet he's so foul
One would scarce touch him with a sword he loved,
And made account of; so most deadly venomous,
He would go near to poison any weapon
That should draw blood on him, one must resolve
Never to use that sword again in fight,   20
In way of honest manhood, that strikes him;
Some river must devour't, 'twere not fit
That any man should find it.—What, again?

Enter Deflores.

He walks a' purpose by, sure to choke me up,
To infect my blood.
Deflores.   My worthy noble Lord.
Tomazo. Dost offer to come near and breathe upon me?   [*Strikes him.*]
Deflores. A blow?   [*Draws.*]
Tomazo.   Yea, are you so prepar'd?
I'll rather like a soldier die by th'sword
Than like a politician by thy poison.   [*Draws.*]
Deflores. Hold, my Lord, as you are honourable.   30
Tomazo. All slaves that kill by poison, are still cowards.
Deflores. [*Aside*] I cannot strike, I see his brother's wounds
Fresh bleeding in his eye, as in a crystal.
—I will not question this, I know y'are noble.
I take my injury with thanks given, sir,
Like a wise lawyer; and as a favour,
Will wear it for the worthy hand that gave it.
[*Aside*] Why this from him, that yesterday appear'd
So strangely loving to me?
Oh but instinct is of a subtler strain,   40
Guilt must not walk so near his lodge again,
He came near me now.   *Exit.*
Tomazo. All league with mankind I renounce for ever,
Till I find this murderer; not so much
As common courtesy, but I'll lock up:
For in the state of ignorance I live in,
A brother may salute his brother's murderer,
And wish good speed to th' villain in a greeting.

Enter Verman: Ali: *and* Isabella.

15 give ... him] cause me to challenge him   16 he] i.e., one, the subject of the clause

Vermandero. Noble Piracquo.

Tomazo.   Pray keep on your way, sir,
    I've nothing to say to you.

Vermandero.   Comforts bless you sir.   50

Tomazo. I have forsworn compliment, in troth I have, sir:
    As you are merely man, I have not left
    A good wish for you, nor any here.

Vermandero. Unless you be so far in love with grief
    You will not part from't upon any terms,
    We bring that news will make a welcome for us.

Tomazo. What news can that be?

Vermandero.   Throw no scornful smile
    Upon the zeal I bring you, 'tis worth more sir;
    Two of the chiefest men I kept about me
    I hide not from the law, or your just vengeance.   60

Tomazo. Ha!

Vermandero. To give your peace more ample satisfaction,
    Thank these discoverers.

Tomazo.   If you bring that calm,
    Name but the manner I shall ask forgiveness in
    For that contemptuous smile upon you:
    I'll perfect it with reverence that belongs
    Unto a sacred altar.   *[Kneels.]*

Vermandero.   Good sir, rise;   *[Raises him.]*
    Why now you overdo as much a'this hand,
    As you fell short a't'other. Speak, Alibius.

Alibius. 'Twas my wive's fortune, (as she is most lucky   70
    At a discovery) to find out lately
    Within our hospital of fools and madmen,
    Two counterfeits slipt into these disguises;
    Their names Franciscus and Antonio.

Vermandero. Both mine sir, and I ask no favour for 'em.

Alibius. Now that which draws suspicion to their habits,
    The time of their disguisings agrees justly
    With the day of the murder.

Tomazo.   O blest revelation!

Vermandero. Nay more, nay more sir, I'll not spare mine own
    In way of justice; they both feign'd a journey   80
    To Bramata, and so wrought out their leaves;
    My love was so abus'd in't.

81 Bramata] i.e., Briamata; apparently a slip (cf. IV. ii. 7–8)

Tomazo.   Time's too precious
　　To run in waste now; you have brought a peace
　　The riches of five kingdoms could not purchase.
　　Be my most happy conduct, I thirst for 'em,
　　Like subtle lightning will I wind about 'em,
　　And melt their marrow in 'em.   *Exeunt.*

[SCENE III]

Enter Alsemero *and* Jasperino.

Jasperino. Your confidence, I'm sure, is now of proof.
　　The prospect from the garden has show'd
　　Enough for deep suspicion.
Alsemero.   The black mask
　　That so continually was worn upon't,
　　Condemns the face for ugly ere't be seen——
　　Her despite to him, and so seeming bottomless.
Jasperino. Touch it home then, 'tis not a shallow probe
　　Can search this ulcer soundly, I fear you'll find it
　　Full of corruption, 'tis fit I leave you,
　　She meets you opportunely from that walk: 10
　　She took the back door at his parting with her.   *Ex.* Jas.
Alsemero. Did my fate wait for this unhappy stroke
　　At my first sight of woman?—She's here.

Enter Beatrice.

Beatrice. Alsemero!
Alsemero.   How do you?
Beatrice.   How do I?
　　Alas! how do you? you look not well.
Alsemero. You read me well enough, I am not well.
Beatrice. Not well sir? Is't in my power to better you.
Alsemero. Yes.
Beatrice.   Nay, than y'are cur'd again.
Alsemero. Pray resolve me one question, Lady.
Beatrice.   If I can.
Alsemero. None can so sure. Are you honest?   20
Beatrice. Ha, ha, ha, that's a broad question, my Lord.
Alsemero. But that's not a modest answer, my Lady:
　　Do you laugh? My doubts are strong upon me.

V. iii, 1 of proof] on the point of being put to the proof   3 black mask] i.e., Beatrice's
show of dislike for Deflores

Beatrice. 'Tis innocence that smiles, and no rough brow
  Can take away the dimple in her cheek.
  Say I should strain a tear to fill the vault,
  Which would you give the better faith to?
Alsemero. 'Twere but hypocrisy of a sadder colour,
  But the same stuff, neither your smiles nor tears
  Shall move or flatter me from my belief,   30
  You are a whore.
Beatrice.   What a horrid sound it hath!
  It blasts a beauty to deformity;
  Upon what face soever that breath falls,
  It strikes it ugly: oh you have ruin'd
  What you can ne'er repair again.
Alsemero.   I'll all
  Demolish and seek out truth within you,
  If there be any left, let your sweet tongue
  Prevent your heart's rifling; there I'll ransack
  And tear out my suspicion.
Beatrice.   You may sir,
  'Tis an easy passage, yet if you please,   40
  Show me the ground whereon you lost your love.
  My spotless virtue may but tread on that
  Before I perish.
Alsemero.   Unanswerable,
  A ground you cannot stand on, you fall down
  Beneath all grace and goodness, when you set
  Your ticklish heel on't; there was a vizor
  O'er that cunning face, and that became you,
  Now impudence in triumph rides upon't;
  How comes this tender reconcilement else
  'Twixt you and your despite, your rancorous loathing   50
  Deflores?
  He that your eye was sore at sight of, he's now
  Become your arm's supporter, your lip's saint.
Beatrice. Is there the cause?
Alsemero. Worse, your lust's devil, your adultery.
Beatrice. Would any but your self say that,
  'Twould turn him to a villain.

---

26 vault] sky   37–8 let your . . . rifling] let your tongue come before the rifling (by telling
the truth); or (if the quarto is right to put a comma after 'tongue'), stop your sweet (and
deceitful) tongue and thereby prevent your heart from being further maltreated   54 there]
i.e., in what he has just told her

Alsemero.   'Twas witnest by
    The counsel of your bosom, Diaphanta.
Beatrice. Is your witness dead then?
Alsemero.   'Tis to be fear'd
    It was the wages of her knowledge, poor soul,   60
    She liv'd not long after the discovery.
Beatrice. Then hear a story of not much less horror,
    Than this your false suspicion is beguil'd with;
    To your bed's scandal, I stand up innocence,
    Which even the guilt of one black other deed
    Will stand for proof of, your love has made me
    A cruel murd'ress.
Alsemero.   Ha.
Beatrice.   A bloody one.
    I have kiss'd poison for't, strok'd a serpent;
    That thing of hate, worthy in my esteem
    Of no better imployment, and him most worthy   70
    To be so imploy'd, I caus'd to murder
    That innocent Piracquo, having no
    Better means than that worst, to assure
    Your self to me.
Alsemero.   Oh the place it self e'er since
    Has crying been for vengeance, the temple
    Where blood and beauty first unlawfully
    Fir'd their devotion, and quencht the right one;
    'Twas in my fears at first, 'twill have it now;
    Oh thou art all deform'd.
Beatrice.   Forget not sir,
    It for your sake was done; shall greater dangers   80
    Make the less welcome?
Alsemero.   Oh thou should'st have gone
    A thousand leagues about to have avoided
    This dangerous bridge of blood, here we are lost.
Beatrice. Remember I am true unto your bed.
Alsemero. The bed it self's a charnel, the sheets shrouds
    For murdered carcases. It must ask pause
    What I must do in this, mean time you shall
    Be my prisoner only, enter my closet,   *Exit* Beatrice.
    I'll be your keeper yet. Oh in what part
    Of this sad story shall I first begin?—   90
    Ha, this same fellow has put me in—Deflores.

64-6 To your . . . proof of] I am innocent of scandal to your bed, as is proved by the other
black deed

Enter Deflores.

Deflores. Noble Alsemero!

Alsemero.   I can tell you
    News sir, my wife has her commended to you.

Deflores. That's news indeed my Lord, I think she would
    Commend me to the gallows if she could,
    She ever lov'd me so well; I thank her.

Alsemero. What's this blood upon your band, Deflores?

Deflores. Blood? No sure, 'twas washt since.

Alsemero. Since when, man?

Deflores.   Since t'other day I got a knock
    In a sword and dagger school; I think 'tis out.   100

Alsemero. Yes, 'tis almost out, but 'tis perceiv'd tho'.
    I had forgot my message; this it is,
    What price goes murder?

Deflores.   How sir?

Alsemero.   I ask you sir;
    My wife's behind hand with you, she tells me,
    For a brave bloody blow you gave for her sake
    Upon Piracquo.

Deflores.   Upon? 'Twas quite through him sure:
    Has she confest it?

Alsemero.   As sure as death to both of you,
    And much more than that.

Deflores.   It could not be much more,
    'Twas but one thing, and that—she's a whore.

Alsemero. It could not choose but follow; oh cunning devils!   110
    How should blind men know you from fair-fac'd saints?

Beatrice within. He lies, the villain does belie me.

Deflores.   Let
    Me go to her, sir.

Alsemero.   Nay, you shall to her.
    Peace, crying crocodile, your sounds are heard,
    Take your prey to you; get you into her sir.   *Exit* Def.
    I'll be your pander now, rehearse again
    Your scene of lust, that you may be perfect
    When you shall come to act it to the black audience
    Where howls and gnashings shall be music to you.
    Clip your adult'ress freely, 'tis the pilot   120
    Will guide you to the *Mare mortuum*,
    Where you shall sink to fadoms bottomless.

97 band] collar   104 behind hand] in debt   120 clip] embrace   121 *Mare mortuum*]
the sea of the dead

Enter Vermandero, Alibius, Isabella, Tomazo, Franciscus, *and* Antonio.

Vermandero. Oh Alsemero. I have a wonder for you.
Alsemero. No sir, 'tis I, I have a wonder for you.
Vermandero. I have suspicion near as proof it self
    For Piracquo's murder.
Alsemero.   Sir, I have proof
    Beyond suspicion, for Piracquo's murder.
Vermandero. Beseech you hear me, these two have been disguis'd
    E'er since the deed was done.
Alsemero.   I have two other
    That were more close disguis'd than your two could be,   130
    E'er since the deed was done.
Vermandero. You'll hear me—these mine own servants——
Alsemero. Hear me: those nearer than your servants
    That shall acquit them, and prove them guiltless.
Franciscus. That may be done with easy truth, sir.
Tomazo. How is my cause bandied through your delays!
    'Tis urgent in blood, and calls for haste;
    Give me a brother alive or dead;
    Alive, a wife with him, if dead for both
    A recompense for murder and adultery.   140
Beatrice within. Oh, oh, oh.
Alsemero.   Hark, 'tis coming to you.
Deflores within. Nay, I'll along for company.
Beatrice within.   Oh, oh.
Vermandero. What horrid sounds are these?
Alsemero. Come forth, you twins of mischief.

    Enter Deflores *bringing in* Beatrice [*wounded*].

Deflores. Here we are; if you have any more
    To say to us, speak quickly, I shall not
    Give you the hearing else, I am so stout yet,
    And so I think that broken rib of mankind.
Vermandero. An host of enemies ent'red my citadel
    Could not amaze like this—Joanna, Beatrice, Joanna!   150
Beatrice. O come not near me sir, I shall defile you;
    I am that of your blood was taken from you
    For your better health, look no more upon't,
    But cast it to the ground regardlessly,
    Let the common sewer take it from distinction.

147 so stout] strong enough for that   148 that...mankind] i.e., Beatrice   152-3 I am...
health] I am that diseased part cut off for your health's sake   155 take...distinction]
remove all signs of its existence

Beneath the stars, upon yon meteor
Ever hung my fate, 'mongst things corruptible,
I ne'er could pluck it from him, my loathing
Was prophet to the rest, but ne'er believ'd;
Mine honour fell with him, and now my life.   160
Alsemero, I am a stranger to your bed,
Your bed was coz'ned on the nuptial night,
For which your false bride died.
Alsemero.   Diaphanta!
Deflores. Yes, and the while I coupled with your mate
    At barley-brake; now we are left in hell.
Vermandero. We are all there, it circumscribes here.
Deflores. I lov'd this woman in spite of her heart,
    Her love I earn'd out of Piracquo's murder.
Tomazo. Ha, my brother's murtherer.
Deflores.   Yes, and her honour's prize
Was my reward, I thank life for nothing   170
But that pleasure, it was so sweet to me
That I have drunk up all, left none behind
For any man to pledge me.
Vermandero.   Horrid villain!
Keep life in him for further tortures.
Deflores.   No,
I can prevent you, here's my penknife still,
It is but one thread more, [*stabs himself*]—and now 'tis cut.
Make haste Joanna, by that token to thee.
Canst not forget, so lately put in mind,
I would not go to leave thee far behind.   *Dies.*
Beatrice. Forgive me Alsemero, all forgive,   180
    'Tis time to die, when 'tis a shame to live.   *Dies.*
Vermandero. Oh, my name is ent'red now in that record,
    Where till this fatal hour 'twas never read.
Alsemero. Let it be blotted out, let your heart lose it,
    And it can never look you in the face,
    Nor tell a tale behind the back of life
    To your dishonour; justice hath so right
    The guilty hit, that innocence is quit
    By proclamation, and may joy again.
    Sir, you are sensible of what truth hath done,   190
    'Tis the best comfort that your grief can find.

156 yon meteor] i.e., Deflores; a volatile meteor would contrast with the fixity of the stars
165 barley-brake] cf. III. ii. 151   177–9] The syntax of these lines is obscure: Deflores'
death is a token to Beatrice that she should not delay her own.   188 innocence is quit]
the innocent are acquitted

Tomazo. Sir, I am satisfied, my injuries
    Lie dead before me, I can exact no more,
    Unless my soul were loose, and could o'ertake
    Those black fugitives, that are fled from thence
    To take a second vengeance; but there are wraths
    Deeper than mine ('tis to be fear'd) about 'em.

Alsemero. What an opacous body had that moon
    That last chang'd on us! here's beauty chang'd
    To ugly whoredom: here servant obedience   200
    To a master-sin, imperious murder.
    I, a suppos'd husband, chang'd embraces
    With wantonness, but that was paid before;
    Your change is come too, from an ignorant wrath
    To knowing friendship. Are there any more on's?

Antonio. Yes sir, I was chang'd too, from a little ass as I was, to a great fool
    as I am; and had like to ha' been chang'd to the gallows, but that you
    know my innocence always excuses me.

Franciscus. I was chang'd from a little wit to be stark mad, almost for the
    same purpose.   210

Isabella. Your change is still behind, but deserve best your transformation.
    You are a jealous coxcomb, keep schools of folly, and teach your scholars
    how to break your own head.

Alibius. I see all apparent, wife, and will change now into a better husband,
    and never keep scholars that shall be wiser than my self.

Alsemero. Sir, you have yet a son's duty living,
    Please you accept it, let that your sorrow
    As it goes from your eye, go from your heart,
    Man and his sorrow at the grave must part.

EPILOGUE

Alsemero. All we can do, to comfort one another,
    To stay a brother's sorrow for a brother,
    To dry a child from the kind father's eyes
    Is to no purpose, it rather multiplies:
    Your only smiles have power to cause re-live
    The dead again, or in their rooms to give
    Brother a new brother, father a child;
    If these appear, all griefs are reconcil'd.   *Exeunt omnes.*

FINIS.

203 that ... before] i.e., by Diaphanta's death   204 Your] i.e., Tomazo's   208 innocence]
punning on the senses of guiltlessness and simple-mindedness   211 Your] i.e., Alibius'
211 behind] to come   212–3 teach ... head] let your inmates cuckold you   Ep., 5 *Your
only smiles*] only your (the audience's) smiles

WOMEN BEWARE WOMEN
by
THOMAS MIDDLETON

THOMAS MIDDLETON (1580–1627)

Women Beware Women

Written perhaps about 1623; printed in 1657

[*Works of Thomas Middleton*, ed. Alexander Dyce, 1840; ed. A. H. Bullen, 1885. Included in *The Best Plays of Thomas Middleton*, ed. A. C. Swinburne & H. Ellis, 1887.]

Women Beware Women was first printed in a volume called *Two New Plays*, the other being *More Dissemblers besides Women*, a comedy and likewise by Middleton. The following address, by the bookseller, Humphrey Moseley, is prefixed to the volume:

TO THE READER

When these amongst others of Mr. Thomas Middleton's excellent poems came to my hands, I was not a little confident but that his name would prove as great an inducement for thee to read as me to print them; since those issues of his brain that have already seen the sun have by their worth gained themselves a free entertainment amongst all that are ingenious: and I am most certain that these will no way lessen his reputation nor hinder his admission to any noble and recreative spirits. All that I require at thy hands is to continue the author in his deserved esteem, and to accept of my endeavours, which have ever been to please thee.

Farewell.

WOMEN

BEWARE
WOMEN.

A
TRAGEDY;
BY
Tho. Middleton, Gent.

LONDON:
Printed for *Humphrey Moseley*, 1657.

UPON THE TRAGEDY OF MY FAMILIAR ACQUAINTANCE,
THO. MIDDLETON

Women beware Women; 'tis a true text
Never to be forgot; drabs of state vext
Have plots, poisons, mischiefs that seldom miss,
To murder virtue with a venom-kiss.
Witness this worthy tragedy, exprest
By him that well deserv'd among the best
Of poets in his time: he knew the rage,
Madness of women cross'd, and for the stage
Fitted their humours; hell-bred malice, strife
Acted in state, presented to the life.
I that have seen't can say, having just cause,
Never came tragedy off with more applause.

NATH. RICHARDS.

[DRAMATIS PERSONAE]

Duke of Florence
Lord Cardinal, brother to the Duke.
Two Cardinals more.
A Lord.
Fabritio, father to Isabella.
Hippolito, brother to Fabritio.
Guardiano, uncle to the foolish ward.
The Ward, a rich young heir.
Leantio, a factor, husband to Bianca.
Sordido, the Ward's man.

Livia, sister to Fabritio.
Isabella, niece to Livia.
Bianca, Leantio's wife.
Widow, his mother.

States of Florence.
Citizens.
A prentice.
Boys.
Messengers.
Servants.
[Ladies.]

The Scene FLORENCE.

Bianca] In the quarto, the name appears throughout as *Brancha*; but as Bullen notes, wherever the name occurs, a trisyllable is needed, and all editors have accepted the amendment of Dyce, who comments: 'Her family name, as we learn from act iii, sc. i, was Capello. —Most readers will recollect the celebrated *Bianca Capello*, second wife of Francis de Medici, grand duke of Tuscany: the earlier events in her history, and in that of the Bianca of the tragedy, have a sort of resemblance; both fled from Venice to Florence, &c.'
   States] nobles (i.e., estates)

Enter Leantio *with* Bianca, *and* Mother.

Mother. Thy sight was never yet more precious to me;
    Welcome with all the affection of a mother,
    That comfort can express from natural love:
    Since thy birth-joy, a mother's chiefest gladness
    After sh'as undergone her curse of sorrows,
    Thou wast not more dear to me, than this hour
    Presents thee to my heart. Welcome again.
Leantio. [*Aside*] 'Las poor affectionate soul, how her joys speak to me!
    I have observ'd it often, and I know it is
    The fortune commonly of knavish children   10
    To have the loving'st mothers.
Mother.   What's this gentlewoman?
Leantio. Oh you have nam'd the most unvaluedst purchase,
    That youth of man had ever knowledge of.
    As often as I look upon that treasure,
    And know it to be mine, (there lies the blessing)
    It joys me that I ever was ordain'd
    To have a being, and to live 'mongst men;
    Which is a fearful living, and a poor one;
    Let a man truly think on't.
    To have the toil and griefs of fourscore years   20
    Put up in a white sheet, ti'd with two knots;
    Methinks it should strike earthquakes in adulterers,
    When ev'n the very sheets they commit sin in
    May prove, for aught they know, all their last garments.
    Oh what a mark were there for women then!
    But beauty able to content a conqueror,
    Whom earth could scarce content, keeps me in compass;
    I find no wish in me bent sinfully
    To this man's sister, or to that man's wife:
    In love's name let 'em keep their honesties,   30
    And cleave to their own husbands, 'tis their duties.
    Now when I go to church, I can pray handsomely;
    Not come like gallants only to see faces,
    As if lust went to market still on Sundays.

12 unvaluedst] invaluable

I must confess I am guilty of one sin, Mother,
More than I brought into the world with me;
But that I glory in: 'tis theft, but noble
As ever greatness yet shot up withal.
Mother. How's that?
Leantio.   Never to be repented (Mother,)
Though sin be death; I had di'd, if I had not sinn'd,   40
And here's my masterpiece: do you now behold her!
Look on her well, she's mine, look on her better:
Now say, if't be not the best piece of theft
That ever was committed; and I have my pardon for't:
'Tis seal'd from heaven by marriage.
Mother.   Married to her!
Leantio. You must keep counsel, Mother, I am undone else;
If it be known, I have lost her; do but think now
What that loss is, life's but a triffle to't.
From Venice, her consent and I have brought her
From parents great in wealth, more now in rage;   50
But let storms spend their furies, now we have got
A shelter o'er our quiet innocent loves,
We are contented; little money sh'as brought me.
View but her face, you may see all her dowry,
Save that which lies lockt up in hidden virtues,
Like jewels kept in cabinets.
Mother.   Y'are to blame,
If your obedience will give way to a check,
To wrong such a perfection.
Leantio.   How?
Mother.   Such a creature,
To draw her from her fortune, which no doubt,
At the full time, might have prov'd rich and noble: 60
You know not what you have done; my life can give you
But little helps, and my death lesser hopes.
And hitherto your own means has but made shift
To keep you single, and that hardly too.
What ableness have you to do her right then
In maintenance fitting her birth and virtues?
Which ev'ry woman of necessity looks for,
And most to go above it, not confin'd
By their conditions, virtues, bloods, or births,
But flowing to affections, wills, and humours.   70

37-8 noble . . . withal] as noble as ever brought greatness (to a commoner)   48 triffle]
trifle

Leantio. Speak low, sweet Mother; you are able to spoil as many
    As come within the hearing: if it be not
    Your fortune to mar all, I have much marvel.
    I pray do not you teach her to rebel,
    When she's in a good way to obedience,
    To rise with other women in commotion
    Against their husbands, for six gowns a year,
    And so maintain their cause, when they're once up,
    In all things else that require cost enough.
    They are all of 'em a kind of spirits soon rais'd,   80
    But not so soon laid (Mother). As for example,
    A woman's belly is got up in a trice,
    A simple charge ere it be laid down again:
    So ever in all their quarrels, and their courses,
    And I'm a proud man I hear nothing of 'em,
    They're very still, I thank my happiness,
    And sound asleep; pray let not your tongue wake 'em.
    If you can but rest quiet, she's contented
    With all conditions that my fortunes bring her to;
    To keep close as a wife that loves her husband;   90
    To go after the rate of my ability,
    Not the licentious swinge of her own will,
    Like some of her old school-fellows; she intends
    To take out other works in a new sampler,
    And frame the fashion of an honest love,
    Which knows no wants, but, mocking poverty,
    Brings forth more children, to make rich men wonder
    At divine Providence, that feeds mouths of infants,
    And sends them none to feed, but stuffs their rooms
    With fruitful bags, their beds with barren wombs.   100
    Good Mother, make not you things worse than they are,
    Out of your too much openness; pray take heed on't;
    Nor imitate the envy of old people,
    That strive to mar good sport, because they are perfit.
    I would have you more pitiful to youth,
    Especially to your own flesh and blood.
    I'll prove an excellent husband, here's my hand,
    Lay in provision, follow my business roundly,
    And make you a grandmother in forty weeks.
    Go, pray salute her, bid her welcome cheerfully.   110

71 spoil] i.e., by putting ideas into their heads   83 simple charge] a burden, but possibly referring to the doctor's fees   85–6 'em, They're] i.e., women's quarrels and courses (in Bianca's case)   99 them . . . their] i.e., the rich men   104 perfit] finished, played out

Mother. Gentlewoman, thus much is a debt of courtesy   *[greeting her]*
   Which fashionable strangers pay each other
   At a kind meeting; then there's more than one
   Due to the knowledge I have of your nearness.
   I am bold to come again, and now salute you
   By th' name of daughter, which may challenge more
   Than ordinary respect.
Leantio. [*Aside*]   Why, this is well now,
   And I think few mothers of threescore will mend it.
Mother. What I can bid you welcome to, is mean;
   But make it all your own; we are full of wants,   120
   And cannot welcome worth.
Leantio. [*Aside*]   Now this is scurvy,
   And spake as if a woman lack'd her teeth.
   These old folks talk of nothing but defects,
   Because they grow so full of 'em themselves.
Bianca. Kind Mother, there is nothing can be wanting
   To her that does enjoy all her desires.
   Heaven send a quiet peace with this man's love,
   And I am as rich, as virtue can be poor;
   Which were enough after the rate of mind,
   To erect temples for content plac'd here;   130
   I have forsook friends, fortunes, and my country,
   And hourly I rejoice in't. Here's my friends,
   And few is the good number; thy successes,
   How e'er they look, I will still name my fortunes,
   Hopeful or spiteful, they shall all be welcome:
   Who invites many guests has of all sorts,
   As he that traffics much drinks of all fortunes,
   Yet they must all be welcome, and us'd well.
   I'll call this place the place of my birth now,
   And rightly too; for here my love was born,   140
   And that's the birth-day of a woman's joys.
   You have not bid me welcome since I came.
Leantio. That I did questionless.
Bianca.   No sure, how was't?
   I have quite forgot it.
Leantio.   Thus.   *[Kisses her.]*
Bianca.   Oh Sir, 'tis true;
   Now I remember well: I have done thee wrong,
   Pray take't again Sir.   *[Kisses him.]*

---

129 after the rate of mind] according as we rate the qualities of mind

Leantio.   How many of these wrongs
    Could I put up in an hour, and turn up
    The glass for twice as many more!
Mother.   Wilt please
    You to walk in, Daughter?
Bianca.   Thanks, sweet Mother;
    The voice of her that bare me is not more pleasing.   *Exeunt.*
                    [*Manet* Leantio.]

Leantio. Though my own care, and my rich master's trust,   151
    Lay their commands both on my factorship,
    This day and night, I'll know no other business
    But her and her dear welcome. 'Tis a bitterness
    To think upon tomorrow, that I must leave her
    Still to the sweet hopes of the week's end,
    That pleasure should be so restrain'd and curb'd
    After the course of a rich work-master,
    That never pays till Saturday night. Marry,
    It comes together in a round sum then,   160
    And does more good, you'll say. Oh fair-ey'd Florence!
    Didst thou but know what a most matchless jewel
    Thou now art mistress of, a pride would take thee,
    Able to shoot destruction through the bloods
    Of all thy youthful sons; but 'tis great policy
    To keep choice treasures in obscurest places:
    Should we show thieves our wealth, 'twould make 'em bolder;
    Temptation is a devil will not stick
    To fasten upon a saint; take heed of that;
    The jewel is cas'd up from all men's eyes.   170
    Who could imagine now a gem were kept,
    Of that great value under this plain roof?
    But how in times of absence? what assurance
    Of this restraint then? Yes, yes, there's one with her.
    Old mothers know the world; and such as these,
    When sons lock chests, are good to look to keys.   *Exit.*

SCAEN. 2

Enter Guardiano, Fabritio, *and* Livia.

Guardiano. What, has your daughter seen him yet? know you that?
Fabritio. No matter, she shall love him.

147–8 turn up The glass] invert the hour-glass (and so gain another hour)   158 course]
manner

Guardiano.   Nay, let's have fair play;
   He has been now my ward some fifteen year,
   And 'tis my purpose (as time calls upon me)
   By custom seconded, and such moral virtues,
   To tender him a wife; now sir, this wife
   I'd fain elect out of a daughter of yours.
   You see my meaning's fair; if now this daughter
   So tendered (let me come to your own phrase, sir)
   Should offer to refuse him, I were hansell'd.   10
   [*Aside*] Thus am I fain to calculate all my words,
   For the meridian of a foolish old man,
   To take his understanding.—What do you answer, sir?
Fabritio. I say still she shall love him.
Guardiano.   Yet again?
   And shall she have no reason for this love?
Fabritio. Why, do you think that women love with reason?
Guardiano. [*Aside*] I perceive fools are not at all hours foolish,
   No more than wisemen wise.
Fabritio.   I had a wife,
   She ran mad for me; she had no reason for't,
   For aught I could perceive: what think you, Lady Sister?   20
Guardiano. [*Aside*] 'Twas a fit match that, being both out of their wits:
   —A loving wife, it seem'd
   She strove to come as near you as she could.
Fabritio. And if her daughter prove not mad for love too,
   She takes not after her, nor after me
   If she prefer reason before my pleasure.
   You're an experienc'd widow, Lady Sister,
   I pray let your opinion come amongst us.
Livia. I must offend you then, if truth will do't,
   And take my niece's part, and call't injustice   30
   To force her love to one she never saw.
   Maids should both see, and like; all little enough
   If they love truly after that, 'tis well
   Counting the time, she takes one man till death,
   That's a hard task, I tell you; but one may
   Enquire at three years' end, amongst young wives,
   And mark how the game goes.

---

10 hansell'd] put to the test   32-4 all . . . death] The text may be corrupt; it seems to
mean that, however little true love there may be later, since maids take a man for life, it is
as well for them to bide their time (and go in with eyes open).

Fabritio.   Why, is not man
  Ti'd to the same observance, Lady Sister,
  And in one woman?
Livia.   'Tis enough for him:
  Besides he tastes of many sundry dishes   40
  That we poor wretches never lay our lips to;
  As obedience forsooth, subjection, duty, and such
  Kickshaws, all of our making, but serv'd in
  To them; and if we lick a finger then
  Sometimes, we are not to blame: your best cooks use it.
Fabritio. Th'art a sweet Lady, Sister, and a witty——
Livia. A witty! Oh the bud of commendation
  Fit for a girl of sixteen; I am blown, man,
  I should be wise by this time; and for instance,
  I have buried my two husbands in good fashion,   50
  And never mean more to marry.
Guardiano.   No, why so, Lady?
Livia. Because the third shall never bury me:
  I think I am more than witty; how think you, sir?
Fabritio. I have paid often fees to a counsellor
  Has had a weaker brain.
Livia.   Then I must tell you,
  Your money was soon parted.
Guardiano.   Like enow.
Livia. Brother,
  Where is my niece? let her be sent for straight,
  If you have any hope 'twill prove a wedding;
  'Tis fit i'faith she should have one sight of him,   60
  And stop upon't, and not be join'd in haste,
  As if they went to stock a new found land.
Fabritio. Look out her uncle, and y'are sure of her,
  Those two are nev'r asunder, they've been heard
  In argument at midnight, moon-shine nights
  Are noondays with them; they walk out their sleeps;
  Or rather at those hours appear like those
  That walk in 'em, for so they did to me.
  Look you, I told you truth; they're like a chain,
  Draw but one link, all follows.

  Enter Hippolito, *and* Isabella *the niece.*

44 them] i.e., our husbands   56 Like enow] The quarto reads 'Light her now Brother';
I have adopted Bullen's conjecture.   61 stop upon't] pause to survey him   62] a reference
to the settling of Massachusetts, or perhaps to Newfoundland itself

Guardiano.   Oh affinity,   70
What piece of excellent workmanship art thou!
'Tis work clean wrought; for there's no lust, but love in't,
And that abundantly: when in stranger things,
There is no love at all, but what lust brings.
Fabritio. On with your mask; for 'tis your part to see now,
And not be seen: go to, make use of your time;
See what you mean to like; nay, and I charge you,
Like what you see: do you hear me? there's no dallying:
The gentleman's almost twenty, and 'tis time
He were getting lawful heirs, and you a-breeding on 'em.   80
Isabella. Good Father!
Fabritio.   Tell me not of tongues and rumours.
You'll say the gentleman is somewhat simple—
The better for a husband, were you wise;
For those that marry fools, live ladies' lives.
On with the mask, I'll hear no more, he's rich;
The fool's hid under bushels.
Livia.   Not so hid neither
But here's a foul great piece of him methinks;
What will he be, when he comes altogether?

Enter the Ward *with a trap-stick, and* Sordido *his man.*

Ward. Beat him?
I beat him out o'th'field with his own cat-stick,   90
Yet gave him the first hand.
Sordido.   Oh strange!
Ward.   I did it,
Then he set jacks on me.
Sordido.   What, my lady's tailor?
Ward. Ay, and I beat him too.
Sordido.   Nay, that's no wonder,
He's used to beating.
Ward.   Nay, I tickl'd him
When I came once to my tippings.
Sordido. Now you talk on 'em, there was a poulterer's wife made a great
complaint of you last night to your guardianer, that you struck a bump
in her child's head, as big as an egg.
Ward. An egg may prove a chicken, then in time
the poulterer's wife will get by't. When I am in game, I am furious;
came my mother's eyes in my way, I would not lose a fair end: no,

73 stranger] less closely related   90 cat-stick] The references throughout are to the game
of tip-cat, in which a cat (or pointed piece of wood) is struck with a cat-stick and made to
spring up.   92 jacks] fellows   97 guardianer] guardian

were she alive, but with one tooth in her head, I should venture the
striking out of that. I think of no body, when I am in play, I am so ear-
nest. Coads me, my guardianer!   104
    Prethee lay up my cat and cat-stick safe.
Sordido. Where, sir, i'th'chimney-corner?
Ward. Chimney-corner!
Sordido. Yes sir, your cats are always safe i'th'chimney-corner, unless they
burn their coats.
Ward. Marry, that I am afraid on!   110
Sordido. Why, then I will bestow your cat i'th'gutter,
    And there she's safe I am sure.
Ward.   If I but live
    To keep a house, I'll make thee a great man,
    If meat and drink can do't. I can stoop gallantly,
    And pitch out when I list: I'm dog at a hole.
I mar'l my guardianer does not seek a wife for me; I protest I'll have a
bout with the maids else, or contract my self at midnight to the larder-
woman, in presence of a fool, or a sack-posset.
Guardiano. Ward.
Ward. I feel my self after any exercise.   120
    Horribly prone: let me but ride, I'm lusty,
    A cock-horse straight i'faith.
Guardiano.   Why, Ward, I say.
Ward. I'll forswear eating eggs in moon-shine nights;
    There's never a one I eat, but turns into a cock
    In four and twenty hours; if my hot blood
    Be not took down in time, sure 'twill crow shortly.
Guardiano. Do you hear, sir? follow me, I must new school you.
Ward. School me? I scorn that now, I am past schooling.
    I am not so base to learn to write and read;
    I was born to better fortunes in my cradle.
                    Exit [*with* Sordido *and* Guardiano].
Fabritio. How do you like him, girl? this is your husband.   131
    Like him, or like him not, wench, you shall have him,
    And you shall love him.
Livia. Oh soft there, Brother! though you be a justice,
    Your warrant cannot be serv'd out of your liberty;
    You may compel, out of the power of a father,

---

104 Coads me] exclamation of surprise; a variation of 'Ecod'   115 dog at a hole] like a
terrier   116 mar'l] marvel   118 fool] playing on 'fowl'   121 ride] playing on the
sexual meaning of the word   124 cock] again playing on the slang meaning of 'penis'
135 your liberty] the range of your jurisdiction

Things merely harsh to a maid's flesh and blood;
But when you come to love, there the soil alters;
Y'are in an other country, where your laws
Are no more set by, than the cacklings   140
Of geese in Rome's great Capitol.

Fabritio.   Marry him she shall then,
Let her agree upon love afterwards.   *Exit.*

Livia. You speak now, Brother, like an honest mortal
That walks upon th'earth with a staff; you were
Up i'th'clouds before, you'd command love,
And so do most old folks that go without it.
My best and dearest Brother, I could dwell here;
There is not such another seat on earth,
Where all good parts better express themselves.

Hippolito. You'll make me blush anon.   150

Livia. 'Tis but like saying grace before a feast then,
And that's most comely; thou art all a feast,
And she that has thee, a most happy guest.
Prethee cheer up thy niece with special counsel.   *Exit.*

Hippolito. [*Aside*] I would 'twere fit to speak to her what I would; but
'Twas not a thing ordain'd, Heaven has forbid it,
And 'tis most meet, that I should rather perish
Than the decree divine receive least blemish:
Feed inward, you my sorrows, make no noise,
Consume me silent, let me be stark dead   160
Ere the world know I'm sick. You see my honesty;
If you befriend me, so.

Isabella. [*Aside*]   Marry a fool!
Can there be greater misery to a woman
That means to keep her days true to her husband,
And know no other man! so virtue wills it.
Why; how can I obey and honour him,
But I must needs commit idolatry?
A fool is but the image of a man,
And that but ill-made neither: oh the heart-breakings
Of miserable maids, where love's enforc'd!   170
The best condition is but bad enough;
When women have their choices, commonly
They do but buy their thraldoms, and bring great portions
To men to keep 'em in subjection,

141 geese . . . Capitol] alluding to the sacred geese kept at the Temple of Juno in the
Capitol, which were said to have given warning by their cackling of an attack by the Gauls

As if a fearful prisoner should bribe
The keeper to be good to him, yet lies in still,
And glad of a good usage, a good look sometimes.
By'r Lady, no misery surmounts a woman's.
Men buy their slaves, but women buy their masters;
Yet honesty and love makes all this happy,   180
And next to angels', the most blest estate.
That Providence, that has made ev'ry poison
Good for some use, and sets four warring elements
At peace in man, can make a harmony
In things that are most strange to human reason.
Oh but this marriage!—What, are you sad too, Uncle?
Faith, then there's a whole household down together:
Where shall I go to seek my comfort now
When my best friend's distress'd? what is't afflicts you, sir?
Hippolito. Faith, nothing but one grief that will not leave me,   190
    And now 'tis welcome; ev'ry man has something
    To bring him to his end, and this will serve
    Join'd with your father's cruelty to you,
    That helps it forward.
Isabella.   Oh be cheer'd, sweet Uncle!
    How long has't been upon you? I never spi'd it:
    What a dull sight have I, how long I pray, sir?
Hippolito. Since I first saw you, Niece, and left Bologna.
Isabella. And could you deal so unkindly with my heart,
    To keep it up so long hid from my pity?
    Alas, how shall I trust your love hereafter?   200
    Have we past through so many arguments,
    And miss'd of that still, the most needful one?
    Walk'd out whole nights together in discourses,
    And the main point forgot? We are to blame both;
    This is an obstinate wilful forgetfulness,
    And faulty on both parts: let's lose no time now,
    Begin, good Uncle, you that feel't; what is it?
Hippolito. You of all creatures, Niece, must never hear on't,
    'Tis not a thing ordain'd for you to know.
Isabella. Not I, sir! all my joys that word cuts off;   210
    You made profession once you lov'd me best;
    'Twas but profession!
Hippolito.   Yes, I do't too truly,
    And fear I shall be chid for't. Know the worst then:
    I love thee dearlier than an uncle can.
Isabella. Why, so you ever said, and I believ'd it.

Hippolito. [*Aside*] So simple is the goodness of her thoughts,
　　They understand not yet th'unhallowed language
　　Of a near sinner: I must yet be forced
　　(Though blushes be my venture) to come nearer.
　　—As a man loves his wife, so love I thee.   220
Isabella. What's that?
　　Methought I heard ill news come toward me,
　　Which commonly we understand too soon,
　　Then over-quick at hearing. I'll prevent it,
　　Though my joys fare the harder; welcome it:
　　It shall nev'r come so near mine ear again.
　　Farewell all friendly solaces and discourses,
　　I'll learn to live without ye, for your dangers
　　Are greater than your comforts; what's become
　　Of truth in love, if such we cannot trust,   230
　　When blood that should be love, is mix'd with lust?   *Exit.*
Hippolito. The worst can be but death, and let it come,
　　He that lives joyless, ev'ry day's his doom.   *Exit.*

SCAEN. 3

Enter Leantio *alone.*

Leantio. Methinks I'm ev'n as dull now at departure,
　　As men observe great gallants the next day
　　After a revels; you shall see 'em look
　　Much of my fashion, if you mark 'em well.
　　'Tis ev'n a second hell to part from pleasure,
　　When man has got a smack on't: as many holidays,
　　Coming together, makes your poor heads idle
　　A great while after, and are said to stick
　　Fast in their fingers' ends, ev'n so does game
　　In a new-married couple; for the time   10
　　It spoils all thrift, and indeed lies abed
　　To invent all the new ways for great expenses.   Bianca *and* Mother
　　See, and she be not got on purpose now   *above.*
　　Into the window to look after me.
　　I have no power to go now, and I should be hang'd:
　　Farewell all business, I desire no more
　　Than I see yonder; let the goods at key
　　Look to themselves; why should I toil my youth out?
　　It is but begging two or three year sooner,
　　And stay with her continually; is't a match?   20

I. iii, 12 s.d.] Bianca and the Mother appear on the stage balcony   13, 15 and] an, if
17 at key] on the quay (or conceivably, locked up)

O fie, what a religion have I leap'd into!
Get out again for shame; the man loves best
When his care's most, that shows his zeal to love.
Fondness is but the idiot to affection,
That plays at hot-cockles with rich merchants' wives;
Good to make sport withal when the chest's full,
And the long warehouse cracks. 'Tis time of day
For us to be more wise; 'tis early with us,
And if they lose the morning of their affairs,
They commonly lose the best part of the day: 30
Those that are wealthy, and have got enough,
'Tis after sun-set with 'em, they may rest,
Grow fat with ease, banket, and toy and play,
When such as I enter the heat o'th'day,
And I'll do't cheerfully.

Bianca.   I perceive sir,
Y'are not gone yet, I have good hope you'll stay now.
Leantio. Farewell, I must not.
Bianca.   Come, come, pray return;
Tomorrow, adding but a little care more,
Will dispatch all as well; believe me 'twill, sir.
Leantio. I could well wish my self where you would have me;   40
But love that's wanton must be rul'd awhile
By that that's careful, or all goes to ruin;
As fitting is a government in love,
As in a kingdom; where 'tis all mere lust,
'Tis like an insurrection in the people
That, rais'd in self-will, wars against all reason:
But love that is respective for increase
Is like a good king, that keeps all in peace.
Once more farewell.
Bianca.   But this one night, I prethee.
Leantio. Alas I'm in for twenty, if I stay,   50
And then for forty more; I've such a luck to flesh,
I never bought a horse, but he bore double.
If I stay any longer, I shall turn
An everlasting spendthrift; as you love
To be maintain'd well, do not call me again,

24-5 Fondness... wives] Fondness, such as is shown by those who play fast and loose with
rich merchants' wives, is idiotic when compared with real affection   28-30 'tis early...
day] we (who are not rich) still have to work to earn our rest   33 banket] banquet
47 that... increase] that looks forward to its own growth

    For then I shall not care which end goes forward:
    Again farewell to thee.   *Exit.*
Bianca.   Since it must, farewell too.
Mother. 'Faith, Daughter, y'are to blame, you take the course
    To make him an ill husband, troth you do,
    And that disease is catching, I can tell you,   60
    Ay, and soon taken by a youngman's blood,
    And that with little urging. Nay fie, see now,
    What cause have you to weep? would I had no more
    That have liv'd threescore years; there were a cause
    And 'twere well thought on; trust me y'are to blame,
    His absence cannot last five days at utmost.
    Why should those tears be fetch'd forth? cannot love
    Be ev'n as well express'd in a good look,
    But it must see her face still in a fountain?
    It shows like a country maid dressing her head   70
    By a dish of water: come, 'tis an old custom
    To weep for love.

Enter two or three Boys, *and a* Citizen *or two, with an* Apprentice.

Boys. Now they come, now they come.
2. Boy.   The Duke!
3. Boy.   The States!
Citizen. How near, boy?
1. Boy.   I'th'next street sir, hard at hand.
Citizen. You sirrah, get a standing for your mistress,
    The best in all the city.
Apprentice.   I have't for her sir,
    'Twas a thing I provided for her over night,
    'Tis ready at her pleasure.
Citizen.   Fetch her to't then,
    Away sir!
Bianca.   What's the meaning of this hurry,
    Can you tell, Mother?
Mother.   What a memory   80
    Have I! I see by that years come upon me.
    Why, 'tis a yearly custom and solemnity,
    Religiously observ'd by th'Duke and State
    To St. Mark's Temple, the fifteenth of April:
    See if my dull brains had not quite forgot it.

65 And] if   69 fountain] i.e., of her tears   71 old] out-of-date, old-fashioned

'Twas happily question'd of thee, I had gone down else,
Sat like a drone below, and never thought on't.
I would not to be ten years younger again
That you had lost the sight; now you shall see
Our Duke, a goodly gentleman of his years.   90
Bianca. Is he old then?
Mother.   About some fifty-five.
Bianca. That's no great age in man, he's then at best
For wisdom, and for judgment.
Mother.   The Lord Cardinal,
His noble brother, there's a comely gentleman,
And greater in devotion than in blood.
Bianca. He's worthy to be mark'd.
Mother.   You shall behold
All our chief states of Florence, you came fortunately
Against this solemn day.
Bianca.   I hope so always.   *Music.*
Mother. I hear 'em near us now, do you stand easily?
Bianca. Exceeding well, good Mother.
Mother.   Take this stool.   100
Bianca. I need it not, I thank you.
Mother.   Use your will then.

Enter in great solemnity six Knights *bare-headed, then two* Cardinals, *and
then the* Lord Cardinal, *then the* Duke; *after him the* States of Florence *by
two and two, with variety of music and song.*   *Exeunt.*

Mother. How like you, Daughter?
Bianca.   'Tis a noble state.
Methinks my soul could dwell upon the reverence
Of such a solemn and most worthy custom.
Did not the Duke look up? me-thought he saw us.
Mother. That's ev'ry one's conceit that sees a duke:
If he looks steadfastly, he looks straight at them,
When he perhaps, good careful gentleman,
Never minds any; but the look he casts
Is at his own intentions, and his object   110
Only the public good.
Bianca.   Most likely so.
Mother. Come, come, we'll end this argument below.   *Exeunt.*

ACT. 2.   SCAEN. 1

Enter Hippolito, *and Lady* Livia *the Widow.*

Livia. A strange affection (Brother) when I think on't!
  I wonder how thou cam'st by't.
Hippolito.   Ev'n as easily
  As man comes by destruction, which oft-times
  He wears in his own bosom.
Livia.   Is the world
  So populous in women, and creation
  So prodigal in beauty and so various,
  Yet does love turn thy point to thine own blood?
  'Tis somewhat too unkindly; must thy eye
  Dwell evilly on the fairness of thy kinred,
  And seek not where it should? it is confin'd   10
  Now in a narrower prison than was made for't:
  It is allow'd a stranger, and where bounty
  Is made the great man's honour, 'tis ill husbandry
  To spare, and servants shall have small thanks for't.
  So he heaven's bounty seems to scorn and mock,
  That spares free means, and spends of his own stock.
Hippolito. Never was man's misery so soon sew'd up,
  Counting how truly.
Livia.   Nay, I love you so,
  That I shall venture much to keep a change from you
  So fearful as this grief will bring upon you.   20
  'Faith it even kills me, when I see you faint
  Under a reprehension, and I'll leave it,
  Though I know nothing can be better for you:
  Prethee (sweet Brother) let not passion waste
  The goodness of thy time, and of thy fortune:
  Thou keep'st the treasure of that life I love
  As dearly as mine own; and if you think
  My former words too bitter, which were minist'red
  By truth and zeal, 'tis but a hazarding
  Of grace and virtue, and I can bring forth   30
  As pleasant fruits as sensuality wishes
  In all her teeming longings: this I can do.

7 point] with a sexual quibble   8 unkindly] with a quibble on 'kind' in the sense of 'kin'
14 spare] be sparing   17 sew'd] The quarto has 'sow'd'; later editors read 'summ'd', but
the emendation seems unnecessary.   19 a change] i.e., in her

Hippolito. Oh nothing that can make my wishes perfect!
Livia. I would that love of yours were pawn'd to't, Brother,
   And as soon lost that way as I could win.
   Sir, I could give as shrewd a lift to chastity
   As any she that wears a tongue in Florence.
   Sh'ad need be a good horse-woman, and sit fast,
   Whom my strong argument could not fling at last.
   Prethee take courage, man; though I should counsel   40
   Another to despair, yet I am pitiful
   To thy afflictions, and will venture hard;
   I will not name for what, 'tis not handsome;
   Find you the proof, and praise me.
Hippolito.   Then I fear me
   I shall not praise you in haste.
Livia.   This is the comfort,
   You are not the first (Brother) has attempted
   Things more forbidden than this seems to be:
   I'll minister all cordials now to you,
   Because I'll cheer you up sir.
Hippolito.   I am past hope.
Livia. Love, thou shalt see me do a strange cure then,   50
   As e'er was wrought on a disease so mortal,
   And near akin to shame; when shall you see her?
Hippolito. Never in comfort more.
Livia.   Y'are so impatient too.
Hippolito. Will you believe? death, sh'has forsworn my company,
   And seal'd it with a blush.
Livia.   So, I perceive
   All lies upon my hands then; well, the more glory
   When the work's finish'd.—How now sir, the news!

   Enter Servant.

Servant. Madam, your niece, the virtuous Isabella,
   Is lighted now to see you.
Livia.   That's great fortune;
   Your stars bless you.—Simple, lead her in.   *Exit* Servant.
Hippolito. What's this to me?
Livia.   Your absence, gentle brother;   61
   I must bestir my wits for you.
Hippolito.   Ay, to great purpose.   *Exit* Hippolito.

36 give . . . chastity] as cunningly trap the chaste (into unchastity)   44 Find . . . proof]
when you find the proof   59 lighted] alighted   60] The text may be corrupt, and the
quarto, which reads, 'bless; you simple' certainly needs re-punctuating.

Livia. Beshrew you, would I lov'd you not so well:
 I'll go to bed, and leave this deed undone:
 I am the fondest where I once affect;
 The careful'st of their healths, and of their ease forsooth,
 That I look still but slenderly to mine own.
 I take a course to pity him so much now,
 That I have none left for modesty and my self.
 This 'tis to grow so liberal; y'have few sisters   70
 That love their brothers' ease 'bove their own honesties:
 But if you question my affections,
 That will be found my fault.

 Enter Isabella *the Niece.*

         Niece, your love's welcome.
 Alas, what draws that paleness to thy cheeks?
 This enforc'd marriage towards?
Isabella.   It helps, good Aunt,
 Amongst some other griefs; but those I'll keep
 Lock'd up in modest silence; for they're sorrows
 Would shame the tongue more than they grieve the thought.
Livia. Indeed, the Ward is simple.
Isabella.   Simple! that were well:
 Why, one might make good shift with such a husband. 80
 But he's a fool entail'd, he halts downright in't.
Livia. And knowing this, I hope 'tis at your choice
 To take or refuse, Niece.
Isabella.   You see it is not.
 I loathe him more than beauty can hate death
 Or age her spiteful neighbour.
Livia.   Let 't appear then.
Isabella. How can I, being born with that obedience,
 That must submit unto a father's will?
 If he command, I must of force consent.
Livia. Alas poor soul! Be not offended prethee,
 If I set by the name of niece awhile,   90
 And bring in pity in a stranger fashion:
 It lies here in this breast would cross this match.
Isabella. How, cross it, Aunt?
Livia.   Ay, and give thee more liberty
 Than thou hast reason yet to apprehend.
Isabella. Sweet Aunt, in goodness keep not hid from me
 What may befriend my life.

75 towards] at hand

Livia.   Yes, yes, I must,
    When I return to reputation,
    And think upon the solemn vow I made
    To your dead mother, my most loving sister;
    As long as I have her memory 'twixt mine eye-lids,   100
    Look for no pity now.
Isabella.   Kind, sweet, dear Aunt——
Livia. No, 'twas a secret I have took special care of,
    Delivered by your mother on her death-bed,
    That's nine years now, and I'll not part from't yet,
    Though nev'r was fitter time, nor greater cause for't.
Isabella. As you desire the praises of a virgin——
Livia. Good sorrow! I would do thee any kindness,
    Not wronging secrecy, or reputation.
Isabella. Neither of which (as I have hope of fruitness)
    Shall receive wrong from me.
Livia.   Nay 'twould be your own wrong,   110
    As much as any's, should it come to that once.
Isabella. I need no better means to work persuasion then.
Livia. Let it suffice, you may refuse this fool,
    Or you may take him, as you see occasion
    For your advantage; the best wits will do't;
    Y'have liberty enough in your own will,
    You cannot be enforc'd; there grows the flow'r,
    If you could pick it out, makes whole life sweet to you.
    That which you call your father's command's nothing;
    Then your obedience must needs be as little.   120
    If you can make shift here to taste your happiness,
    Or pick out aught that likes you, much good do you:
    You see your cheer, I'll make you no set dinner.
Isabella. And trust me, I may starve for all the good
    I can find yet in this: sweet Aunt, deal plainlier.
Livia. Say I should trust you now upon an oath,
    And give you in a secret that would start you,
    How am I sure of you, in faith and silence?
Isabella. Equal assurance may I find in mercy,
    As you for that in me.
Livia.   It shall suffice.   130
    Then know, however custom has made good,
    For reputation's sake, the names of niece
    And aunt 'twixt you and I, w'are nothing less.

127 that] what   133 w'are nothing less] there's nothing that we are less (than aunt and niece)

Isabella. How's that?

Livia.   I told you I should start your blood.
        You are no more alli'd to any of us,
        Save what the courtesy of opinion casts
        Upon your mother's memory and your name,
        Than the mer'st stranger is, or one begot
        At Naples, when the husband lies at Rome;
        There's so much odds betwixt us. Since your knowledge   140
        Wish'd more instruction, and I have your oath
        In pledge for silence, it makes me talk the freelier.
        Did never the report of that fam'd Spaniard,
        Marquess of Coria, since your time was ripe
        For understanding, fill your ear with wonder?

Isabella. Yes, what of him? I have heard his deeds of honour
        Often related when we liv'd in Naples.

Livia. You heard the praises of your father then.

Isabella. My father!

Livia.   That was he: but all the business
        So carefully and so discreetly carried,   150
        That fame receiv'd no spot by't, not a blemish;
        Your mother was so wary to her end,
        None knew it, but her conscience, and her friend,
        Till penitent confession made it mine,
        And now my pity yours: it had been long else,
        And I hope care and love alike in you,
        Made good by oath, will see it take no wrong now:
        How weak his commands now, whom you call father!
        How vain all his enforcements, your obedience,
        And what a largeness in your will and liberty,   160
        To take, or to reject, or to do both!
        For fools will serve to father wise men's children:
        All this y'have time to think on. O my wench!
        Nothing o'erthrows our sex but indiscretion,
        We might do well else of a brittle people,
        As any under the great canopy:
        I pray forget not but to call me aunt still;
        Take heed of that, it may be mark'd in time else,
        But keep your thoughts to your self, from all the world,
        Kinred, or dearest friend, nay, I entreat you,   170
        From him that all this while you have call'd uncle;

___

165 We might . . . people] otherwise we might do as well as anyone who is capable of being hurt (or perhaps damned)

And though you love him dearly, as I know
His deserts claim as much ev'n from a stranger,
Yet let not him know this, I prethee do not;
As ever thou hast hope of second pity
If thou should'st stand in need on't, do not do't.
Isabella. Believe my oath, I will not.
Livia.   Why, well said.
[*Aside*] Who shows more craft t'undo a maidenhead,
I'll resign my part to her.

Enter Hippolito.

                              —She's thine own, go.   *Exit.*
Hippolito. Alas, fair flattery cannot cure my sorrows!   180
Isabella. [*Aside*] Have I past so much time in ignorance,
And never had the means to know my self
Till this blest hour? Thanks to her virtuous pity
That brought it now to light; would I had known it
But one day sooner, he had then receiv'd
In favours what (poor gentleman) he took
In bitter words; a slight and harsh reward
For one of his deserts.
Hippolito. [*Aside*]   There seems to me now
More anger and distraction in her looks.
I'm gone, I'll not endure a second storm;   190
The memory of the first is not past yet.
Isabella. [*Aside*] Are you return'd, you comforts of my life,
In this man's presence? I will keep you fast now,
And sooner part eternally from the world,
Than my good joys in you.—Prethee forgive me,
I did but chide in jest; the best loves use it
Sometimes, it sets an edge upon affection:
When we invite our best friends to a feast,
'Tis not all sweet-meats that we set before them,
There's somewhat sharp and salt, both to whet appetite,   200
And make 'em taste their wine well: so me thinks,
After a friendly, sharp and savoury chiding,
A kiss tastes wondrous well, and full o'th'grape.   [*Kisses him.*]
How think'st thou, does't not?
Hippolito.   'Tis so excellent,
I know not how to praise it, what to say to't.
Isabella. This marriage shall go forward.

175 second pity] i.e., from heaven

Hippolito.   With the ward?
    Are you in earnest?
Isabella.   'Twould be ill for us else.
Hippolito. [*Aside*] For us? how means she that?
Isabella.   Troth I begin
    To be so well methinks, within this hour,
    For all this match able to kill one's heart.   210
    Nothing can pull me down now; should my father
    Provide a worse fool yet (which I should think
    Were a hard thing to compass) I'd have him either;
    The worse the better, none can come amiss now,
    If he want wit enough: so discretion love me,
    Desert and judgment, I have content sufficient.
    She that comes once to be a house-keeper
    Must not look every day to fare well, sir,
    Like a young waiting gentlewoman in service,
    For she feeds commonly as her lady does;   220
    No good bit passes her, but she gets a taste on't;
    But when she comes to keep house for her self,
    She's glad of some choice cates then once a week,
    Or twice at most, and glad if she can get 'em:
    So must affection learn to fare with thankfulness.
    Pray make your love no stranger, sir, that's all,
    [*Aside*] Though you be one your self, and know not on't,
    And I have sworn you must not.   *Exit.*
Hippolito.   This is beyond me!
    Never came joys so unexpectedly
    To meet desires in man; how came she thus?   230
    What has she done to her, can any tell?
    'Tis beyond sorcery this, drugs, or love-powders;
    Some art that has no name sure, strange to me
    Of all the wonders I e'er met withal
    Throughout my ten years' travels; but I'm thankful for't.
    This marriage now must of necessity forward;
    It is the only veil wit can devise
    To keep our acts hid from sin-piercing eyes.   *Exit.*

220 feeds] The word was commonly slang for sexual intercourse.   223 cates] dishes

SCAEN. 2

Enter Guardiano *and* Livia.

Livia. How sir? a gentlewoman, so young, so fair
 As you set forth, spi'd from the widow's window?
Guardiano. She!
Livia. Our Sunday-dinner woman?
Guardiano. And Thursday-supper woman, the same still.
 I know not how she came by her, but I'll swear
 She's the prime gallant for a face in Florence;
 And no doubt other parts follow their leader:
 The Duke himself first spi'd her at the window,
 Then in a rapture, as if admiration   10
 Were poor when it were single, beck'ned me,
 And pointed to the wonder warily,
 As one that fear'd she would draw in her splendour
 Too soon, if too much gaz'd at: I nev'r knew him
 So infinitely taken with a woman,
 Nor can I blame his appetite, or tax
 His raptures of slight folly, she's a creature
 Able to draw a state from serious business,
 And make it their best piece to do her service:
 What course shall we devise? h'as spoke twice now. 20
Livia. Twice?
Guardiano. 'Tis beyond your apprehension
 How strangely that one look has catch'd his heart:
 'Twould prove but too much worth in wealth and favour
 To those should work his peace.
Livia.   And if I do't not,
 Or at least come as near it (if your art
 Will take a little pains, and second me)
 As any wench in Florence of my standing,
 I'll quite give o'er, and shut up shop in cunning.
Guardiano. 'Tis for the Duke, and if I fail your purpose,
 All means to come, by riches or advancement,   30
 Miss me, and skip me over.
Livia.   Let the old woman then
 Be sent for with all speed, then I'll begin.
Guardiano. A good conclusion follow, and a sweet one
 After this stale beginning with old ware!
 Within there!
 Enter Servant.

16–17 tax . . . folly] tax him for being enraptured foolishly 34 old ware] i.e., the Mother

Servant.   Sir, do you call?
Guardiano.   Come near, list hither.   [*Whispers.*]
Livia. I long my self to see this absolute creature,
     That wins the heart of love and praise so much.
Guardiano. Go sir, make haste.
Livia.   Say I entreat her company;
     Do you hear, sir?
Servant.   Yes, Madam.   *Exit.*
Livia.   That brings her quickly.
Guardiano. I would 'twere done, the Duke waits the good hour,   40
     And I wait the good fortune that may spring from't.
     I have had a lucky hand these fifteen year
     At such court passage with three dice in a dish.
     Signor Fabritio!

     Enter Fabritio.

Fabritio.   Oh sir, I bring
     An alteration in my mouth now.
Guardiano. [*Aside*] An alteration! no wise speech I hope;
     He means not to talk wisely, does he, trow?
     —Good! what's the change, I pray, sir?
Fabritio.   A new change.
Guardiano. Another yet! 'faith, there's enough already.
Fabritio. My daughter loves him now.
Guardiano.   What, does she, sir?   50
Fabritio. Affects him beyond thought, who but the Ward forsooth!
     No talk but of the Ward; she would have him
     To choose 'bove all the men she ever saw.
     My will goes not so fast, as her consent now;
     Her duty gets before my command still.
Guardiano. Why then sir, if you'll have me speak my thoughts,
     I smell 'twill be a match.
Fabritio.   Ay, and a sweet young couple,
     If I have any judgment.
Guardiano. [*Aside*]   'Faith, that's little.
     —Let her be sent tomorrow before noon,
     And handsomely trick'd up; for 'bout that time   60
     I mean to bring her in, and tender her to him.
Fabritio. I warrant you for handsome, I will see
     Her things laid ready, every one in order,
     And have some part of her trick'd up tonight.

---

40 waits] is impatient for   43 court passage] Passage is an old dicing game, in which two
players alternately throw for doublets with three dice.   47 trow?] do you think?

Guardiano. Why, well said.

Fabritio.   'Twas a use her mother had,
    When she was invited to an early wedding;
    She'd dress her head o'ernight, sponge up her self,
    And give her neck three lathers.

Guardiano. [*Aside*]   Ne'er a halter?

Fabritio. On with her chain of pearl, her ruby bracelets,
    Lay ready all her tricks and jiggam-bobs.   70

Guardiano. So must your daughter.

Fabritio.   I'll about it straight, sir.

                                            Exit Fabritio.

Livia. How he sweats in the foolish zeal of fatherhood,
    After six ounces an hour, and seems
    To toil as much as if his cares were wise ones!

Guardiano. Y'have let his folly blood in the right vein, Lady.

Livia. And here comes his sweet son-in-law that shall be;
    They're both ally'd in wit before the marriage;
    What will they be hereafter, when they are nearer?
    Yet they can go no further than the fool:
    There's the world's end in both of 'em.

Enter Ward *and* Sordido, *one with a shittlecock, the other a battledore.*

Guardiano.   Now, young heir.   80

Ward. What's the next business after shittlecock now?

Guardiano. Tomorrow you shall see the gentlewoman
    Must be your wife.

Ward.   There's even another thing too
    Must be kept up with a pair of battledores.
    My wife! what can she do?

Guardiano. Nay, that's a question you should ask your self, Ward,
    When y'are alone together.

Ward.   That's as I list.
    A wife's to be ask anywhere, I hope;
    I'll ask her in a congregation,
    If I have a mind to't, and so save a license: [Guardiano *and* Livia
    My guardiner has no more wit than an herb-woman,   *talk apart.*]
    That sells away all her sweet herbs and nosegays,   92
    And keeps a stinking breath for her own pottage.

---

70 tricks] ornaments   73 after] more than   78 nearer] closelier related   88 ask] asked
89–90] By asking for the banns to be read in church he will avoid the need for a special
licence.   91 guardiner] The spelling here may be intended to suggest a pun on 'gardener',
which would associate with 'herb-woman' (but at line 101 the quarto has the same spelling
where no such quibble is possible).

Sordido. Let me be at the choosing of your beloved,
   If you desire a woman of good parts.
Ward. Thou shalt, sweet Sordido.
Sordido. I have a plaguy guess; let me alone to see what she is; if I but look
   upon her—'way, I know all the faults to a hair, that you may refuse her for.
Ward. Dost thou! I prethee let me hear 'em, Sordido.
Sordido. Well, mark 'em then; I have 'em all in rhyme.   100
   The wife your guardiner ought to tender
   Should be pretty, straight and slender;
   Her hair not short, her foot not long,
   Her hand not huge, nor too too loud her tongue:
   No pearl in eye, nor ruby in her nose,
   No burn or cut, but what the catalogue shows.
   She must have teeth, and that no black ones,
   And kiss most sweet when she does smack once:
   Her skin must be both white and plumpt,
   Her body straight, not hopper-rumpt,   110
   Or wriggle sideways like a crab;
   She must be neither slut nor drab,
   Nor go too splay-foot with her shoes,
   To make her smock lick up the dews.
   And two things more, which I forgot to tell ye,
   She neither must have bump in back, nor belly.
   These are the faults that will not make her pass.
Ward. And if I spy not these, I am a rank ass.
Sordido. Nay more; by right, sir, you should see her naked,
   For that's the ancient order.
Ward.   See her naked?   120
   That were good sport i'faith: I'll have the books turn'd over;
   And if I find her naked on record,
   She shall not have a rag on: but stay, stay,
   How if she should desire to see me so too?
   I were in a sweet case then—such a foul skin!
Sordido. But y'have a clean shirt, and that makes amends, sir.
Ward. I will not see her naked for that trick, though.   *Exit.*
Sordido. Then take her with all faults, with her clothes on!
   And they may hide a number with a bum-roll.

---

97 plaguy guess] conceivably a shrewd perception; or more literally, a troublesome apprehension   105 pearl in eye] whitish spots said to have been caused by smallpox   105 ruby]
pimple   106 what . . . shows] what there ought to be   110 hopper-rumpt] with a behind
like a funnel   116 bump . . . in belly] i.e., she must be neither hump-backed nor pregnant
121–2 I'll . . . record] I'll have this checked   127 trick] fashion   129 bum-roll] hoop
(for supporting a farthingale)

'Faith, choosing of a wench in a huge farthingale is like the buying of ware
under a great pent-house. What with the deceit of one, and the false light
of th'other, mark my speeches, he may have a diseas'd wench in's bed,
and rotten stuff in's breeches.   *Exit.*

Guardiano. It may take handsomely.

Livia.   I see small hindrance.   134
    How now, so soon return'd?

Enter Mother.

Guardiano.   She's come.

Livia.   That's well.
    Widow, come, come, I have a great quarrel to you,
    'Faith I must chide you, that you must be sent for!
    You make your self so strange, never come at us;
    And yet so near a neighbour, and so unkind;
    Troth y'are to blame, you cannot be more welcome   140
    To any house in Florence, that I'll tell you.

Mother. My thanks must needs acknowledge so much, Madam.

Livia. How can you be so strange then? I sit here
    Sometimes whole days together without company,
    When business draws this gentleman from home,
    And should be happy in society,
    Which I so well affect as that of yours.
    I know y'are alone too; why should not we,
    Like two kind neighbours, then, supply the wants
    Of one another, having tongue discourse,   150
    Experience in the world, and such kind helps
    To laugh down time, and meet age merrily?

Mother. Age (Madam): you speak mirth; 'tis at my door,
    But a long journey from your Ladyship yet.

Livia. My faith I'm nine and thirty, ev'ry stroke, wench,
    And 'tis a general observation
    'Mongst knights' wives or widows, we accompt our selves
    Then old, when young men's eyes leave looking at's:
    'Tis a true rule amongst us, and ne'er fail'd yet
    In any but in one, that I remember;   160
    Indeed she had a friend at nine and forty;

---

131 pent-house] here probably an awning or canopy (making the inside of the shop dark)
133 rotten . . . breeches] with a quibble on venereal disease   135 s.d.] Perhaps the
servant comes in too, but Livia's question does not demand his entry.   147 affect] like
157 'Mongst . . . widows] The text is perhaps corrupt: the quarto has ' 'Mongst Knights,
Wives, or Widdows'; I take Livia to refer to the gentry among whom she lives.

    Marry, she paid well for him, and in th'end
    He kept a quean or two with her own money,
    That robb'd her of her plate, and cut her throat.
Mother. She had her punishment in this world (Madam)
    And a fair warning to all other women,
    That they live chaste at fifty.
Livia.   Ay, or never, wench:
    Come, now I have thy company I'll not part with't
    Till after supper.
Mother.   Yes, I must crave pardon (Madam).
Livia. I swear you shall stay supper; we have no strangers, woman,   170
    None but my sojourners and I; this gentleman
    And the young heir his ward; you know our company.
Mother. Some other time, I will make bold with you, Madam.
Guardiano. Nay, pray stay, widow.
Livia.   'Faith, she shall not go.
    Do you think I'll be forsworn?   *Table and Chess.*
Mother.   'Tis a great while
    Till supper time; I'll take my leave then now (Madam)
    And come again i'th'evening, since your Ladyship
    Will have it so.
Livia.   I'th'evening? by my troth, wench,
    I'll keep you while I have you; you have great business, sure,
    To sit alone at home; I wonder strangely   180
    What pleasure you take in't! were't to me now,
    I should be ever at one neighbour's house
    Or other all day long; having no charge,
    Or none to chide you, if you go, or stay,
    Who may live merrier, ay, or more at heart's-ease?
    Come, we'll to chess, or draughts; there are an hundred tricks
    To drive out time till supper, never fear't, wench.
Mother. I'll but make one step home, and return straight (Madam).
Livia. Come, I'll not trust you; you use more excuses
    To your kind friends than ever I knew any.   190
    What business can you have, if you be sure
    Y'have lock'd the doors? and that being all you have,
    I know y'are careful on't: one afternoon
    So much to spend here! say I should entreat you now
    To lie a night or two, or a week with me,
    Or leave your own house for a month together,

171 sojourners] (habitual) guests   175 s.d.] The timing of this stage direction seems
arbitrary, but perhaps Livia is supposed to make a sign to a servant; it may however be a
prompter's reminder of what is needed ahead.

It were a kindness that long neighbourhood
And friendship might well hope to prevail in:
Would you deny such a request i'faith?
Speak truth, and freely.
Mother.   I were then uncivil, Madam.   200
Livia. Go to then, set your men; we'll have whole nights
Of mirth together, ere we be much older, wench.
Mother. [*Aside*] As good now tell her then, for she will know't;
I have always found her a most friendly lady.
Livia. Why widow, where's your mind?
Mother.   Troth, ev'n at home, Madam.
To tell you truth, I left a gentlewoman
Ev'n sitting all alone, which is uncomfortable,
Especially to young bloods.
Livia.   Another excuse!
Mother. No, as I hope for health, Madam, that's a truth;
Please you to send and see.
Livia.   What gentlewoman? pish.   210
Mother. Wife to my son indeed, but not known (Madam)
To any but your self.
Livia.   Now I beshrew you,
Could you be so unkind to her and me,
To come and not bring her? 'Faith, 'tis not friendly.
Mother. I fear'd to be too bold.
Livia.   Too bold? Oh what's become
Of the true hearty love was wont to be
'Mongst neighbours in old time?
Mother.   And she's a stranger (Madam).
Livia. The more should be her welcome; when is courtesy
In better practice than when 'tis employ'd
In entertaining strangers? I could chide i'faith.   220
Leave her behind, poor gentlewoman, alone too!
Make some amends, and send for her betimes, go.
Mother. Please you command one of your servants, Madam.
Livia. Within there.

    Enter Servant.

Servant.   Madam.
Livia.   Attend the gentlewoman.
Mother. It must be carried wondrous privately
From my son's knowledge, he'll break out in storms else.
Hark you, sir.   [*Whispers to* Servant, *who goes out.*]

201 men] i.e., chessmen

Livia. [*To* Guar.]   Now comes in the heat of your part.
Guardiano. True, I know it (Lady) and if I be out,
    May the Duke banish me from all employments,
    Wanton or serious.
Livia.   So, have you sent, widow?   230
Mother. Yes (Madam) he's almost at home by this.
Livia. And 'faith let me entreat you, that henceforward
    All such unkind faults may be swept from friendship,
    Which does but dim the lustre; and think thus much
    It is a wrong to me, that have ability
    To bid friends welcome, when you keep 'em from me,
    You cannot set greater dishonour near me;
    For bounty is the credit and the glory
    Of those that have enough: I see y'are sorry,
    And the good mends is made by't.
Mother.   Here she's, Madam.   240

   Enter Bianca, *and* Servant.   [*Exit* Servant.]

Bianca. [*Aside*] I wonder how she comes to send for me now?
Livia. Gentlewoman, y'are most welcome, trust me y'are,
    As courtesy can make one, or respect
    Due to the presence of you.
Bianca.   I give you thanks, Lady.
Livia. I heard you were alone, and 't had appear'd
    An ill condition in me, though I knew you not,
    Nor ever saw you, (yet humanity
    Thinks ev'ry case her own) to have kept your company
    Here from you, and left you all solitary:
    I rather ventur'd upon boldness then   250
    As the least fault, and wish'd your presence here;
    A thing most happily motion'd of that gentleman,
    Whom I request you, for his care and pity,
    To honour and reward with your acquaintance,
    A gentleman that ladies' rights stands for,
    That's his profession.
Bianca.   'Tis a noble one,
    And honours my acquaintance.
Guardiano.   All my intentions
    Are servants to such mistresses.
Bianca.   'Tis your modesty,
    It seems, that makes your deserts speak so low, sir.

240 mends] amends   248 your company] her who keeps you company

Livia. Come widow: look you, Lady, here's our business;   260
                          [Livia *and* Mother *sit down to chess.*]
    Are we not well employ'd, think you! an old quarrel
    Between us, that will never be at an end.
Bianca. No, and methinks there's men enough to part you (Lady).
Livia. Ho! but they set us on, let us come off
    As well as we can, poor souls, men care no farther.
    I pray sit down forsooth, if you have the patience
    To look upon two weak and tedious gamesters.
Guardiano. 'Faith Madam, set these by till evening,
    You'll have enough on't then; the gentlewoman,
    Being a stranger, would take more delight   270
    To see your rooms and pictures.
Livia.   Marry, good sir,
    And well rememb'red, I beseech you show 'em her;
    That will beguile time well; pray heartily do, sir,
    I'll do as much for you; here take these keys,
    Show her the monument too, and that's a thing
    Every one sees not; you can witness that, widow.
Mother. And that's worth sight indeed, Madam.
Bianca.   Kind lady,
    I fear I came to be a trouble to you.
Livia. Oh nothing less forsooth.
Bianca.   And to this courteous gentleman,
    That wears a kindness in his breast so noble   280
    And bounteous to the welcome of a stranger.
Guardiano. If you but give acceptance to my service,
    You do the greatest grace and honour to me
    That courtesy can merit.
Bianca.   I were to blame else,
    And out of fashion much. I pray you lead, sir.
Livia. After a game or two, w'are for you, gentlefolks.
Guardiano. We wish no better seconds in society
    Than your discourses, Madam, and your partner's there.
Mother. I thank your praise, I listen'd to you, sir;
    Though when you spoke, there came a paltry rook   290
    Full in my way, and chokes up all my game.
                          Exit Guardiano *&* Bianca.
Livia. Alas poor widow, I shall be too hard for thee.
Mother. Y'are cunning at the game, I'll be sworn (Madam).
Livia. It will be found so, ere I give you over:
    She that can place her man well——
Mother.   As you do (Madam).

Livia. ——As I shall (wench) can never lose her game;
  Nay, nay, the black king's mine.
Mother.   Cry you mercy (Madam).
Livia. And this my queen.
Mother.   I see't now.
Livia.   Here's a duke
  Will strike a sure stroke for the game anon;
  Your pawn cannot come back to relieve it self.   300
Mother. I know that (Madam).
Livia.   You play well the whilst;
  How she belies her skill! I hold two ducats,
  I give you check and mate to your white king:
  Simplicity it self, your saintish king there.
Mother. Well, ere now, Lady,
  I have seen the fall of subtilty: jest on.
Livia. Ay, but simplicities receives two for one.
Mother. What remedy but patience!

    Enter above Guardiano *and* Bianca.

Bianca.   Trust me, sir,
  Mine eye nev'r met with fairer ornaments.
Guardiano. Nay, livelier, I'm persuaded, neither Florence   310
  Nor Venice can produce.
Bianca.   Sir, my opinion
  Takes your part highly.
Guardiano.   There's a better piece
  Yet than all these.   —*The* Duke *above.*
Bianca.   Not possible, sir!
Guardiano.   Believe it,
  You'll say so when you see't: turn but your eye now,
  Y'are upon't presently.   *Exit.*
Bianca.   Oh sir.
Duke.   He's gone, beauty!
  Pish, look not after him: he's but a vapour,
  That, when the sun appears, is seen no more.
Bianca. Oh treachery to honour!
Duke.   Prethee tremble not;
  I feel thy breast shake like a turtle panting
  Under a loving hand that makes much on't;   320

298 duke] rook   302 I hold two ducats] Presumably Livia, having won, keeps the two
stakes; or perhaps ducats, like dukes, are rooks.   307 simplicities . . . one] simplicity falls
twice as often as subtlety   313 s.d. *above*] i.e., on a balcony or upper stage
315 presently] directly

    Why art so fearful? as I'm a friend to brightness,
    There's nothing but respect and honour near thee:
    You know me, you have seen me; here's a heart
    Can witness I have seen thee.
Bianca.   The more's my danger.
Duke. The more's thy happiness. Pish, strive not, sweet;
    This strength were excellent employ'd in love now,
    But here 'tis spent amiss; strive not to seek
    Thy liberty, and keep me still in prison.
    I'faith you shall not out, till I'm release now;
    We'll be both freed together, or stay still by't;   330
    So is captivity pleasant.
Bianca.   Oh my Lord.
Duke. I am not here in vain; have but the leisure
    To think on that, and thou'lt be soon resolv'd:
    The lifting of thy voice is but like one
    That does exalt his enemy, who proving high,
    Lays all the plots to confound him that rais'd him.
    Take warning, I beseech thee; thou seem'st to me
    A creature so compos'd of gentleness,
    And delicate meekness; such as bless the faces
    Of figures that are drawn for goddesses,   340
    And makes art proud to look upon her work:
    I should be sorry the least force should lay
    An unkind touch upon thee.
Bianca.   Oh my extremity!
    My Lord, what seek you?
Duke.   Love.
Bianca.   'Tis gone already,
    I have a husband.
Duke.   That's a single comfort,
    Take a friend to him.
Bianca.   That's a double mischief,
    Or else there's no religion.
Duke.   Do not tremble
    At fears of thine own making.
Bianca.   Nor, great Lord,
    Make me not bold with death and deeds of ruin,
    Because they fear not you; me they must fright,   350
    Then am I best in health. Should thunder speak,
    And none regard it, it had lost the name,

336 Lays all . . . him] foils all the plots and so confounds him that aroused the enemy
350 fear] frighten

And were as good be still. I'm not like those
That take their soundest sleeps in greatest tempests,
Then wake I most, the weather fearfullest,
And call for strength to virtue.
Duke.   Sure I think
  Thou know'st the way to please me. I affect
  A passionate pleading, 'bove an easy yielding,
  But never pitied any, (they deserve none)
  That will not pity me: I can command,   360
  Think upon that; yet if thou truly knewest
  The infinite pleasure my affection takes
  In gentle, fair entreatings, when love's businesses
  Are carried courteously 'twixt heart and heart,
  You'd make more haste to please me.
Bianca.   Why should you seek, sir,
  To take away that you can never give?
Duke. But I give better in exchange: wealth, honour;
  She that is fortunate in a duke's favour
  Lights on a tree that bears all women's wishes:
  If your own mother saw you pluck fruit there,   370
  She would commend your wit, and praise the time
  Of your nativity. Take hold of glory:
  Do not I know y'have cast away your life
  Upon necessities, means merely doubtful
  To keep you in indifferent health and fashion,
  (A thing I heard too lately, and soon pitied)
  And can you be so much your beauty's enemy,
  To kiss away a month or two in wedlock,
  And weep whole years in wants for ever after?
  Come play the wise wench, and provide for ever;   380
  Let storms come when they list, they find thee shelter'd:
  Should any doubt arise, let nothing trouble thee;
  Put trust in our love for the managing
  Of all to thy heart's peace. We'll walk together,
  And show a thankful joy for both our fortunes.   *Exeunt above.*
Livia. Did not I say my duke would fetch you over (widow)?
Mother. I think you spoke in earnest when you said it (Madam).
Livia. And my black king makes all the haste he can too.
Mother. Well (Madam) we may meet with him in time yet.
Livia. I have given thee blind mate twice.

357 affect] take pleasure in   369 Lights] alights   380 wise] The quarto has 'wife'; the
f is probably a misprint for a long *s*, but the quarto reading is possible (implying that this
is how all wives provide for themselves).

Mother.   You may see (Madam)   390
    My eyes begin to fail.
Livia.   I'll swear they do, wench.

    Enter Guardiano.

Guardiano. [*Aside*] I can but smile as often as I think on't,
    How prettily the poor fool was beguil'd:
    How unexpectedly; it's a witty age,
    Never were finer snares for women's honesties
    Than are devis'd in these days; no spider's web
    Made of a daintier thread than are now practis'd
    To catch love's flesh-fly by the silver wing:
    Yet to prepare her stomach by degrees
    To Cupid's feast, because I saw 'twas queasy,   400
    I show'd her naked pictures by the way;
    A bit to stay the appetite. Well, advancement!
    I venture hard to find thee; if thou com'st
    With a greater title set upon thy crest,
    I'll take that first cross patiently, and wait
    Until some other comes greater than that.
    I'll endure all.
Livia.   The game's ev'n at the best now;
    You may see, widow, how all things draw to
    An end.
Mother.   Ev'n so do I, Madam.
Livia.   I pray
    Take some of your neighbours along with you.   410
Mother. They must be those are almost twice your years then,
    If they be chose fit matches for my time, Madam.
Livia. Has not my duke bestirr'd himself?
Mother.   Yes 'faith, Madam;
    H'as done me all the mischief in this game.
Livia. H'as show'd himself in's kind.
Mother.   In's kind, call you it?
    I may swear that.
Livia.   Yes 'faith, and keep your oath.
Guardiano. [*To* Livia.] Hark, list, there's somebody coming down; 'tis she.

    Enter Bianca.

398 flesh-fly] blow-fly (but the word is used only for its connexion with flesh)   415 in's
kind] in his true colours

Bianca. [*Aside*] Now bless me from a blasting; I saw that now,
  Fearful for any woman's eye to look on;
  Infectious mists and mildews hang at's eyes: 420
  The weather of a doomsday dwells upon him.
  Yet since mine honour's leprous, why should I
  Preserve that fair that caus'd the leprosy?
  Come poison all at once.—[*To* Guardiano] Thou in whose baseness
  The bane of virtue broods, I'm bound in soul
  Eternally to curse thy smooth-brow'd treachery,
  That wore the fair veil of a friendly welcome,
  And I a stranger; think upon't, 'tis worth it.
  Murders pil'd up upon a guilty spirit
  At his last breath will not lie heavier   430
  Than this betraying act upon thy conscience:
  Beware of off'ring the first-fruits to sin;
  His weight is deadly who commits with strumpets,
  After they have been abas'd, and made for use;
  If they offend to th'death, as wise men know,
  How much more they then that first make 'em so!
  I give thee that to feed on; I'm made bold now,
  I thank thy treachery; sin and I'm acquainted,
  No couple greater; and I'm like that great one,
  Who, making politic use of a base villain,   440
  He likes the treason well, but hates the traitor;
  So hate I thee, slave.
Guardiano.   Well, so the Duke love me,
  I fare not much amiss then; two great feasts
  Do seldom come together in one day;
  We must not look for 'em.
Bianca.   What, at it still, Mother?
Mother. You see we sit by't; are you so soon return'd?
Livia. [*Aside*] So lively, and so cheerful, a good sign that.
Mother. You have not seen all since, sure?
Bianca.   That have I, Mother,
  The monument and all: I'm so beholding
  To this kind, honest, courteous gentleman,   450
  You'd little think it (Mother) show'd me all,
  Had me from place to place, so fashionably;
  The kindness of some people, how't exceeds!

---

418 bless . . . blasting] preserve me from damnation 421 him] presumably the Duke, but possibly Guardiano 433 His . . . deadly] he is weighted down with mortal sin 435 they] i.e., strumpets 435 offend . . . death] sin mortally 448 since] yet

'Faith, I have seen that I little thought to see,
  I'th'morning when I rose.
Mother.   Nay, so I told you
  Before you saw't, it would prove worth your sight.
  I give you great thanks for my daughter, sir,
  And all your kindness towards her.
Guardiano.   O good widow!
  Much good may't do her; [*Aside*] forty weeks hence, i'faith.

  Enter Servant.

Livia. Now sir.
Servant.   May't please you, Madam, to walk in?   460
  Supper's upon the table.
Livia.   Yes, we come;   [*Exit* Servant.]
  Will't please you, gentlewoman?
Bianca.   Thanks virtuous lady,
  (Y'are a damn'd bawd) I'll follow you forsooth,
  Pray take my mother in, [*Aside*] an old ass go with you;
  This gentleman and I vow not to part.
Livia. Then get you both before.
Bianca.   There lies his art.
                              Exeunt [Bianca & Guardiano].
Livia. Widow, I'll follow you. [*Exit* Mother.] Is't so, damn'd bawd?
  Are you so bitter? 'Tis but want of use;
  Her tender modesty is sea-sick a little,
  Being not accustom'd to the breaking billow   470
  Of woman's wavering faith, blown with temptations.
  'Tis but a qualm of honour, 'twill away,
  A little bitter for the time, but lasts not.
  Sin tastes at the first draught like wormwood water,
  But drunk again, 'tis nectar ever after.   *Exit*.

ACT. 3.   SCAEN. 1

  Enter Mother.

Mother. I would my son would either keep at home,
    Or I were in my grave;
    She was but one day abroad, but ever since,
    She's grown so cutted, there's no speaking to her:
    Whether the sight of great cheer at my Lady's,

III. i, 4 cutted] querulous

And such mean fare at home, work discontent in her,
I know not; but I'm sure she's strangely alter'd.
I'll nev'r keep daughter-in-law i'th'house with me
Again, if I had an hundred: when read I of any
That agreed long together, but she and her mother   10
Fell out in the first quarter! nay, sometime
A grudging of a scolding the first week, by'r Lady;
So takes the new disease, methinks, in my house;
I'm weary of my part, there's nothing likes her;
I know not how to please her, here a-late;
And here she comes.

Enter Bianca.

Bianca.   This is the strangest house
For all defects, as ever gentlewoman
Made shift withal, to pass away her love in:
Why is there not a cushion-cloth of drawn work,
Or some fair cut-work pinn'd up in my bedchamber?   20
A silver and gilt casting-bottle hung by't?
Nay, since I am content to be so kind to you,
To spare you for a silver basin and ew'r,
Which one of my fashion looks for of duty;
She's never offered under, where she sleeps.
Mother. She talks of things here my whole state's not worth.
Bianca. Never a green silk quilt is there i'th'house, Mother,
To cast upon my bed?
Mother.   No by troth is there,
Nor orange tawny neither.
Bianca.   Here's a house
For a young gentlewoman to be got with child in.   30
Mother. Yes, simple though you make it, there has been three
Got in a year in't, since you move me to't;
And all as sweet-fac'd children, and as lovely,
As you'll be mother of; I will not spare you:
What, cannot children be begot, think you,
Without gilt casting-bottles? Yes, and as sweet ones.
The miller's daughter brings forth as white boys,
As she that bathes her self with milk and bean-flour.

12 A grudging of a scolding] Perhaps we should read 'or' for 'of'; but she may mean that
the daughter grudges the scolding of the mother.   13 new disease] of insubordination?
19 drawn work] ornamental weaves made by drawing out some threads from warp and woof
20 cut-work] openwork embroidery, lace   25 She's never . . . sleeps] she is always given
as much in her bedroom   37 white boy] a term of endearment   38 bean-flour] used
as a cosmetic

'Tis an old saying, one may keep good cheer
In a mean house; so may true love affect   40
After the rate of princes in a cottage.
Bianca. Troth you speak wondrous well for your old house here;
   'Twill shortly fall down at your feet to thank you,
   Or stoop when you go to bed, like a good child
   To ask you blessing. Must I live in want,
   Because my fortune matcht me with your son?
   Wives do not give away themselves to husbands,
   To the end to be quite cast away; they look
   To be the better us'd and tender'd rather,
   Highlier respected, and maintain'd the richer;   50
   They're well rewarded else for the free gift
   Of their whole life to a husband. I ask less now
   Than what I had at home when I was a maid,
   And at my father's house, kept short of that
   Which a wife knows she must have, nay, and will;
   Will, Mother, if she be not a fool born;
   And report went of me, that I could wrangle
   For what I wanted when I was two hours old,
   And by that copy, this land still I hold.
   You hear me, Mother.   *Exit.*
Mother.   Ay, too plain methinks;   60
   And were I somewhat deafer when you spake,
   'Twere nev'r a whit the worse for my quietness:
   'Tis the most sudden'st, strangest alteration,
   And the most subtilest that ev'r wit at threescore
   Was puzzled to find out: I know no cause for't; but
   She's no more like the gentlewoman at first,
   Than I am like her that nev'r lay with man yet,
   And she's a very young thing where'er she be;
   When she first lighted here, I told her then
   How mean she should find all things; she was pleas'd forsooth,   70
   None better: I laid open all defects to her,
   She was contented still; but the devil's in her,
   Nothing contents her now. Tonight my son
   Promis'd to be at home, would he were come once,
   For I'm weary of my charge, and life too:
   She'd be serv'd all in silver by her good will,
   By night and day; she hates the name of pewterer,

40–41 affect . . . rate] contrive to be as high as that   46 fortune] fate (not wealth)
59 copy] quibbling on 'copyhold', tenure at the will of the lord of the manor   62 quiet-
ness] peace of mind

More than sick men the noise, or diseas'd bones
That quake at fall o'th'hammer, seeming to have
A fellow-feeling with't at every blow: 80
What course shall I think on? she frets me so. *Exit.*

Enter Leantio.

Leantio. How near am I now to a happiness,
That earth exceeds not! not another like it;
The treasures of the deep are not so precious,
As are the conceal'd comforts of a man,
Lockt up in woman's love. I scent the air
Of blessings when I come but near the house;
What a delicious breath marriage sends forth!
The violet-bed's not sweeter. Honest wedlock
Is like a banqueting-house built in a garden, 90
On which the spring's chaste flowers take delight
To cast their modest odours; when base lust,
With all her powders, paintings, and best pride,
Is but a fair house built by a ditch-side.
When I behold a glorious dangerous strumpet,
Sparkling in beauty and destruction too,
Both at a twinkling, I do liken straight
Her beautifi'd body to a goodly temple
That's built on vaults where carcasses lie rotting,
And so by little and little I shrink back again, 100
And quench desire with a cool meditation,
And I'm as well methinks. Now for a welcome
Able to draw men's envies upon man:
A kiss now that will hang upon my lip,
As sweet as morning dew upon a rose,
And full as long; after a five days' fast
She'll be so greedy now, and cling about me,
I take care how I shall be rid of her;
And here't begins.

[*Enter* Bianca *and* Mother.]

Bianca.   Oh sir, y'are welcome home
Mother. Oh is he come? I am glad on't.
Leantio.   Is that all? 110
Why, this is as dreadful now as sudden death
To some rich man, that flatters all his sins
With promise of repentance when he's old,

111 this is as] Quarto: 'this? as'.

And dies in the midway before he comes to't.
Sure y'are not well, Bianca. How dost, prethee?
Bianca. I have been better than I am at this time.
Leantio. Alas, I thought so.
Bianca.   Nay, I have been worse too,
Than now you see me, sir.
Leantio.   I'm glad thou mend'st yet,
I feel my heart mend too: how came it to thee?
Has any thing dislik'd thee in my absence?   120
Bianca. No certain, I have had the best content
That Florence can afford.
Leantio.   Thou makest the best on't.
Speak Mother, what's the cause? you must needs know.
Mother. Troth I know none, son, let her speak her self;
Unless it be the same gave Lucifer
A tumbling cast; that's pride.
Bianca.   Methinks this house
Stands nothing to my mind; I'd have
Some pleasant lodging i'th'high street, sir,
Or if 'twere near the court, sir, that were much better;
'Tis a sweet recreation for a gentlewoman,   130
To stand in a bay-window, and see gallants.
Leantio. Now I have another temper, a mere stranger
To that of yours, it seems; I should delight
To see none but your self.
Bianca.   I praise not that:
Too fond is as unseemly as too churlish;
I would not have a husband of that proneness,
To kiss me before company, for a world:
Beside, 'tis tedious to see one thing still (sir),
Be it the best that ever heart affected;
Nay, were't your self, whose love had power, you know,   140
To bring me from my friends, I would not stand thus,
And gaze upon you always: troth I could not, sir;
As good be blind, and have no use of sight,
As look on one thing still: what's the eye's treasure,
But change of objects? You are learned, sir,
And know I speak not ill; 'tis full as virtuous
For woman's eye to look on several men,
As for her heart (sir) to be fix'd on one.
Leantio. Now thou com'st home to me; a kiss for that word.

120 dislik'd] annoyed   132 temper] attitude   138, 144 still] always   146 'tis] Quarto: "till'.

Bianca. No matter for a kiss, sir, let it pass,   150
    'Tis but a toy, we'll not so much as mind it,
    Let's talk of other business, and forget it.
    What news now of the pirates, any stirring?
    Prethee discourse a little.
Mother. [*Aside*]   I am glad he's here yet
    To see her tricks himself; I had lied monstrously,
    If I had told 'em first.
Leantio.   Speak, what's the humour (sweet)
    You make your lip so strange? this was not wont.
Bianca. Is there no kindness bewixt man and wife,
    Unless they make a pigeon-house of friendship,
    And be still billing? 'tis the idlest fondness   160
    That ever was invented, and 'tis pity
    It's grown a fashion for poor gentlewomen;
    There's many a disease kiss'd in a year by't,
    And a French curtsy made to't. Alas, sir,
    Think of the world, how we shall live, grow serious;
    We have been married a whole fortnight now.
Leantio. How? a whole fortnight! why, is that so long?
Bianca. 'Tis time to leave off dalliance; 'tis a doctrine
    Of your own teaching, if you be rememb'red,
    And I was bound to obey it.
Mother. [*Aside*]   Here's one fits him;   170
    This was well catch'd i'faith, son, like a fellow
    That rids another country of a plague,
    And brings it home with him to his own house.   *Knock within.*
    ——Who knocks?
Leantio.   Who's there now? withdraw you Bianca,
    Thou art a gem no stranger's eye must see,
    Howev'r thou pleas'd now to look dull on me.

                          Exit [Bianca, *with* Mother.]

    Enter Messenger.

    Y'are welcome, sir; to whom your business, pray?
Messenger. To one I see not here now.
Leantio.   Who should that be, sir?
Messenger. A young gentlewoman, I was sent to.
Leantio.   A young gentlewoman?
Messenger. Ay sir, about sixteen; why look you wildly, sir?   180
Leantio. At your strange error: y'have mistook the house, sir.
    There's none such here, I assure you.

164 French curtsy] alluding to 'French disease' or syphilis   170 fits him] strikes home

Messenger.   I assure you too,
  The man that sent me cannot be mistook.
Leantio. Why, who is't sent you, sir?
Messenger.   The Duke.
Leantio.   The Duke?
Messenger. Yes, he entreats her company at a banquet
  At Lady Livia's house.
Leantio.   Troth, shall I tell you, sir,
  It is the most erroneous business
  That e'er your honest pains was abus'd with;
  I pray forgive me, if I smile a little
  (I cannot choose i'faith, sir) at an error   190
  So comical as this (I mean no harm though).
  His grace has been most wondrous ill inform'd,
  Pray so return it (sir). What should her name be?
Messenger. That I shall tell you straight too: Bianca Capella.
Leantio. How sir, Bianca? What do you call th'other?
Messenger. Capella; sir, it seems you know no such then?
Leantio. Who should this be? I never heard o'th'name.
Messenger. Then 'tis a sure mistake.
Leantio.   What if you enquir'd
  In the next street, sir? I saw gallants there
  In the new houses that are built of late.   200
  Ten to one, there you find her.
Messenger.   Nay, no matter,
  I will return the mistake, and seek no further.
Leantio. Use your own will and pleasure, sir, y'are welcome.   *Exit*
  What shall I think of first? Come forth Bianca,   Messenger.
  Thou art betray'd, I fear me.

    Enter Bianca [*and* Mother].

Bianca.   Betray'd, how sir?
Leantio. The Duke knows thee.
Bianca.   Knows me! how know you that, sir?
Leantio. H'as got thy name.
Bianca. [*Aside*]   Ay, and my good name too,
  That's worse o'th'twain.
Leantio.   How comes this work about?
Bianca. How should the Duke know me? can you guess, Mother?
Mother. Not I with all my wits, sure we kept house close.   210
Leantio. Kept close! not all the locks in Italy
  Can keep you women so; you have been gadding,
  And ventur'd out at twilight, to th'court-green yonder,

And met the gallant bowlers coming home;
Without your masks too, both of you, I'll be hang'd else;
Thou hast been seen, Bianca, by some stranger;
Never excuse it.

Bianca.   I'll not seek the way, sir;
Do you think y'have married me to mew me up
Not to be seen? what would you make of me?

Leantio. A good wife, nothing else.

Bianca.   Why, so are some   220
That are seen ev'ry day, else the devil take 'em.

Leantio. No more then; I believe all virtuous in thee,
Without an argument; 'twas but thy hard chance
To be seen somewhere, there lies all the mischief;
But I have devis'd a riddance.

Mother.   Now I can tell you, son,
The time and place.

Leantio.   When, where?

Mother.   What wits have I!
When you last took your leave, if you remember,
You left us both at window.

Leantio.   Right, I know that.

Mother. And not the third part of an hour after,
The Duke pass'd by in a great solemnity,   230
To St. Mark's temple, and to my apprehension
He look'd up twice to th'window.

Leantio.   Oh, there quick'ned
The mischief of this hour!

Bianca. [*Aside*]   If you call't mischief,
It is a thing I fear I am conceiv'd with.

Leantio. Look'd he up twice, and could you take no warning?

Mother. Why, once may do as much harm, son, as a thousand;
Do not you know one spark has fir'd an house,
As well as a whole furnace?

Leantio.   My heart flames for't:
Yet let's be wise, and keep all smother'd closely;
I have bethought a means; is the door fast?   240

Mother. I lockt it my self after him.

Leantio.   You know, Mother,
At the end of the dark parlour there's a place
So artificially contriv'd for a conveyance,

---

14 bowlers] i.e., those who have been playing bowls   217 excuse] deny

No search could ever find it: when my father
Kept in for man-slaughter, it was his sanctuary;
There will I lock my life's best treasure up.
Bianca!

Bianca.   Would you keep me closer yet?
Have you the conscience? y'are best ev'n choke me up, sir!
You make me fearful of your health and wits,
You cleave to such wild courses; what's the matter?   250

Leantio. Why, are you so insensible of your danger
To ask that now? the Duke himself has sent for you
To Lady Livia's, to a banquet forsooth.

Bianca. Now I beshrew you heartily, has he so!
And you the man would never yet vouchsafe
To tell me on't till now: you show your loyalty
And honesty at once; and so farewell, sir.

Leantio. Bianca, whether now?

Bianca.   Why, to the Duke, sir.
You say he sent for me.

Leantio.   But thou dost not mean
To go, I hope.

Bianca.   No? I shall prove unmannerly,   260
Rude, and uncivil, mad, and imitate you.
Come Mother, come, follow his humour no longer,
We shall be all executed for treason shortly.

Mother. Not I, i'faith; I'll first obey the Duke,
And taste of a good banquet, I'm of thy mind.
I'll step but up, and fetch two handkerchiefs
To pocket up some sweet-meats, and o'ertake thee.   *Exit.*

Bianca. [*Aside*] Why, here's an old wench would trot into a bawd now,
For some dry sucket, or a colt in march-pane.   *Exit.*

Leantio. Oh thou the ripe time of man's misery, wedlock;   270
When all his thoughts, like overladen trees,
Crack with the fruits they bear, in cares, in jealousies.
Oh that's a fruit that ripens hastily,
After 'tis knit to marriage; it begins,
As soon as the sun shines upon the bride,
A little to show colour. Blessed powers!
Whence comes this alteration? the distractions,
The fears and doubts it brings are numberless,
And yet the cause I know not. What a peace
Has he that never marries! if he knew   280

258 whether] whither   269 sucket] succade, sweetmeat   269 colt in march-pane]
fancifully shaped marzipan sweet

The benefit he enjoy'd, or had the fortune
To come and speak with me, he should know then
The infinite wealth he had, and discern rightly
The greatness of his treasure by my loss:
Nay, what a quietness has he 'bove mine,
That wears his youth out in a strumpet's arms,
And never spends more care upon a woman
Than at the time of lust; but walks away,
And if he find her dead at his return,
His pity is soon done, he breaks a sigh   290
In many parts, and gives her but a piece on't!
But all the fears, shames, jealousies, costs and troubles,
And still renew'd cares of a marriage-bed,
Live in the issue, when the wife is dead.

   Enter Messenger.

Messenger. A good perfection to your thoughts.
Leantio.   The news, sir?
Messenger. Though you were pleas'd of late to pin an error on me,
   You must not shift another in your stead too:
   The Duke has sent me for you.
Leantio.   How, for me, sir?
   [*Aside*] I see then 'tis my theft; w'are both betray'd:
   Well, I'm not the first has stol'n away a maid,   300
   My countrymen have us'd it.—I'll along with you, sir.   *Exeunt*.

SCAEN. 2

   A banquet prepared: enter Guardiano *and* Ward.

Guardiano. Take you especial note of such a gentlewoman,
   She's here on purpose, I have invited her,
   Her father, and her uncle, to this banquet;
   Mark her behaviour well, it does concern you;
   And what her good parts are, as far as time
   And place can modestly require a knowledge of,
   Shall be laid open to your understanding.
   You know I'm both your guardian and your uncle,
   My care of you is double, ward and nephew,
   And I'll express it here.
Ward.   'Faith, I should know her   10
   Now by her mark among a thousand women:
   A lettle pretty deft and tidy thing, you say?

294 issue] children   III. ii, 12 lettle] little

Guardiano. Right.

Ward.   With a lusty sprouting sprig in her hair.

Guardiano. Thou goest the right way still; take one mark more,
    Thou shalt nev'r find her hand out of her uncle's,
    Or else his out of hers, if she be near him:
    The love of kinred never yet stuck closer
    Than theirs to one another; he that weds her
    Marries her uncle's heart too.

Ward.   Say you so, sir?
    Then I'll be ask'd i'th'church to both of them.   *Cornets* [*within*].

Guardiano. Fall back, here comes the Duke.

Ward.   He brings a gentlewoman,
    I should fall forward rather.

   Enter Duke, Bianca, Fabritio, Hippolito, Livia, Mother, Isabella, *and*
Attendants.

Duke.   Come Bianca,   22
    Of purpose sent into the world to show
    Perfection once in woman; I'll believe
    Hence forward they have ev'ry one a soul too
    'Gainst all the uncourteous opinions
    That man's uncivil rudeness ever held of 'em.
    Glory of Florence, light into mine arms!

   Enter Leantio.

Bianca. Yon comes a grudging man will chide you, sir;
    The storm is now in's heart, and would get nearer,   30
    And fall here if it durst, it pours down yonder.

Duke. If that be he, the weather shall soon clear.
    List, and I'll tell thee how.   [*Whispers* Bianca.]

Leantio. [*Aside*]   A-kissing too?
    I see 'tis plain lust now; adultery bold'ned;
    What will it prove anon, when 'tis stufft full
    Of wine and sweetmeats, being so impudent fasting?

Duke. We have heard of your good parts, sir, which we honour
    With our embrace and love; is not the captainship
    Of Rouans citadel, since the late deceas'd,
    Suppli'd by any yet?

Gentleman.   By none, my Lord.   40

Duke. Take it, the place is yours then, and as faithfulness
    And desert grows, our favour shall grow with't: [Leantio *kneels*.]
    Rise now the captain of our fort at Rouans.

13 sprig] probably an ornament in the form of a spray of flowers   39 Rouans] 'A misprint,
I presume; but qy. for what?' (*Dyce*)

Leantio. The service of whole life give your Grace thanks.
Duke. Come sit, Bianca.
Leantio. [*Aside*]   This is some good yet,
   And more than ev'r I look'd for, a fine bit
   To stay a cuckold's stomach: all preferment
   That springs from sin and lust, it shoots up quickly,
   As gardeners' crops do in the rotten'st grounds;
   So is all means rais'd from base prostitution,   50
   Ev'n like a sallet growing upon a dunghill:
   I'm like a thing that never was yet heard of,
   Half merry, and half mad, much like a fellow
   That eats his meat with a good appetite,
   And wears a plague-sore that would fright a country;
   Or rather like the barren hard'ned ass,
   That feeds on thistles till he bleeds again;
   And such is the condition of my misery.
Livia. Is that your son, widow?
Mother.   Yes, did your Ladyship
   Never know that till now?
Livia.   No, trust me, did I,   60
   [*Aside*] Nor ever truly felt the power of love,
   And pity to a man, till now I knew him;
   I have enough to buy me my desires,
   And yet to spare; that's one good comfort.—Hark you,
   Pray let me speak with you, sir, before you go.
Leantio. With me, Lady? you shall, I am at your service:
   [*Aside*] What will she say now, trow, more goodness yet?
Ward. [*Aside*] I see her now, I'm sure; the ape's so little,
   I shall scarce feel her; I have seen almost
   As tall as she sold in the fair for ten pence.   70
   See how she simpers it, as if marmalade would not
   Melt in her mouth; she might have the kindness i'faith
   To send me a gilded bull from her own trencher,
   A ram, a goat, or somewhat to be nibbling.
   These women, when they come to sweet things once,
   They forget all their friends, they grow so greedy;
   Nay, oftentimes their husbands.
Duke.   Here's a health now, gallants,
   To the best beauty at this day in Florence.
Bianca. Whoe'er she be, she shall not go unpledg'd, sir.
Duke. Nay, you're excus'd for this.
Bianca.   Who, I, my Lord?   80

51 sallet] salad   56 barren] dull-witted   73 gilded bull] cf. III. i. 269

Duke. Yes, by the law of Bacchus; plead your benefit,
    You are not bound to pledge your own health, Lady.
Bianca. That's a good way, my Lord, to keep me dry.
Duke. Nay, then I will not offend Venus so much,
    Let Bacchus seek his mends in another court,
    Here's to thy self, Bianca.
Bianca.   Nothing comes
    More welcome to that name than your Grace.
Leantio. [*Aside*]   So, so:
    Here stands the poor thief now that stole the treasure,
    And he's not thought on; ours is near kin now
    To a twin-misery born into the world.   90
    First the hard-conscienc'd worldling, he hoards wealth up,
    Then comes the next, and he feasts all upon't;
    One's dam'd for getting, th'other for spending on't:
    Oh equal justice, thou hast met my sin
    With a full weight, I'm rightly now opprest,
    All her friends' heavy hearts lie in my breast.
Duke. Methinks there is no spirit amongst us, gallants,
    But what divinely sparkles from the eyes
    Of bright Bianca; we sat all in darkness,
    But for that splendour. Who was't told us lately   100
    Of a match-making right, a marriage-tender?
Guardiano. 'Twas I, my Lord.
Duke.   'Twas you indeed: where is she?
Guardiano. This is the gentlewoman.
Fabritio.   My Lord, my daughter.
Duke. [*Aside*] Why, here's some stirring yet.
Fabritio.   She's a dear child to me.
Duke. That must needs be; you say she is your daughter.
Fabritio. Nay, my good Lord, dear to my purse I mean,
    Beside my person, I nev'r reckon'd that.
    She has the full qualities of a gentlewoman;
    I have brought her up to music, dancing, what not,
    That may commend her sex, and stir her husband.   110
Duke. And which is he now?
Guardiano.   This young heir, my Lord.
Duke. What is he brought up to?
Hippolito. [*Aside*]   To cat and trap.

---

85 mends] amends   101 right] perhaps a misprint for 'rite'   104 here's ... yet]
suggesting to the audience that the Duke is sexually roused by Isabella (cf. l. 110); but it
could mean simply 'something is going on'

Guardiano. My Lord, he's a great ward, wealthy, but simple;
 His parts consist in acres.
Duke.   Oh, wise-acres.
Guardiano. Y'have spoke him in a word, sir.
Bianca.   'Las, poor gentlewoman,
 She's ill bested, unless sh'as dealt the wiselier,
 And laid in more provision for her youth:
 Fools will not keep in summer.
Leantio. [*Aside*]   No, nor such wives
 From whores in winter.
Duke.   Yea, the voice too, sir?
Fabritio. Ay, and a sweet breast too, my Lord, I hope,   120
 Or I have cast away my money wisely;
 She took her pricksong earlier, my Lord,
 Than any of her kinred ever did:
 A rare child, though I say't, but I'd not have
 The baggage hear so much, 'twould make her swell straight:
 And maids of all things must not be puft up.
Duke. Let's turn us to a better banquet then,
 For music bids the soul of a man to a feast,
 And that's indeed a noble entertainment,
 Worthy Bianca's self; you shall perceive, beauty,   130
 Our Florentine damsels are not brought up idlely.
Bianca. They are wiser of themselves, it seems my Lord,
 And can take gifts, when goodness offers 'em.   *Music.*
Leantio. [*Aside*] True, and damnation has taught you that wisdom,
 You can take gifts too. Oh that music mocks me!
Livia. [*Aside*] I am as dumb to any language now
 But love's, as one that never learn'd to speak:
 I am not yet so old, but he may think of me;
 My own fault, I have been idle a long time;
 But I'll begin the week, and paint tomorrow,   140
 So follow my true labour day by day:
 I never thriv'd so well, as when I us'd it.

SONG [sung by Isabella]

What harder chance can fall to woman,
Who was born to cleave to some man,
Than to bestow her time, youth, beauty,
Life's observance, honour, duty,

113 great] rich, profitable 115ff.] This speech sounds like an aside, but Leantio overhears. 120 breast] voice 122 pricksong] music written or pricked in notes (but with
an inescapable sexual quibble, as in ll. 125f.) 126 puft] puffed 140 paint] make up

On a thing for no use good
But to make physic work, or blood
Force fresh in an old lady's cheek?
She that would be   150
Mother of fools, let her compound with me.

Ward. [*Aside*] Here's a tune indeed; pish, I had rather hear one ballad sung i'th'nose now of the lamentable drowning of fat sheep and oxen, than all these simpering tunes play'd upon cat's-guts, and sung by little kitlings.

Fabritio. How like you her breast now, my Lord?

Bianca. [*To* Duke]   Her breast?
He talks as if his daughter had given suck
Before she were married, as her betters have;
The next he praises sure will be her nipples.

Duke. [*To* Bianca] Methinks now, such a voice to such a husband   160
Is like a jewel of unvalued worth
Hung at a fool's ear.

Fabritio.   May it please your Grace
To give her leave to show another quality?

Duke. Marry, as many good ones as you will, sir,
The more the better welcome.

Leantio. [*Aside*]   But the less
The better practis'd: that soul's black indeed
That cannot commend virtue; but who keeps it?
The extortioner will say to a sick beggar,
'Heaven comfort thee', though he give none himself:
This good is common.

Fabritio.   Will it please you now, sir,   170
To entreat your ward to take her by the hand,
And lead her in a dance before the Duke?

Guardiano. That will I, sir, 'tis needful; hark you, Nephew.

Fabritio. Nay, you shall see, young heir, what y'have for your money,
Without fraud or imposture.

Ward.   Dance with her!
Not I, sweet Guardiner, do not urge my heart to't,
'Tis clean against my blood; dance with a stranger!
Let who will do't, I'll not begin first with her.

Hippolito. [*Aside*] No, fear't not, fool, sh'as took a better order.

152ff.] The quarto prints this speech in double columns alongside the song; is it supposed to be spoken while the song is going on?   155 kitlings] kittens   178 who] The quarto has 'who's', which might conceivably be a misprint for 'who s'' (i.e., 'who so')   179 sh'as ... order] she has already begun first with another (Hippolito)

Guardiano. Why, who shall take her then?

Ward.   Some other gentleman;   180
    Look, there's her uncle, a fine-timber'd reveller,
    Perhaps he knows the manner of her dancing too,
    I'll have him do't before me, I have sworn, Guardiner,
    Then may I learn the better.

Guardiano.   Thou'lt be an ass still.

Ward. I? All that uncle shall not fool me out.
    Pish, I stick closer to my self than so.

Guardiano. I must entreat you, sir, to take your niece
    And dance with her; my ward's a little wilful,
    He would have you show him the way.

Hippolito.   Me, sir?
    He shall command it at all hours, pray tell him so.   190

Guardiano. I thank you for him, he has not wit himself, sir.

Hippolito. Come, my life's peace. [*Aside*] I have a strange office on't here:
    'Tis some man's luck to keep the joys he likes
    Conceal'd for his own bosom; but my fortune
    To set 'em out now, for another's liking,
    Like the mad misery of necessitous man,
    That parts from his good horse with many praises,
    And goes on foot himself; need must be obey'd
    In ev'ry action, it mars man and maid.   *Music.*

    A dance, making honours to the D[uke] *and curtsy to themselves, both before
and after.*

Duke. Signor Fabritio, y'are a happy father,   200
    Your cares and pains are fortunate you see,
    Your cost bears noble fruits. Hippolito, thanks.

Fabritio. Here's some amends for all my charges yet;
    She wins both prick and praise, where e'er she comes.

Duke. How lik'st, Bianca?

Bianca.   All things well, my Lord:
    But this poor gentlewoman's fortune, that's the worst.

Duke. There is no doubt, Bianca, she'll find leisure
    To make that good enough; he's rich and simple.

Bianca. She has the better hope o'th'upper hand indeed,
    Which women strive for most.

Guardiano.   Do't when I bid you, sir.   210

181 fine-timber'd] well built   185] I take 'uncle' to refer to Hippolito, so that the line
means that Hippolito will not make a fool of him; but the quarto reads 'I, all that Uncle',
which might mean 'Ay, I am all that, Uncle', though the sense seems weaker.   199 s.d.
honours] bows   204 prick] The image is from archery, the prick being the centre of the
target, though there is of course a sexual quibble (not recognized by Fabritio).

Ward. I'll venture but a hornpipe with her, Guardiner,
Or some such married man's dance.
Guardiano.   Well, venture something, sir.
Ward. I have rhyme for what I do.
Guardiano.   But little reason, I think.
Ward. Plain men dance the measures, the cinquepace the gay:
Cuckolds dance the hornpipe; and farmers dance the hay:
Your soldiers dance the round, and maidens that grow big:
Your drunkards the canaries; your whore and bawd the jig.
Here's your eight kind of dancers, he that finds
The ninth, let him pay the minstrels.
Duke. Oh here he appears once in his own person;   220
I thought he would have married her by attorney,
And lain with her so too.
Bianca.   Nay, my kind Lord,
There's very seldom any found so foolish
To give away his part there.
Leantio. [Aside]   Bitter scoff!
Yet I must do't; with what a cruel pride
The glory of her sin strikes by my afflictions!   *Music.*

    Ward *and* Isabella *dance, he ridiculously imitates* Hippolito.

Duke. This thing will make shift (sirs) to make a husband,
For aught I see in him; how think'st, Bianca?
Bianca. 'Faith, an ill-favoured shift, my Lord, methinks;
If he would take some voyage when he's married,   230
Dangerous, or long enough, and scarce be seen
Once in nine year together, a wife then
Might make indifferent shift to be content with him.
Duke. A kiss; that wit deserves to be made much on.
Come, our caroche.
Guardiano.   Stands ready for your Grace.
Duke. My thanks to all your loves. Come, fair Bianca,
We have took special care of you, and provided
Your lodging near us now.
Bianca.   Your love is great, my Lord.
Duke. Once more our thanks to all.
Omnes.   All blest honours guard you.
                    Exe. all but Leantio *and* Livia; *cornets flourish.*

212 married man's dance] cf. l. 215   214 measures] a grave or stately dance   214 the
cinquepace the gay] gay people dance the cinquepace or galliard, a lively dance
215 hornpipe] danced of course by one person (a quibble also on the cuckold's horns)
215 hay] a country dance with a serpentine movement   217 canaries] a lively Spanish
dance (with a quibble on Canary wine)   226 strikes by] disregards   235 caroche] coach

Leantio. [*Aside*] Oh hast thou left me then, Bianca, utterly!   240
    Bianca! now I miss thee; oh return,
    And save the faith of woman! I nev'r felt
    The loss of thee till now; 'tis an affliction
    Of greater weight than youth was made to bear;
    As if a punishment of after-life
    Were fall'n upon man here; so new it is
    To flesh and blood, so strange, so insupportable,
    A torment, ev'n mistook, as if a body
    Whose death were drowning, must needs therefore suffer it
    In scalding oil.
Livia.   Sweet sir!
Leantio. [*Aside*]   As long as mine eye saw thee,   250
    I half enjoy'd thee.
Livia.   Sir?
Leantio. [*Aside*]   Canst thou forget
    The dear pains my love took, how it has watcht
    Whole nights together, in all weathers for thee,
    Yet stood in heart more merry than the tempests
    That sung about mine ears (like dangerous flatterers
    That can set all their mischief to sweet tunes),
    And then receiv'd thee from thy father's window,
    Into these arms at midnight, when we embrac'd
    As if we had been statues only made for't,
    To show art's life, so silent were our comforts,   260
    And kiss'd as if our lips had grown together?
Livia. [*Aside*] This makes me madder to enjoy him now.
Leantio. [*Aside*] Canst thou forget all this? and better joys
    That we met after this, which then new kisses
    Took pride to praise?
Livia. [*Aside*]   I shall grow madder yet.—Sir!
Leantio. [*Aside*] This cannot be but of some close bawd's working.
    —Cry mercy, Lady. What would you say to me?
    My sorrow makes me so unmannerly,
    So comfort bless me, I had quite forgot you.
Livia. Nothing but ev'n in pity to that passion   270
    Would give your grief good counsel.
Leantio.   Marry, and welcome, Lady,
    It never could come better.
Livia.   Then first, sir,
    To make away all your good thoughts at once of her,
    Know most assuredly, she is a strumpet.

270 that passion] i.e., sorrow

Leantio. Ha: most assuredly! Speak not a thing
    So vilde so certainly, leave it more doubtful.
Livia. Then I must leave all truth, and spare my knowledge,
    A sin which I too lately found and wept for.
Leantio. Found you it?
Livia.   Ay, with wet eyes.
Leantio.   Oh perjurious friendship!
Livia. You miss'd your fortunes when you met with her, sir.   280
    Young gentlemen, that only love for beauty,
    They love not wisely; such a marriage rather
    Proves the destruction of affection;
    It brings on want, and want's the key of whoredom.
    I think y'had small means with her.
Leantio.   Oh not any, Lady.
Livia. Alas poor gentleman, what meant'st thou, sir,
    Quite to undo thy self with thine own kind heart?
    Thou art too good and pitiful to woman:
    Marry, sir, thank thy stars for this blest fortune
    That rids the summer of thy youth so well   290
    From many beggars that had lain a-sunning
    In thy beams only else, till thou hadst wasted
    The whole days of thy life in heat and labour.
    What would you say now to a creature found
    As pitiful to you, and as it were
    Ev'n sent on purpose from the whole sex general,
    To requite all that kindness you have shown to't?
Leantio. What's that, Madam?
Livia.   Nay, a gentlewoman, and one able
    To reward good things, ay, and bears a conscience to't;
    Couldst thou love such a one, that (blow all fortunes)   300
    Would never see thee want?
    Nay more, maintain thee to thine enemy's envy,
    And shalt not spend a care for't, stir a thought,
    Nor break a sleep, unless love's music wak'd thee;
    No storm of fortune should. Look upon me,
    And know that woman.
Leantio.   Oh my life's wealth, Bianca!
Livia. [*Aside*] Still with her name? will nothing wear it out?
    —That deep sigh went but for a strumpet, sir.
Leantio. It can go for no other that loves me.
Livia. [*Aside*] He's vext in mind; I came too soon to him;   310
    Where's my discretion now, my skill, my judgment?

276 vilde] vile   291 many beggars] i.e., his future children

I'm cunning in all arts but my own love:
'Tis as unseasonable to tempt him now
So soon, as for a widow to be courted
Following her husband's corse, or to make bargain
By the grave-side, and take a young man there:
Her strange departure stands like a hearse yet
Before his eyes; which time will take down shortly.   *Exit.*

Leantio. Is she my wife till death? yet no more mine?
That's a hard measure; then what's marriage good for?   320
Me thinks by right I should not now be living,
And then 'twere all well: what a happiness
Had I been made of, had I never seen her!
For nothing makes man's loss grievous to him,
But knowledge of the worth of what he loses;
For what he never had he never misses:
She's gone for ever, utterly; there is
As much redemption of a soul from hell,
As a fair woman's body from his palace.
Why should my love last longer than her truth?   330
What is there good in woman to be lov'd,
When only that which makes her so has left her?
I cannot love her now, but I must like
Her sin, and my own shame too, and be guilty
Of law's breach with her, and mine own abusing;
All which were monstrous: then my safest course,
For health of mind and body, is to turn
My heart, and hate her, most extremely hate her;
I have no other way: those virtuous powers,
Which were chaste witnesses of both our troths,   340
Can witness she breaks first, and I'm rewarded
With captainship o'th'fort; a place of credit
I must confess, but poor; my factorship
Shall not exchange means with't: he that di'd last in't,
He was no drunkard, yet he di'd a beggar
For all his thrift; besides, the place not fits me;
It suits my resolution, not my breeding.

Enter Livia.

---

314 as for a widow] Quarto: 'as a widow'.   332 only that which] that which alone
333-5 I cannot . . . with her] I cannot love her now except by approving her sin and my
shame, and being guilty of compliance with her in breaking the law (of God)   344 shall
not . . . with't] i.e., is above it in value

Livia. [*Aside*] I have tri'd all ways I can, and have not power
    To keep from sight of him.—How are you now, sir?
Leantio. I feel a better ease, Madam.
Livia.   Thanks to blessedness!   350
    You will do well, I warrant you, fear it not, sir;
    Join but your own good will to't; he's not wise
    That loves his pain or sickness, or grows fond
    Of a disease, whose property is to vex him,
    And spitefully drink his blood up. Out upon't, sir,
    Youth knows no greater loss; I pray let's walk, sir.
    You never saw the beauty of my house yet,
    Nor how abundantly fortune has blest me
    In worldly treasure; trust me, I have enough, sir,
    To make my friend a rich man in my life,   360
    A great man at my death; your self will say so:
    If you want any thing, and spare to speak,
    Troth I'll condemn you for a wilful man, sir.
Leantio. Why, sure
    This can be but the flattery of some dream.
Livia. Now by this kiss, my love, my soul and riches,
    'Tis all true substance.   [*Kisses him.*]
    Come, you shall see my wealth, take what you list,
    The gallanter you go, the more you please me:
    I will allow you too your page and footman,   370
    Your racehorses, or any various pleasure
    Exercis'd youth delights in; but to me
    Only, sir, wear your heart of constant stuff:
    Do but you love enough, I'll give enough.
Leantio. Troth then, I'll love enough, and take enough.
    Then we are both pleas'd enough.   *Exeunt.*

SCAEN. 3

    Enter Guardiano *and* Isabella *at one door, and the* Ward *and* Sordido *at another.*

Guardiano. Now Nephew, here's the gentlewoman again.
Ward. Mass, here she's come again; mark her now, Sordido.
Guardiano. This is the maid my love and care has chose
    Out for your wife, and so I tender her to you;
    Your self has been eye-witness of some qualities
    That speak a courtly breeding, and are costly.

362 spare to speak] do not say so

I bring you both to talk together now,
'Tis time you grew familiar in your tongues;
Tomorrow you join hands, and one ring ties you,
And one bed holds you; (if you like the choice)   10
Her father and her friends are i'th'next room,
And stay to see the contract ere they part;
Therefore dispatch, good Ward, be sweet and short;
Like her, or like her not, there's but two ways;
And one your body, th'other your purse pays.

Ward. I warrant you, Guardiner, I'll not stand all day thrumming,
But quickly shoot my bolt at your next coming.

Guardiano. Well said: good fortune to your birding then.   *Exit.*

Ward. I never miss'd mark yet.

Sordido. Troth I think, master, if the truth were known,   20
You never shot at any but the kitchen-wench,
And that was a she-woodcock, a mere innocent,
That was oft lost, and cri'd at eight-and-twenty.

Ward. No more of that meat, Sordido, here's eggs o'th'spit now,
We must turn gingerly: draw out the catalogue
Of all the faults of women.

Sordido.   How, all the faults!
Have you so little reason to think so much paper will lie in my breeches?
Why, ten carts will not carry it, if you set down but the bawds. All the
faults? pray let's be content with a few of 'em; and if they were less, you
would find 'em enough, I warrant you: look you, sir.   30

Isabella. [*Aside*] But that I have th'advantage of the fool,
As much as woman's heart can wish and joy at,
What an infernal torment 'twere to be
Thus bought and sold, and turn'd and pri'd into,
When alas
The worst bit is too good for him! and the comfort is
H'as but a cater's place on't, and provides
All for another's table; yet how curious
The ass is, like some nice professor on't,
That buys up all the daintiest food i'th'markets,   40
And seldom licks his lips after a taste on't!

Sordido. Now to her, now y'have scann'd all her parts over.

Ward. But at which end shall I begin now, Sordido?

Sordido. Oh ever at a woman's lip, while you live, sir; do you ask that
question?

18 birding] hawking or shooting   22 woodcock] simpleton   23 cri'd] i.e., by the public
crier   24 eggs o'th'spit] The phrase, implying daintier meat, plays on 'turn' in the next line.
37 cater] caterer   38 curious] careful in his examination   43 at which end] Quarto: 'at end'.

Ward. Methinks, Sordido, sh'as but a crabbed face to begin with.

Sordido. A crabbed face? that will save money.

Ward. How! save money, Sordido?

Sordido. Ay, sir: for having a crabbed face of her own, she'll eat the less
verjuice with her mutton; 'twill save verjuice at year's end, sir.   50

Ward. Nay, and your jests begin to be saucy once, I'll make you eat your
meat without mustard.

Sordido. And that in some kind is a punishment.

Ward. Gentlewoman, they say 'tis your pleasure to be my wife, and you
shall know shortly whether it be mine or no to be your husband; and
thereupon thus I first enter upon you. [*Kisses her.*] Oh most delicious
scent! Methinks it tasted as if a man had stept into a comfit-maker's
shop to let a cart go by, all the while I kiss'd her. It is reported, gentlewoman, you'll run mad for me, if you have me not.

Isabella. I should be in great danger of my wits, sir,   60
   For being so forward. [*Aside*] Should this ass kick backward now!

Ward. Alas poor soul! And is that hair your own?

Isabella. Mine own, yes sure, sir, I owe nothing for't.

Ward. 'Tis a good hearing, I shall have the less to pay when I have married
you. Look, does her eyes stand well?

Sordido. They cannot stand better than in her head, I think, where would
you have them? And for her nose, 'tis of a very good last.

Ward. I have known as good as that has not lasted a year though.

Sordido. That's in the using of a thing; will not any strong bridge fall down
in time, if we do nothing but beat at the bottom? A nose of buff would not
last always, sir, especially if it came into th'camp once.   71

Ward. But Sordido, how shall we do to make her laugh, that I may see what
teeth she has? For I'll not bate her a tooth, nor take a black one into
th'bargain.

Sordido. Why, do but you fall in talk with her, you cannot choose but one
time or other make her laugh, sir.

Ward. It shall go hard, but I will. Pray, what qualities have you beside
singing and dancing? can you play at shittlecock forsooth?

Isabella. Ay, and at stool-ball too, sir; I have great luck at it.

Ward. Why, can you catch a ball well?   80

Isabella. I have catcht two in my lap at one game.

Ward. What, have you woman? I must have you learn
   To play at trap too, then y'are full and whole.

---

50 verjuice] sour sauce often made from crab-apples   53 in some kind] going without
a sauce (mustard) is a punishment in kind for being saucy   67 last] in the sense of a
cobbler's last   70 buff] tough leather made from ox's hide and used for military uniforms
79 stool-ball] an old game something like cricket (a sexual quibble is of course present;
cf. l. 81)

Isabella. Any thing that you please to bring me up to,
  I shall take pains to practise.
Ward. 'Twill not do, Sordido, we shall never get her mouth open'd wide
  enough.
Sordido. No, sir? that's strange! then here's a trick for your learning.

                He yawns.
     [Isabella *likewise, but covers her face with a handkerchief.*]
  Look now, look now; quick, quick there.
Ward. Pox of that scurvy mannerly trick with handkerchief! It hind'red
  me a little, but I am satisfied. When a fair woman gapes, and stops her
  mouth so, it shows like a cloth-stopple in a cream-pot; I have fair hope
  of her teeth now, Sordido.   93
Sordido. Why then, y'have all well, sir; for aught I see,
  She's right and straight enough, now as she stands;
  They'll commonly lie crooked, that's no matter:
  Wise gamesters
  Never find fault with that, let 'em lie so still.
Ward. I'd fain mark how she goes, and then I have all: for of all creatures
  I cannot abide a splay-footed woman, she's an unlucky thing to meet in a
  morning; her heels keep together so, as if she were beginning an Irish
  dance still, and the wriggling of her bum playing the tune to't. But I have
  bethought a cleanly shift to find it; dab down as you see me, and peep of
  one side, when her back's toward you; I'll show you the way.   104
Sordido. And you shall find me apt enough to peeping,
  I have been one of them has seen mad sights
  Under your scaffolds.
Ward.   Will it please you walk forsooth,
  A turn or two by your self? you are so pleasing to me,
  I take delight to view you on both sides.
Isabella. I shall be glad to fetch a walk to your love, sir;   110
  'Twill get affection a good stomach, sir,
  [*Aside*] Which I had need to have, to fall to such coarse victuals.

                   [*Walks.*]

Ward. Now go thy ways for a clean-treading wench,
  As ever man in modesty peept under.
Sordido. I see the sweetest sight to please my master:
  Never went Frenchman righter upon ropes
  Than she on Florentine rushes.
Ward.   'Tis enough forsooth.
Isabella. And how do you like me now, sir?

91 gapes] yawns 92 stopple] stopper 98 still] always 99 goes] walks 103 dab]
duck 107 scaffolds] presumably stages in the theatre 116 ropes] tightropes; presumably an allusion to visiting French troupes.

Ward.   '*Faith*, so well,
   I never mean to part with thee, sweet-heart,
   Under some sixteen children, and all boys.   120
Isabella. You'll be at simple pains, if you prove kind,
   And breed 'em all in your teeth.
Ward.   Nay by my faith,
   What serves your belly for? 'twould make my cheeks
   Look like blown bagpipes.

   Enter Guardiano.

Guardiano.   How now, Ward and Nephew,
   Gentlewoman and Niece! speak, is it so or not?
Ward. 'Tis so, we are both agreed, sir.
Guardiano.   Into your kinred then;
   There's friends, and wine, and music waits to welcome you.
Ward. Then I'll be drunk for joy.
Sordido.   And I for company,
   I cannot break my nose in a better action.   *Exeunt.*

ACT. 4.   SCAEN. 1

   Enter Bianca *attended by two* Ladies.

Bianca. How goes your watches, Ladies? what's a-clock now?
1. Lady. By mine full nine.
2. Lady.   By mine a quarter past.
1. Lady. I set mine by St. Mark's.
2. Lady.   St. Anthony's, they say,
   Goes truer.
1. Lady.   That's but your opinion, Madam,
   Because you love a gentleman o'th'name.
2. Lady. He's a true gentleman then.
1. Lady.   So may he be
   That comes to me tonight, for aught you know.
Bianca. I'll end this strife straight: I set mine by the sun,
   I love to set by th'best, one shall not then
   Be troubled to set often.
2. Lady.   You do wisely in't.   10

---

122 breed . . . teeth] 'alluding to a superstition that an affectionate husband had the tooth-
ache while his wife was breeding' (*Dilke*)

Bianca. If I should set my watch, as some girls do,
    By ev'ry clock i'th'town, 'twould nev'r go true;
    And too much turning of the dial's point,
    Or tamp'ring with the spring, might in small time
    Spoil the whole work too; here it wants of nine now.
1. Lady. It does indeed forsooth; mine's nearest truth yet.
2. Lady. Yet I have found her lying with an advocate,
    Which show'd
    Like two false clocks together in one parish.
Bianca. So now I thank you, Ladies, I desire   20
    A while to be alone.
1. Lady.   And I am nobody,
    Methinks, unless I have one or other with me.
    [*Aside*] 'Faith, my desire and hers will nev'r be sisters.

                                  Exeunt Ladies.

Bianca. How strangely woman's fortune comes about!
    This was the farthest way to come to me,
    All would have judg'd, that knew me born in Venice
    And there with many jealous eyes brought up,
    That never thought they had me sure enough,
    But when they were upon me; yet my hap
    To meet it here, so far off from my birth-place,   30
    My friends, or kinred; 'tis not good, in sadness,
    To keep a maid so strict in her young days;
    Restraint
    Breeds wand'ring thoughts, as many fasting days
    A great desire to see flesh stirring again:
    I'll nev'r use any girl of mine so strictly;
    Howev'r they're kept, their fortunes find 'em out,
    I see't in me; if they be got in court,
    I'll never forbid 'em the country, nor the court,
    Though they be born i'th'country: they will come to't,   40
    And fetch their falls a thousand mile about,
    Where one would little think on't.

    Enter Leantio [*richly dressed*].

Leantio. [*Aside*] I long to see how my despiser looks,
    Now she's come here to court; these are her lodgings,
    She's simply now advanc'd: I took her out
    Of no such window, I remember, first;
    That was a great deal lower, and less carv'd.
Bianca. How now! What silkworm's this, i'th'name of pride?
    What, is it he?

31 in sadness] seriously   41 fetch their falls] come to rest   45 simply] truly

Leantio.   A bow i'th'ham to your greatness;
    You must have now three legs, I take it, must you not?   50
Bianca. Then I must take another, I shall want else
    The service I should have; you have but two there.
Leantio. Y'are richly plac'd.
Bianca.   Methinks y'are wondrous brave, sir.
Leantio. A sumptuous lodging.
Bianca.   Y'ave an excellent suit there.
Leantio. A chair of velvet.
Bianca.   Is your cloak lin'd through, sir?
Leantio. Y'are very stately here.
Bianca.   'Faith, something proud, sir.
Leantio. Stay, stay, let's see your cloth-of-silver slippers.
Bianca. Who's your shoemaker? h'as made you a neat boot.
Leantio. Will you have a pair?
    The Duke will lend you spurs.
Bianca.   Yes, when I ride.   60
Leantio. 'Tis a brave life you lead.
Bianca.   I could nev'r see you
    In such good clothes in my time.
Leantio.   In your time?
Bianca. Sure I think, sir,
    We both thrive best asunder.
Leantio.   Y'are a whore.
Bianca. Fear nothing, sir.
Leantio.   An impudent spiteful strumpet.
Bianca. Oh sir, you give me thanks for your captainship;
    I though you had forgot all your good manners.
Leantio. And to spite thee as much, look there, there read,   [*Gives letter.*]
    Vex, gnaw, thou shalt find there I am not love-starv'd.
    The world was never yet so cold, or pitiless,   70
    But there was ever still more charity found out
    Than at one proud fool's door; and 'twere hard, 'faith,
    If I could not pass that. Read to thy shame there;
    A cheerful and a beauteous benefactor too,
    As ev'r erected the good works of love.
Bianca. [*Aside*] Lady Livia!
    Is't possible? Her worship was my pandress.
    She dote, and send and give, and all to him!
    Why, here's a bawd plagu'd home.—Y'are simply happy, sir,
    Yet I'll not envy you.

50 legs] obeisances   53 brave] richly dressed   60 ride] with a sexual quibble

Leantio.   No, court-saint, not thou!   80
  You keep some friend of a new fashion;
  There's no harm in your devil, he's a suckling,
  But he will breed teeth shortly, will he not?
Bianca. Take heed you play not then too long with him.
Leantio. Yes, and the great one too: I shall find time
  To play a hot religious bout with some of you,
  And perhaps drive you and your course of sins
  To their eternal kennels; I speak softly now,
  'Tis manners in a noble woman's lodgings,
  And I well know all my degrees of duty.   90
  But come I to your everlasting parting once,
  Thunder shall seem soft music to that tempest.
Bianca. 'Twas said last week there would be change of weather,
  When the moon hung so, and belike you heard it.
Leantio. Why, here's sin made, and nev'r a conscience put to't;
  A monster with all forehead, and no eyes.
  Why do I talk to thee of sense or virtue,
  That art as dark as death? and as much madness
  To set light before thee, as to lead blind folks
  To see the monuments, which they may smell as soon   100
  As they behold; marry, oft-times their heads,
  For want of light, may feel the hardness of 'em.
  So shall thy blind pride my revenge and anger,
  That canst not see it now; and it may fall
  At such an hour, when thou least seest of all;
  So to an ignorance darker than thy womb
  I leave thy perjur'd soul: a plague will come.   *Exit.*
Bianca. Get you gone first, and then I fear no greater,
  Nor thee will I fear long; I'll have this sauciness
  Soon banish'd from these lodgings, and the rooms   110
  Perfum'd well after the corrupt air it leaves:
  His breath has made me almost sick in troth:
  A poor base start-up! Life! because he's got
  Fair clothes by foul means, comes to rail, and show 'em.

  Enter the Duke.

Duke. Who's that?
Bianca.   Cry you mercy, sir.
Duke.   Prethee who's that?

91 your everlasting parting] parting eternally from you; or perhaps, your death   113 start-
up] upstart

Bianca. The former thing, my Lord, to whom you gave
    The captainship; he eats his meat with grudging still.
Duke. Still!
Bianca.   He comes vaunting here of his new love,
    And the new clothes she gave him; Lady Livia—
    Who but she now his mistress?
Duke.   Lady Livia?   120
    Be sure of what you say.
Bianca.   He show'd me her name, sir,
    In perfum'd paper, her vows, her letter,
    With an intent to spite me; so his heart said,
    And his threats made it good; they were as spiteful
    As ever malice utter'd, and as dangerous,
    Should his hand follow the copy.
Duke.   But that must not:
    Do not you vex your mind; prethee to bed, go,
    All shall be well and quiet.
Bianca.   I love peace, sir.
Duke. And so do all that love; take you no care for't,
    It shall be still provided to your hand.   *Exit* [Bianca].
    Who's near us there?

    Enter Messenger.

Messenger.   My Lord.
Duke.   Seek out Hippolito,   131
    Brother to Lady Livia, with all speed.
Messenger. He was the last man I saw, my Lord.
Duke.   Make haste.
                                        Exit [Messenger].
    He is a blood soon stirr'd, and as he's quick
    To apprehend a wrong, he's bold, and sudden
    In bringing forth a ruin: I know likewise
    The reputation of his sister's honour's
    As dear to him as life-blood to his heart;
    Beside, I'll flatter him with a goodness to her,
    Which I now thought on, but nev'r meant to practise   140
    (Because I know her base), and that wind drives him.
    The ulcerous reputation feels the poise
    Of lightest wrongs, as sores are vext with flies:
    He comes. Hippolito, welcome.

126 Should . . . copy] should he copy in deeds the intent of his words   141 that wind]
i.e., flattery   142 poise] weight

Enter Hippolito.

Hippolito.   My lov'd Lord.
Duke. How does that lusty widow, thy kind sister?
    Is she not sped yet of a second husband?
    A bed-fellow she has, I ask not that,
    I know she's sped of him.
Hippolito.   Of him, my Lord?
Duke. Yes, of a bed-fellow; is the news so strange to you?
Hippolito. I hope 'tis so to all.
Duke.   I wish it were, sir;   150
    But 'tis confest too fast; her ignorant pleasures,
    Only by lust instructed, have receiv'd
    Into their services an impudent boaster,
    One that does raise his glory from her shame,
    And tells the midday sun what's done in darkness;
    Yet, blinded with her appetite, wastes her wealth,
    Buys her disgraces at a dearer rate,
    Than bounteous housekeepers purchase their honour.
    Nothing sads me so much, as that in love
    To thee, and to thy blood, I had pickt out   160
    A worthy match for her, the great Vincentio,
    High in our favour, and in all men's thoughts.
Hippolito. Oh thou destruction of all happy fortunes,
    Unsated blood! Know you the name, my Lord,
    Of her abuser?
Duke.   One Leantio.
Hippolito.   He's
    A factor.
Duke.   He nev'r made so brave a voyage,
    By his own talk.
Hippolito.   The poor old widow's son.
    I humbly take my leave.
Duke. [*Aside*]   I see 'tis done.
    —Give her good counsel, make her see her error,
    I know she'll hearken to you.
Hippolito.   Yes, my Lord,   170
    I make no doubt, as I shall take the course,
    Which she shall never know till it be acted;
    And when she wakes to honour, then she'll thank me for't.
    I'll imitate the pities of old surgeons
    To this lost limb, who, ere they show their art,

146 is she not sped yet of] has she not attained yet   158 honour] reputation   167 By]
to judge by

    Cast one asleep, then cut the diseas'd part.
    So out of love to her I pity most,
    She shall not feel him going till he's lost,
    Then she'll commend the cure.   *Exit.*

Duke.   The great cure's past;
    I count this done already; his wrath's sure,   180
    And speaks an injury deep; farewell Leantio.
    This place will never hear thee murmur more.
    Our noble brother, welcome!

Enter Lord Cardinal *attended.*

Cardinal.   Set those lights down:
    Depart till you be call'd.   [*Exeunt* Attendants.]
Duke. [*Aside*]   There's serious business
    Fix'd in his look, nay, it inclines a little
    To the dark colour of a discontentment.
    —Brother, what is't commands your eye so powerfully?
    Speak, you seem lost.
Cardinal.   The thing I look on seems so
    To my eyes, lost for ever.
Duke.   You look on me.
Cardinal. What a grief 'tis to a religious feeling,   190
    To think a man should have a friend so goodly,
    So wise, so noble, nay, a duke, a brother,
    And all this certainly damn'd!
Duke.   How!
Cardinal.   'Tis no wonder,
    If your great sin can do't; dare you look up
    For thinking of a vengeance? dare you sleep
    For fear of never waking but to death,
    And dedicate unto a strumpet's love
    The strength of your affections, zeal and health?
    Here you stand now; can you assure your pleasures,
    You shall once more enjoy her, but once more?   200
    Alas you cannot; what a misery 'tis then
    To be more certain of eternal death
    Than of a next embrace! nay, shall I show you
    How more unfortunate you stand in sin
    Than the low private man? all his offences,

179 cure's] Perhaps we should read 'care's'; but the two were used indiscriminately.
199 assure] ensure   205 low] The quarto reads 'love', and 'love-private' (i.e., one who
keeps his love to himself or within what is allowed him) is just possible; but Dyce's
amendment seems to make better sense.

Like inclos'd grounds, keep but about himself,
And seldom stretch beyond his own soul's bounds;
And when a man grows miserable, 'tis some comfort
When he's no further charg'd than with himself;
'Tis a sweet ease to wretchedness: but, great man,   210
Ev'ry sin thou commit'st shows like a flame
Upon a mountain, 'tis seen far about,
And with a big wind made of popular breath,
The sparkles fly through cities: here one takes,
Another catches there, and in short time
Waste all to cinders: but remember still,
What burnt the valleys first came from the hill;
Ev'ry offence draws his particular pain,
But 'tis example proves the great man's bane.
The sins of mean men lie like scatter'd parcels   220
Of an unperfect bill; but when such fall,
Then comes example, and that sums up all:
And this your reason grants, if men of good lives,
Who by their virtuous actions stir up others
To noble and religious imitation,
Receive the greater glory after death,
As sin must needs confess, what may they feel
In height of torments, and in weight of vengeance,
Not only they themselves not doing well,
But sets a light up to show men to hell?   230
Duke. If you have done, I have; no more, sweet Brother.
Cardinal. I know time spent in goodness is too tedious;
This had not been a moment's space in lust now;
How dare you venture on eternal pain,
That cannot bear a minute's reprehension?
Methinks you should endure to hear that talkt of
Which you so strive to suffer. Oh my brother!
What were you, if you were taken now!
My heart weeps blood to think on't; 'tis a work
Of infinite mercy (you can never merit)   240
That yet you are not death-struck, no not yet:
I dare not stay you long, for fear you should not
Have time enough allow'd you to repent in.
There's but this wall betwixt you and destruction,

219 'tis ... bane] the great man is brought to destruction by setting an example
220-22] The idea of the metaphor of accountancy here is that the fall of the mean is
explained by the example of the great.   227 they] i.e., who set an evil example
244 this wall] his body

When y'are at strongest, and but poor thin clay.
Think upon't, Brother; can you come so near it,
For a fair strumpet's love, and fall into
A torment that knows neither end nor bottom
For beauty but the deepness of a skin,
And that not of their own neither? Is she a thing   250
Whom sickness dare not visit, or age look on,
Or death resist? does the worm shun her grave?
If not (as your soul knows it), why should lust
Bring man to lasting pain, for rotten dust?
Duke. Brother of spotless honour, let me weep
The first of my repentance in thy bosom,
And show the blest fruits of a thankful spirit;
And if I e'er keep woman more unlawfully,
May I want penitence at my greatest need!
And wisemen know there is no barren place   260
Threatens more famine than a dearth in grace.
Cardinal. Why, here's a conversion is at this time, Brother,
Sung for a hymn in heaven; and at this instant
The powers of darkness groan, makes all hell sorry.
First, I praise heaven, then in my work I glory.
Who's there attends without?

   Enter Servants.

Servant.   My Lord!
Cardinal. Take up those lights; there was a thicker darkness,
When they came first. The peace of a fair soul
Keep with my noble brother!   *Exit* Cardinal, &c.
Duke.   Joys be with you, sir.
She lies alone tonight for't, and must still,   270
Though it be hard to conquer, but I have vow'd
Never to know her as a strumpet more,
And I must save my oath; if fury fail not,
Her husband dies tonight, or at the most,
Lives not to see the morning spent tomorrow;
Then will I make her lawfully mine own,
Without this sin and horror. Now I'm chidden,
For what I shall enjoy then unforbidden,
And I'll not freeze in stoves; 'tis but a while:
Live like a hopeful bridegroom, chaste from flesh,   280
And pleasure then will seem new, fair and fresh.   *Exit.*

279 freeze] as he does now, being denied access to Bianca, though in her presence

SCAEN. 2

Enter Hippolito.

Hippolito. The morning so far wasted, yet his baseness
    So impudent? See if the very sun
    Do not blush at him!
    Dare he do thus much, and know me alive!
    Put case one must be vicious, as I know my self
    Monstrously guilty, there's a blind time made for't;
    He might use only that, 'twere conscionable:
    Art, silence, closeness, subtlety, and darkness
    Are fit for such a business; but there's no pity
    To be bestow'd on an apparent sinner,   10
    An impudent daylight lecher; the great zeal
    I bear to her advancement in this match
    With Lord Vincentio, as the Duke has wrought it,
    To the perpetual honour of our house,
    Puts fire into my blood, to purge the air
    Of this corruption, fear it spread too far,
    And poison the whole hopes of this fair fortune.
    I love her good so dearly, that no brother
    Shall venture farther for a sister's glory
    Than I for her preferment.

   Enter Leantio, *and a* Page.

Leantio. [*Aside*]   Once again   20
    I'll see that glist'ring whore, shines like a serpent
    Now the court sun's upon her.—Page!
Page.   Anon, sir!
Leantio. [*Aside*] I'll go in state too.—See the coach be ready.   [*Exit* Page.]
    I'll hurry away presently.
Hippolito.   Yes, you shall hurry,
    And the devil after you; take that at setting forth.   [*Strikes him.*]
    Now, and you'll draw, we are upon equal terms, sir.
    Thou took'st advantage of my name in honour,
    Upon my sister; I nev'r saw the stroke
    Come, till I found my reputation bleeding;
    And therefore count it I no sin to valour   30
    To serve thy lust so. Now we are of even hand,   [Leantio *draws.*]
    Take your best course against me. You must die.

10 apparent] self-evident   16 fear] for fear   26 and] if

Leantio. How close sticks envy to man's happiness!
    When I was poor, and little car'd for life,
    I had no such means offer'd me to die,
    No man's wrath minded me. Slave, I turn this to thee,
    To call thee to account, for a wound lately
    Of a base stamp upon me.
Hippolito.   'Twas most fit
    For a base mettle. Come and fetch one now
    More noble then, for I will use thee fairer   40
    Than thou hast done thine soul, or our honour;   [*Fight*.]
    And there I think 'tis for thee.   [Leantio *falls*.]
Within.   Help, help! Oh part 'em.
Leantio. False wife! I feel now th'hast pray'd heartily for me;
    Rise, strumpet, by my fall, thy lust may reign now;
    My heart-string, and the marriage-knot that ty'd thee,
    Breaks both together.   [*Dies*.]
Hippolito.   There I heard the sound on't,
    And never lik'd string better.

   Enter Guardiano, Livia, Isabella, Ward, *and* Sordido.

Livia.   'Tis my brother.
    Are you hurt, sir?
Hippolito.   Not any thing.
Livia.   Bless'd fortune!
    Shift for thy self; what is he thou hast kill'd?
Hippolito. Our honour's enemy.
Guardiano.   Know you this man, Lady?   50
Livia. Leantio? My love's joy? Wounds stick upon thee
    As deadly as thy sins; art thou not hurt
    (The devil take that fortune) and he dead?
    Drop plagues into thy bowels without voice,
    Secret, and fearful! Run for officers,
    Let him be apprehended with all speed,
    For fear he scape away; lay hands on him,
    We cannot be too sure, 'tis wilful murder;
    You do heaven's vengeance, and the law just service.
    You know him not as I do, he's a villain,   60
    As monstrous as a prodigy, and as dreadful.

---

36 this] i.e., his sword   39 mettle] So quarto; but there is an obvious pun on 'metal' (the two words were originally the same).   42 *Within*] Perhaps this line is to be spoken by people who have seen from a balcony, for they cannot reasonably enter before l. 47, yet must be presumed to see what is happening.   52 thou] i.e., Hippolito

Hippolito. Will you but entertain a noble patience,
   Till you but hear the reason, worthy Sister?
Livia.The reason! that's a jest hell falls a-laughing at:
   Is there a reason found for the destruction
   Of our more lawful loves? and was there none
   To kill the black lust 'twixt thy niece and thee,
   That has kept close so long?
Guardiano.   How's that, good Madam?
Livia. Too true, sir, there she stands, let her deny't;
   The deed cries shortly in the midwife's arms,   70
   Unless the parents' sin strike it still-born;
   And if you be not deaf, and ignorant,
   You'll hear strange notes ere long. Look upon me, wench!
   'Twas I betray'd thy honour subtilly to him
   Under a false tale; it lights upon me now;
   His arm has paid me home upon thy breast,
   My sweet belov'd Leantio!
Guardiano.   Was my judgment,
   And care in choice, so dev'lishly abus'd,
   So beyond shamefully?—All the world will grin at me.
Ward. Oh Sordido, Sordido, I'm damn'd, I'm damn'd!   80
Sordido. Damn'd? why, sir?
Ward. One of the wicked; dost not see't? a cuckold, a plain reprobate cuckold.
Sordido. Nay, and you be damn'd for that, be of good cheer, sir! Y'have
   gallant company of all professions; I'll have a wife next Sunday too,
   because I'll along with you my self.
Ward. That will be some comfort yet.
Livia. You sir, that bear your load of injuries,
   As I of sorrows, lend me your griev'd strength
   To this sad burthen; who in life wore actions,
   Flames were not nimbler: we will talk of things   90
   May have the luck to break our hearts together.
Guardiano. I'll list to nothing, but revenge and anger,
   Whose counsels I will follow.   *Exeunt* Livia *and* Guardiano,
                                  [*with* Leantio's *body*].
Sordido.   A wife quoth 'a?
   Here's a sweet plum-tree of your guardiner's graffing!
Ward. Nay, there's a worse name belongs to this fruit yet,
   And you could hit on't, a more open one:
  for he that marries a whore looks like a fellow bound all his lifetime to a

89–90 actions, Flames] actions than which flames   94 guardiner] The pun on 'gardener'
is clear here.   94 graffing] grafting

medlar-tree, and that's good stuff; 'tis no sooner ripe, but it looks rotten;
and so do some queans at nineteen. A pox on't,
    I thought there was some knavery abroach,   100
    For something
    Stirr'd in her belly, the first night I lay with her.
Sordido. What, what, sir!
Ward. This is she brought up so courtly, can sing, and dance, and tumble
too, methinks; I'll never marry wife again that has so many qualities.
Sordido. Indeed they are seldom good, Master; for likely when they are
taught so many, they will have one trick more of their own finding out.
Well, give me a wench but with one good quality, to lie with none but her
husband, and that's bringing up enough for any woman breathing.
Ward. This was the fault, when she was tend'red to me;   110
    You never look'd to this.
Sordido. Alas, how would you have me see through a great farthingal, sir? I can-
not peep through a mill-stone, or in the going, to see what's done i'th'bottom.
Ward. Her father prais'd her breast, sh'ad the voice forsooth;
    I marvell'd she sung so small indeed, being no maid.
    Now I perceive there's a young querister in her belly:
    This breeds a singing in my head, I'm sure.
Sordido. 'Tis but the tune of your wive's cinquapace,
    Danc'd in a featherbed.
    'Faith, go lie down, Master—but take heed your horns do not make holes
in the pillowbers. [*Aside*] I would not batter brows with him for a hogs-
head of angels, he would prick my skull as full of holes as a scrivener's
sand-box.   *Exeunt* Ward *and* Sordido.
Isabella. [*Aside*] Was ever maid so cruelly beguil'd   124
    To the confusion of life, soul, and honour,
    All of one woman's murd'ring! I'd fain bring
    Her name no nearer to my blood than woman,
    And 'tis too much of that. Oh shame and horror!
    In that small distance, from yon man to me,
    Lies sin enough to make a whole world perish.   130
    —'Tis time we parted, sir, and left the sight
    Of one another, nothing can be worse
    To hurt repentance; for our very eyes
    Are far more poisonous to religion,
    Than basilisks to them; if any goodness
    Rest in you, hope of comforts, fear of judgments,

116 querister] chorister   121 pillowbers] pillowcases   122 angels] gold coins
123 sand-box] a pierced tray from which sand was shaken to dry the ink on manuscripts
126–7 I'd fain ... woman] I'd rather she were no closelier related to me than by our
common sex   135 basilisk] the fabulous beast whose look was said to be fatal

My request is, I nev'r may see you more;
And so I turn me from you everlastingly.
So is my hope to miss you; but for her,
That durst so dally with a sin so dangerous,   140
And lay a snare so spitefully for my youth,
If the least means but favour my revenge,
That I may practise the like cruel cunning
Upon her life, as she has on mine honour,
I'll act it without pity.
Hippolito. [*Aside*]   Here's a care
Of reputation, and a sister's fortune,
Sweetly rewarded by her: would a silence,
As great as that which keeps among the graves,
Had everlastingly chain'd up her tongue;
My love to her has made mine miserable.   150

   Enter Guardiano *and* Livia.

Guardiano. If you can but dissemble your heart's griefs now,
Be but a woman so far.
Livia.   Peace! I'll strive, sir.
Guardiano. As I can wear my injuries in a smile;
Here's an occasion offer'd, that gives anger
Both liberty and safety to perform
Things worth the fire it holds, without the fear
Of danger, or of law; for mischiefs acted
Under the privilege of a marriage-triumph
At the Duke's hasty nuptials, will be thought
Things merely accidental; all's by chance,   160
Not got of their own natures.
Livia.   I conceive you, sir,
Even to a longing for performance on't;
And here behold some fruits.   [*Kneels to* Hippolito & Isabella.]
                 Forgive me both:
What I am now, return'd to sense and judgment,
Is not the same rage and distraction
Presented lately to you; that rude form
Is gone for ever. I am now my self,
That speaks all peace, and friendship; and these tears
Are the true springs of hearty penitent sorrow
For those foul wrongs, which my forgetful fury   170
Sland'red your virtues with. This gentleman
Is well resolv'd now.

172 resolv'd] satisfied

Guardiano.   I was never otherways,
    I knew (alas) 'twas but your anger spake it,
    And I nev'r thought on't more.
Hippolito.   Pray rise, good Sister.
Isabella. [*Aside*] Here's ev'n as sweet amends made for a wrong now,
    As one that gives a wound, and pays the surgeon;
    All the smart's nothing, the great loss of blood,
    Or time of hindrance: well, I had a mother,
    I can dissemble too.—What wrongs have slipt
    Through anger's ignorance (Aunt) my heart forgives.   180
Guardiano. Why, this is tuneful now!
Hippolito.   And what I did, Sister,
    Was all for honour's cause, which time to come
    Will approve to you.
Livia.   Being awak'd to goodness,
    I understand so much, sir, and praise now
    The fortune of your arm, and of your safety;
    For by his death y'have rid me of a sin
    As costly as ev'r woman doted on:
    'T has pleas'd the Duke so well too, that (behold, sir)
    Has sent you here your pardon, which I kist
    With most affectionate comfort; when 'twas brought,   190
    Then was my fit just past, it came so well, me thought,
    To glad my heart.
Hippolito.   I see his Grace thinks on me.
Livia. There's no talk now but of the preparation
    For the great marriage.
Hippolito.   Does he marry her then?
Livia. With all speed, suddenly, as fast as cost
    Can be laid on with many thousand hands.
    This gentleman and I had once a purpose
    To have honour'd the first marriage of the Duke
    With an invention of his own; 'twas ready,
    The pains well past, most of the charge bestow'd on't;   200
    Then came the death of your good mother (Niece)
    And turn'd the glory of it all to black:
    'Tis a device would fit these times so well too,
    Art's treasury not better; if you'll join,
    It shall be done, the cost shall all be mine.

---

181 Why . . . now!] Quarto: 'Why thus tuneful now!' It is just possible that this is a
question (question- and exclamation-marks are used indiscriminately in this quarto); it
would then be an aside, suspicious of Isabella's changed tune.   183 approve] prove

Hippolito. Y'have my voice first, 'twill well approve my thankfulness
  For the Duke's love and favour.
Livia.   What say you, Niece?
Isabella. I am content to make one.
Guardiano.   The plot's full then;
  Your pages, Madam, will make shift for Cupids.
Livia. That will they, sir.
Guardiano.   You'll play your old part still.   210
Livia. What is't? good troth, I have ev'n forgot it.
Guardiano. Why Juno Pronuba, the marriage goddess.
Livia. 'Tis right indeed.
Guardiano.   And you shall play the nymph,
  That offers sacrifice to appease her wrath.
Isabella. Sacrifice, good sir?
Livia.   Must I be appeased then?
Guardiano. That's as you list your self, as you see cause.
Livia. Methinks 'twould show the more state in her deity
  To be incenst.
Isabella.   'Twould, but my sacrifice
  Shall take a course to appease you, [*Aside*] or I'll fail in't,
  And teach a sinful bawd to play a goddess.   [*Exit.*]
Guardiano. For our parts, we'll not be ambitious, sir;   221
  Please you walk in, and see the project drawn,
  Then take your choice.
Hippolito.   I weigh not, so I have one.   *Exit.*
Livia. How much ado have I to restrain fury
  From breaking into curses! Oh how painful 'tis
  To keep great sorrow smother'd! sure I think
  'Tis harder to dissemble grief, than love:
  Leantio, here the weight of thy loss lies,
  Which nothing but destruction can suffice.   *Exeunt.*

SCAEN. 3

Hoboys. Enter in great state the Duke *and* Bianca, *richly attir'd, with*
Lords, Cardinals, Ladies, *and other* Attendants. *They pass solemnly over.*
Enter Lord Cardinal *in a rage, seeming to break off the ceremony.*

Lord Cardinal. Cease, cease! Religious honours done to sin
  Disparage virtue's reverence, and will pull
  Heaven's thunder upon Florence; holy ceremonies

218 incenst] There is a quibble here on 'angry' and 'perfumed with incense'.   223 weigh]
care   223 so] so long as   223 s.d. *Exit*] So quarto: perhaps Guardiano goes out here too.
229 suffice] i.e., to revenge   IV. iii, s.d. *Hoboys*] oboes (the instrument was more like
a shawm than the modern oboe)

    Were made for sacred uses, not for sinful.
    Are these the fruits of your repentance, Brother?
    Better it had been you had never sorrow'd,
    Than to abuse the benefit, and return
    To worse than where sin left you.
    Vow'd you then never to keep strumpet more,
    And are you now so swift in your desires,   10
    To knit your honours, and your life fast to her?
    Is not sin sure enough to wretched man,
    But he must bind himself in chains to't? Worse!
    Must marriage, that immaculate robe of honour,
    That renders virtue glorious, fair, and fruitful
    To her great Master, be now made the garment
    Of leprosy and foulness? is this penitence
    To sanctify hot lust? what is it otherways
    Than worship done to devils? is this the best
    Amends that sin can make after her riots?   20
    As if a drunkard, to appease heaven's wrath,
    Should offer up his surfeit for a sacrifice:
    If that be comely, then lust's offerings are
    On wedlock's sacred altar.
Duke.   Here y'are bitter
    Without cause, Brother: what I vow'd I keep,
    As safe as you your conscience, and this needs not;
    I taste more wrath in't than I do religion;
    And envy more than goodness; the path now
    I tread is honest, leads to lawful love,
    Which virtue in her strictness would not check: 30
    I vow'd no more to keep a sensual woman:
    'Tis done,
    I mean to make a lawful wife of her.
Cardinal. He that taught you that craft,
    Call him not master long, he will undo you:
    Grow not too cunning for your soul, good Brother;
    Is it enough to use adulterous thefts,
    And then take sanctuary in marriage?
    I grant, so long as an offender keeps
    Close in a privileg'd temple, his life's safe;   40
    But if he ever venture to come out,
    And so be taken, then he surely dies for't:

26 this needs not] this (i.e., the Cardinal's reproof) is unnecessary   31 sensual woman]
for the senses (only)   37 enough] i.e., for complete protection

So now y'are safe; but when you leave this body,
Man's only privileg'd temple upon earth,
In which the guilty soul takes sanctuary,
Then you'll perceive what wrongs chaste vows endure,
When lust usurps the bed that should be pure.

Bianca. Sir, I have read you over all this while
In silence, and I find great knowledge in you,
And severe learning, yet 'mongst all your virtues   50
I see not charity written, which some call
The first-born of religion, and I wonder
I cannot see't in yours. Believe it, sir,
There is no virtue can be sooner miss'd,
Or later welcom'd; it begins the rest,
And sets 'em all in order; heaven and angels
Take great delight in a converted sinner.
Why should you then, a servant and professor,
Differ so much from them? If ev'ry woman
That commits evil should be therefore kept   60
Back in desires of goodness, how should virtue
Be known and honour'd? From a man that's blind
To take a burning taper, 'tis no wrong,
He never misses it: but to take light
From one that sees, that's injury and spite.
Pray, whether is religion better serv'd,
When lives that are licentious are made honest,
Than when they still run through a sinful blood?
'Tis nothing virtue's temples to deface;
But build the ruins, there's a work of grace.   70

Duke. I kiss thee for that spirit; thou hast prais'd thy wit
A modest way. On, on there.   *Hoboys.*
Cardinal.   Lust is bold,
And will have vengeance speak, ere't be controll'd.   *Exeunt.*

ACT. 5.   SCAEN. 1

Enter Guardiano *and* Ward.

Guardiano. Speak, hast thou any sense of thy abuse?
Dost thou know what wrong's done thee?
Ward.   I were an ass else.
I cannot wash my face but I am feeling on't.

58 professor] of this religion   71 prais'd] set a value on

Guardiano. Here take this galtrop then, convey it secretly
    Into the place I show'd you; look you sir,
    This is the trap-door to't.
Ward. I know't of old, Uncle, since the last triumph; here rose up a devil
    with one eye, I remember, with a company of fireworks at's tail.
Guardiano. Prethee leave squibbing now, mark me, and fail not;
    But when thou hear'st me give a stamp, down with't: 10
    The villain's caught then.
Ward.   If I miss you, hang me.
    I love to catch a villain, and your stamp shall go current, I warrant you.
    But how shall I rise up, and let him down too, all at one hole? that will be
    a horrible puzzle. You know I have a part in't, I play Slander.
Guardiano. True, but never make you ready for't.
Ward. No? my clothes are bought and all, and a foul fiend's head with a
    long contumelious tongue i'th'chaps on't, a very fit shape for Slander
    i'th'out-parishes.
Guardiano. It shall not come so far, thou understand'st it not.
Ward. Oh, oh!
Guardiano.   He shall lie deep enough ere that time,   20
    And stick first upon those.
Ward.   Now I conceive you, Guardiner.
Guardiano. Away, list to the privy stamp, that's all thy part.
Ward. Stamp my horns in a mortar if I miss you, and give the powder in
    white wine to sick cuckolds, a very present remedy for the headache.
                                                   Exit Ward.

Guardiano. If this should any way miscarry now,
    As, if the fool be nimble enough, 'tis certain,
    The pages that present the swift-wing'd Cupids
    Are taught to hit him with their shafts of love,
    Fitting his part, which I have cunningly poison'd;
    He cannot 'scape my fury; and those ills   30
    Will be laid all on fortune, not our wills,
    That's all the sport on't; for who will imagine
    That at the celebration of this night
    Any mischance that haps can flow from spite?   *Exit*.

---

4 galtrop] 'a caltrop; or iron engine of war, made with four pricks, or sharp points, whereof
one, howsoever it is cast, ever stands upward' (Cotgrave's *Dictionary*)   9 squibbing]
letting off squibs (literal or metaphorical)   10 stamp] quibbling on the sense of a piece
of money   17 out-parishes] In the suburbs slander spread proverbially fast.   21 those]
i.e., the points of the caltrop   22 privy] secret   24 headache] i.e., one caused by being
cuckolded   26 certain] i.e., certain not to miscarry

SCAEN. 2

Flourish. Enter above, Duke, Bianca, L. Cardinal, Fabritio, *and other* Cardinals, Lords *and* Ladies *in State.*

Duke. Now, our fair Duchess, your delight shall witness
         How y'are belov'd and honour'd; all the glories
         Bestow'd upon the gladness of this night
         Are done for your bright sake.
Bianca.   I am the more
         In debt, my Lord, to loves and courtesies,
         That offer up themselves so bounteously
         To do me honour'd grace, without my merit.
Duke. A goodness set in greatness; how it sparkles
         Afar off like pure diamonds set in gold!
         How perfect my desires were, might I witness   10
         But a fair noble peace 'twixt your two spirits!
         The reconcilement would be more sweet to me,
         Than longer life to him that fears to die.
         Good sir!
Cardinal.   I profess peace, and am content.
Duke. I'll see the seal upon't, and then 'tis firm.
Cardinal. You shall have all you wish.   [*Kisses* Bianca's *hand.*]
Duke.   I have all indeed now.
Bianca. [*Aside*] But I have made surer work; this shall not blind me;
         He that begins so early to reprove,
         Quickly rid him, or look for little love;
         Beware a brother's envy, he's next heir too.   20
         Cardinal, you die this night, the plot's laid surely:
         In time of sports death may steal in securely;
         Then 'tis least thought on:
         For he that's most religious, holy friend,
         Does not at all hours think upon his end;
         He has his times of frailty, and his thoughts
         Their transportations too, through flesh and blood,
         For all his zeal, his learning, and his light,
         As well as we, poor souls, that sin by night.
Duke. What's this, Fabritio?
Fabritio.   Marry, my Lord, the model   30
         Of what's presented.

s.d. *above*] The masque is played on the stage, the spectators watching from the upper
works, which must have been crowded.   29 souls] Quarto: 'soul'.

Duke.   Oh, we thank their loves;
    Sweet Duchess, take your seat, list to the argument.
    Reads.
    There is a Nymph that haunts the woods and springs,
    In love with two at once, and they with her;
    Equal it runs; but to decide these things,
    The cause to mighty Juno they refer,
    She being the marriage-goddess; the two lovers
    They offer sighs, the Nymph a sacrifice,
    All to please Juno, who by signs discovers
    How the event shall be, so that strife dies: 40
    Then springs a second; for the man refus'd
    Grows discontent, and, out of love abus'd,
    He raises Slander up, like a black fiend,
    To disgrace th'other, which pays him i'th'end.
Bianca. In troth, my Lord, a pretty pleasing argument,
    And fits th'occasion well; envy and slander
    Are things soon rais'd against two faithful lovers;
    But comfort is, they are not long unrewarded.   *Music.*
Duke. This music shows they're upon entrance now.
Bianca. Then enter all my wishes.   50

    Enter Hymen *in yellow,* Ganymed *in a blue robe powdered with stars, and* Hebe *in a white robe with golden stars, with covered cups in their hands: they dance a short dance, then bowing to the* Duke, &c. Hymen *speaks.*

Hymen. To thee fair bride Hymen offers up
    Of nuptial joys this the celestial cup.
    Taste it, and thou shalt ever find
    Love in thy bed, peace in thy mind.
Bianca. We'll taste you sure, 'twere pity to disgrace
    So pretty a beginning.
Duke.   'Twas spoke nobly.
Ganymed. Two cups of Nectar have we begg'd from Jove;
    Hebe, give that to innocence, I this to love.
    Take heed of stumbling more, look to your way;
    Remember still the Via Lactea.   [Duke & Cardinal *drink.*]
Hebe. Well, Ganymed, *you have more faults, though not so known;*   61
    I spill'd one cup, but you have filch'd many a one.
Hymen. No more, forbear for Hymen's sake;
    In love we met, and so let's part.   *Exeunt* [Masquers].

39 *discovers*] reveals   60 Via Lactea] Milky Way

Duke. But soft! here's no such persons in the argument,
    As these three, Hymen, Hebe, Ganymed.
    The actors that this model here discovers
    Are only four, Juno, a nymph, two lovers.
Bianca. This is some antimasque belike, my Lord,
    To entertain time. [*Aside*] Now my peace is perfect: 70
    Let sports come on apace.—Now is their time, my Lord.   *Music.*
    Hark you, you hear from 'em!
Duke.   The nymph indeed.

Enter two drest like Nymphs, bearing two tapers lighted; then Isabella *drest with flowers and garlands, bearing a censer with fire in it; they set the censer and tapers on Juno's altar with much reverence; this ditty being sung in parts.*

Ditty.
    Juno nuptial goddess, thou that rul'st o'er coupled bodies,
    Ti'st man to woman, never to forsake her, thou only powerful marriage-
        maker,
    Pity this amaz'd affection; I love both, and both love me,
    Nor know I where to give rejection, my heart likes so equally,
        Till thou set'st right my peace of life,
        And with thy power conclude this strife.

Isabella. *Now with my thanks depart you to the springs,*
    I to these wells of love. Thou sacred goddess,   [*Exeunt* Nymphs.]
    And queen of nuptials, daughter to great Saturn,   81
    Sister and wife to Jove, imperial Juno,
    Pity this passionate conflict in my breast,
    This tedious war, 'twixt two affections;
    Crown me with victory, and my heart's at peace.

Enter Hippolito *and* Guardiano, *like shepherds.*

Hippolito. *Make me that happy man, thou mighty goddess.*
Guardiano. *But I live most in hope, if truest love*
    Merit the greatest comfort.
Isabella.   *I love both*
    With such an even and fair affection,
    I know not which to speak for, which to wish for,   90
    Till thou, great arbitress, 'twixt lovers' hearts
    By thy auspicious grace, design the man;
    Which pity I implore.

---

69 antimasque] a grotesque interlude or introduction in a masque (in this case engineered by Bianca)   92 *design*] point out

Both.   *We all implore it.*
Isabella. *And after sighs, contritions, truest odours,*
   I offer to thy powerful deity
   This precious incense, may it ascend peacefully!
   [*Aside*] And if it keep true touch, my good Aunt Juno,
   'Twill try your immortality ere't be long:
   I fear you'll never get so nigh heaven again,
   When you're once down.

Livia *descends like Juno* [*attended by* Pages *as* Cupids].

Livia.   *Though you and your affections*   100
   Seem all as dark to our illustrious brightness
   As night's inheritance, hell, we pity you,
   And your requests are granted. You ask signs;
   They shall be given you, we'll be gracious to you.
   He of those twain which we determine for you
   Love's arrows shall wound twice, the later wound
   Betokens love in age; for so are all,
   Whose love continues firmly all their lifetime,
   Twice wounded at their marriage; else affection
   Dies when youth ends. [*Aside*] This savour overcomes me.   110
   —*Now for a sign of wealth and golden days,*
   Bright-ey'd prosperity, which all couples love,
   Ay, and makes love—take that: *our brother Jove*
   Never denies us of his burning treasure,
   T'express bounty.   [Isabella *falls and dies.*]
Duke.   She falls down upon't.
   What's the conceit of that?
Fabritio.   As overjoy'd belike:
   Too much prosperity overjoys us all,
   And she has her lapful, it seems, my Lord.
Duke. This swerves a little from the argument though:
   Look you, my Lords.
Guardiano. [*Aside*]   All's fast; now comes my part   120
   To toll him hither; then with a stamp given,
   He's dispatch'd as cunningly.

100 s.d.] she descends on some device which maintains her poised above the stage until
l. 129   110 savour] The quarto has 'favour', which is possible but is more likely a misreading of the long *s*.   113 take that] I have adopted, though without much conviction,
Dyce's amendment to the original pointing ('Ay, and makes love take that:'); Dyce's idea
is that 'that' is some unspecified means by which Livia does away with Isabella, whose death
is otherwise unaccounted for.   121 toll] entice

Hippolito.   Stark dead:
   O treachery! cruelly made away! How's that?
                  [*The trap-door opens and* Guardiano *falls through.*]
Fabritio. Look, there's one of the lovers dropt away too.
Duke. Why, sure this plot's drawn false, here's no such thing.
Livia. Oh I am sick to th'death, let me down quickly;
   This fume is deadly: oh 't'has poison'd me!
   My subtilty is sped, her art has quitted me;
   My own ambition pulls me down to ruin.   [*Falls and dies.*]
Hippolito. Nay, then I kiss thy cold lips, and applaud   130
   This thy revenge in death.   [*Kisses* Isabella.]
Fabritio.   Look, Juno's down too: Cupids *shoot.*
   What makes she there? her pride should keep aloft.
   She was wont to scorn the earth in other shows:
   Methinks her peacocks' feathers are much pull'd.
Hippolito. Oh death runs through my blood, in a wild flame too:
   Plague of those Cupids; some lay hold on 'em.
   Let 'em not 'scape, they have spoil'd me; the shaft's
   Deadly.
Duke.   I have lost my self in this quite.
Hippolito. My great Lords, we are all confounded.
Duke.   How?
Hippolito. Dead; and I worse.
Fabritio.   Dead? my girl dead? I hope   140
   My sister Juno has not serv'd me so.
Hippolito. Lust, and forgetfulness has been amongst us,
   And we are brought to nothing. Some blest charity
   Lend me the speeding pity of his sword
   To quench this fire in blood. Leantio's death
   Has brought all this upon us (now I taste it)
   And made us lay plots to confound each other;
   The event so proves it, and man's understanding
   Is riper at his fall, than all his lifetime.
   She, in a madness for her lover's death,   150
   Reveal'd a fearful lust in our near bloods,
   For which I am punish'd dreadfully and unlook'd for;
   Prov'd her own ruin too, vengeance met vengeance,
   Like a set match; as if the plagues of sin
   Had been agreed to meet here altogether.

123 s.d.] This, like most of the s.d. in this scene, must be supplied: why Guardiano's plot
fails is not clear, but see below l. 177; perhaps the Ward opens the trap at the word 'stamp'
in l. 121.   128 her] Isabella's   128 quitted] repaid   132 there] i.e., on the stage (not
aloft)   134 peacocks' feathers] Juno's chariot was drawn by peacocks.

But how her fawning partner fell, I reach not,
Unless caught by some spring of his own setting
(For, on my pain, he never dream'd of dying):
The plot was all his own, and he had cunning
Enough to save himself; but tis the property   160
Of guilty deeds to draw your wisemen downward.
Therefore the wonder ceases.—Oh this torment!

Duke. Our guard below there!

Enter a Lord *with a* Guard.

Lord.   My Lord.
Hippolito.   Run and meet death then,
And cut off time and pain.   [*Runs on a sword and dies.*]
Lord.   Behold, my Lord,
H'as run his breast upon a weapon's point.

Duke. Upon the first night of our nuptial honours,
Destruction play her triumph, and great mischiefs
Mask in expected pleasures, 'tis prodigious!
They're things most fearfully ominous: I like 'em not.
Remove these ruin'd bodies from our eyes.   [Guard *removes the
                                                    dead bodies.*]

Bianca. [*Aside*] Not yet, no change? when falls he to the earth?   171

Lord. Please but your Excellence to peruse that paper,   [*Gives paper.*]
Which is a brief confession from the heart
Of him that fell first, ere his soul departed;
And there the darkness of these deeds speaks plainly.
'Tis the full scope, the manner, and intent;
His ward, that ignorantly let him down,
Fear put to present flight at the voice of him.

Bianca. [*Aside*] Nor yet?

Duke. Read, read; for I am lost in sight and strength.   180

Cardinal. My noble Brother!

Bianca.   Oh the curse of wretchedness!
My deadly hand is fall'n upon my lord:
Destruction take me to thee, give me way;
The pains and plagues of a lost soul upon him,
That hinders me a moment.

Duke. My heart swells bigger yet; help here, break't ope,
My breast flies open next.   [*Dies.*]

Bianca.   Oh with the poison,
That was prepar'd for thee, thee, Cardinal!
'Twas meant for thee.

Cardinal.   Poor prince!

Bianca.   Accursed error!
    Give me thy last breath, thou infected bosom,   190
    And wrap two spirits in one poison'd vapour.   [*Kisses* Duke.]
    Thus, thus, reward thy murderer, and turn death
    Into a parting kiss: my soul stands ready at my lips,
    Ev'n vext to stay one minute after thee.
Cardinal. The greatest sorrow and astonishment
    That ever struck the general peace of Florence
    Dwells in this hour.
Bianca.   So my desires are satisfied,
    I feel death's power within me.
    Thou hast prevail'd in something (cursed poison)
    Though thy chief force was spent in my lord's bosom;   200
    But my deformity in spirit's more foul;
    A blemish'd face best fits a leprous soul.
    What make I here? these are all strangers to me,
    Not known but by their malice, now th'art gone;
    Nor do I seek their pities.   [*Drinks from the poisoned cup.*]
Cardinal.   O restrain
    Her ignorant wilful hand!
Bianca.   Now do; 'tis done.
    Leantio: now I feel the breach of marriage
    At my heart-breaking. Oh the deadly snares
    That women set for women, without pity
    Either to soul or honour! Learn by me   210
    To know your foes: in this belief I die,
    Like our own sex we have no enemy!
Lord. See, my Lord,
    What shift sh'as made to be her own destruction.
Bianca. Pride, greatness, honours, beauty, youth, ambition,
    You must all down together, there's no help for't:
    Yet this my gladness is, that I remove,
    Tasting the same death in a cup of love.   [*Dies.*]
Cardinal. Sin, what thou art, these ruins show too piteously.
    Two kings on one throne cannot sit together,   220
    But one must needs down, for his title's wrong;
    So where lust reigns, that prince cannot reign long.   *Exeunt.*

FINIS.

212 no enemy] The quarto repeats these words.